The Color of Sunlight

A TRUE STORY OF UNCONDITIONAL ACCEPTANCE BETWEEN A RURAL RN AND A BLIND, TERMINALLY-ILL TRANSSEXUAL

MICHELLE ALEXANDER, RN
AND
MICHELLE DIANE ROSE

This book is dedicated with love to our mothers:

Judith Ann Painter Klapperich

and

Mary Louise Babcock Roser.

If not for their strength and courage,

we would not be the women we are today.

Contents

Caveat Emptor

The events, people and places depicted in this narrative are real, insofar as memory, emotion and skill can recall them. Some incidents have been conflated; intertwined into a single scene; others compressed or expanded both in time and space. For the most part; the timeline remains constant throughout this book. Some conversations between the author and her patient have been reconstructed, but most are reported verbatim.

Some of the words and their definitions used in this book may in some cases cause distress to members of the transgender community and their allies. The authors would like to gently remind those well-meaning folk that these events occurred over three years ago and the landscape and vocabulary of the trans community has changed considerably since then. Additionally, the subject of this memoir did not have the resources nor the education available to the trans community then or now. Therefore; those words are solely hers and the definitions hers alone. The authors firmly reject alteration of the events as recounted in favor of political correctness.

As with nearly all memoirs, this book is not so much a dry reporting of facts as it is an impression; a moving portrait through the mind's eye of the events surrounding the last days of a singularly unique person. It is not *her* life that this book is concerned with however, as it is the author's four and a half months spent with her; a tragically short period that irrevocably changed the author's life, for which she is and will be forever deeply grateful.

Prologue:

August Twenty-second, 2006

I'd never been to the police station before. I guess there's a first time for everything.

There aren't any parking spaces; not even a parking lot. Road parking only. I backed the Toyota into a spot and shut off the engine then took a deep breath, grabbed my purse and got out.

I was early by about fifteen minutes. I hate tardiness; so arrest me for that too, why don't you? Waiting next to the flagpole out front, I scowled at the concrete block building that housed Kalispell's finest and did the same for my general surroundings. Where the hell was Dave?

At five minutes 'till, I dug my cellphone out of my bag and flipped it open.

"Dave, are you almost here? I'm waiting. Don't frickin' be late!" I snapped it closed with a muttered curse and listened to my heart do the mambo.

Arms folded, I waited, just long enough for my heart to flirt with tachycardia. At about two minutes past one, his white Ford pickup pulled into a spot across the road and he emerged, our laptop in one hand and a plastic bag in the other.

The look on his face was enough to raise the little hairs up and down my arms. I pointed at the bag as he approached me.

"What's that?"

"Those letters from the Crusillo," he said anxiously. "I thought they might be useful."

I considered it. "Well, they certainly can't do any harm."

Together, we entered the lion's den.

It smelled like old paper: musty, dusty and long past its prime. There wasn't a soul in sight in the foyer, if you can call it that. We wandered down a short hall, our footsteps echoing and came to a glassed-in office area. A female clerk looked up as we approached. She slid open a slot in the glass.

"Can I help you?"

"I'm Michelle Alexander. I'm here to see Detective Scott Wardell."

She buzzed us in and I've never heard such an ugly sound as that buzzer. Dave politely held the door open for me and we went in.

There wasn't much to see: two chairs midway down a hallway floored with tile that looked older than me. Two doors: one into the clerk's office and another with a name plate. *Detective Wardell* it said and I glanced at it and shuddered.

We sat down. The chairs were hard and unyielding. My palms were sweating. I looked at Dave. He was frowning at the floor.

I wanted to say something, anything. But nothing came to me and anyway my throat was too tight for conversation.

It was five minutes that felt like five hours. When the door before us finally opened, we nearly jumped out of our shoes.

"Mrs. Alexander? I'm Detective Wardell."

I looked up. He didn't look much like a cop. In fact, he looked rather like a schoolteacher: jeans, button-down shirt, a round, pleasant face that lacked any expression I could see and opaque brown eyes that missed nothing. No badge or identification tag and I would have never guessed he was a cop if I'd bumped into him at the grocery store.

"Would you come with me, please?"

I stood. Detective Wardell held the door for me and I glanced back at Dave.

I've never seen such stark terror on my husband's face, not even when I was in the delivery room.

The door closed behind me with a heavy finality and I was on my own. I suddenly realized I'd forgotten both the laptop and the letters.

To hell with it, I thought. *If he wants them, he can ask me for them. Nicely.*

He ushered me into a plain office that was equipped with a bare minimum of furniture: a steel desk littered with paperwork and a computer, two chairs and a file cabinet.

As interrogation rooms go, it wasn't particularly impressive.

I sat. He sat. We stared at each other.

"Do you know why you're here, Mrs. Alexander?"

I took a deep breath. "Yes. I'm being investigated for the murder of Mishelle Woodring."

He shook his head. "No, not exactly. Assisted suicide. It's not classed as murder. Manslaughter One, actually."

"Which is pretty much the same damn thing, isn't it?" I snapped.

He nodded. "It does carry a heavy penalty, yes. I want to inform you immediately that you don't have to say anything to me and that you're entitled to an attorney if you wish."

"Am I under arrest?"

He shook his head. "No. Not yet, anyway."

"I'd better not be!"

"Well, that remains to be seen. Would you like to tell me what happened Friday the eleventh of this month?"

I held up my hand. "Wait just a minute. If you really want to know what happened, we're going to have to back up some. There was so much more to it than that last day."

"Go ahead."

"We'll have to back up to the week before she died."

"I'm listening."

I paused for a long, long moment, gathering my thoughts. Then I said: "Maybe even further. Like four months ago. . ."

PART ONE

Intersections

CHAPTER ONE

New Horizons

E ARLY SPRING WEATHER in Flathead Valley is predictable: gray and gloomy, with every day holding a promise of becoming a day much like those before it. Thick gray clouds had rolled in overnight, obscuring the sharp but brief sunshine of yesterday; assuring the return of more rain and wind; perfect weather for this time of year.

I peered up at them through my windshield as I came to a stop at a red light. The first fat, soft drops of rain began to patter on the glass inches from my nose.

Montana has *weather* and I've grown to like it. I expect it when the clouds bunch up at the edge of the big sky as they did that day; teetering over the mountains circling Kalispell, blending with the snowcaps until you can't define them as separate anymore.

I've learned that nothing is separate, here on this Earth and certainly elsewhere, too. Where others see differences, I see the similarities and I like to think I'm richer for it.

I'm also thankful that I live in a small rural community. I've been to the city. I'll take the country anytime.

Yes, especially on those magical days when the sun comes out and the mountains surrounding Flathead Valley somehow seem closer in the crystalline air; the color of the sunlight changed and the color of everything else changed with it: vivid beyond belief and so beautiful it hurts.

Days like that make you very glad to be alive.

I'm a nurse, a Home Health Care provider, one of those perennially cheerful women with a degree, a sensible car that always needs washing and a big black bag that's somewhat heavier than it looks.

I love my job.

I was one of the first to arrive at the office that gloomy, briskly cold day in March of 2006. I like to get in early, get the paperwork on my patients in order and get out on the road as soon as possible. Office hub-bub is distracting to me. I don't like chit-chat and gossip. I prefer folks to do their job; to be unobtrusive and predictable, if possible.

But when I pulled into the parking lot that morning, I was a bit sur-prised to see Jodie's car already there, unusual for my supervisor.

Unusual, I later discovered, didn't even begin to describe it.

I barely had time to take off my coat when Jodie spotted me and made a beeline across the room toward me, her face set in an expression I had come to think of as surprise party.

It's an uncomfortable combination of a cold smile and a frown. It would look right at home on a stern headmistress or an irritable nun. She gets that look whenever she has an assignment she thinks no one will like and she's usually right. It's too bad that it clashes so with her appearance because she's a nice looking woman.

I've always wondered why she went into management. I was manage-ment too, long ago, and I hated it. I think she hates it, too.

She didn't waste any time: "'Morning! Michelle, you're going to be admitting and case-managing an unusual patient today. Her name is Mishelle Woodring. She's on a seven-day course of IV antibiotics for a respiratory infection. She's going to be on our service for only a week and then we discharge her."

She looked at me soberly. "She's blind, Michelle. And somewhat needy, if you follow me. We've had her before and she's a bit of a prob-lem child. Don't get caught up in her drama! Just get in and get out."

She looked down and didn't say anything for a moment while I digested that. I'd never had a blind patient before. I found myself racking my brain for the basics from school and it kept coming up with absolutely nothing except: *This could be interesting.*

Jodie looked up and her expression was strange. Her smile was gone and she looked almost apologetic; strange, for her. "One more thing. I hope you're okay with this: she's transgender."

I stared. "Oh. Really? That's . . . unusual."

She eyed me narrowly. "You okay with that?"

I literally had no idea what she was talking about. "Of course. Not a problem at all."

She looked relieved. "Good. Some of us . . . never mind. If it does bother you—and it might—keep in mind that it's only for a week." There was that strange expression again, so out of place on her face: "Just get in and get out. It's better that way, believe me."

I nodded and watched her stroll off, the slant of her shoulders and her no-nonsense stride telling me that she was pretty happy to have that little problem off her plate this morning, yes ma'am.

I sighed and headed for the case files cabinet. I found her file immediately and opened it, looking for the H&P report. History & Physical is often the best snapshot of a patient's condition.

I frowned at the date: the previous year.

Reading further, my frown grew. Mishelle had been admitted to the ER with severe shortness of breath and a fever. The ER physician's diagnosis was COPD, Chronic Obstructive Pulmonary Disease, usually referred to as emphysema.

I winced a little. COPD is a death sentence, the long, slow kind. The alveoli in the lungs become scarred and inflamed, the cilia in the airways—the little hairs that sweep away microscopic junk in the air—die and aren't replaced. The patient slowly but surely becomes weaker and more unable to walk or move or perform even the slightest exertion without gasping for breath.

Eventually, most patients end up chained to an oxygen tank and find themselves in a wheelchair or bedridden not long after the initial diagnosis. Respiratory infections are common with patients with COPD and Mishelle apparently had had a whopper when she'd been admitted last year.

I kept frowning at that date. A year. Why no follow-up?

I flipped through the file.

There was more, of course. Mishelle also had a fractured vertebra, resulting in chronic back pain. I nodded. This poor dear had a most unenviable history: COPD, chronic back pain and . . .

I came to the end of the report. There was a notation from that ER physician referencing her as a transvestite.

I stared at that word.

Transgender? Transvestite? One and the same? Different? I knew what a transvestite was; my mother had taken me to Darcelle's in Portland, Oregon shortly after I'd graduated from nursing school. At the time, I'd been amazed at how good some of those men looked dressed up as women. In fact, if I hadn't *known* they were men, I would have been completely fooled by most of them. I assumed then that they were gay men expressing their notion of femininity.

Mom thought it was a hoot: "I brought you here to broaden your horizons!" she whooped in the middle of their opening number. "What do you think so far?"

I don't remember what I said to her. I remember thinking only that I found it a bit weird but that was the extent of it. It was a memory almost twenty years old and it meant little, if anything.

I shook my head and came back to the present. The file was spread open before me and I looked again at that word: transvestite, knowing somehow that it was wrong.

My mom raised me in a pretty liberal fashion. She taught me to see people as people, not symbols. Given that my profession has also trained me to be objective and to leave my personal feelings about a patient at the door, it didn't bother me then that Mishelle was a transvestite.

But somehow I knew that it wasn't accurate.

And what was *transgender*? A new definition for a man who wears a dress? Well, it was a new one for me, anyway.

I couldn't shake my uneasy feeling and I thought I knew why: I didn't understand that word. What I don't understand makes me uneasy. I'd never heard the word before and my quick response to Jodie's question was simply because I didn't want to look stupid to my supervisor.

But I don't waste time wondering about what I don't know or understand. I *learn*, quickly, because knowledge can be the difference between life and death and life is infinitely more preferable.

Or so I've been taught.

I stared at Mishelle's chart, not really seeing it, as my mind raced along at top speed. I had a million questions and all of them made me uneasy.

Questions such as: what kind of person was this Mishelle who spelled her name with an s?

What was her lifestyle all about?

Was she gay? Was she just a man living as a woman? Did she have a partner? Another male or . . .?

I tried to imagine a man living as a woman living with a real woman and I gave up that line of thinking as it was too much, too soon for me.

Instead, I thought about her as a patient and that helped.

It occurred to me that there might be a lot of anger there due to her condition. People with a fatal condition like COPD or cancer or AIDS go through several clearly defined stages in coming to terms with their situation. Anger is always one of those, a stage some never fully pass through because they never come to the final stage: acceptance. An angry patient is always the hardest to treat because anger is very often far more debilitating than the disease itself.

I didn't want an angry patient. Right then, I told myself that it was the root of my apprehension about this new assignment.

But I think, even then, that I knew it wasn't true.

I tucked her file under my arm, slowly made my way back to my desk and sat down, still thinking hard. I looked at the phone and hesitated.

I made myself a promise in that moment; a promise that I would give Mishelle with an s the very best care within my abilities to provide.

I might be uncomfortable with her lifestyle. I might be uncomfortable with someone the likes of which I'd seen only on a stage almost twenty years before.

But I was determined to give her—I was trying hard not to put mental quotation marks around that female pronoun—the very best care and respect I could muster.

If she was uncomfortable with me, that was a bridge I would cross when it was time and not before. I remembered Jodie's comment about not getting involved with her drama.

I shrugged. Gravely ill people and drama go together like hand in glove. I could handle that.

I picked up the phone and dialed.

"Hello?" It was a high-pitched yet gravelly voice. I knew right then it was her.

"Hi, this is Michelle from Home Health. Is Mishelle there?"

"This is Mishelle," the gravelly voice responded.

I swallowed a giggle. Her voice sounded like my husband trying to imitate a woman. "Hi, Mishelle. I have you on my schedule today to admit you to Home Health. It sounds like you could use some antibiotics. Would it work for you if I came over in about an hour?"

Her voice dropped a bit in pitch: "That would be fine."

"Okay, see you then. 'Bye!"

I hung up the phone and let the giggle escape. Two or three of its minor siblings fled with it.

"The voice thing isn't working, sweetie," I told the phone. Still chuckling, I stuffed her file into my bag and made my own escape from the office.

On the drive to her place, I mused further about those questions.

What did she *look* like? Would she be like those men at Darcelle's, all glammed up and in ridiculously high heels, hair halfway to the ceiling?

Was she in fact gay?

Gay people didn't bother me but maybe that was because I'd never been around any long enough to care. I knew there were a few in Kalispell but that's *all* I knew.

I vaguely remembered reading about a gay student in Wyoming that had been beaten and left tied to a fence to die. I sincerely doubted that something like *that* could ever happen here in my quaint little town.

On the other hand, it was just as unlikely that I'd ever witness them parading down Main Street on Gay Pride Day.

I tried to remember all the gay people I'd ever met in my life and realized with a slight shock that I could probably count them all on the fingers of one hand.

I guess that qualifies me as a conservative, even though I've never had much use for labels on people, myself or anyone else. That's my mother's influence, too.

Transgender people? Another label, one I'd never seen before. I could tell I was due for some education, if nothing else.

I pulled into the parking lot of her apartment complex. It was one of those simple but nicely laid-out subsidized senior-living places: newly constructed and very tidy. The paint, a pleasant muted lemon color, was still relatively unscarred by our harsh winter. Young shrubbery planted at corners and nooks and insets throughout the complex pushed back defiantly at their weakening burden of snow.

I parked close to her door and got out, lugging my bag after me. A license plate—no, just a sign—was attached to the door: *Reserved for Elvis Fans.*

I grinned at it. *That's fine*, I thought. *I've always been kinda fond of the King.*

I knocked. From within, I heard that same pseudo-soprano voice call out: "Come in!" followed by a cough.

I turned the knob, pushed and another part of my life began in that instant.

Looking back over three years, I realize now that the door was more than just a slab of wood, more than just an entrance and far more than merely a barrier to keep the world at bay.

The door swung slowly inward, just missing a small end table. My eyes followed the arc of its movement and focused on the person sitting in a recliner next to the table, a table littered with junk: keys, a half-filled water glass, hand lotion, two or three remote controls and a nebulizer.

But my attention was fixed on the person in that chair: her and the dachshund standing arrogantly on her knees in full defense mode, barking his adorable little head off.

"Hi," I said cheerfully. "Mishelle? Can I . . .?"

"Hello, yes. Please come in. Nicholas!" she admonished, soothing him. "Be nice, now. It's just our nurse. Shh . . ."

She petted him; his yapping subsiding into irritable growls as she rhythmically stroked his fur. His eyes never left me as I came in and put my bag down on the coffee table in front of them.

I had to smile. I've known a few wiener dogs and every one of them was cursed with that dreaded small dog syndrome: the notion that the whole world is a threat and by golly, I'm not scared of anything!

But I knew Nicholas would turn into a pussy-cat once he relaxed long enough to let me rub his chest. No dog in the world can resist that.

I sat down on the loveseat under the window, facing them. Speaking of pussy-cats: a sleekly beautiful gray kitty with dazzling blue eyes sauntered in from somewhere and proceeded to rub against my legs before casually levitating to her place of honor next to Nicholas.

When I looked down to pet her, I noticed that the front of the loveseat, the part where your legs rest was wrapped with sheet plastic and secured with duct tape.

Odd, I thought.

I looked up at my patient and my first thought was that no one could possibly mistake her for a performer at Darcelle's.

For one thing, she had on absolutely no make-up; not a stitch as far as I could tell. Her graying blonde hair looked like it hadn't been brushed in two or three days and she was wearing a nightgown in black and red satin.

It was a pretty sexy nightie, actually; not what I'd consider appropriate for greeting a visitor.

Hmm, kinky, I thought with some disapproval and then noticed that her bra strap—clashing in pink—peeked out above what looked like some authentic and ample cleavage.

I stared openly. Real breasts? Not falsies?

I don't know what I'd been expecting. Yes, I did, but it wasn't anything like this.

I covered my astonishment and embarrassment with a little small talk. It helps to break the ice with new patients but I was getting the feeling that this person (this *woman?*) didn't need any help in that direction.

There was an aura of something I could only think of as serenity around her. I've seen that sort of thing before in terminal patients who know things we don't; things they can't really talk about anymore because it's so much a part of them, it's like blood and bone: an integral component of their existence, for whatever existence remains to them.

I've always found it both troubling and humbling.

I cleared my throat. "Um, have you lived in Kalispell very long, Mishelle?"

"I've lived here on and off since I was a teenager. I've been back now for about four years. I used to live in Seattle."

That gravelly voice was so at odds with the person sitting before me but all I could think right then was: *why on Earth would you move back here, of all places?*

"Have you had Home Health care before?"

"Oh, someone came last year but only a few times." Her gravelly voice sounded wry although I could sense the pain beneath those careless words.

"Well, as you know, the first visit is usually the longest. Medicare requires a lot of questions and even if they seem redundant, I still have to ask them. I hope you don't mind?"

"No, go ahead: ask. It's okay. It's just nice to have some company, even for a little while."

I nodded and felt foolish, realizing she couldn't see me. Yes, this whole case would require some serious adjustments on my part.

I began with the usual things about her medical history and was startled to learn she'd had a mitral valve replacement some sixteen years previous. Looking closer, I saw the faint scar starting at the top of her sternum.

I didn't probe into her transgender status. I said nothing at all about it. At the time, I wasn't even aware that it was actually a medical condition so I avoided that, thinking that she didn't need me poking my nose into her lifestyle choices.

She was very pleasant, answering all my questions completely and concisely but her detachment still bothered me. Generally, I have no trouble developing rapport with my patients but this was different. I felt I was walking on eggshells, choosing my words with the utmost of care.

Later, I realized it was because I was trying to avoid mentioning her transgender status and that was my first mistake: trying to separate what she was from whom she was, as if the two weren't one and the same.

I could tell that there was a core of reluctance within her too, some wariness that kept her from opening up fully. *Pain*, I thought. *She's had a lot of pain in her life.*

"Do you experience a lot of pain, Mishelle? In your back, for instance?"

She grimaced quickly and the expression vanished in the next heartbeat, leaving that placid look on her face. It was almost detached, as if I was talking to someone no longer quite connected to this Earth. "All the time. I take Oxycontin three times a day for it. Oxycodone in between if I need it."

"Yes, I saw that on your chart. Mishelle, I need to do a physical assessment, if that's okay. That means your vitals: blood pressure, temperature and so forth. May I?"

She nodded and muttered "Yes," and I was again struck by how detached she seemed.

As I was getting my equipment out of my bag, I glanced here and there around her apartment, noting details:

An enormous entertainment center dominated the rear wall; two huge speakers perched on either side like a pair of buzzards waiting for their dinner to die. The stereo system itself would have made my youngest son tap-dance with glee but the enormous television set gave me momentary pause. Why would a blind person need a TV?

A glance into the dining room area revealed a large armoire and two big cabinets housing computer equipment and electronic miscellanea I didn't recognize. I was somehow reminded of something you'd see on *Star Trek* but I didn't look too closely.

Past that was the kitchenette: cramped and tiny as those in senior apartments usually are, made even more so with all the clutter covering every square inch of countertop. There was barely enough room for a microwave oven, an espresso machine, and a dish drying rack.

There was a refrigerator and a large freezer that stuck partway out into the dining room. The result was a tiny space between the fridge and the sink about the size of an old-fashioned phone booth.

Thermometer in hand, I looked back at Mishelle and paused. Something from school finally popped into my head: *preparation*. Blind people can do just fine for themselves if they know what to expect and where things are.

"Mishelle, I need to take your temperature. Here's the thermometer."

She reached out both hands like a child in a high chair. I immediately noticed her rings: two on the right, one a plain gold band, the other small and delicate with what looked like a sapphire setting. On the left ring finger was a gaudy diamond or rhinestone ring that reminded me of one of my grandmother's costume jewelry pieces.

She placed the thermometer in her mouth and I finally had the opportunity to closely examine her face.

Her eyes were a pale blue and the right eye wandered disconcertingly while the left was fixed, staring straight ahead as if probing. Dark circles beneath marred what was otherwise a good complexion but she was so thin!

Her Adam's apple seemed larger than normal and her jaw and chin jutted out like a Fifties movie idol. She had beautiful cheekbones: high and well shaped.

A nice face, for all that she was so obviously ill. Not pretty in the conventional sense but certainly pleasant enough, I thought.

I recorded the temperature reading and told her I would be taking her blood pressure. She stretched a long arm toward me and things jangled.

The left wrist bore a silver charm bracelet, the dangling charms tinkling like sleigh bells. Her arms were well-muscled, not like a woman who visits the gym on a regular basis but certainly not masculine either. Tattoos on both: the left, a crudely done outline of a wizard, colored in black and red, the right bearing a beautifully executed bouquet of yellow flowers, obviously professionally applied.

Her arms somehow reminded me of my husband's but unlike my husband's; completely hairless, not even a fine fuzz like mine. I took her blood pressure and marveled how smooth and soft her skin was: very much like mine.

"I'm going to listen to your lungs now, Mishelle. Can you lean forward for me?"

"Sure thing. That's usually how I sit anyway."

I knew what she meant. People with advanced COPD find it easier to breathe if they lean forward a bit. It braces the diaphragm and adds a bit of leverage, making it easier to draw a breath and takes the strain out of using the lower mesentery muscles.

I placed the stethoscope on her back and began to listen. My gaze wandered over her shoulder and to my embarrassment, I found myself staring down at her cleavage and wondering if they were real.

They sure *looked* real. My face felt suddenly hot and then my attention was seized by her coughing fit which sounded like cannon-fire in my earpieces. I winced and pulled them free of my ears.

"Do you cough a lot, Mishelle?"

"No more than anyone else who's smoked for forty-some years," she said dryly and then coughed again, an explosive sound that drew another wince from me.

"But is it worse than usual? Do you cough up any phlegm?"

"Yes, the cough is worse than usual. The problem is that I can't cough up the stuff. It's like it's stuck." She let loose another painful bark, as if to illustrate.

I got up to get her a glass of water, ignoring the one already on the side table. I wanted to give her time to catch her breath. Answering my question while she was coughing would only worsen it.

As I rummaged around in her cabinets, looking for a glass, I noticed they were crammed with food and medicines. A note posted to the side of the cupboard read: *Please put everything back exactly as you found it so Mishelle knows where it is.*

I nodded at it. Preparation again. I found a glass, filled it and brought it back to her.

While she drank, I inspected her ankles for edema or swelling. She was barefoot and almost imperceptibly digging her long toes into the carpet. She had big feet and kept them tightly together, lined up like a soldier's.

By contrast, her legs were long and slender; runway legs only slightly marred by somewhat bony knees which she kept tightly closed like a Catholic schoolgirl. Her legs looked very much like mine right after I've shaved them in the shower: soft and smooth. I spotted another tattoo on the outside of her left ankle: a lovely bouquet of yellow roses almost five inches across, similar to the one on her left arm.

Once she finished coughing and caught her breath, I proceeded with my assessment. I inquired about her bowel and urinary functions, secretly wondering how she urinated. Did she have a penis and was it functional? Had she ever had a sex change operation?

She smiled wryly and said: "My plumbing works just fine, thanks."

So I didn't ask those questions after all. *That's a relief.*

"Mishelle, do you have a scale?"

"Yes, it's in the bathroom, down the hall."

Before I could stop her, she reached forward and grabbed hold of a white pole near the recliner, anchored to both the ceiling and the floor. There was a scarf tied to the middle of it and for some reason, I was reminded of a stripper's pole. She hoisted herself up with some effort while I stood with my arms out, ready to catch her if she fell.

My assumption was that the white pole was there to assist Mishelle with her navigation and finding her home position; a pretty safe guess under the circumstances.

When she stood up, she towered over me, and as she swayed to catch her balance, I was afraid she might fall. She didn't fall and hurried down the hallway into the bathroom with her arms outstretched.

I trailed her, looking down when she said, "Watch out for the land mines!" Nicholas the protector was sniffing two separate piles of hardened dog turds on the floor.

The hallway was like an obstacle course. There were three large pieces of furniture pushed up against the wall. First: a glass curio cabinet with multiple shelves almost blocking the entrance to the hallway. On each shelf, cleaning products were arranged meticulously with price tags facing out, as if they were for sale. Next to the curio cabinet was a cart full of DVD's and VCR tapes, incongruous in a blind person's apartment. The third set of shelves was packed tightly with books and portable oxygen tanks.

I glanced to the left and noticed a single small bedroom. The full size bed was piled high with clean laundry and numerous stuffed animals. It appeared as if the bed hadn't been slept in for a long time, no surprise there as most patients with COPD are unable to lie flat due to their compromised breathing.

I saw an antique dresser covered with papers and what looked like a very old computer. Next to that was a portable air conditioner, the kind that can be placed temporarily in a window.

I realized that Mishelle's recliner truly was her home base.

We made it into a tiny bathroom crowded with a cat box and her oxygen concentrator. Mishelle felt with her foot for the scale and deftly stepped up onto it. In a harsh, robotic voice, the scale belched: "One hundred and seventy three pounds."

I asked her: "How tall are you?"

"Six feet, four inches," she replied with that wry smile.

A big girl, I thought.

"Is there anything else we need to do in here?" Mishelle whispered.

"No, that's about it."

She returned to her recliner. I noticed it wasn't as fast as the journey to the bathroom.

As we settled back down into our seats, I saw that she was slowly panting, rather like a dog. She grabbed her inhaler, shook it vigorously, took two puffs and then leaned forward with her elbows on her knees.

I sat quietly for almost five minutes as she caught her breath, wondering if this was her norm or if her shortness of breath was aggravated by the infection.

I began to prepare the IV antibiotics and asked for her arm again.

"Give me just another moment," she murmured, still panting.

"Well, I was going to bring the scale to you, but you move way too fast!"

She laughed weakly. "A girl's got to get her exercise."

I finished my visit by administering the IV antibiotics and reviewing all of the other medication that she was taking. I inquired about her caregivers and found that she had two that alternated for five hours every day. They helped her with the cooking, cleaning, laundry, errands, transportation and most importantly: companionship.

Even though she did have some help, her ability to live alone, given her compromised medical condition and her blindness amazed me.

We said our goodbyes and I told her that I would be back the next day for another round of antibiotics.

As I was opening the front door, I noticed another note: *Turn off all of the lights and close the blinds before you leave.*

I was relieved that the first visit was complete. At least now I knew what to expect the next day. I felt that our visit had gone smoothly, considering how ill at ease I'd felt.

As I was driving away from her apartment, the internal questions began again: *If I hadn't been told, I wonder if I would have known that Mishelle was born a male?*

Yes. Her size, her voice, her facial features all said that genetically she was really a male.

But make-up can do wonders. Think of those guys from Darcelle's.

Well, even the best make-up wouldn't make much difference in her case and for some reason, I felt sad about that.

But the dead give-away was her medications. She was taking female hormones at *six times* the dose that a post-menopausal woman would normally take.

Other questions flooded my mind: her blindness and her life as a transgender person.

What was it like to live a life in complete darkness? How long had she been blind?

Why would she choose this lifestyle and subject herself to harsh judgment and possible rejection?

Why Kalispell of all places? What brought her here from Seattle four years ago?

Did she have any friends? Did she have any family?

Did they accept her?

How long had she been like this?

I doubted that I would ever get the answers to these questions since she wasn't going to be on our service for more than a week.

My curiosity had been thoroughly well-piqued. I sighed, partly from frustration and partly from what I thought was pity for someone so obviously alone and cut off from a normal life.

But I was feeling awfully judgmental, too.

Because if I wasn't judging her, then why would I be uncomfortable around her? That made me wonder how the other new people she met perceived her.

It also made me feel some empathy for what she may have been through and was probably still going through with each new person. She couldn't see a person's facial expressions when they met. She had to judge a person's impression by her instincts alone.

Just how good were her instincts, really? I'd done my best throughout our visit to conceal my own discomfort but I wondered if she'd sensed it.

I finished my other visits rather quickly. I was looking forward to getting home and talking about this with my husband Dave.

Yes, I was well aware that this was a breach of confidentiality, but at the time, I just didn't consider that.

I'm still not sure why. I've gone over it in my mind a thousand times since then and the only thing that comes to me is:

Culture shock.

I had just met someone who was utterly unlike anyone I'd ever met before. I had no reference points at all except those three or four hours at Darcelle's.

Mishelle was nothing like that. I felt I needed to share with someone and who else but the man in my life and the father of my sons?

Dave was already home when I arrived, tending to our two boys Zach and Chris. Something that smelled delicious was simmering on the stove but I was too excited to notice. I bolted through the door, set my purse down and started right in:

"Boy, I admitted a *very* different patient today."

"Oh, yeah?"

"Yeah! My new patient's name is Mishelle too, only she spells it with an s. And guess what? She's blind. I mean, *totally* blind. And guess what else? She's a transgender!"

He blinked at me. "She's a *what?*"

"You know, like those guys at Darcelle's that dress up like women?"

"Seriously?"

"Uh huh. But the weird thing was: it looked like she had boobs! I couldn't tell if they were falsies or if they were the real thing."

"Now, *that's* just downright weird."

I continued with details of the visit. Dave's right eyebrow went up and pretty much stayed there while we talked.

"Did he look like a male or a female?"

"Definitely a guy dressed up as a woman." I hesitated. "Not very well, but jeez, I've seen worse-looking women, I suppose."

"Well, I'm glad that you'll only be in there for a week. That's just . . . weird."

Even though I considered Mishelle an odd character, I was actually looking forward to seeing her again. It never occurred to me that I was crossing lines by thinking of her as something other than a patient.

In some ways, I had already begun to think of her as a friend, someone new and pretty exotic: a visitor from some far-off land I'd only heard of or seen on TV.

Culture shock. She was from a different world, one I never knew existed.

I wanted to know more.

Who was she, really? How had she come to be this way and why was she here in Kalispell, Montana?

I had a million questions and I hoped that perhaps some of them had answers.

CHAPTER TWO

Take a Giant Step

EARLY THE NEXT MORNING, I approached the door to the office with slowly diminishing steps. Once again, Jodie's car was parked in its spot an hour earlier than usual.

I knew she was going to ask me about Mishelle and for some reason, I just didn't want to discuss it with her. I didn't want to discuss it with anyone, for that matter.

I was working toward a concept new to me, a different way of seeing people although I didn't know it at the time. It was something I'd never done before, at least not with someone like Mishelle.

It was taking up an awful lot of my attention.

Jodie had other plans, though. Less than ten minutes at my desk and she was there in front of me, an expectant expression on her face.

It didn't look any more pleasant than her surprise party expression.

"Well, how did it go with Mishelle?"

"Good, good," I said with what I hoped was a nonchalant air. "No problems."

She eyed me the same way she had the day before. "You sure?"

I tried for non-committal: "Of course. Well, she *is* quite a character . . ." I let my voice trail off deliberately.

She nodded knowingly. "Oh, yeah. If you let her, she'll drag you right into her drama. Better to keep her at arm's length."

Wish I could keep you *at arm's length*, I said to myself. Aloud, I said, "Well, she *is* doing very poorly, in my assessment. Her infection seems pretty severe and her COPD appears fairly well advanced. I'll keep regular and complete notes, of course."

She nodded. "Good. Anything else?"

I shook my head.

"Okay, then," and she marched off, her day beginning very well, thank you and mine with a lot of thinking yet to do. I studied her departing rear end, musing that a swift kick in that region might just do her a world of good.

Reluctantly, I looked back at the paperwork on my desk. It was a slow day; three patients including Mishelle. I stared at the case files spread across my desk without seeing them: thinking.

I had encountered someone completely out of my experience. I didn't know it then but my world-view had been fairly well shaken by meeting Mishelle. At the time, all I felt was something I thought of as sympathy and an overwhelming urge to know more about my new patient.

I picked up the phone and dialed Mishelle's number. She answered in that affected high voice and I was more successful in swallowing giggles this time. They stayed well submerged as I confirmed the second appointment for her antibiotic treatments.

It occurred to me though, as I listened to her, that her natural voice was neither masculine nor feminine, really. Pleasant, when she didn't affect that higher pitch.

So: *why?*

I wanted to know more.

When I got to her apartment, I knocked with rather more force than was necessary and Nicholas set up a barrage of barking within.

She opened the door; confirming me again as a member of Elvis fandom and greeted me cordially. I was a little surprised to see her out of her chair, but I stepped past her to put my bag down on the coffee table.

I turned and saw that she had a guest.

"Hi! I'm Julie," the other woman announced cheerfully. We shook hands.

"Michelle Alexander. I'm Mishelle's nurse from Home Health."

"Yeah, I figured."

"Julie spent the night with me," Mishelle offered with just a touch of a titter. She was smirking like the proverbial cat. I could almost see a feather hovering around her lips. I raised an eyebrow.

"Oh?"

Julie giggled and playfully poked my patient in the ribs. Mishelle giggled back "It's not like *that*," she protested. "Mishelle just needed someone to stay with her, 'cause of her coughing, y'know? Makes for a long night and she needed the company."

I nodded, relaxing. "Yes, that was very nice of you to do that."

"Glad to. So, is she getting any better?"

"Oh, he's not responding to the antibiotics yet . . . *She*. I mean *she!*"

And with *that*, I figured, I had just shot down in flames any possible chance I might have had in building rapport with Mishelle.

Just like that. One word, one single, solitary pronoun.

One lousy damn pronoun that meant nothing from me and everything to her.

I stood there, my face beet red for what felt like a full minute, but couldn't have been any more than a few seconds. Julie eyed me and nodded abruptly.

Face flaming, I glanced at Mishelle, expecting to see that withdrawn look settling onto her face and there it was, by golly.

"I gotta go, Mishelle," Julie said. She sounded tired. "You gonna be okay?"

Mishelle nodded. "I'll be fine, hon. Thanks for staying with me."

They hugged each other and with another cool glance in my direction, Julie left.

I tried to cover my embarrassment by getting out my equipment and setting up for an assessment. Mishelle settled back into her chair as I took her blood pressure and pulse.

I fussed for a few minutes, setting up her antibiotic and making small talk. She answered me in a friendly enough manner, but I could tell (anyone could, I think) that my mistake had caused her to withdraw from the here and now.

It made me feel worse.

"How long have you known Julie?"

"A few years. We met right after I moved back here."

"She seems awfully nice."

"She is. She accepts me for who I am."

And there it was. The answer, staring me in the face: accept me for who I am, what I am. Not for what you think I should be.

I was in the process of readying the dose of antibiotic. I glanced at her face. It was serene; placid and perhaps not as withdrawn, so I took a chance.

"Mishelle, how long you been blind?"

She smiled. "Since I was eighteen months old."

I stopped what I was doing, staring at her. "That's . . . really young. You weren't born blind?"

"Oh, no. I can kind of remember being able to see. I like to think so, anyway."

"What happened?"

"They thought I had measles, so they tried to treat it with a massive dose of penicillin. But since it was rheumatic fever, not measles, all it did was make me blind." She chuckled. "The rheumatic fever turned out to have some side effects, too."

My gaze traced the faint scar running from the top of her sternum down between her breasts. "Your mitral valve?"

"Right." Her face started to close up again. I tried a different tack:

"Do you see shadows or anything?"

"Nope, not a thing." Another chuckle: "I can see with other than my eyes, you know."

"I know." I finished laying out the necessary items and stood. A digitized voice coming from behind me made my head snap around:

"*Mishelle, you have email.*"

"What's *that?*"

Mishelle grinned. "Oh, that's Krystal. She's my email robot. Since I can't see, I don't know when I've got new mail so my computer guru hooked her up for me. Cool, huh?"

"I guess. Hey, don't get up yet. I have to give you your antibiotic."

"But I gotta answer my mail."

I'd been through this sort of thing before with my sons, usually right in the middle of dinner. "It can wait a few minutes," I said firmly. "I don't want you to accidentally pull this needle loose. Just stay right where you are, young lady."

I knelt again and got busy with the catheter: a regular 20 gauge butterfly needle. Nicholas stood up on her knees as I cleaned her left arm. He eyed me like I was a juicy cut of porterhouse. I squinted back at him.

"Mishelle, Nicholas won't bite me, will he?"

"No, no." Right handed, she took hold of his collar and he growled softly, his eyes never leaving me as I uncapped the needle.

It went in smoothly, thank heavens. Nicholas didn't look especially pleased. I decided I would rub his chest later.

Her email robot announced the arrival of more messages. She shifted as if to rise and I laid a hand on her knee. Nick's growl shifted up a third in pitch.

I pulled my hand back. "Please hold still until we're done, Mishelle. Please. And keep Nicholas back."

"Aw . . . Okay." She fidgeted in the chair, Nicholas tucked under her right arm while I loaded the syringe.

It was an IV push per doctor's orders, rather than a bag, which would have been easier but also would have taken much longer. It was a darn big dose, too: ten cc. I uncapped the needle, pulled the alcohol pad off the catheter and let her have it.

"Ooh! Ow, that *burns*!" Nicholas growled in harmony with his mistress and the hint of fangs showed behind his thin black lips.

"Yes, I know." I tried to soothe her and stroked her arm with my free hand, noticing again how smooth it was. "Just be patient, Mishelle. It'll be over soon."

"Ugh." She squirmed again in her chair, her respiration rate visibly increasing. "My arm's on fire." She grimaced. Nicholas rolled his eyes.

"Half done. One more minute." I kept a slow, constant pressure on the plunger. No infiltrations for me, thank you. I saw that happen once and it was pretty ugly.

At last I was done. I backed the syringe out and capped it, tucked it in my portable sharps container. The catheter had to stay in place for the next few days so I wrapped it carefully and stood.

"Don't rub that, dear." She was reaching for her arm, a relieved expression settling across her features. "Okay, show me this robot secretary of yours."

Her discomfort apparently forgotten, Mishelle set Nicholas on the floor and eagerly lifted herself with her stripper pole, went to her computer chair and sat down.

Her hands *flew* over the keyboard. She was obviously in her element. Krystal the voice program repeated the name of each key she touched like some crazed high-speed version of Simon-Says. She clicked onto her email and Krystal read it to her in a very stilted, robotic voice.

"Amazing," I commented. "I would have never thought that a blind person could use a computer so fast."

Mishelle snickered. "Honey, I used to be able to type a hundred and twenty three words per minute. My Russian hands and Roman fingers are good for *something*." She held up her hands to me, stretched them toward me and I looked, really *looked* at them.

They were her eyes, her voice on the Net and the core of the only skills she possessed that this society could accept. They were long and lean and they radiated strength: surgeon's hands or concert pianist's hands.

I was fascinated. Absurdly, I wanted to hold them in mine in that moment.

"My pinkies are so crooked," she complained. "Look at them. They work great for the space bar, though." She grinned and I couldn't help but grin back at her, never mind that she couldn't see me.

"I'd be lost without my gadgets," she said and I believed her. She slid her chair to the right, her hands questing across the tabletop until they came to a gadget that resembled nothing so much as an electric piano: black and rectangular, with keys and controls that only confused me.

"This is my Braille embosser." Mishelle ran her long, strong fingers over the surface of it, caressingly. "If I want to read my email in, I just push a button and it prints it out here in Braille. I can also print letters and my own emails to review before I send them. And I can even scan books into the computer and I can have Krystal either read the book to me or print it out in Braille."

"Yeah, but that voice," I protested. "Don't tell me you *like* how she sounds?"

She laughed. "Oh, I don't mind. It puts me right to sleep, in fact. My computer guru told me once he could modify her voice to make it sound more human but he never shared that secret with me." She looked resigned for a moment. "You know how computer nerds can be sometimes."

"*The time is Twelve pm. The temperature is forty-two degrees.*" It was a different robot voice, more harsh than Krystal's. I turned, looking for the source.

"Okay, now who was *that*?"

Mishelle giggled. "I haven't named that one yet."

She got up and headed for the kitchenette and as she passed a file cabinet tucked under the dining room window, she bumped it. Cat food was suddenly everywhere. Blue the kitty jumped up and nosed among the kibble as Mishelle began righting the overturned items.

I knew without being told that this was commonplace and that saying anything, even offering to help would not endear me to either Mishelle or her kitty. She knew what had just happened and who was *I* to step in and tell her: "Hey, what a mess! Let me help."

Sometimes the best help amounts to just staying the hell out of the way.

She finished straightening the items but left about a bowlful of kibble still scattered on the floor and table. I stayed silent as she continued into the kitchenette and got a glass of water.

Mishelle returned to her chair, panting now, obviously winded from even that little exertion. Her color was blotchy and I felt a surge of alarm.

But I kept quiet, waiting and listening to the voices of her gadgets: Krystal the email robot, the time and date robot, even a caller ID program that announced the number of every caller.

It was strange and more than a little eerie. Her front room sounded like an electronics convention with all the attendees wired for sound: bells, whistles and speech borrowed from those with warmer hearts.

I wasn't altogether comfortable with it. I think I've always preferred a human's voice to one generated by silicon.

Watching Mishelle catch her breath, I noticed a mesh bag hanging from the side of her recliner that contained a small arsenal of remote controls. When she'd finally caught her breath, I inquired about them:

"Don't tell me you use *all* of those? I can barely use the one we have for our DVD player."

Mishelle grinned again and it struck me how the age and fatigue dropped away from her face when she smiled. "Of course," she replied. I could tell she was very pleased that I'd asked. She pulled them out, randomly as far as I could tell, and proceeded to demonstrate:

"This is the DVD control. I like it 'cause it's got a dial-type fast forward and reverse. The button kind is too slow and the buttons wear out too fast. Here's the dish control for the satellite receiver and here's the TV itself. This one's for the air conditioner—can't live without that one—and this one is for the cat collar,"

"Eh?"

"It zaps Blue. Little buzzy sensation on the inside; keeps her off the equipment so she doesn't knock over anything. Here's the CD player control. I really like the recall and shuffle modes on it. This one," she held up another, almost identical to them all as far as I could see. "This is the stereo control. It has EQ presets on it so I can change the tone controls for whatever kind of music I'm listening to. Station presets too, of course, mostly talk radio."

"Really?" I wasn't particularly surprised. "Who do you listen to?"

She grinned again, wickedly this time. "Believe it or not, I like listening to Rush Limbaugh. I love to yell back at that asshole. It's a great tension reliever."

I giggled, envisioning a big, blind transgender woman yelling at the country's biggest archconservative. "What about the music stations?"

Mishelle sniffed. "Too redneck. I'm a classic rocker chick, y'know? Check out my CD collection."

My patient waved a hand toward the racks of compact discs. There might have been hundreds. "Pink Floyd. Beatles. Crosby, Stills and Nash. Jefferson Airplane, though I kinda like the Starship, too. Janis Joplin, Zeppelin! *Love* them. Classics! Back when rock was real and they didn't use computers."

"*You* use computers," I pointed out.

She smiled. "Ya got me there. I'd hate to do without them, though."

"I see your point."

For a moment, I was bewildered. This woman, blind nearly all her life, had more physical dexterity than me and a far greater working knowledge than I of electronic devices that left me, for the most part, utterly baffled.

My world view was being stood on its ear and shaken, none too gently.

I cleared my throat. "Wow. That's . . . Mishelle, that's amazing. *You're* amazing."

She smiled again and I felt warm clear through. "Aw, shucks. T'ain't nothin', really."

"Yeah, it is. Really." I took a deep breath and sat down on the love-seat. "Hey, I have to tell you something. You'll have a different nurse tomorrow."

She looked resigned. "Yeah, that happens a lot. And a different one after that, I suppose."

"No, not this time. I'm a part-timer, but I'm still the primary nurse on your case so I made arrangements to make sure that the same nurse will always be here when I'm not. Her name is Judy and she's really nice. You'll like her."

"Not as much as I like you." It was said so matter-of-fact that I blinked, not knowing what to say for a moment.

"Oh. Well, uh, I'm . . . That's nice. I'll be back on Friday to see you. Okay?"

She smiled but it was a little dimmed this time. "Sure. I'll be looking forward to it."

I shook her hand and told her to stay in her chair as I let myself out. I got into my messy little Toyota. Started it and with the engine idling, I stared through the windshield at the Elvis license plate, letting my thoughts chase each other for a few minutes.

I was in a state and its name was Confusion.

I had somehow fallen into the habit of making mistakes on this case and referring to Mishelle as a *he* was only one of my mistakes. I don't like making mistakes. They can be very costly in terms of lives.

I'd made a fairly typical mistake, I think, that most people make when dealing with blind folk. We assume that they're helpless when in fact the very opposite is more often true. That person in there could run rings around me with computers, stereos, satellite receivers, Braille technology and who knew what else?

But the mistake that nagged at me the most was one I was having the most trouble admitting, much less dealing with: I didn't like this transgender issue at all.

It bothered me, like a cut on the inside of your cheek bothers you and you can't keep from touching it with your tongue, no matter how sore it is.

I didn't like the transgender issue because I couldn't wrap my mind around the two realities: she was a woman and she was also a man.

It made me feel as if my eyeballs were about to roll around in their sockets. My head hurt and my stomach felt kind of queasy, too.

Woman, yet man. Man, but really a woman.

Ouch.

One thing was abundantly clear: I was not without prejudice in this one. Bluntly, I was one judgmental asshole, myself. Move over, Rush Limbaugh. A conservative like the fat man from Fox would call her lifestyle seedy or even perverse and right then, I might've agreed, God forgive me.

It made me feel like a great big phony because I wanted her to like me. But did I really like her? Did I?

Nothing and no one answered.

Did I accept her for whom and what she was?

Well, that was simple enough: no. I could not, would not accept this two people in one body thing. My mind kept veering away.

My runaway mouth was ample proof of that.

I shrugged mentally, put the car in gear and backed away from her apartment. There were other questions more pressing than whom or what my patient was, inside or out.

Truth be told, she would only be on the service for a little while longer and then the matter would be out of my hands.

Wouldn't it? I braked for a stoplight and nibbled at my lower lip.

Another truth to be told: I wanted to like her, but I didn't know her well enough, not just yet. A painful thought mingled with that one and they bounced around inside my head like drops of water on a hot griddle: I was *ashamed*.

The answers to those questions made it perfectly clear to me that there were reserves of prejudice and bigotry deep inside myself; dark, ugly things that made my face feel hot when I thought about them.

Perhaps when I saw Mishelle next, there would be better answers.

CHAPTER THREE

Authenticity

THAT WEEKEND PASSED. A previously dormant part of my brain was nibbling away at the notion of my bias about Mishelle's lifestyle. I wasn't distracted exactly, but my patient and her somewhat bizarre existence was never far from my mind. In retrospect, I can see now that I was on the verge of taking steps over that professional line of demarcation that separates patient from friend. I often wonder what my life would be like if I'd just shrugged it off and relegated her to that file in my head marked *Beyond Help*.

It's a small file though, and I don't put people there unless there's absolutely no hope at all. Sometimes I think that hope is the only thing that distinguishes us from everything else living on this good, green Earth.

Tuesday morning, I called her to let her know I'd be coming that day. She surprised me by answering: "Hi, Michelle."

"Hi! Hey, how did you know it was me?"

"I have your phone number memorized," she said, not without some pride.

"Oh." I was both flattered and flustered. "Well, I'm on my way to your place. How are you feeling?"

"The same: not so good."

I bit my lip. Not the answer I was hoping for . . . "I'll be there as soon as I can."

I might have exceeded the speed limit a little getting there. I pulled up to her place, hopped out and knocked.

"It's open!" was followed by a bubbly, painful-sounding cough. I winced and pushed the door. Nicholas barked at once and then recognized me, transforming his bark into a tail wag. I set my bag down and took a look at her.

She was using the nebulizer which is a wonderful gadget if you have an ordinary cold or even pneumonia. With the right medication, usually Xopenex, it can loosen sticky mucous in the lungs and bronchi, ease breathing and bring relief to some serious congestion in most patients.

The operative word here is *most*. I could tell, just by looking at Mishelle that neither the nebulizer nor her antibiotics were having much effect on her infection. Her face was drawn and sallow and there were dark circles under her eyes; much worse than usual.

I felt a chill, looking at her.

Speaking of cold—I looked down and saw that she wasn't wearing socks or slippers. I raised an eyebrow.

"Aren't your feet freezing?" I asked as I was getting out my stethoscope and blood pressure cuff.

"A little," she admitted. "But I don't notice it much anymore and besides, bare feet help me navigate around this apartment."

"Oh." I hadn't thought of that, but it made perfect sense. Feet are like hands that we walk on, after all.

I wrapped the cuff around her arm and noticed that she had on the same skirt she'd been wearing during my last visit. A few extra stains had been added since then.

I shook my head in distaste and noted her blood pressure—unusually good for *anyone*—and undid the cuff, began listening to her lungs.

Yuck. Gurgles and crackles. It sounded like a bowl of Rice Krispies in there.

"So you're not feeling any better?"

She shook her head. "I can't seem to cough any of it up. It's like it's stuck." As if to illustrate her point, she coughed: a wet, hacking noise. I winced again.

"How did your doctor's appointment go yesterday?"

She scowled. "It didn't. I had to cancel it."

Uh-oh. "Why?"

"Because I didn't have a caregiver yesterday," she snapped. "Won't have one today, either."

"Why not?"

She sighed. "Lynn had surgery and can't be here until next week and Nicky had babysitting issues or something." She scowled again. "It's always *something* with her," she muttered. Louder: "It ticks me off!"

"So what do you do when that happens?" I asked.

She shrugged. "I make do the best I can." She stuck the nebulizer mouthpiece back into her mouth and sucked deep on it, even though it had to be empty by then.

Carefully, feeling like I was picking my way though a minefield, I said, "Well, tomorrow is the last of your IV antibiotics, Mishelle. I need to talk to your doctor and discuss your options. You haven't responded to the antibiotics as you should have and the infection is still present."

She took the mouthpiece out. "What options?"

"Well, we should consider hospitalization where you can receive more aggressive treatment."

"I will *not* go back there! I'd rather die!" Her words might have been forged from red-hot steel. It was the first time I'd ever heard her shout and for a moment, I was afraid it might set off another serious coughing fit.

"Why not?" I pitched my voice as soothingly as possible. Asking her to calm down would just make her more upset.

"I was there last year and they absolutely humiliated me, especially the nurses." I'd never heard such venom and pain before in one person's voice.

"The nurses? Really?" I must have sounded doubtful.

"Yes! That damned place needs more compassionate people like *you*."

For a moment, I was taken aback. I'd been thinking that she was able to somehow see through me and spot my professional demeanor as a cover-up for my discomfort with her lifestyle.

That she actually regarded me as compassionate or caring left me speechless for a moment.

She went on: "Michelle, my life is such a fucked-up mess, sometimes I wish I could just *die*." A strange expression crossed her face, something I'd never seen before on anyone. In a dull voice, empty of emotion, she added: "Sometimes when I get really depressed, I beat myself. That's what happened last night."

Gently: "Did you hurt yourself?"

"Oh, I'm okay," she said sullenly.

I stared at her, Jodie's word's echoing in my head: *Don't get caught up in her drama.*

I'd hit a wall and for the first time in my professional career, I didn't know what to do or say. I knew I should have asked her if she was feeling suicidal or at least pursued some line of inquiry about her beating herself, but I just couldn't do that.

I looked at her drawn, empty face and I knew that it would have been a waste of time. Asking her anything would just drive her deeper into that dark place within where no one, not even me, would ever be welcome.

So I chickened out and let it go, saying only: "Well, let's just wait and see how you're doing tomorrow. I'll call your doctor and we'll go from there. Okay?"

Listlessly, she nodded. I packed up my things and beat a hasty retreat. I left her apartment without even asking her if there was anything that she needed or if I could do something to help her.

I've never felt more ashamed than in that moment. *And you call yourself a nurse.*

As I pulled away, it dawned on me why she'd had on the same clothes as she'd worn three days before: she was too short of breath to get up and go change into clean ones.

I had allowed myself to be fooled into thinking that her COPD wasn't that bad. She was still able to get up from her chair and walk into the kitchen or the bathroom, but I saw now how much effort it cost her and I saw too, that it was all for my benefit.

She didn't want to appear weak.

But with the clarity that comes from admitting to yourself that you've been wrong, that you've been deceived by your own expectations, I could see now that she was constantly short of breath, even just sitting in her chair and doing nothing.

Her condition, as we say in my profession, was guarded.

More: there was no way that she would be discharged from Home Health anytime soon. Not possible.

And *I* would still be her case manager. Me? I saw this woman as bizarre and beyond my comprehension. I disapproved of her lifestyle, her behavior and still I knew practically nothing about her.

I was thinking so hard, I almost ran a stoplight. I slammed on the brakes and my car screeched to a stop. A horn sounded behind me but I hardly noticed.

Bottom line, Michelle: are you really disapproving?

Or just scared?

The light changed. I didn't notice that either until the horn blared behind me again. I snapped out of it, gave the car some gas and got out of the way, pulled over and stopped.

Education. I needed to know more about this, about my patient and who she really was. But to do that, I had to lose all of my preconceptions, all of the innate notions I had about the concept of gender, what little I did know.

Did it matter who or what Mishelle was? Did it matter that she was a man who lived as a woman?

All I could see was someone seriously ill, a patient who needed my help. Why should it bother me how she chose to live her life?

I didn't have to agree with it or live that way myself but I had a duty, a sworn responsibility to provide the best care possible and I knew that I was failing miserably in that regard.

Why was I finding this so hard to accept?

I realized that I was practically strangling the steering wheel. I relaxed my grip and in that moment I realized that I *was* scared: scared of something different, something bizarre, something I'd never experienced before.

Somehow that made it easier. I made up my mind to ask her. Why not? The most she could do was tell me to mind my own business and I had a hunch she wouldn't do that.

Jodie had called her needy and I snorted in disgust. Well, of course she was needy. She was blind and alone. Anyone would be needy in that space, that condition and being transgender had nothing to do with it.

I put the car in gear and drove home, feeling a little better. Okay: education and acceptance. With a little patience and luck, one would bring the other.

Dave was puttering around in the kitchen. He looked up when I came in.

"Hi, hon. How did it go today?"

I put my bag down and gave him a kiss. "Not so good. Mishelle's not doing very well. We're going to have to keep her on service for a while longer."

He frowned. "Meaning you, of course."

"Well, of course."

"Hmm."

I let it pass. I've known my husband long enough to know that when he makes those noises, it means he's not happy. I also know him well enough to know when to leave him alone to figure things out in his own way and in his own time.

I knew, even if I wasn't fully aware of it right then. I was coming to regard Mishelle as someone more than just a patient.

Maybe I was afraid, just a little, of what my man might say about someone I was beginning to respect and even admire.

* * *

Rolling out of bed the next day, I felt totally energized. I had a plan and the means to execute it:

I would see Mishelle that morning, ask some of those questions that had been haunting me and finally get to the bottom of this transgender thing that had been keeping me at arms length from my patient in the few short days I'd known her.

For openers, I was determined to apologize for my shameful behavior the day before.

It was the seventh day of her antibiotic treatment, the day she was supposed to be to be discharged, but I knew it wasn't going to happen. All of her symptoms indicated that the infection was firmly entrenched. It was going to require an especially powerful antibiotic regimen to eliminate it and what little I knew of pharmacology told me that the selections were diminishing.

I called her doctor from the office that morning and we had a short, somewhat depressing conversation. He confirmed my evaluation and prescribed two more oral antibiotics for her. I made sure the pharmacy would deliver them that day, looked in on one of my other patients and then headed off to visit Mishelle.

When I arrived, I could hear the TV going full-blast inside. I stopped with my knuckles poised over the *Elvis Fans* sign and then shrugged. Well, this would answer at least one of my questions.

I knocked and Nicholas barked in response from within.

There was no other answer, so I let myself in. What I saw made me grin with delight.

Mishelle was listening to the *Today* show so intently; I was instantly reminded of that RCA dog. At her feet was Nicholas, dancing about impatiently and barking up a storm.

When he saw me, his bark seemed to change from *Warning* to *Welcome*. He danced in my direction and I bent down to stroke him and rub his big chest. His tail wagged madly so I was fairly sure that he had accepted me but what about his mistress?

I looked up at her.

She didn't acknowledge me but there was a faint smile on her face as she listened to the TV.

"Good morning!" I announced cheerfully. "What's new with Katie and Matt?"

Her smile deepened. "I love Katie Couric," she said over a commercial. "She has a soothing voice. I'll bet she has a nice smile."

"She does and so do you," I responded. I set my bag on the coffee table and looked her over.

She looked better. The dark circles under her eyes weren't as pronounced and her color seemed less pale. She was wearing a clean dress: a very good sign.

It was time to put my plan into action. "Say, can I get you anything before we start?"

She nodded and slipped her hand into the mesh bag containing the remotes. Without any fumbling whatsoever, she pulled out the TV remote and turned the sound down.

"How 'bout heating up my coffee for me?"

I nodded back, immediately felt foolish and said, "Sure thing." I grabbed her coffee cup and water jug and went into the kitchen.

The coffee cup went into the microwave and I nuked it on high for sixty seconds while I filled her water jug. Blue the kitty strolled in and began rubbing against my leg. When I glanced down, she moved away and jumped up to her food dish. It was empty. She nosed it and then meowed at me plaintively.

"Mishelle, did you have a caregiver yesterday?" I called out.

"Nicky was here for a little while. She fixed me something to eat and helped me change clothes."

"Well, that's good. Where's your cat food? I think Blue is hungry."

"Lower cabinet left of the sink. Plastic storage container. It's marked."

I looked and there it was, right where she'd said. I filled Blue's dish and noticed Nicholas's water dish was empty so I filled that and put it on the floor for him.

He raced to it, tail wagging madly and began lapping greedily. Poor dear, he was thirsty.

Her coffee was done so I carried it and the water jug back into the front room. I happened to glance down the hall and noticed something that made me compress my lips into a thin line: the hallway was positively littered with dog turds.

Yuck. I set her water jug and coffee cup within reach and went back into the kitchen.

"What are you doing?" she called.

"Cleaning up the landmines," I said, a bit grimly. I grabbed a roll of paper towels and started scooping up the piles, shooting Nicholas a glare.

He looked embarrassed and slunk away, head down and tail between his legs. "Yeah, you should be," I whispered at him.

"What?"

"Nothing. Garbage can under the sink?"

"Yes. You don't have to do that, you know. That's not your job."

"I know but I don't want you to step in them."

"Well, it's happened before," she said cheerfully.

"Not while *I'm* here," I muttered. I dropped the mess into the garbage can, giving thanks that Nicholas had left neat little piles and then washed my hands.

I returned to the front room. "There. All done. How are you feeling?"

She shrugged. "About the same."

I sat down on the loveseat, feeling the plastic crinkle behind my legs, and dug out my stethoscope and blood pressure cuff. Blue jumped up next to me and made herself comfortable. "Why does Nicholas do that, anyway? Isn't he housebroken?"

She looked embarrassed, too. "Well, he *was* but when I was in the hospital last year, nobody came over to let him out and he got into some bad habits. Since I can't see him when he does it, I can't discipline him. He's a good boy despite that. He's what they call a therapy dog, a home companion and he's my friend, too. I just can't bear to spank him for something that's not his fault, not really."

I looked down at the plastic behind my legs. "Is that why you have the loveseat wrapped like this?"

"Yep. That damn dog pees on every corner in this place."

I was kind of surprised her place didn't smell like a kennel. "I'll make sure he gets a chance to go out before I leave."

"Thanks." She still looked a little embarrassed, so I changed the subject:

"I spoke to your doctor this morning before I came over. He's pre-scribed two oral antibiotics and the pharmacy is going to deliver them today."

I took a deep breath. "He knows how reluctant you are about going into the hospital and he's willing to try this approach first"—in fact, I had all but begged him to—"but he wants you to know that if this doesn't do the trick, then you'd better reconsider your decision."

"Well," she said firmly, "Then these had better work because I am *not* going back there, not for any reason."

I was silent for a few moments, thinking about that and studying her face and the sheer, immutable stubbornness I saw there.

She certainly had the right to refuse hospitalization and the right to stop taking the antibiotics altogether, but did she really understand the consequences of her actions?

Yes. Looking at her, I was suddenly and completely sure of that. She knew, even more than I, what that meant and for a moment, my eyes stung terribly as I fought my emotions to a standstill.

My surge of feeling subsided and receded as quickly as it had come. I took another deep breath.

It was time to ask some of those questions, starting with that thorny transgender issue. I opened my mouth . . .

And nothing came out. I knew, somehow, that now was not the time. Whatever the reason, I couldn't go there right then.

"You're awfully quiet," Mishelle remarked. "Trying to think of a way to talk me into it?"

I cleared my throat. "Uh, no. Actually, I was wondering if you'd mind answering a few questions about your blindness."

She smiled from ear to ear. "I'd love to. Ask me anything."

"Okay. Do you see colors in your mind?"

"All the time. I see colors, yes, but you know something? I'm never sure if the color is right, like the colors *you* see."

"How do you mean?"

She seemed to settle back in her chair and relax. "Well, I know I dream in color. I think I remember the color red and the color green. We had a barn that was red and my dad had a green tractor."

"When I say red to you, what does it make you think of?"

"Fire. Heat. Energy."

"Blue?"

She smiled. "That's my favorite color. Calmness and serenity. The color of the sky."

"Yellow?"

"Ah, that's the color of sunlight. Roses. My favorite roses are yellow."

I hesitated. *What the hell*, I thought. "What do you think *I* look like?"

Her smile turned shy. "You're little. Light-colored hair: blonde, I think, with dark streaks in it and your eyes are blue."

I stared at her. "Exactly right. How . . . How did you know?"

Her smile was rather smug, now. "I told you that I can see with more than just my eyes."

I was more than a bit stunned. "I guess so."

"Y'know, I can do a lot of things even if I am blind." Her voice wasn't boastful at all, just matter-of-fact.

"Like what, for example?"

"I used to drive a car."

My jaw dropped. "You're *kidding*!"

"Nope. I only crashed once and that was into a fence. I can do pretty well if I have a good navigator with me."

My astonishment was growing, along with a strange sense of excitement. "What else?"

"I went skydiving once."

"Oh my *God*! Really?"

"Uh-huh." Her expression turned dreamy. "It was so wonderful. I felt like I was floating with nothing but the wind to keep me company." She giggled. "They told me to pull the ripcord after ten seconds but I didn't want to. I wanted to keep on floating."

I swallowed with some difficulty. "Good thing you did, else we wouldn't be here talking about it. The ground can be awfully hard."

"Don't I know it!" She sighed. "I'd love to do that again someday."

I've never understood skydiving. People who *want* to jump out of a perfectly good airplane have always struck me as a little crazy. I had a psych instructor in nursing school who told us that skydiving sublimates the fear of falling into that part of our brains which makes us laugh.

Crazy. But this woman was not crazy, not in the least. "What else have you done?"

"I used to water-ski with my family when I was a teenager." Another giggle: "That was easy!"

I enjoy waterskiing myself and I could not imagine how waterskiing blind could possibly be easy. "How in the world did you avoid wakes from other boats?"

"One toot on the horn means a wave is coming. Two toots means go left, three toots means go right. Four toots means let go!"

I could not take my eyes from the expressions playing across her face: joy and satisfaction and an amazing sense of self that told me to let go, too.

Just: *let go*.

"You've led an exciting life, Mishelle. Except for when you lived in Seattle, have you always lived here in Kalispell?"

She nodded. "Mostly. I was born in Kansas though, and once I hitchhiked down from Kansas to Florida. Just me and my white cane. Didn't have any trouble getting rides."

I thought of the many horrible ways a blind person could be abused or taken advantage of while hitchhiking and shuddered. "Weren't you worried that someone might have robbed you or hurt you?"

She shrugged. "Being blind kind of makes most people treat you with respect, I guess. I wasn't scared at all, traveling by myself. I wanted to see the world and that's what I did."

See the world. Yes, she did. Even though blind, she could see the world in ways I could only imagine and not very well at that.

I shook myself, feeling like I was awakening from a daydream. I glanced at my watch and saw with a shock that it was close to noon. I'd been there at Mishelle's apartment for almost two hours.

I needed to be home, with my husband and my boys. More: I needed time for myself, time to think about all that I'd heard, time to understand it and fit all of this into the concept of Mishelle that was slowly taking shape within my mind.

"Mishelle, it's time I went home. Can I get you something to eat before I leave?"

She shook her head, a sad and resigned expression surfacing for just a moment across her weathered features. "No, I'm not hungry right now." She touched her wristwatch and I was startled to see her flip open the crystal and delicately touch the hands on its face. "You're right, it's almost noon. Nicky should be here soon to fix me something to eat. You should be home with your family."

I swallowed the lump that had suddenly appeared in my throat. "Yes, you're right. I should. Do you . . . Do you see your family much? Do they ever visit you?"

She smiled wistfully. "Not as much as I'd like. We don't agree on much, you know. What's your family like?"

"I have two sons. Chris is nine and Zach is twelve."

That wistful smile was beginning to tear at my heart. "You have two boys? How lovely. I always wanted to have children but it never happened, even though I was married two times."

I stared at her. "You *were*? You'll have to tell me about that."

"Maybe I will. Someday."

I could see the doors in her face closing, gently but inexorably forcing me out of her world. So I fell back into my nurse persona; took her vitals quickly and then let Nicholas out as I'd promised.

When I packed up my things, she was listening to the TV again, the sound turned up good and loud, letting me know that it was time for me to leave; time for me to give her the space she needed.

I took her hand and it was as if I wasn't there. Her long, strong fingers lay limply within mine, unwilling to acknowledge my presence.

"I'll see you tomorrow," I whispered and I wasn't sure that she'd heard me for a moment then she nodded, once.

I wanted to kiss her hand but I refrained. The line was back and we both knew it.

I gave Nicholas a brief pat on his little head and let myself out, closing the door gently behind me.

I drove home, my thoughts a jumble. I was struggling for perspective, something that could give me some sort of handle on my feelings and all that I'd heard that day.

Nothing came to me. I had about given up when I pulled into my driveway and then it burst into my consciousness like some sort of magnificent fireworks display, accompanied by a silent voice that was impossible to ignore:

How could she know she was a woman when she'd never seen herself?

I sat stunned, staring blindly through the windshield of my little Toyota and listened to that voice with something very much like awe.

Mishelle could not possibly compare herself with other women and know that she wanted to look like that or be like that. She would never be able to actually *see* herself as feminine.

It had to be something else; something that could only be described as a deep sense of *self*. Psychologists and psychiatrists and scientists and researchers alike have been trying to define *self* ever since mankind emerged from the caves and began to build a civilization.

Mishelle knew herself as no one else I'd ever met.

She knew with a certainty that shook me to my very core that she was female. Yet she had never seen herself, never had a role model or something to compare herself to and say: "*That's* what I am. *That's* what I want to be."

Open-mouthed, I sat in my driveway, shivering as this knowledge swept over me like surf in a tropical storm.

She knew she was female because she *felt* it in a way that most of us could never comprehend. We humans tend to take our sense of self for granted because it's such an integral part of our very existence that questioning it almost isn't worth the effort for most people.

Most people would call Mishelle confused and bizarre at best, weird or kinky at worst. She was instead the most self-aware individual I'd ever met.

By extension, she could only be thought of as completely, wonderfully, gloriously *sane*.

Not crazy. Not bizarre or weird or kinky.

Sane.

Possibly the sanest, most authentic person I'd ever met. And her sanity had been hard-fought and her authentic self won through years of struggle that I was only now coming to understand.

Shocked, I saw that her strengths were my own weaknesses. I utterly lacked her courage in facing my own identity, my own sense of self.

I'd spent many years being a nurse, a housewife and a mother; never once questioning my roles and my identity; accepting all that those labels meant; accepting the labels attached to me by others as if they were a self-fulfilling prophecy: the only path to fulfillment and happiness.

I'd never questioned it, any of it. Until now.

My eyes stung. I brushed at them impatiently, knowing that I had a family to face and my own life to live.

Knowing too, that her life was now bound up inextricably with mine and knowing as well that I had no idea where all this would take me. If she could undertake that journey with such consummate courage than who was I to cringe at the thought?

I had much to learn but I was sure that she would teach me, if I asked.

FIRST INTERLUDE

"Do you think you violated policy then?"

I swallowed a big lump in my throat. "Yes. I did."

"Your supervisors knew about this, I take it?"

I shook my head. "Not . . . Not all of it, no."

He eyed me. "But you're going to tell me all of it, aren't you?"

I nodded. "Oh, yes. All of it . . ."

PART TWO

Learning Curve

CHAPTER FOUR

Apples and Oranges

ONCE AGAIN, I STOOD before the *Elvis Fans* sign, fist poised over the door and wondering what I'd find on the other side. Was she better? Worse? I hesitated again.

I'd been worrying about my strange, sad and utterly unique patient. The last few days had passed in a blur for me. Dave had noticed and so had my sons:

There is a tree in my backyard that I sit beneath in summer, my spine against its rough bark and my bare feet stretched out before me or dug into the coarse grass of our lawn. When I have the time, I go there to relax and take my mind off the day and its stresses and pressures.

It's a good tree, with a strong, thick trunk that holds one end of my hammock and provides just the right amount of shade on warm sunny days. I go there when I can and turn off my mind and let the rest of the world drift by. It sounds silly but the tree seems to accept me, as if it trusted me to not prune it drastically or carve my initials into its trunk.

Five days into my patient's new antibiotic regime, I stood inside looking out through the tall windows at the south end of our family room, staring at the tree through the slushy snow of a miserable March, wishing with all my heart that summer was here again and I could go out there to just sit and let all this drift away.

"Mom?"

I turned to see Chris, my youngest son.

"Yes, baby?"

"Is something wrong?" He had an anxious expression on his cherubic face. I shook my head.

"No, dear. I'm just thinking."

"You've been standing there an awful long time."

I smiled. "And just how long have you been watching me, sweetie?"

He shrugged. "Not long." I could see that he was struggling to get the words out, wrestling with a very adult kind of concern.

My little boy was growing up and my heart melted; seeing his expression. Too soon and too fast they grow. It seemed like just a few short weeks since I'd held him in my arms; wrapped in his blanket, fussing over him and making those silly sounds that mothers make to newborns.

"Come here, Cee-Boo." It's my pet name for him. He came to me obediently, because both of my boys are good kids and they nearly always do what they're told.

I guess I'm lucky, considering how some kids turn out these days.

I put my arms around him, kissed the top of his head and then mussed his hair. He hates that, which is probably why I do it.

"I'm okay. I'm just thinking about a new patient I have."

He pulled back a little and looked up into my face. "Is she okay?"

I frowned a bit, looking down at him. "How did you know it was a she?"

"I heard you and Dad talking about her last night. He sounded kinda mad or something."

I sighed. "No, he's not mad. He's just . . . concerned. That's all."

"Oh. Is she gonna be okay?"

I sighed again. "I don't know, Cee-Boo. I hope so. I really do."

Two days later; standing before her door; fist poised to knock; I thought about that. *Hope.*

I was beginning to think that hope was becoming a very important part of this case, maybe the most important part.

I knocked.

A strange voice I didn't recognize yelled something unintelligible within and Nicholas barked, once. Brow furrowed, I turned the knob, thinking: *Doesn't she ever lock this door?*

"Hello?" I called. A short, plump woman with flaming red hair came around the corner of the hallway and stopped, smiling at me.

"Hi!" she said in a loud, almost brassy voice. "You must be Michelle!"

"That's right. And you must be . . . Lynn?"

"That's me," she said cheerfully. "Pleased to meet you!"

We shook hands while I looked her over. She seemed like the kind of woman you'd see at a church social; serving the punch and glad-handing every new arrival; one of those boisterous volunteer types that has a different kind of welcome for every kind of person.

I liked her immediately.

Mishelle was in her chair, the faint half-smile that was her usual expression in place. I patted her on the leg, said hello and set my bag down on the coffee table.

Lynn headed out the door, a red-headed whirlwind forever in motion, saying: "Michelle hon, I'm going to the store to pick up a few things. I'll be back soon. Nice to meet you, Michelle Number Two!"

I couldn't help grinning at her as she bustled out. "Nice meeting you too, Lynn!" I called at her. The door closed behind her and the whirlwind was gone. I could almost imagine the curtains slowly settling back into place.

I sat down on the loveseat and regarded my patient. "How are you today, Mishelle?"

"A little better, actually. My cough isn't as bad, even though I still can't cough up much. Maybe the antibiotics are finally kicking in."

She leaned forward to catch her breath and I grabbed my bag, took out my stethoscope and stood.

"Well, let's find out, shall we?" I leaned over her to listen to her lungs and noticed that she was wearing a purple bra.

"Hey, nice bra, Mishelle. Very colorful. Victoria's Secret?"

"Nah, Lane Bryant. You like that, do ya?"

I chuckled. "Well, maybe I'm envious. Mine are all boring white. Take some deep breaths, please."

She complied as best as she could and I listened intently. There was still a lot of crud in there, but they did sound better. I felt a surge of relief tempered by caution.

"They *do* sound better. Have you been able to cough anything up?"

"Not really. Why?"

I stood up and took the earpieces out. "Well, the color of the phlegm might tell us some things about the nature of the infection. Was it dark or light colored?"

Mishelle leaned back, adjusting her blouse and smiled up at me. "How should *I* know? I can't see, remember?"

I couldn't believe I'd just said that. Face hot, I said, "Uh, sorry. I . . . forgot. *Duh*." I laughed weakly. "Well, could you, like, save some in a Kleenex or something when you do cough some up? It would help a lot."

"Whatever you want, sweetie," she said cheerfully.

I sighed, feeling a knot of something loosen within my chest and my embarrassment was gone, just like that. My patient had a way of putting me at ease that rivaled my own interpersonal skills. That aura of serenity and repose was again draped around her shoulders and it was strangely relaxing just to be in her presence.

I took the blood pressure cuff out of my bag and began taking her vitals. "Lynn seems pretty nice," I said.

She nodded. "She and I go back a long ways," she declared. "Almost seventeen years."

"Really? Well, how long has she been your caregiver, then?" I noted her blood pressure; remarkably low as always.

"About two years. When I started to really need help, I went to an agency that sent caregivers to my home." She pursed her lips and for a moment I was afraid she might spit. "What a disaster! A different one almost every day and not one of them give a damn about me. Most of them either ripped me off or left after humiliating me."

She sighed and I didn't have to be wearing the stethoscope to hear the crackles in her lungs. "I went another route."

"How's that?" I noted her pulse: 68, a nice low rate but a bit higher than it should have been for someone resting in an easy chair.

A smug smile: "I hire my own caregivers now. It's a program called self-directed care. The State pays *me* instead of paying them and it works out a lot better."

"I can imagine. How does it work?"

Mishelle stopped to catch her breath and I waited patiently. Presently she said, "Basically, I'm the boss. They fill out a time card and I pay them at the end of the week. There's only one problem." She stopped to pant gently.

I couldn't resist. I blurted: "What's that?"

"I'm a lousy boss." She smiled again. "I let too many things slide."

I nodded and immediately felt foolish. "Like what?"

Mishelle paused to cough ineffectively and bowed her head for a moment. I waited more patiently this time. When she was done, I asked, "Anything come up?"

She shook her head and reached for her water bottle. I didn't try to help. I knew she had to do it herself.

When she finally recovered a little, I asked again: "What do you let slide, Mishelle?"

She grinned wryly. "The usual. Lateness, sloppiness, overlooking things. I love Lynn dearly but she doesn't have it in her to do any housekeeping. She cleans only when the dust sets off the fire alarm. Nicky . . . Nicky would be late to her own hanging, I think."

I said: "I think we're on the same page here. I once had to supervise thirty-three caregivers for a home-care program."

I winced at the memory and was secretly glad that Mishelle couldn't see my expression. "Worst experience of my life. Oh, don't get me wrong. Some of the people who worked for me were absolutely wonderful but for the most part, I really doubt if most of them had ever heard of a work ethic."

Mishelle smiled again. "But everybody has their strengths and weaknesses, you know. Nicky's a good housekeeper. She likes things nice and tidy and that helps me a lot. Lynn's a great cook but Nicky can't even boil water."

She leaned forward to pant. Then: "I have to take the bad with the good." A shrug: "It evens out, I guess. Nobody's perfect."

She turned her face up to me and her expression was utterly open and trusting. "Except you, I think."

I snorted. "*Me?* I don't think so, sweetie. I put my panties on one leg at a time too, you know."

Her expression didn't change. "If you say so, Michelle. I still think you're pretty terrific and I've only known you a little while." A shy smile surfaced. "You accept me for who I am. That counts for a lot."

I was silent for a long moment.

Blind. Transgender. What a horribly vulnerable existence. Almost helpless, yet she was still willing to trust anyone who could see the thing that was most important to her.

The problem for me was that I wasn't entirely sure that I had come to a full acceptance of this transgender thing, at least to my satisfaction.

"Actually, I met Nicky a few years ago," I said. I knew I was just covering that disquiet. I think she did, too. "She was the primary caregiver for one of our patients with Home Health. I thought she did a pretty good job."

She was silent for a long moment, too. Then: "The thing I like about Nicky is her spunk. She can be a lot of fun, you know. We have some great conversations and she's really funny."

She laughed and it turned into a cough. When it subsided, she said, "When she came to work for me, she was really curious about me. I like that. I told her that if she wanted to know anything about me then all she had to do was just ask."

She put out her hand and I took it. "The same goes for you, you know."

"Really?"

She nodded. "Really. If you have the courage to ask, then I have the courage to answer."

Okay, I thought. *Here goes*: "Are your boobs real?"

She cackled like Janis Joplin but didn't cough, fortunately. "Of all the questions you could have asked . . .! Are you *serious*?"

I was still holding her hand. I gave it a squeeze. "Yeah, I am."

To this day, I don't know why I asked that one first. It just popped out.

"Whoo! Never saw that one coming." She sat up straight and arched her back so they stood out proudly. "Yes ma'am, they certainly are. They may not be much but they're all mine. The doctors told me that they wouldn't grow when I started taking the hormones but I proved 'em wrong."

Her grin was infectious and entirely unselfconscious. "Took seven years, but I did it."

I was fascinated. "I didn't think that was possible."

"Neither did the doctors. Just goes to show ya: if you're determined and you believe in yourself enough, you can do almost anything."

My fascination deepened, if anything. "You sound like a crusader or something."

She nodded. "I am." It was a simple, straightforward declaration and I was jolted to my core at the naked honesty of her tone, her whole demeanor. "I feel that one of the reasons I was put on this Earth was to educate others about transgender people."

Mishelle smiled and held out her hand again. I took it, a little hesitantly. "And you are my latest pupil. How about that?"

I shrugged, a little helplessly. "I . . . Well, Heaven knows I need some education. The only time I ever encountered anyone like you was at Darcelle's."

"Oh, I know that place. Downtown Portland. Darcelle was really nice to me."

I nodded, unsurprised. I knew somehow that she could feel it through our joined hands. "My mom took me there when I was just out of nursing school, almost twenty years ago."

She chuckled. "Yeah, I was in one of those shows once in Seattle."

I let go of her hand as my jaw dropped. "You're kidding! How in the world . . .? What was the name of the club? Were you like a regular performer or something?"

She shook her head. "No, it was just a fashion show for us T's. I don't remember the name of the club."

I rolled my eyes, stifling a snicker. "A *fashion* show?"

She laughed. "Yeah! They put me in this sequined evening gown that must have weighed ten pounds!" She sighed, lungs crackling with congestion. "It felt absolutely delicious! I felt like a queen, not some dude in a dress. The other girls piled my hair up and put layers of makeup on me and put me in a pair of heels that had to be over three inches high!"

"Holy smokes, Mishelle. That would make you six feet seven inches tall! How in the world did you walk in those?"

"Oh, it took a little practice but it was fun." She giggled. "And I have a great swish, too. I rehearsed a lot: ten steps forward, turn left, head down the runway ten more steps, turn around and come back. Simple, right?"

"It *sounds* simple," I said, a little dubiously.

"Well, I fell off the stage anyway." She giggled again as my eyes grew big. I think I must have uttered a squeak of horror. "Don't worry, I wasn't hurt. Being blind makes you used to tripping and taking falls. It did put an end to my pageantry days, though."

I found my voice. "Oh my God, that must have been *so* embarrassing."

She smiled sweetly. "Actually, I thought it was pretty funny. I think I must have miscalculated the number of steps because of the high heels or maybe it was all those cocktails I drank before I went on."

"But didn't you have your cane?" I blurted and was instantly mortified.

"Models don't use canes, Michelle," she chided me, very gently.

"Uh," was all I could manage to say, right then. You could have used my cheeks as stop signs.

I think she might have been enjoying my discomfort. "Anything else you want to ask me?"

Mortified or not, my curiosity got the best of me. "Yes. Why did you move here, to Kalispell of all places? Seattle is . . ."

"More trans-friendly?" I think she must have sensed my nod. She sighed again. It threatened to turn into a coughing fit but I could see her fight it down. "I've often asked myself the same question." She shrugged. "My family is here. I came back because I wanted to be closer to them. I wanted them to accept me."

Family? I was astonished, to put it mildly and my embarrassment forgotten. Where were they? Why weren't they here, helping her? "And do they? Accept you?"

Sadness seemed to settle over her; a gray shadow never far away. "Not really. Mom and I are pretty close and my sister, well, she's a real sweetie. She's a lot younger than me, almost twenty years. I really wish she had more time to see me but she's always so busy."

"What about your Dad?"

She actually hung her head. "No. We've never gotten along. My three brothers are just like him, too." Mishelle shifted painfully in her chair.

Her color by now was quite blotchy. I could hear her breathing increase until she was panting.

It was stressing her terribly to speak of this. I realized that I'd finally gone too far. Changing the subject, I said, "Well, it could be worse, you know. You could be living in Butte, where I come from."

Her head lifted and there was a smirk on her face. "A Butte chick, huh? I hear you gals like to party."

A little nettled, I said, "Well, I've done my share, I guess."

"Yeah, well, they would have run me out of Butte on a rail, sweetie." She took a breath and again somehow managed to keep from coughing. "Anything else you wanna know? Better ask now, 'cause I'm getting kind of tired."

I hesitated, chewing my lip. *Oh, well*: "Do you, I mean, are you attracted to men or women?"

She grinned again but I could see the fatigue-deepened lines around her mouth. "Oh, that's an easy one. Males. Don't worry, Michelle. You're safe with me."

"Well, thanks for that, I guess."

I glanced at my watch and saw that I was running behind; more patients to see that day and I'd spent almost two hours talking to her.

I think I could have spent all day. I stowed my gear and as I shouldered my bag, she lifted her head and turned it in my direction.

"There's something I want you to read for me."

I stopped. "What?" I was thinking she meant something in the newspaper or her mail, but she surprised me again.

"On the bookshelf over my computer. Top shelf, third from the left."

Curious, I went to the shelf and pulled the book down: *She's Not There—A Life in Two Genders* by Jennifer Finney Boylan.

"Looks interesting," I commented, leafing through it.

"It is. Very interesting. It might help explain some of this uninvited dilemma you find yourself in."

I looked sharply at her, but those doors were closing again behind her face and all I could see now was someone who badly needed a nap. I shrugged and tucked the book into my bag. "Thanks."

"You're welcome." She lifted her water bottle and took a deep swallow. That seemed to be the end of our conversation for the day and none too soon, I realized. I patted her on the knee as I went past on my out the door.

"See you in a few days, Mishelle."

She nodded and rubbed her face with the back of her hand. She looked so tired that I wanted to do more than pat her knee.

For a moment, I wanted to hug her and thank her and . . .

I don't know. It was time for me to go. I closed the door gently behind me and got into my Toyota, started it and drove away; my thoughts a furious, barely contained jumble.

If I'd thought this woman was strange and complex before, I could see now that I didn't know the half of it, not even a tenth of it. My patient was the most fascinating person I'd ever met and I'd known her for less than three weeks.

I stopped for the light and tried to bring some order to my conflicted thoughts and emotions. *Accept me*, she'd said and that was really all Mishelle was seeking, had ever been seeking, all her life.

In that, she was no different than anyone else. No matter who or what we are, we just want to be part of something: society, family or just to be with friends and people like ourselves.

"Think about it," I said to myself softly and I was, so hard that I almost missed the green light. Fortunately, this time no one was behind me to lean on their horn, but I kind of gunned it harder than necessary anyway.

Obviously, there was no one here in Kalispell, Montana anything like Mishelle Woodring. She was utterly unique, as far as I could tell.

Family? I'd seen neither hide nor hair of any of them and no one had mentioned them; not Jodie nor Lynn or Nicky. Apparently, they'd all but abandoned her.

I was beginning feel a certain anger about that.

You don't abandon your own flesh and blood, no matter what. That was another thing I'd learned from my own mother and she'd stuck by me through everything in my life.

But I was more astonished by Mishelle's complete candor with me. She was treating me as if I was her own family. I was touched and humbled and a little awed at how open she'd been.

It was as if she'd been waiting for someone to come along, just so she could tell her story; someone who could listen and not judge her and hold her to some impossible set of standards.

I remembered what she'd said: "*I was put here to educate others about transgender people.*"

I was certainly getting an education.

Something else came to me: I dug into my bag with one hand and got out my cellphone, the other gripping the wheel as I drove out of town. I dialed Mishelle's number, keeping an eye on the road as it was still rather slushy and icy in spots.

Later, I realized what a mistake that was, but again: curiosity got the better of me.

"Hello?" I winced at that artificial phone voice of hers.

"Hi. It's Michelle. I just wanted to ask one more question."

Her voice shifted down into normal range. "Sure. Go ahead."

"What was your name before, you know, your transition?"

There was a pause. Then: "Why?"

"It's . . . You said to ask you anything, right?"

Warily: "Yeah. That's right."

"Okay. I really want to know. It's . . . It's important."

There was another pause, longer this time. Then:

"Mike."

CHAPTER FIVE
One Room Schoolhouse

What is in your mind?

W This ran through my own mind while I read *She's Not There*. For the next four days, I could *not* put that book down.

I do most of my reading after my chores are done; after work and dinner is finished and the dishes done and put away. I park myself on the couch; ignore the TV, the kids, my husband: everything. Then I read, voraciously.

It wasn't hard to do with that book.

From the opening scene to the very end, I wanted to know more. It was my first time inside a trans person's head: able to see finally the pain of being born into the wrong body.

I saw the sadness and longing for peace, the deep, abiding yearning and the unmistakable connection trans women have with the concept of femininity. Born female, I'd kind of taken all of what that meant for granted: a state I later learned is called cis-gender. Those of us who are comfortable in our bodies, who never question our gender, to whom it never occurs that there could be any other sort of condition; tend to see this as a subject too obvious even to discuss.

Jenny Boylan changed my mind very quickly about that. In less than four days, as a matter of fact.

What struck me was that she didn't know much more about this transgender thing than I did. Oh, she could—and did—discuss the specifics and the details (some of them pretty hair-raising!) and how it felt, but she couldn't say exactly what it *is*.

What causes it? Nobody knows.

Is there some common thread to trans people, some unifying detail or details that make them unique and instantly recognizable? No, not really.

Is there a test or series of tests that specifically identifies a trans person? No: testing amounts to individual subjective observations by the very few trained specialists in the field of gender psychology.

Is there a way to help these people become who they truly are?

Yes. They're called the Harry Benjamin Standards of Care.

But even those are only approximations. And it depends entirely on that series of subjective observations and always on the honesty of the patient herself.

She's Not There answered a lot of questions but left me with even more questions yet unanswered. Education: it's a never-ending process, I think.

I wanted to discuss this with Mishelle and ask her some of those questions but weirdly, I didn't want to seem nosy. It seemed to me that for one thing, these were questions I shouldn't have to ask—*accept me*, she'd said—and for another, it seemed that I should find out for myself.

I would see her again on Tuesday and in the meantime; I buried my nose in that book and educated myself.

Tuesday finally arrived. I called her from my office to let her know what time I'd be arriving at her apartment. I deliberately scheduled the appointment around my lunchtime so I would have more time to discuss some of this material and see if what I'd learned matched what I knew of Mishelle.

I knocked on the *Elvis Fans* door and when I went in; I knew immediately that all of that would have to wait.

My patient's condition had worsened.

At first, we didn't talk much that day except to exchange the bare pleasantries. That was just as well because I didn't want her to talk and she really didn't have the strength to disagree.

I took her vitals and listened to her lungs.

They sounded awful: gurgles and crackles, as if someone were blowing bubbles through a straw in a water glass within her chest. Her pulse had picked up as well in an attempt to boost circulation to her lungs to clear the secretions. She was running a temperature—101 degrees—and frankly, she looked terrible: sallow complexion, bags beneath her eyes from lack of sleep and fatigue lines etched down the sides of her nose.

She was visibly and deeply depressed. I was listening to her lungs, most of my attention precisely focused on the areas of congestion—about sixty percent, I estimated—when I heard her say it.

I might not have heard it at all had I not had the diaphragm against her upper back.

I took the earpieces out. I leaned forward. "What did you say?" I asked quietly.

"I said I want to die."

A sliver of ice slid down my back. I stood, knees trembling. With some effort, I went to my bag and stowed my stethoscope and cuff. My back to her, I said:

"You know that your infection has worsened, don't you?"

"Yes."

I turned. My legs still trembled so I sat on the loveseat and regarded her soberly. "Mishelle, it's not likely to get any better. You've had three full courses of antibiotics, one of them intravenous and they've done no good. That's just not normal."

"Hey, nothing I do is normal." She coughed.

"Very funny. You need to consider your options. Soon."

She turned her face away. "You know that I'm not going back to the hospital."

"I know. I respect that. I just want you to understand the consequences of that decision."

"Like what?"

"You just told me that you wanted to die. Do you really mean that?"

Her response was a series of coughs. When she'd caught her breath, I went on:

"Because if you do, then all you have to do is stop taking the antibiotics."

That got her attention. I could almost see her ears prick up. "What?" she gasped and reached for her water bottle.

"Just what I said: you always have the option of not continuing your treatment."

My voice was flat and calm and without inflection. I remember that I was trying to seem compassionate but now, today, I think I must have seemed detached more than anything and I was.

It hurt to say that then and it hurts to remember what I said. My eyes smarted from the tears that threatened to flow then, just as they sting now; remembering:

"You can let nature take its course. But if you do that, then you should consider letting Hospice come out to take care of you for your final days."

She found her breath and a ragged, hoarse thing it was: "What's Hospice? Is that here at home or in the hospital?"

"Here. Not the hospital. It's a program like Home Health but with an emphasis on symptom management, not aggressive medical treatment."

"You mean end of life care?"

"Exactly."

"Are you saying that I'm terminally ill?" she asked in a small voice that had nothing to do with her lack of air.

"If you decide to quit taking the antibiotics then yes, that's what I'm saying. If your course of treatment is not effective and you decide to discontinue it and you don't want to be hospitalized then terminal care would be . . . Appropriate."

It was like a game of cat and mouse with her, I realized. Neither of us wanted to say the words. Perhaps she was stronger than me because she said:

"You mean I'm going to die? If I stop taking these useless drugs then I'll *die*?"

I closed my eyes and sat silent for a moment. We both were silent for what seemed like ages: one woman who could not see but knew, and another who knew but would not see.

My eyes threatened to overflow, but I opened them and said, in the calmest, most compassionate tone I could muster:

"Yes. If you stop treatment, then there's a strong possibility that you'll die."

I studied her face as well as I could through eyes blurred with tears. There was no expression there. She spoke.

"Well, that certainly gives me something to think about, doesn't it?"

"Are you scared?" I asked quietly.

"Hell, yes!"

"I'm sorry. I don't want to scare you. I just want you to know the truth. You do have options but only you can decide what's best for yourself. And I need to know so I can help guide your care, no matter what you decide."

"I need to think about this," she said in that same small voice.

"Of course. For now, let's just take it one day at a time, okay?"

"Okay." Again in that small voice and my heart ached and my eyes threatened to overflow.

"I want to call your doctor and get you another round of antibiotics. Do I have your permission to do that?"

Mishelle struggled: for air and with that decision. Finally: "Yes."

"Okay." I wanted to relax, hearing that small victory but I couldn't. "Do you have any questions?"

"Yeah. I have an appointment in about two weeks with a pulmonologist. Can you help me figure out what questions to ask him? About what I should do?"

"I'd be glad to. Anything else?"

She hesitated, struggling with this and I so badly wanted to hold her. But I sat: hands folded; heart racing; my eyes overflowing. A tear ran down my cheek as she said:

"If I get lucky and the new meds actually work this time, then what? What's my . . .?" She fumbled for the word.

"Prognosis?"

"Yeah. That. What's my prognosis?"

I shrugged. "I can't tell you that now. And I'm not allowed to say because I'm a nurse, not a doctor." I took a deep breath. "Your pulmonologist can tell you, but first you have to see him and you'll have to stay on the meds for that."

She nodded. "Fair enough."

None of this was fair. I wiped away the treacherous tears on my cheeks and said, "Okay." Even that single word betrayed me because my voice broke a little on those two syllables.

I leaned forward and put a hand on her knee and she covered it with her hand; her strong, slender, amazingly talented hand. She said:

"Are you okay?"

I nodded. "I'm fine. Really."

But we both knew it wasn't true.

CHAPTER SIX

Class in Session

THE NEXT DAY, the first thing Mishelle said to me was: "Did you read that book?"

I finished stowing my stethoscope and blood pressure cuff. I smiled down at her, hoping that my expression showed in the tone of my voice.

"Yup. Can you hang on for a few minutes while we finish up here? I need to draw some blood and I can't concentrate if we chat about something like this."

"Okay, but I need to know what you thought."

I scrubbed her arm with an alcohol prep pad. "My, but you're feeling frisky, aren't you? I'm glad to see you've improved a bit. How do you feel, overall?"

She took a swallow from her water bottle before answering. It seemed to me that her hoarseness had receded somewhat. "Better. I don't feel so hot and sweaty anymore."

"Ladies don't sweat, Mishelle," I said absently, my concentration on finding the right angle in her vein. Nicholas was snoozing in the bathroom and that made my job a bit easier. "They glow."

She chuckled. "I knew that."

I got the needle in and slid the collection tube into place. Bright red blood began to fill the glass ampoule. I released the rubber tourniquet from her arm. "Okay, almost done. Hold still another minute while I fill another. Doctor J wants two good samples today."

Another chuckle: "He can bite me on the neck if he wants. I think he's kinda cute."

I looked up at her and smiled again. "And how would *you* know, young lady?"

She smiled back complacently. "I can tell."

The truth was; her primary doctor *was* kind of cute in a big brotherly sort of way. Not my type, but it takes all kinds, I suppose. "Your pulmonologist is kind of a hunk, too."

"Yeah, I think so, too. He's really sweet. But Doctor J always says he likes my perfume." She sighed. "And he has such gentle hands."

The second sample ampoule filled and I pulled it free of the needle and carefully stowed them both. I slid the needle out of the vein and held a cotton ball over it with my thumb and dropped the needle into a portable sharps container. Then a Band-Aid and we were done.

"Okay! That's all for now and thank you for being such a cooperative patient, Miss Woodring."

She giggled. I was heartened to hear very little crackle in that sound. "You're welcome, Nurse Alexander. Now can we talk?"

I sat down on the loveseat, facing her. "Yes, we certainly can. Shall I go first?"

"Please."

I didn't hesitate. "Okay, I *loved* it. The book, I mean. Professor Boylan is a really good writer and it made me feel . . ." I stopped, searching for the words. "Sad but glad. I was so happy for her but I hated what happened to her friend Melanie. That was awful! How could anyone *do* that to a relative?"

A little grimly, Mishelle said: "It happens."

I flushed. "Sorry. Anyway, I guess I'm still confused, maybe just as confused as Jenny was, at least at the beginning. What *is* a transgender person?" I lifted my hands helplessly. "There're so many words. Transgender. Transvestite. Transsexual. I can't keep them all straight. Are they all they same thing?"

She shook her head. "Not at all. Transgender is kind of a blanket term for all of us, even though it doesn't apply equally. Transgender means being born into the wrong body, mostly."

"Well, I got that part right, I think. But what's the difference between a transvestite and a transsexual?"

"A transvestite is a male who enjoys dressing like a woman. Some get turned-on from it or at least a kind of a pleasant feeling. A transsexual is someone who feels that they want to fully transition to a different gender." A corner of her mouth lifted in that sad half-smile. "Like me. What they're wearing doesn't matter mostly, but it sure does to *me*."

"Fully transition. You mean surgery?"

"Yes." She sipped at her water bottle. "Most transvestites would run for the hills if you offered them surgical options. They like being female, but not always on a permanent basis." She added gently: "We don't use that word much. It's kind of a put-down. Some of us use tranny or T-girl but those are kind of unwelcome, too. Tranny is probably least offensive but I wouldn't call a cross-dresser a tranny to her face if I were you."

"Then what's a drag queen?"

Mishelle gave me a big sweet smile. "*Anyone* can be a drag queen, honey. It's kind of a universal condition, y'know? There's a little bit in everybody whether they like to admit it or not." She took another sip of water. "Mostly they're gay guys doing parodies, but some pre-ops and even a few post-ops do it too; for the tips. Some of them were my best friends in Seattle."

Now she had the most intriguing smirk on her face, as if to say: *Gotcha!* It would have been annoying if the subject matter didn't have me fully occupied:

"I'm still confused. Those guys I saw at Darcelle's in Portland; were they transvestites or drag queens? And what's a pre-op?"

"Pre-operative transsexual. Before the bottom surgery. Some people who should know better sometimes use the term she-male, but those are mostly hookers and porno actresses. And that's a term you *never* use unless she uses it first." She shrugged. "It could have been both queens and regular trannys. Some of the weekend girls were married guys with nine-to-five jobs. There was a pre-op or two in the club I went to a lot."

"I never would have guessed they were *all* guys. Some of them looked pretty convincing." I made a face. "Not sure I like that word: transsexual. Nothing sexual about this; as far as I can tell. Transgender seems, I dunno, more accurate, somehow. All these people: transvestites and drag queens and cross dressers; these are all transgender?"

She nodded and sipped again at her water bottle. Her color was better today, I noted. "For the most part. But not all of them, I'm sure." That smirk was actually quite friendly, I realized; a sharing kind of smirk: *Psst. I've got a secret . . .* "It's a spectrum, Michelle."

"Did you spend a lot of time in those kinds of clubs in Seattle?"

Her smile broadened. "Those kinds? *Drag* clubs, Michelle. Say it with me: *drag* clubs."

"Ha-ha. Well?"

She nodded. "Sure. I gravitated to clubs like those because it made me feel accepted. I was just another girl there and I felt like I belonged." Her eyes grew sad: brows lowered and her questing right eye stilled for a moment. "For a while, I didn't feel like an island in the middle of a vast ocean." She bowed her head. "It became so shallow, though. Just another beauty pageant. Who's got the best hair? The biggest boobs? God, they were so catty, sometimes. So mean."

"Sounds like high school," I commented.

"Yeah. It turned into a competition for attention and money, mostly from sugar daddies." She made a face of her own. "Some of the girls were just looking for a rich guy who would pay for their implants or the bottom surgery."

"You mean the sex change operation?" It sounded stupid as soon as I'd said it.

"The correct name is sexual reassignment surgery." Her mouth turned down: wry and sad. "Me, I'll *always* be a pre-op."

"Why?" As I said that, I knew: "Your heart surgery? The Coumadin . . ." She was taking blood thinners along with her estrogen.

"That's right." She smiled wistfully. "I had it all ready to go: the money saved, the doctors picked out, even the dates scheduled. And then they told me at one of my physicals that I had a terrible murmur in my mitral valve and that it had to be done first or I might never survive the SRS."

I stared at her. "But post-surgery . . . the blood thinners . . ."

"Right again. No surgeon would touch me after that. They all said there was too great a risk I'd die on the table." She smiled in my direction and if she'd been able to see, she would have looked me right in the eye. "What a way to go."

Very quietly, I said: "That's an awful thing to say. "

Just as quietly: "No, it's *not*. I did it once already, you know."

"Did . . . *What?*"

"Died on the operating table. They had to resuscitate me. And I wished they hadn't because I saw Heaven."

After a moment, I said, "It's called an NDE. Near death experience."

"I know what it's called. I saw a beautiful place with a bright blue sky and flowers of every shape and color all around me." Her voice was calm, casual. "Did you hear me, Michelle? I could *see*."

"I heard you."

"I spoke with my grandmother." Still in that calm, detached, almost amused voice; somehow unencumbered by infection and quietly confident: "She told me that I wasn't done yet, that I had more to do here."

I learned long ago to humor any possible delusion a patient might entertain but this sounded like something else entirely. "You mean educating people."

"Yes, which would be you." Her grin was wide and pure *gotcha*.

I didn't know how to respond to that. Instead, I glanced at my watch and saw with a shock that I was almost a half hour late for my next appointment. Where did the time go when I was with this woman? "Well, class is dismissed for the day, teacher. I've got four more patients to see today. I'll see you again in a few days."

She reached down next to her chair and lifted a stack of four videos and another book, all secured with a big rubber band and ready to go. She held it out. "In that case, here's your homework for the next few days. Test next week."

I took the pile and looked at her. "Gee, thanks."

"Don't mention it. Any other questions before you go?"

"About a million, I think." I paused. "No, actually just one. If there are so many transgender people in this country—*She's Not There* hinted at *thousands*—why don't we see them? Where *are* they?"

She shifted in her chair, leaning forward a bit to ease her breathing. "The books and videos tell you that, too. It's called stealth." She stopped to pant gently. "Most transgender people want to blend in, to just be normal. Being read is a common nightmare for all of us. Nobody likes being treated like a freak, Michelle."

"I guess not." I tucked the DVD's and book—*A Soldier's Girl, Southern Comfort*, two Discovery Channel videos and *Dress Codes* by Noelle Howey—into my bag. "Thanks, teacher. See you in a few days."

I let myself out and drove off to the next patient, my mind in a whirl as usual. The rest of the day was interrupted at regular intervals with thoughts of my homework and our conversation, but I managed to drag my concentration back into focus each time and pay attention to my other responsibilities: frail and elderly folk in equal need of a gentle hand, quiet reassurance and competent technique.

It works every time, but I'm just well-trained, I think.

When I got home that night, I badly needed to share. Dave was in the kitchen when I walked in, the DVD's and book already in my hand.

"Look what *I* got," I announced. He had a skillet and spatula in his hands so I placed them on the counter.

He craned his head to look at them while flipping potatoes. "What're those?"

"Homework!"

He peered at me over the tops of his glasses. "Mishelle?"

"Uh-huh. Want to watch the videos with me?"

"I dunno. Are they family-friendly?"

"Well yeah, I'm sure they are." I looked down at *A Soldier's Girl.* "Except maybe this one, I think." I looked up. "You interested?"

"Maybe later. You going to have them for a while?"

I was a bit disappointed. "Yeah, at least four days." *Oh, well . . .* "What's for dinner?"

"I dunno. I'm just making it up as I go along. You look tired. Why don't you pour yourself a glass of wine and relax for a while?"

"Where are the boys?"

"Doing homework. Zach already set the table. Sit down," he urged. "I got this, okay?"

"How long 'till dinner?"

"About an hour, I hope. Go take a bath and relax. You look like you need it."

It sounded like a good suggestion, so I poured myself a glass of chardonnay and went into the bedroom to dump my things. I started a bath.

Our house has some wonderful creature comforts and our bathroom is perhaps the best example: the Jacuzzi tub alone is worth the price of admission. Clean up your mess when you're done and you're welcome to it.

If I'm not already in it, that is. I dumped a handful of foaming bath beads into the roaring jets and went back into the bedroom to strip down.

When it was good and full of warm water and fragrant suds, I relaxed into it, my hair pinned up, the chardonnay on the edge of the tub and *Dress Codes* held carefully out of the way. I leaned back, took a sip of wine and buried my nose in the book.

In one word: fascinating. It was the story of a trans person's daughter and her reaction to the dissolution of her parent's marriage; her grief and confusion at watching her father become a woman and her resolve to never abandon her love for the person who sired her, even as he became she.

It examined the love the couple had for each other as seen through the eyes of their daughter even as their love melted and morphed into something the word friendship could never describe.

Their daughter changed, too. A nervous breakdown described with dizzying detail that occurred not long after her father's surgery made it very clear to me how the ripple effects from patients with this condition can touch everyone and anyone.

Briefly, I wondered about the ripple effects encircling me even now, decided that they were awfully minor and resumed reading.

It was this book, I think, that convinced me how slippery the concept of gender is and how much of a spectrum the definition really encompassed. Or, closer: a series of Venn diagrams; overlapping circles or areas of gender that blurred into each other. I could see differentiation now among the possible variations of gender expression when before it had all been pretty black and white to me.

They call that gender bipolarity and it's about as useful in describing the human condition as a sundial is in telling the time of day.

I'm a fast reader. I was already on chapter three when Dave called me for dinner. The glass of chardonnay was barely touched. I bookmarked *Dress Codes* and dried off, thinking that school had never before been so enjoyable.

* * *

I called her four days later, using a different cellphone. I got her soprano voice.

"Hello?"

"Hi!" I said. "Gotcha. I was testing your memorization skills. You committed the other two numbers to memory, let's see if you can do it for this one."

"No problem," she said in her regular voice; rather dryly, I thought. "Give me a hard one next time. And bring an apple, too."

"Okay, but I'm out of apples, teacher. Can I pick up anything else for you on my way over?"

"Sure. How 'bout a caramel latte?"

"I can do that. Whipped cream?"

"Of course."

At Norm's News, I threw in an apple danish for symbolic reasons. I put my foot down on the gas pedal and was on her doorstep ten minutes later.

She was using the nebulizer when I came in. I dropped my bag, said hello as I gave her the latte and pastry and set about at what had become my routine in the last couple of weeks: pet the dog and cat; feed them; pick up the landmines; load the dishwasher and fill her water bottle.

A fast wipe-through in the kitchen and I proceeded on to the official business: her vitals and chart-notes. She was still short of breath despite the session on the nebulizer and I was careful not to stress her too much.

At last we were done with all the minutiae and school was in session.

"Did you do your homework?"

"I did. I watched all the videos and I'm on chapter ten in the book." I bit my lip. "*Soldier's Girl* was so *sad*. But I have a million questions for you."

She grinned and sipped her latte. "Of course." Crumbs from the pastry dotted her lips and I moistened a paper towel, leaned forward to dab at her mouth. "Thanks. Okay, go ahead."

"When did you decide you were a girl?"

"I never *decided*. It just was always that way. I didn't know I *wasn't* a girl until I was about four or five."

She thought it over. "I had a cousin: Linda. I used to go over to her house and play dress-up. She had all kinds of dresses and girl-stuff for me to try on. I didn't talk about it much with my folks because it just seemed so natural. Linda and I were about the same size and when mom went shopping, she'd try the stuff she was buying for Linda on me."

Mishelle shrugged. "I don't know, I thought it was okay, I guess. Up until I was about eight or nine, I think."

"What happened then?"

"Nothing really dramatic. Mom used to tell me to keep my jeans zipped or she'd put me in a dress—I *hated* wearing jeans—so of course I left them unzipped as much as possible." She wore an impish grin, complete with dimples.

"But you were . . . a crossdresser?"

She sighed hoarsely. "I suppose so. I didn't have much choice where and when not long after that. Dad was pretty . . . dead set against it."

"Then how old were you when you made the transition?"

"Thirty-eight."

"Thirty . . .!" I stared. "That's a long time to wait."

Her grin turned wry. "A few things got in the way."

"Uh, but you knew you were transgender all that time?"

"I knew there was something wrong with me. I just didn't know what it was called." She took a reflective sip of her latte. "I was listening to a program on *Geraldo*. They had a group of transgender people and transsexuals on. When I heard that, it was such a sense of *relief*. All that time I'd thought I was the only one with this problem."

"Yeah, it must have been pretty comforting, knowing that there were others like you out there."

"Sure, but my problem then was to find them. And find out more about this condition I had." She sighed and followed it with a non-productive cough. "Being blind, it was almost impossible. But I found out enough to know that transition was what I had to do, no matter what. I wrote letters! Even if most of what I got back wasn't in Braille. I wrote one to Geraldo to thank him for having them on his show and asking for more information."

"Did you get a reply?"

"The form letter kind, yeah." She sniffed. "That's okay, I found out what I needed to know, anyway. Even if it was in bits and pieces. But I got on the Standard and stuck to it for ten years before I tried to get my SRS."

"The Standard? Benjamin Standards for Care?"

Another of her *gotcha* smirks: "Go to the head of the class, Michelle. That's the one." She stopped to pant gently. Then: "Tell me what they are."

I ticked them off on my fingers: "Live full-time for a year in your preferred gender, on hormones for at least a year, undergo counseling with a licensed psychiatrist during that time and be assessed as transsexual by the psychiatrist and another licensed physician; preferably an internal medicine specialist, like an endocrinologist."

Her expression was sad. "Good job. But you left out having a healthy heart."

I was embarrassed. "Sorry."

"Not your fault. Gold star otherwise, sweetie. Next question."

"When did you go full-time?"

"Twenty years ago. I was living here, in Kalispell. One day I just gathered up all my boy clothes and carried them out to the dumpster, dropped them inside and set them on fire, so I wouldn't change my mind later."

"Nothing like burning your bridges," I commented.

"No, nothing like that," she sneered. "Then I put on a dress and my makeup, strolled on down to Norm's News and got myself some coffee." She lifted her cup toward me in salute.

I looked at the cup in her hand. "I take my kids there for milkshakes. I've never seen you there before this."

A shrug: "We missed each other, I guess. And I moved to Seattle in '91."

"Oh." I hadn't returned to Kalispell until 1995. Suddenly, I burst out: "Hey! How the *hell* did you put on your own makeup?"

(I misplace my manners, sometimes, when I'm stunned. It happens.)

She snickered: *gotcha!* "Wondered if you'd notice that. I dunno. I just went by feel." She cackled like a hen laying a big one. "I'd imagine the folks down at Norm's might have had some things to say but I didn't hear much."

"Even if they were used to seeing you as . . ." I hesitated. "Mike?"

Another cackle that turned into a cough: "I guess it's a good thing I couldn't see their faces, huh?"

I thought about that. I also thought about something that caused me to groan involuntarily.

"Something wrong?"

"This was in the early Eighties?"

"Yeah. Why?"

I thought about the kind of makeup I used or saw used in the early Eighties and another groan escaped me: bright, glossy red lipstick, industrial strength mascara and metallic blue eye shadow.

"Please don't tell me you wore any blue eye shadow," I whispered very sincerely.

"Okay, I won't."

"*Ugh.*"

"Well, you asked. Besides, my drag queen buddies in Seattle once told me that you can never have too much blue eye shadow!" She cackled again.

It was a really good time to change the subject, I decided. "So, this book: *Dress Codes*, it's about a married couple and their relationship during and after the husband's transition, right?"

"Uh-huh. Told by their daughter."

"Right. And they try to stay together . . ." I stopped. "How often does *that* happen?"

"Not very. More about that later. Go on."

"Well, wouldn't that make them lesbians, even if she, I mean the wife, didn't know it at first?" English just didn't have the words, I realized. Or if it did, I needed to learn them. "If they were intimate, I mean. How does everything work in a situation like that?"

"What do you mean?" The edges of her mouth curved up.

"On the . . . other woman. The husband. Former husband. Whatever."

She grinned broadly. "Having a little trouble with this?"

I sighed. "It's the pronouns. I can't keep them straight."

"Relax; you're not the only one. Don't chase your tail, Michelle." Her smile turned distant. "I was married, too. For about five years." She shook her head. "If she could see me now . . ." she murmured.

I shifted uncomfortably. "Yeah, you told me that. What was she like?"

"Sharon? We were college sweethearts."

"You went to college?" There was a distant buzzing in my ears that told me my saturation point was rapidly approaching.

"Yes, audio engineering. Three years. I wish I'd finished."

"How did you take notes?" Then I nodded, sure I knew: "You taped it, right?"

"Not exactly." She put her hand down into the mesh bag holding her arsenal of remotes and pulled out something blocky and metallic. "I Brailled my notes with this. I can read faster than hearing things on a tape."

"Uh," I managed. The buzzing was becoming more distinct. "Sharon. Your wife?"

Mishelle sipped her latte, her expression still somewhere far away. "I knew it was the wrong thing to do but I so wanted to fit it, to make it all go away and let me live a normal life." A corner of her mouth tipped up. "And I was a virgin, too. With girls, anyway."

"Did she know?" I asked quietly.

"I think she suspected. She found out soon enough." She stopped to pant gently.

"Maybe we should continue this another time," I suggested.

She straightened up. "No! I have to . . . to tell you . . . *ack*! Something . . ."

Alarmed, I started to get up but she waved me back. "I'm all right. Hand me my inhaler."

I plucked it off the side table and pressed it into her palm. She gave herself two quick blasts and sat there, panting. I watched her color slowly return.

"Okay?" I asked after a decent interval.

"Yeah. About Sharon . . . I couldn't make love to her. My wedding night was . . . a disaster. I think she knew, then. I didn't want to be . . . male with her."

"You wanted to take the female role." I was having trouble with my own breathing; I was holding it so tight.

Mishelle nodded and sucked air in little gulps for about ten seconds. Then: "She was unfaithful. With one of my friends." Her mouth was pursed: something bitter just behind her lips. "*I* never was but I guess I was glad someone could make her happy that way."

Her eyes closed. In a monotone, she said: "But I got her pregnant anyway. So she said."

In the softest voice I could manage: "I'm so sorry."

"Save your sympathy for the baby. She aborted it, all by herself."

As if a switch had been thrown, the buzzing sound within my head ended. It was suddenly very quiet. I could hear my own heart beat. I looked into her face and anyone else might have called it serene.

"God, Mishelle . . ."

"Yes, *He* has her now. When I'm done here, I'll get to see her." I could see muscles twitch in her movie-idol jaw. "The doctor . . . He told Sharon that my genes were bad and that the baby would inherit my . . . problem. But it was a girl, or so she said."

I sat. I said nothing.

After a long moment, she said in clinical tones: "I suppose it officially ended when she came home and found me in her wedding dress. About two weeks later, she did it in the tub when I wasn't home."

She turned her head to me: "You know something, Michelle? Apart from being female, the thing I've wanted most was a boring life."

Somehow, my eyes remained dry. "Boring might be nice."

The door suddenly swung open and I almost jumped out of my shoes. It was Nicky. She looked at us, her curiosity evident.

"Hi! What are you two up to?"

"Just talking," I said defensively. "How are you?"

She eyed me with suspicion. "Great, really great. You just get here?"

"No, actually I was just leaving." I stood up, barely able to conceal the trembling in my legs.

"Oh, well, cool. How's our patient?"

You mean client, I thought. *I get to call her patient, you don't.* Aloud, I said: "Still a lot of congestion. She's had Xopenex via nebulizer and two doses from the inhaler. Call me or the doctor if her breathing gets any worse."

Nicky nodded and disappeared into the kitchenette. I turned to Mishelle.

"Thanks." I couldn't think of anything else to say.

She nodded and held out a thick manila folder jammed with typewritten pages. "Take this. I was going to save it for your term final but we may not have enough time."

I took it gingerly. A lot of the pages were yellowed with age and crumbling at the edges. "What is it?"

"My journal." Her face was turned toward mine as if she was trying to study my expression but with what? "It'll answer a lot more questions than I can right now. And then maybe you'll see why my life is such a fucked-up mess. Be careful, some of the pages are falling apart."

She grinned suddenly and it was like sunshine breaking through the clouds for a moment. "I typed it on a regular typewriter but it's mostly readable, I think."

"Not a Braille typewriter?"

"Nope. Didn't have one yet. Don't worry; I was a pretty good touch typist, even then."

Carefully, I said, "I don't think it's fucked-up. And thank you. I'm very honored."

"Yeah, *I* haven't even looked at it. How does *she* rate?"

I turned my head. Nicky was scowling at us, fists firmly planted on her hips. I felt a flash of irritation.

"Hey, I'll let you borrow it when I'm done. Good enough?"

"I suppose." She flounced back into the kitchen. I looked at my patient.

"I truly am honored," I said, very quietly. I carefully placed the folder on the coffee table and leaned over to give her a hug. "You are a child of God," I whispered in her ear.

When I pulled back a bit, she patted me on the cheek. "And you are a beautiful person," she whispered.

CHAPTER SEVEN

Outside the Lines

Leaning against the glass of the tall windows in our front room, I watched the rising sun paint salmon and lemon morning tints against the snowy white crags of the mountains of Glacier Park to the north of town.

I shifted the scalding cup of coffee in my hand, took a cautious sip and scorched a few taste buds. With a slow, careful exhale, I considered my feelings. There was much to consider.

Most of it was still being processed but I knew one thing for sure: I was not the same person I'd been the day before.

Coffee-warmed moisture misted across the window and I wrote *hi* with a fingertip, backwards so that my departing former self, whose reflection I could see dimly in that window in the light of the morning sun would know I still cared. Then I drew a heart around the word to show that I meant it and went to get dressed.

About an hour later, I let myself in her door and put my bag down. Nicholas yapped once and then subsided, his tail whipping eagerly back and forth as I went to scratch him.

"Hi, there."

"Well, *hi*."

I bent and hugged her; kissed her on the cheek. When I stood, she was smiling.

"What was that for?" Blue had been on her lap during that hug and the kitty's scandalously blue eyes seemed very wide in similar surprise. She uttered an interrogative mew in chorus with Mishelle. I stroked her ears while her mistress and I re-introduced ourselves to each other.

"I just felt like doing it. And you looked like you needed one."

"Maybe I did." Her smile grew. "You read the journal, didn't you?"

"Yup, the whole thing." I looked around the apartment. "Give me a few minutes, will you? Then we'll talk."

"All of it in one night? My, aren't you fast?"

"When I'm motivated. Hang on for a few minutes and then we can talk."

I went to work. Fortunately, there wasn't much to do. I finished the domestic stuff in record time and started in on her vitals. While I was taking her pulse and blood pressure, we chatted about her condition:

"How are you feeling?"

"Not very well. I felt better yesterday but today this cough is driving me crazy." As if to illustrate, she let go with one that sounded like a sea lion's bark. I winced.

"Are the antibiotics giving you any relief?"

"Some," she admitted. "As long as I'm still taking them. When I run out, I feel worse than before."

"Well, you have that appointment tomorrow with your pulmonologist. Have you given any thought to those questions?"

She nodded. "Yes." She hesitated. "I really want to know about my prognosis but I think I'm afraid of what he's going to tell me."

My fingers were on her wrist, taking her pulse. She turned her hand over to touch mine. "I don't want to hear if I'm going to die, Michelle," she said softly.

"You aren't going to die," I said firmly. "From what I know of your pulmonologist, he's a straight shooter. He'll tell you the truth."

"That's what I'm afraid of," she muttered.

Our hands were still linked. I swallowed the lump in my throat. "Why don't you just wait and hear what he has to say? What other questions do you have?"

She sighed and I heard the crackles within. "Mostly if this damned infection will ever go away!" She coughed. "I'm so sick of being sick."

"You have every reason to be. Any other questions you've thought of?"

Mishelle shrugged. In a subdued voice: "I just want to know where I am with this disease and what my options are."

"I'm sure he can do that. Do you think you're prepared for what he might say?"

Another shrug: "I guess so." She gave me a wan smile. "Is anyone ever prepared to hear the worst?"

"It probably won't be as bad as you think." I squeezed her hand. "Listen to me. You have to keep a positive attitude about this. Your self-talk, your internal dialog has to change if you're going to get through this.

You're doing as much harm to yourself as this infection is by believing it can't or won't get any better."

She sighed. There was a world of hurt in that sigh.

"I know it's hard, Mishelle. But you have to try. Don't give up on me, not now. Now that I've gotten to know you. Reading your journal . . ." I hesitated. "I think I like you even more than I did when we first met."

"Huh. Really? I kind of thought you might think I was totally messed-up."

I shook my head, still holding her hand and I knew she could feel the motion through our linked fingers. "Not at all. You aren't giving yourself nearly enough credit. You've had some major traumas in your life and you couldn't have survived those unless you were an amazingly strong and courageous person. You *are*, you know." I shook my head again. "I can't imagine going through what you've been through, especially here in Kalispell."

The corners of her mouth twisted. "Girl, you can say *that* again. They call this a choice, but who would ever choose to do this?" She bowed her head. "We don't choose it," she said softly, more to herself than anyone. "It chooses us."

"I think I'm finally beginning to understand. Your journal explained a lot."

Her head lifted. "Did it? Did it explain the mental torture I felt, struggling with being two people at once?"

"Pretty well, actually. Do you want to talk about that some more?"

Her mouth twisted again. "Would it help?"

"That's up to you, I think. I take it you're still struggling with this? Being two people at once?"

"Not anymore. I used to think of myself as two people: Mishelle and Mike." Her jaw tightened. "God, how I hated him."

"You saw him as destructive and wanting to keep you somehow stuck."

She nodded. "He was an asshole," she declared. "He was angry all the time." Her expression changed and a faraway look settled onto her features.

"I had a vision when I began my transition," she said, her tone soft and dreamy. "I wanted to be kind and gentle: a generous and positive person. It was so wonderful; that vision. I knew that I could if only I reached out and took what was offered me."

I sat, not speaking. She turned her head to me as if seeking my face. "Do you believe me?"

I folded my hands in my lap and studied her face for a moment before replying. The lines there had smoothed out and it was perhaps the most serene expression I'd seen on anyone.

"I think you believe what you're saying." I hesitated, choosing my words carefully. "Was this like your NDE? Your vision of Heaven?"

"Yes and no." She smiled like the Mona Lisa. "It was more like my real self emerging. I could see what I wanted to be, what I *had* to be if I was going to survive."

"And you think you've been successful so far? Letting your real self come out?"

"Mostly." The Mona Lisa smile turned wry. "I still struggle with the positive part, I think."

"Don't we all?"

She cocked her head. I had the strangest feeling she could actually see my expression. "Don't tell me you struggle with being positive, too? You? Little Miss Perky?"

I burst out laughing and covered my mouth. "Oh, my God! Is that how you think of me?"

Her smile was altogether friendly. "Michelle, you're the most upbeat and positive person I've ever met. That's why I like you so much. You make me smile just being around you."

"Well, thank you." I was embarrassed. "But I struggle, too. It's part of being human, I think. I'm just trying to be the best person I can be."

She reached out to me again and I took her hand. "Same here. Even if it means being humiliated and rejected because people think I'm just a dude in a dress."

"You *aren't* a dude in a dress," I stated most firmly. "I read your journal. I know what you are; who you are and if others could read it, they'd know too."

"Maybe they will. Someday." Her smile was tinged with regret. "I just wish I had more time."

I compressed my lips. Time. *Time to change the subject* . . . "Can I ask you some more questions about your childhood? Your background?"

"Sure." Mishelle coughed abruptly and leaned forward. "If you'll get me some more coffee, that is. All this talking makes me thirsty."

"Water might be better," I suggested.

She fumbled on the table and silently held up her water bottle. Another cough that sounded terribly painful to my ears. Alarmed, I got up and put my arm around her. I could feel her shoulders shake as she struggled for air.

"Do you need your inhaler?"

"Uh-huh." Another racking cough that sounded desperate. Reflexively, I slapped her back; open-palmed as if swatting a new-born, carefully avoiding her spine.

Amazingly, it worked. Mishelle said: "*Ock!*" or something like it and leaned forward suddenly. I snagged a tissue and thrust it into her hands. What was within her mouth went into the tissue and she passed it to me with a trembling hand.

Still crouching next to her, I spread the tissue and looked at it: about 30 cc in volume; dark green and terribly jelly-like in appearance; speckled with blood.

My teeth clenched.

I looked up to see her color slowly returning to normal, so I stood, my legs trembling.

"Well, that was exciting. Do me a favor, huh? Don't scare me like that again. I'm not sure my heart can take it."

"*Your* heart?" she wheezed. "I'm the one with the Tinker-Toy valve, remember?"

"How could I forget? I hear it clicking away in there every time I listen to your lungs. Which reminds me . . ." I got out my stethoscope, placed the diaphragm against her back and listened carefully.

Oh, dear. Her congestion was much worse: gurgles and crackles and burbling sounds. Her pulmonologist would have his hands full tomorrow, I decided.

"How's it sound?" she gasped.

"Don't talk for a while," I advised. "About the same." I touched her on the shoulder. "Are you feeling any better?"

She nodded. "How 'bout that coffee?"

"Sure. You just relax and breathe deep as you can. I'll be right back." Carefully, I tucked the tissue into a sample baggie and then into my bag, grabbed her coffee cup off the table and went into the kitchen.

Cream 'n sugar and I topped it off with the black mud Mishelle was pleased to call coffee. (I tried a sip of it once and it was strong enough to make my hair stand on end.)

I went back into the front room, carefully observing her color, which had thankfully returned to normal.

"Here you go." She reached out with both hands and took it, sipping gratefully.

"Thanks."

"You're welcome." I sat down on the loveseat and regarded her. "Well, where were we when we were so rudely interrupted?"

She sipped her coffee. "You were going to ask me about my childhood, I think."

"Where were you born?"

"Liberal, Kansas."

"But you're not in Kansas anymore, are you, Dorothy?"

She laughed. It sounded better. "I love that movie. Nope, I've left the Bible Belt behind me, girlfriend."

"What did your dad do? His job?"

"Oh, he was a farmer, of course. Everybody was around Liberal." She smirked at me. "Green tractor, red barn; remember? I can remember those colors for sure."

"How did your parents discover that you were going blind?"

Her smile turned distant. "I was sitting in my high chair, eating breakfast. Or trying to. My folks told me that I couldn't find my scrambled eggs. They took me to Kansas City a day or two later for testing and that's when they found out that I was blind. I was eighteen months old almost to the day."

I leaned forward and rested my chin on my fist, studying her body language. It was utterly relaxed and open. "What were you like as a kid?"

She dimpled. "At that age, pretty much like any other kid, I would imagine. A lot of energy and adaptability, because my mom told me I adjusted pretty easily to being blind. My dad's family spoiled me rotten though, and I think I became kind of a brat, later on. I didn't like being told what to do."

She paused for a sip of coffee. "Especially when it came to wearing Linda's clothes. She lived with my grandmother and I spent a lot of time at Grandma's house when I was growing up." Her dimples deepened.

"Did your Grandmother know about you?"

"I think so. She certainly didn't mind me prancing about the place in a dress!"

"Did she encourage this?"

"No, not really. I didn't *need* encouragement. We never talked about it, Michelle. There was always this unspoken thing hanging in the air between us and we never voiced it, it just *was*; like a house rule or something. I got to be me while I was there and that's why I always thought that I was a girl when I was growing up."

"What about school? Did you go to a special school for the blind?"

"Not until later. At first, I went to regular kindergarten until it became obvious that I needed extra help." She took a moment to pant, then: "We moved, finally. To Denver. There was a school there. I remember riding the bus with the other disabled kids. There was a pretty good spectrum of special needs and problem children."

My friend grinned wickedly. "But no one could top *me* for being a problem child. They told me that I made a great gang leader. I think they were worried I'd choose a life of crime."

I grinned and patted her knee. "You might have."

She smiled back. "The thought often occurred to me. But I do remember getting into trouble a lot."

"When you were at this school, did you play with boys or girls?"

"Oh, I played with both, but I preferred to play with the girls and do girl things."

"Like what?"

"Like hopscotch, swinging on the swings, dolls; things like that. I s'pose I had a few masculine hobbies, too."

"Such as?" I had a brief vision of her in a batting cage and shuddered.

"Well, I learned to play the accordion."

"The *accordion*? No, that's not exactly feminine," I said with a laugh.

"Says who? Well, I guess I picked it up pretty easily. My Mom taught me how to play. We practiced every night. I remember she was really patient with me, but like I said: I learned really fast."

"I just can't quite see you playing the accordion!" I laughed again. "You seem more like a guitar player to me."

She laughed right back at me. "Oh, I did that too! I got pretty good at the bass guitar, but the constant practice gave me calluses on my fingers. It was really hard to give it up."

"Why did you give it up?"

"It made it impossible for me to read Braille, so I had to stop. Remember, I read with my fingers. Even though I loved playing bass, reading Braille was like my lifeline to the world."

"What other things did you like to do?"

Her grin spread ear to ear. "I loved to play chess!"

"Hmm, not my game. Dave and the boys play it all the time, though. Chris is pretty good. I think he'd enjoy playing you."

"Sure, as long as we use a chessboard that's set up for blind players."

I cocked an eyebrow. "Interesting. How's that?"

"You'll see. Any more questions, Miss Nosy?"

I laughed. "I thought I was Miss Perky?"

"You're both. Nosy *and* perky, which is why I'm willing to answer all these personal questions." Her smile was entirely forgiving. "How do you like the curriculum so far?"

"Pretty well." I was sure of that. "We left off when you were at school in Denver. What happened then?"

Her face fell. "I had to leave home. The worst time of my life, I think."

"Leave home? Why?"

"I left home to live at the school for the blind. I only came home for weekends and the holidays." Her tone was as bleak as the weather just outside her front door. "I was completely blind by then; no shadows or anything." Muscles bunched in her movie-idol jaw. "It was the year everything changed for me."

Her head tilted toward me, chin down and aimed at me. Her true eye was completely still. "Michelle, have you ever been abandoned?"

Taken aback, all I could do was stutter: "N-no . . . Yes! When . . . When my stepfather shot himself. He . . ." I swallowed hard. "I felt sorry for him; that he had to do that. But it was still a shitty thing to do to me and Mom and my brother."

"Ah, then maybe you do understand. My parents abandoned me. My mother had another child by then, my first baby brother and all her time was devoted to him when I was at home. She stopped teaching me accordion, even refused to play songs with me because she was always busy with him."

"What about the school? What was it like there?"

"Hell," she said flatly. "Not now, Michelle."

I couldn't help it, I had to know: "But didn't the school have anything like counselors or psychologists or something? You were completely different from the other kids. It should have been obvious that you weren't really a boy."

I leaned forward, my gaze direct and intense, my words equally heart-felt: "And what about your *parents*?" She shifted uncomfortably. "Didn't you at least talk about this with them, try to reach an understanding?"

"My parents don't talk, Michelle. And no, the school didn't have anything like counselors. We had attendants who looked after us and bullied us and abused us."

Her expression was winter itself; snow piled to the eaves and a cold, thin wind whipping down the chimney, scattering the ashes of a fire that once warmed the heart as well as the body.

After a long pause, I said meekly: "I'm sorry."

She nodded. "You didn't know. We'll talk about it later." She sighed hoarsely. "Getting kind of tired, hon. Anything else you want to ask?"

I shrugged. "I guess . . . what other things did you do as a kid?"

"Kid stuff: riding my bike, swimming, that sort of thing."

I gaped at her. "How in the world did you ride a bike, being blind?"

"Easy. Tie a couple of pop cans to the guy's bike ahead of you. Follow the sound."

"Swimming?" I was aghast: a vision of Mishelle floundering in a swift river.

"Oh, yeah. I used to float for hours in the pool. It felt like freedom itself. I used to swim here in Kalispell, too. Ashley Lake. I swam across that at least once a week before I went to Seattle."

I was staring so hard, my eyeballs felt itchy. "Is this what you meant by being abandoned by your parents? I can't imagine they would let a blind child take such risks."

She said, very quietly and extremely sincerely: "My parents always treated me as if I could see. They didn't baby me which was a good thing; otherwise I would have lived my life with a fear of my disability. I was already living in fear of wondering what was wrong with me. I didn't need any more fear."

"No. I guess not." I sat, limp as a dishrag: done.

"See you next week?"

I started. "Huh? Oh, yeah . . . Yes, next week." Without thinking, I stood and went to her and wrapped her in a hug.

"I'm going to be pondering all this," I said into her ear. She nodded. "Mostly I'm going to be pondering how you managed to live with that load on your shoulders for all that time."

I released her, looked into her face and carefully traced the fatigue lines down each side of her nose. Her hand came up to clasp mine, gently.

"I did what a lot of folks did: a lot of drugs and I drank a lot. Let's not go there right now, okay? I'm tired."

"Deal."

"Hey, do you mind giving me your email address so I can send you some jokes? I got some great ones."

I crossed that line without a blink: not thinking for a second what I was doing, I rattled it off, knowing her well-nigh perfect memory would retain it.

"I'll call you tomorrow to see how your appointment went. 'Kay?"

"Sure."

I let myself out, got in my car and drove away. I was almost to my next patient's address when the enormity of what I had just done struck me. I almost put the brake pedal through the floor.

I had given personal information to a patient.

In twenty years of nursing, I had never before crossed lines or broken barriers like this.

I should have been horrified. I should have been ashamed and disgusted with myself.

I felt just fine, thanks.

The day passed and I took it one hour at a time, one minute following the other. I had five patients that day, mostly elderly folk; each with a unique tale to tell. My patients were and always have been a diverse lot and well worth the extra minutes with each. If it gets me home a little later than most folks, what of it?

It beats working in an office.

It was well past seven when I finally parked the Toyota in the driveway. I stomped through what remained of the slush, put my bag down in the foyer and poked my head into the kitchen. A note on the fridge informed me that Dave and the boys had already eaten and a tasty piece of meatloaf waited within for me if I was hungry.

It could wait, I decided. I could hear the TV and that told me my husband was engrossed in a game, so I went into my office. I logged on to my e-mail and there it was, proof positive of my transgression: an e-mail from Mishelle.

I opened it and began to read. After a bit, I chuckled. Then a giggle. Finally, a full-out guffaw. They *were* good jokes.

"What are you doing?"

I looked up. Dave was in the doorway, his expression midway between curious and irritated.

"Reading an e-mail from Mishelle," I said without thinking. "She sent me some jokes and they're . . ."

I froze.

"She *what*?" He stepped into my office, a thundercloud forming on his forehead. "How the hell did she get your e-mail address?"

"I, uh, I gave it to her. Would you like to read some?" I asked. My baby-blues were wide open in what I desperately hoped was innocence. "They're really funny."

He stopped a few feet from me, his posture stiff and unyielding. "What are you doing, Michelle?" His voice was very quiet.

"What?"

"Don't give me that crap! You're crossing the line here and you know it!"

His voice changed in an instant. I'd never before heard such anger from my husband. "Ignoring the fact for just a moment that this is in violation of regulations, I want you to know that I think that . . . that *person* is a complete mental case!"

"You read her journal," I said tonelessly.

"Damn straight I did!" He waved his hands in the air. "You *asked* me to! And frankly, I'm kind of sorry I did! That . . . he's . . . *she's* one sick puppy!"

"You read all of it?" I asked; my voice still low and toneless.

"No, not all of it. Enough to know that . . . she's . . . a nut case."

I took a deep breath. "Well, when you read all of it, you might change your mind."

"Probably not." Abruptly, his face sagged and I could see the concern beneath the anger. "I'm just worried, sweetheart. You're putting your career at risk here. Your patient isn't the most stable person in the world."

We looked at each other for a long moment. "I'm just trying to be her friend, Dave. She doesn't have many friends. Think about that, will you?"

He scowled. "That's not your job, Michelle."

"In case you haven't noticed, this is more than just a job, Dave."

"I noticed," he growled. "I just hope the hell you know what you're doing."

He stomped out of my office. I looked back at the screen, not really seeing it. There would be the devil to pay tomorrow; the devil and a thin-lipped silence.

But somehow, I just didn't care.

I clicked on *reply* to Mishelle's e-mail and began typing. I wanted to send her some positive messages. I have quite a bit of that sort of thing stashed away in my computer; self-actualization material I've acquired over the years. I sent some of it off to her and was pleasantly surprised to receive a reply almost immediately.

So much for being tired, young lady, I thought and was instantly contrite. She probably couldn't sleep.

There was a small attachment. I opened it, thinking it was more jokes. It was a poem. She'd written it some years ago and forwarded it to me, thinking I might like it.

I did. I read it through to the end and looked at the signature: *Mishelle L. Woodring.*

I clicked on *reply* and typed: *Hey, nice work. What does the L stand for?*

The reply came back within seconds: *Lynn.*

I stared at it for a full minute. My middle name is Lynne.

SECOND INTERLUDE

I squirmed in my chair. His gaze was mild but those opaque brown eyes never left my face, never stopped probing and missed nothing, nothing at all.

"You crossed professional boundaries." It was not a question.

"Yes."

"Those e-mails." He shook his head. "We seized her computers, you know."

I nodded. "I heard."

"I'll be honest with you. What we're looking for is any kind of conversation you and Mishelle might have had about ending her life. And any response or agreement you might have made to assist her. If we find anything . . ." He let the end of the sentence hang in mid-air.

I swallowed again. "You won't. Because it never happened." I looked him squarely in the eyes. "Did you find that e-mail from her that said she wanted to live? The one she wrote just a few weeks before she died?"

"Yes, I read that one." His gaze nailed me to my chair and now he was every inch the tough, unrelenting cop. "What I'm saying is: if there's anything, anything, I should know about, now is the time to tell me."

I shook my head, feeling slightly dizzy. "All I can tell you is what I've been telling you all along. If you'll let me finish."

He studied me, his gaze turning mild again. "You might want to skip over the day to day details. Give me the high points."

I nodded back and took a deep breath.

CHAPTER EIGHT

Meetings and Greetings

SOME PEOPLE LIKE TO SLEEP in on their days off; loll around in bed and read the newspaper; drink coffee or hot chocolate and watch bad daytime TV. To those, dressing before noon is a sin and chores are something to save for the very last minute.

Pity me: I'm not one of those.

I was up by six-thirty; cooked breakfast for three (I had a glass of orange juice and a muffin on the fly); did two loads of laundry and tidied three rooms before I started making phone calls at about eight thirty.

First up was Mishelle's pulmonologist to confirm that she'd made it on time to her appointment. Nicky had promised to take her but you never knew with that girl. I asked the receptionist to tell Mishelle I said hi and that I'd call her later.

Next was my sister in law; Margie. I call her about every other day just to chat and keep in touch because she has such an energizing effect on me.

She's an amazing woman. She loves life, my brother and bling in equal measures. If I'm Little Miss Perky, then Margie has to be Miss Perky Plus. We chatted about inconsequential things for about an hour and then said our goodbyes. I hung up, feeling slightly uneasy.

During the course of our chat, I found myself wanting to tell her about Mishelle, but managed to steer the subject to other areas. Warning bells that I perhaps should have heeded later.

I took a break from the phone and did some more laundry and then called Mishelle's number. She picked up almost immediately, using her high voice and I grinned. *Gotcha!*

"Hi! How did the appointment go?"

There was a pause. "Oh, *hi!* What number are you calling from?"

I flinched. *Oops.* Another line crossed . . . "My home phone. What did your pulmonologist say?"

"Well, he thinks I've still got an infection and he put me on another antibiotic and something else; a steroid, I think."

"Did he answer all your questions?"

I'd never heard her sound so despondent. "Yeah. He says I'm functioning at about twenty percent lung capacity and that I have end stage COPD. He didn't mention Hospice, though."

I chewed my lower lip and didn't say anything. Twenty percent. End stage.

"You still there?"

I started. "Oh, uh, yeah. Still here. You sound . . . kind of down. Do you want to talk about it?"

"No, I just have a lot to think about right now. . ."

That's for sure, I thought.

"And I need some time alone today. See you in a couple of days?"

"You can call me if you change your mind."

"I know. See you Saturday." She hung up.

I hung up and a bit dazed, rose and went to the window. I stood for a while, looking out at the gray day fighting to turn sunny. Blue sky showed at the far edge of the horizon, widening gradually as I watched, winning the battle a bit at a time.

Twenty percent. End stage.

Eventually I moved away, turning my back upon the struggle. I did some things. I don't remember what they were, but my house was remarkably clean that day, including my son's rooms.

Later that night, I checked my e-mails and saw one from her. I opened it:

Dear Michelle:

Thanks for helping me with that list of questions. It was good to be able to get some answers, even if they weren't the ones we were hoping for. We'll talk Saturday. Until then, may the sun always shine brightly on your shoulders.

Love, Mishelle

I re-read the message a half-dozen times, trying to ignore my slowly blurring eyes. Finally, I gave up and touched the screen with my fingertips, just for a moment before I logged off.

* * *

That Saturday morning, I let myself into her place with but a single knock and a single yap from Nicholas. I gave her a warm hug. Hers was equally enthusiastic.

"Hi, there."

"Hi. Good to see you."

"Aha, you *can* see! I knew it all along."

"Smartass."

I grinned at her and patted her cheek. She clasped my hand, pressing it to her face for just a moment and then released it and it was then I felt light stubble on her cheek. I looked closer and saw that she had a minor but definite five o'clock shadow.

I didn't say anything.

I perched on the loveseat and looked down at Nicholas. His tail waved madly. Gently, I picked him up and he nestled next to me, my fingers resting along his muscular back, carefully scratching as she and I talked.

"You're in a good mood."

"Maybe. I made a decision last night."

"Tell me."

"If the doctors say I have to be hospitalized, I'll do it." She shifted, as if her back were bothering her. I frowned.

"You mean that?"

She nodded. "The minute someone calls me sir, I'm calling them out on it, though. I mean it."

I laughed. "Mishelle, if any of those nurses give you crap, I'll come down there and kick some ass. I promise you."

I got a sunny smile in return. "Thanks! Knew I could count on you. Hey, can you tell me more about this steroid medication he gave me?" She reached into the mesh bag hanging from her chair and handed it to me.

I looked at it: Prednisone, 20 milligrams, twice a day. "Yes, this is a steroid. It reduces the inflammation in your lungs and makes it easier for you to breathe."

"It won't make my muscles any bigger, will it?" she asked anxiously.

I looked up at her and grinned. "No, it's not that kind of steroid. It might increase your appetite though, and make you retain water."

"Retain water? Will it make my boobs any bigger?"

I giggled. "No, it won't make your boobs any bigger . . . You're a nut, you know that?"

"Oh, darn. I was hoping for an excuse to go bra shopping." Abruptly, she shifted again in her chair, obviously trying to find a more comfortable position.

"Sheesh. Since when have you needed an excuse to go shopping? Hey, is your back sore? You keep moving around."

"Always." She sighed. "It's because I'm always leaning forward, I think. I don't suppose . . .?"

"Of course." I set Nicholas gently down on the floor. He gave me a reproachful look and plunked his butt down, watching us.

I perched on the arm of her recliner. Her hand lotion was on the side table as always, so I squeezed a dollop into my palm and warmed it as she leaned forward and pulled her blouse up for me.

I started in and she sighed in quiet pleasure as I began kneading her muscles. I don't have any particular technique but I'm gentle and patient. It usually works pretty well.

She groaned and I slowed. "Hurt?"

"Yeah, but it's a *good* hurt."

I resumed kneading. "Okay, then."

"Hey, about the steroid?"

"Hmm?"

"I think it's making the hair grow on me. Can you feel it?"

I started to laugh then quickly stifled it. She was serious. "Where?"

"Along my arms and legs."

I ran both hands down the sides of her arms then slipped off the recliner to do the same on her long legs. Nicholas quickly scooted out of the way and then crept close again to sniff at her. I stood.

"Smooth as a baby's butt."

"You're *sure*?"

I sighed. "Mishelle, I'd love to have skin as smooth as yours. How often do you shave your legs?"

"Uh, I don't."

"You *don't*?" I didn't quite glare at her. "That is *so* not fair."

Meekly: "Sorry. Hey, can you finish my back?"

"Sure." I perched again on the arm of the recliner and resumed thumbing and kneading and gently twisting her muscles into some semblance of a normal state.

It was quite a challenge. She had a lot of adhesions.

"Can I unhook your bra?"

She didn't answer immediately and I was afraid I might have offended her. Then: "Sure, if you buy me a drink first."

"Ha-ha. It'll make this easier."

"Go right ahead, sweetie."

I undid the hooks. There was a bra extension, not surprising and probably necessary, given the size of her ribcage. As her bra came free of her torso, I finally realized that there was no doubt whatsoever about the authenticity of her breasts.

Embarrassed, I glanced at her face in profile and again saw that five o'clock shadow. I bit my lip and perhaps I flinched a bit as well. She must have felt it through my hands.

"What?"

"Uh . . . hair."

"I knew it! Where? On my *back*?"

"No, no. Your face." I whispered: "It's definitely five o'clock, Mishelle."

She muttered something then. I leaned forward but didn't catch it.

"What was that?"

"I said: if anyone else but you had said that!"

"Hey, sorry. I didn't mean . . ."

"No, don't worry. If anyone else *but* you . . . I can't shave every day. I get terrible razor bumps. I usually shave in the bath and tomorrow is bath day."

"Mind if I feel?" At her nod, I reached up and stroked her cheek. I couldn't feel anything except the light stubble I'd noted. "It's not that bad, Mishelle. Really. Do you want me to shave you?"

She didn't answer and again; I thought I'd said something to offend her. Then: "Have you ever done that? Shave someone else?"

"Of course!" I said, lying through my teeth. "I'm a nurse! I've shaved . . . well, *almost* everything."

"Do you have time?" She sounded doubtful.

"Sure!" I said brightly. "I have a light schedule today. I don't have to see anyone until after noon and it's only nine."

Mishelle shifted again. I could hear her wheezing. I knew she was distressed and that it was aggravating her shortness of breath.

So I resumed rubbing her back. I'll be honest: I was enjoying it. We talked while I rubbed. Nicholas watched us, his tongue hanging out, panting and I'd swear he was smiling.

"I'm curious: why did your folks move here to Montana?"

"My dad came through here on a train when he was young and loved the scenery. You know: the big sky and the mountains and Flathead Lake, especially. He used to talk about it all the time when I was growing up. So when I started high school in '64, they moved here to Kalispell."

"They? What about you? They didn't leave you behind in Colorado, did they?"

"Not exactly." She sighed. "They dumped me off at the school for the blind in Great Falls." She fell silent. I waited, knowing there was more. Then she said: "It was the worst years of my life, I think."

"You said that about Denver, too," I reminded her.

"Hah!" It turned into a series of coughs. I kept my hands motionless on her back until they subsided. When she could talk and breathe again, she said: "Denver was a fun party compared to Great Falls. I think it was the first time I really wanted to kill myself, but I didn't have the courage. I kept praying that God would take me, but He didn't."

My hands were kneading her shoulders now. She reached up to grasp one. "I'm glad He didn't, now that I know what He wants me to do."

"I remember," I said, trying to soothe her. "Do you want to talk about what happened in Great Falls?"

The silence grew while I squeezed more lotion into my palm and rubbed my hands together. I was afraid to say anything; the silence was that fragile.

"The House Father abused me."

I resumed kneading her shoulders, moved down to her upper back, carefully avoiding her fractured vertebra in the thoracic region.

"I was going down the hall one night to the bathroom." She drew a hoarse breath and I could feel her heartbeat increase beneath my palms. "I was wearing a nightgown."

"Yours?"

"My mother's. I swiped it from her dresser. I don't think she noticed it was missing. At least, she never mentioned it to me."

"Go on. Please."

"He . . ." She stopped. "This is really hard to talk about, Michelle."

"Okay." I slipped off the arm of the chair and knelt beside her, took her hand. "I don't want to do anything to upset you. I can feel it through my hands when you become upset, you know."

"Really?"

"Yep. Your breathing gets more labored and your heart rate increases noticeably." I hesitated. "You know, there are anti-anxiety medications available for that, like Lorazepam. I'm a little surprised your doctor hasn't prescribed anything like that for you. It would make your breathing easier and make you feel a lot more relaxed. Do you want me to look into that for you?"

Mishelle shrugged, her face lined with sadness. "My doctors treat me like a junkie. I have to beg them for anything that eases the pain in my back." She squeezed my hand. "But if you think you can do anything for me, go for it."

"I will. I promise." I touched her face again, wanting to smooth away those lines and felt the stubble prickle my fingertips. "How about we try that shave? You trust me?"

"Are you kidding? Of course I trust you." She frowned and ran her hand along her jaw. "I just hope I don't break out in bumps. I hate it when that happens."

"I'll put on a nice moisturizer," I reassured her. I knew she had plenty; I'd seen her collection in the bathroom and it was more extensive than my own. "Lancome?"

"Nah, that Sally Hansen stuff works a lot better. Smells nice, too."

"Okay, let me go get it and we'll do this." I rose and went into the bathroom, Nicholas trailing at my heels. The little dachshund seemed to have adopted me and I didn't mind one bit. I like dogs.

I gathered the necessities: a washcloth, the moisturizer and shaving gel. "Where's your razor?" I called.

"In the tub."

I pulled back the curtain and clucked my tongue. As in most senior-living apartments, the tub seemed to have been designed for hobbits. I couldn't imagine Mishelle actually enjoying a bath in such a tiny thing. Even my youngest son Chris would feel cramped.

I thought of our luxurious Jacuzzi tub and the seed of an idea began to flower within me.

The razor and other necessities in hand, I went into the kitchen and found a small metal bowl. I filled it with warm water and went back to the living room.

"Are you ready for this?" I inquired.

"I am if you are."

"Okay, girlfriend. Here we go."

I dampened the washcloth and laid it on her face for a few moments. While her beard softened a bit, I squirted some gel into my hand and rubbed my palms together, working up the lather.

"'At feef's nife."

"Hmm?" I lifted the washcloth.

"That feels nice. The washcloth."

I smiled and began applying the lather. "Good. Let's hope this feels nice, too."

When she was good and smeary with shaving cream, I dunked the razor in the water and mentally saying a brief prayer; began shaving my patient.

I used to watch my dad shave when I was a little girl. He always started at the base of the neck, but Mishelle didn't seem to have any hair there, even though I'd lathered her up pretty well everywhere else.

I shrugged mentally and started on the side, up near the top of her ear.

The razor made little scraping sounds as I went down the side of her face. "Hey, sweetie? Open your mouth a bit so it stretches the skin."

She complied and I finished one side and went on to the other. So far, so good. I got to her lip and paused for a second. "Mishelle? Can you kinda pull your upper lip down so I can get to it?"

"Sure."

I proceeded a little more carefully, making tiny strokes and it seemed to work pretty well. I did below her mouth and then her chin and squinted at the neck again. *Oh, well. Might as well be thorough*, I thought and put a finger under her chin. "Tilt your head back a bit, Mishelle."

Obediently, she leaned her head back and I placed the razor against the base of the neck, as I'd seen my dad do. Mishelle had a fairly prominent Adam's apple and I was determined to take it slow.

But to my utter consternation, I said: "So what happened that night in Great Falls?"

(I could have bitten my tongue right out of my head!)

Mishelle was silent for a moment and then she replied: "Well, since you're holding a razor blade against my throat, I guess I'd better tell you, huh?"

Hastily, I pulled the razor away. "Ohmy*god*, I'm so sorry! I didn't . . ."

"No, it's okay." She sighed deeply, for her, and I could hear the tiny crackles in her lungs. "You might as well know. Hey, don't let the soap dry. It dries out my skin and gives me those bumps."

Infinitely cautious, I resumed shaving her neck. "Okay. Go ahead, if you want to."

Mishelle paused, collecting her thoughts while I slid the razor carefully up her neck, as I'd seen my dad do. She said: "He told me . . . he told me that if I wanted to be a woman, he would show me what that meant." She swallowed and her Adam's apple bobbed.

I paused, waiting; the razor away from the side of her throat.

"And that's just what he did. Every week. For years."

"I'm so sorry," I said quietly.

"Why? It happened. It's over." She shrugged. "I tried to tell my mom and dad what happened when I came home for the weekend but they wouldn't believe me at first. Dad finally did, but he beat me; called me a faggot."

Her voice fairly dripped with bitterness and pain. I felt my heart constrict. "I was such a disgrace, he said. So worthless. And after awhile, I began to believe him."

"*No.*"

"Yes. When you're that young, you kind of believe what you're told, you know."

And the true hell of it was; she was absolutely right. "You can't really mean that; that you think you're worthless."

"No, not that." She smiled wryly. "I do like guys, but I didn't do anything with another man after that. I think I wanted something a little more . . . romantic, I guess."

I gnawed at my lower lip and carefully scraped the other side of her neck. "I can't imagine . . . it took a lot of courage to survive that, sweetie."

Mishelle shrugged again. "I suppose. Dad used to drink heavily in those days. When he sobered up, he didn't beat me any more, but the damage was done, I think."

"Maybe not as bad as you think," I said carefully, just as carefully scraping under her chin. "No, don't talk for a moment. Listen to me. I've never met any rape victims before, but I learned a lot in my rotations on the ER. Rape victims who can at least talk about it afterwards stand a better chance of getting through the PTSD that always accompanies a trauma like that, even if it's an ongoing thing like what you went through."

"PT . . . what?"

"PTSD. Post-Traumatic Stress Disorder. It's a condition that affects anyone who's been through a terrible crisis. We see it a lot in military veterans, police officers who have to use deadly force and . . . rape victims."

She was silent while I finished her and then wiped away traces of shaving cream with the washcloth. I began rubbing in the moisturizer.

"It wasn't all bad, you know. I did have some good times while I was there."

"Tell me about them." I put a dab of moisturizer on her nose and rubbed gently.

"There was this boy I was friends with. No, not like *that*," she added, smiling; almost as if she could read my mind. "He was blind too, although he could still see some shadows. We used to get into trouble a lot. We snuck out of the dorm one night and stole a deaf kid's bike."

"There were deaf kids there, too?"

"Yup. Kind of a full-service school. Anyway, there was always this ongoing rivalry between the blind kids and the deaf ones. We stole a deaf kid's bike and went out for a ride."

"Good grief."

"No, it was a lot of fun! I hung on for dear life while he pedaled like a maniac and we went flying through the night. It felt like we were escaping from it all, I guess."

She giggled as I gently applied moisturizer to her throat. I could feel her pulse and voice beneath my fingers. Her skin was warm and silky smooth. "We did pretty well until we crashed into a parked car."

"Uh-oh."

"You better believe it! We totaled the bike."

"Were you hurt?"

"No, not really. A few scrapes. Anyway, we hoofed it back to the dorm where the teachers were waiting for us." Another giggle: "Oh boy, did we have a rep after that! I got pretty defiant, I think. I used to smoke cigarettes in the dorm, which was a big no-no, and flick the butts out the window."

"And you got caught, I bet."

"Sure. Even when they found the pile of butts outside the window, I just stuck out my tongue at them and said: *Prove it!* Hah!"

She paused and then said, quietly: "I was such a shit in those days. I'm glad I'm not that way anymore."

"Me, too," I said sincerely. I worked some more moisturizer into her chin. "Did you ever discuss your gender issues with anyone at the school?"

"No, but I'm sure they suspected something. I made a big stink in gym class the first time and insisted on being with the girls, mostly because they had swimming, which I really loved. The boys did all the athletic stuff and I hated that. They all thought I was gay, but I knew I wasn't. I knew I was born into the wrong body, that's all."

"Apart from dressing, how did you try to cope with that?"

She shrugged. "Like everyone else there. I smoked pot and drank when we could get our hands on some weed or booze. I buried it, mostly."

Another sigh, followed by her trademark wry smile: "When I was fucked-up, I didn't have to think about how fucked-up I was. I would swipe a bra and panties from my mom's dresser when I went home for the weekend, wear them under my clothes and that made me feel . . . whole, I guess. It felt *right*."

She turned her face up to me. "Do you understand?"

"Yes." I put my hand against her cheek. "Yes, I understand."

"Do you?" She covered mine with hers. "I thought I was crazy, you know. Crazy and all alone. I *couldn't* talk to anyone about it, Michelle.

I was always afraid that they'd me send to some place *worse* than the school."

"I understand, Mishelle." My voice was steady and quiet. "You couldn't trust anyone. And in the Sixties, there weren't a lot of people who knew anything about gender issues. Yes, you were alone. You had to be . . . stealth? Is that the right word?"

"Not really, but that's close. Yeah, I think you *do* understand." Her hand left mine to slide around the rest of her face, feeling it. "Hey, nice job, Michelle."

"As smooth as a baby's butt?" I smiled at her and patted her knee.

"Ooh, yeah! Now I won't have to shave tomorrow. Thanks!"

"You're very welcome." I began to gather up the shaving things.

"There's something else I want you to do."

I looked up at her. "What?"

"There's a trophy on top of the entertainment center. Could you get it down, please?"

I rose and went across the room and took the trophy down, looked at the inscription: *Mike Woodring, 1st Place Traveler's Award.* "What's this for?"

"When I was a senior, the school took a bunch of us blinks down to Billings and gave us an address, then told us where we were. We had to find our way from there to the address they gave us. It took me about four hours to find my way there on foot. I was the first one to find it, so I got an award."

"Blink?"

"Slang for a blind person."

"Well, for heaven's sake . . . How did you even know where North and South were? Had you even been to Billings before?"

"Nope, never. Directions are almost instinctive to a blind person. Kind of like a built-in compass." Mishelle shrugged, but there was a gleeful, almost smug grin on her face. "One of the advantages us blinks have over you sighted folks."

I looked at her and then down at the trophy in my hands. "Amazing. I'm never going to think of blind people as handicapped ever again."

"Yeah, you might be surprised. We can do a lot of things you normal folks can't."

"After meeting you, I'm not sure I'll ever be surprised by *anything*," I said sincerely.

I put the trophy back in its place of honor on the shelf and went to my patient. I bent and kissed her cheek. "You've given me quite an education these past few weeks, Miss Woodring," I whispered in her ear.

She smiled up at me. "Thanks."

"But I really do have to get going soon." I glanced at my wristwatch. "Let me clean up here first."

Her smile dimmed a bit. "I know. But I'll see you again tomorrow?"

"Of course."

I took the shaving things into the bathroom and looked around for a new cartridge pack. I couldn't find one. "Hey, Mishelle? Where are your . . .?"

Just then, I heard Nicholas bark and two voices I didn't recognize. Curious, I came out of the bathroom and stopped dead in my tracks, the razor still in my hand.

Two elderly people were standing in the front room, talking to her. They stared at me.

American Gothic was the first thing that popped into my mind; that classic painting of the farmer and his wife. Give the man before me a pitchfork and they'd be dead ringers for that portrait; even to the overalls and the expressions.

"Hello. I'm Michelle, uh, Mishelle's nurse."

The woman said, in a southern drawl so thick you could have sliced it and spread it on toast: "Ah'm Louise an' this is mah husband Earl. We'ah Mike's parents."

I blinked. *Mike?* "How do you do? It's nice to finally meet you."

We shook hands. Earl's hand was like a piece of knotty oak: gnarled and toughened by decades of hard, back-breaking work. Louise's wasn't far behind in that respect.

Louise said, "Mike, Ah made a pah yesterday and thought you might want a piece." She was talking to Mishelle, I realized. "Ah'll put it in the fridge fo' ya."

"Thanks, Mom," Mishelle piped up. I looked at her. She had an odd expression on her face; part embarrassment and part resignation.

Louise picked up the pie from the coffee table and went into the kitchen. Earl looked at me, his face impassive, just like the painting.

He didn't say a word. I was beginning to get a crawling, creepy feeling between my shoulder blades.

Louise came back from the kitchen and stood beside her husband. Good ol' Earl remained silent, staring at me.

I realized with a start that I was still holding the razor. I put it down on the coffee table.

"I was shaving her," I said in a feeble attempt at conversation. He said nothing and neither did his expression; not even an eye-blink.

Louise spoke. She seemed to be the voice for the both of them. "How's he doin'? Is he gettin' any bettah?"

I gritted my teeth. *He?* Wow, I *had* come a long way in the last few weeks because that pronoun scraped at my nerves like 60-grit sandpaper.

Carefully, I said, "She still has the infection, but she's responding to this series of antibiotics fairly well, I think. The COPD is an ongoing problem, of course, but there are still some options her doctors have yet to explore. Other than that, she's doing pretty well, under the circumstances."

I might as well have been speaking Greek. Louise nodded. "Wey-ull, tha's fahn. Y'all will tell us if'n anythin' changes, wontcha?"

My jaw was beginning to hurt, I was clenching my teeth together so hard. "Of course."

"Thanks." She turned to Mishelle. "We'll see ya later, Mike. You take keer, now."

"Okay. 'Bye, Mom."

They left. Earl hadn't uttered a single word; not a peep.

I looked at Mishelle. That odd expression was still draped uncomfortably across her face.

"Well, *that* was interesting. I hope I didn't scare them off."

"No, don't fret. They're always like that."

"Really? She called you . . ."

"I know." Her eyes closed and now there was nothing but resignation. "It makes my blood boil, it really does. After twenty years, you'd think they'd finally get it right, but *nooo* . . ."

"Well, why don't you *say* something?"

"I have. Thousands of times. It's just the way it is with them."

"Well, if it's any consolation, you look a lot like your mom."

Her eyes opened and she grinned. "Well, thank God for that!"

"Your dad, he's . . . a little scary."

"No kiddin'. I'm still scared of him, even after all these years. He stopped beating on me after he sobered up, but . . ."

Frustration rose in my throat. "Mishelle, I just don't understand! Why can't they accept you? You're their child, for God's sake!"

"Michelle, think about it," she said quietly. "You have kids, right?"

"I told you: two sons."

"Yes, Zach and Chris. Well, what would you do if one of them came to you and said he was trans; that he was really a woman inside and wanted to live that way all his life? What would *you* do?"

I thought about it and that crawly feeling came back in full force. "I think," I said slowly, "That I would be very distressed but I'd try to find some way to accept it." I looked at her. "I love my boys. If either or both were trans, I'd still love them and accept them."

"Well, my folks love me, too. They just don't get the transgender thing, that's all." She sighed and closed her eyes again. "I'm done trying to change them. They don't get it and they never will and that's all there is to it."

I opened my mouth to reply but the phone rang. The robot recited the number and Mishelle's eyes opened.

"That's Nicky," she said.

"You want me to get it for you?"

"No. Wait."

The message machine kicked in and Nicky's voice filled the room: "Hi, Mishelle this is Nicky, I'm runnin' behind and I'm gonna be a little late and I hope you don't mind 'cause I gotta wait for my old man to get back with the car 'cause he's out tonight if ya know what I mean and I think ya *do*." She giggled. "But I'll be over as soon as I can and don't go anywhere 'cause I know you can't and I'll see you soon. 'Bye!"

The machine clicked off.

"Jesus," I muttered.

"Oh, she's always like that."

"I know. I've met her before, remember? I'd just forgotten what a chatterbox she can be." I looked at my watch and flinched. "Whoa, I have to get going! I'm *really* late." I looked up at her. "Are you going to be okay? I don't want to leave you if she's not going to show up."

"No, she'll be here, in her own time and in her own way." That resigned smile was really beginning to tug at me in ways I'd never thought possible. "You go take care of your other patients. I'll be fine."

"Okay." I picked up my bag and crossed the room to pet Nicholas and then kiss his mistress goodbye. "I'll see you tomorrow." Suddenly, I slapped my forehead. "No, wait. I almost forgot: I'm going to that retreat this weekend."

"A retreat?" she inquired.

"Yeah, a spiritual retreat."

Mishelle smiled broadly. "Good. You're looking for God, I guess?"

I was embarrassed and a little reluctant to discuss it. "Well, not exactly. My Dad asked me to go. E-mail me tonight?"

"Sure. Tell me all about it when you get back. 'Bye, Michelle."

"'Bye, sweetie."

* * *

That night, parked in front of my computer, I opened an e-mail from Mishelle:

Hi. I'm really worried that this new medication is making my hair grow back. I can feel it on my legs!

I grinned. Worrywart. I typed in a reply: *Hey, if I have to shave, so should you. It's only fair, you know.*

The reply came back in seconds: *YOU DON'T UNDERSTAND! THIS HAS TAKEN ME YEARS TO ACCOMPLISH! I'M THROWING THE STEROIDS IN THE GARBAGE!*

Stunned, I rapidly typed: *Hey, don't worry. The steroids can't possibly do that. But you do what you need to do. Whatever you choose, I support you.*

I hit *send* and sat back, trying to blink away tears.

It didn't take a genius to realize that she'd rather risk death than lose any part of her femininity.

I think I was finally coming to understand why.

CHAPTER NINE

Gethsemane

"So, it's . . . she was a guy who's now female?" my stepmother said, hesitantly.

From the back seat, I chirped an affirmation. "That's it exactly."

"Has she had surgery?"

"Nope." I looked out the window.

We were on the highway to Big Fork; passing through Somers and right off the highway; I could see the big green trash receptacles I think of as Somers's Mall because some folks like to hang around there on the weekends and go through other folk's garbage. Dumpster diving is considered an Olympic sport by many of our less financially secure citizens here in Flathead Valley.

"It's her fondest wish, of course, but with the replacement valve in her heart and the sheer cost of the procedure, I'm afraid it's out of the question."

There was silence from the front seat. Uneasy, I glanced back and forth at their profiles. My dad's face was like stone and Joyce was compressing her lips. The silence went on for about ten seconds too long and then Joyce said, "Well, that's very interesting, Michelle. You certainly meet the most remarkable people in the field, don't you?"

"Yeah, I guess I do," I said, trying to keep the embarrassment out of my voice. "But they're all good people, especially Mishelle. She's . . ."

"Is he . . . *she* gay?" My father has a deep, bass voice and even when he doesn't mean it, he sometimes sounds disapproving.

"No," I said flatly. "She's never had a consensual relationship with a male, to my knowledge, anyway."

"And you believe that?"

For a moment, I honestly didn't know what to say. "Why shouldn't I?"

"No reason. Just curious."

I had my doubts about that. "Dad, this isn't a case of sexual deviation we're talking about here. Gender identity doesn't have anything to do with sex. It's about who you *are*, not who you sleep with . . ."

"Look, we're here," my father rumbled; a truck running over my words and squashing them flat. "Plenty of parking, it looks like."

I don't need a house to fall on me to know when to shut up. Their Toyota pulled up to the curb and I looked out the window at the church.

It was a nice-looking place: rather rustic in design and very much in keeping with the countrified flavor of Big Fork's architecture. We got out.

I busied myself with my one bag while Dad and Joyce said their good-byes. I kissed him on the cheek, told him I'd look after my step mom and we entered the quaint little Catholic church; the site of the weekend gathering known as a Crusillo.

The Catholic Church rather broadly defines a Crusillo as a gathering by which the word of Christ is spread among both the faithful and the curious. The latter describes me pretty well, I think. I'm not Catholic but I *am* curious about all things spiritual and Dad had asked me to go with Joyce, partly because I think he was a bit afraid she wouldn't go without some sort of support from a family member.

So I agreed. It was kind of impulsive and I've wondered ever since just whose impulse it was in the first place.

A quietly jovial fellow was handing out a printed program of the weekend's activities at the entrance to the church. He welcomed us and his pleasure at seeing us felt awfully genuine.

It was, as it turned out. I met him later, during the workshops, and the air of gentle joviality was always with him, reminding me of especially pleasant cologne.

I looked at the program as we were being introduced. *Love One Another* said the title page. I wondered briefly just how welcome and loved my friend would be, here among these devout Catholics and truth-seekers.

Would these gentle Catholics, heirs to the Kingdom of Christ, welcome and love my strange friend? I could just imagine *that*.

Sometimes I wish my imagination wasn't so active.

But I had no doubt that the Carpenter from Nazareth would have welcomed her with open arms. That belief has never left me and it continues to sustain me to this day. Call it faith. It's as good a word as any.

What was it like, that weekend?

I wish I could say.

Oh, it's not that the telling would be difficult. I could but I *can't*. They asked us not to speak of the details, so I won't. It's one promise I want to keep, for reasons I'd rather not discuss. I'm sorry if that seems mysterious, but that's the truth. Truth was something I was looking for that weekend and I found it.

Or it found me. I'm still not sure about that.

I can give some brief impressions. The church inside was much like the outside: rustic and countrified. We were quartered in the basement, in the school and it felt rather silly at first; sitting in kid's desks while the ceremonies and prayers were conducted. The silly feeling passed away very soon, though.

They took very good care of us. They fed us well, treated us like family members and kept us busy. They entertained us, did their best to educate us and make us feel like we were much more than welcome. For that and so much more, I was very impressed and very, very grateful.

But I'm still dancing around this spiritual thing, aren't I? Forgive me if I just say that I left that Sunday feeling that I'd touched Something much bigger than I could have ever imagined.

Briefly: I was overwhelmed.

There was a lot to process: prayers, ceremonies, skits, and interactions; seemingly simple tasks that caused me to haul out my soul and examine it in minute detail. They challenged me and nudged me and did things to some long-held beliefs that shook me down to the roots of my consciousness.

They didn't convert me, though. I don't think they really intended to. Nor am I trying to convert anyone else. It's none of my business what church *anyone* attends or if they attend one at all. A relationship with the Almighty, whatever it might be, is something I regard as completely and utterly private.

Dad dropped me off at home that Sunday afternoon. Dave and the boys were gone, so I had the place to myself. In a daze, I unpacked my few things and went outside to my garden.

I wandered around, touching my flowers and smelling them, listening to the birdsong and the comforting hum of bees; just being in the moment and not really thinking at all. I don't recall what triggered it. Perhaps it was the bird that alighted on the branches of a tree a few feet away or maybe it was the scents and sights of a beautiful spring day in Montana: the vast blue sky overhead and the pristine white clouds gathering at the crests of the mountains so far away but seemingly close enough to touch in the still, clear air.

I found myself weeping.

No, it was not grief. I did not feel sad or unhappy or even a sense of loss. It was acceptance. A single thought had arisen within me and I confronted it or it confronted me and all I could do was stand before it: mute; accepting; weeping.

She will die.

It was a fact. Mishelle would die, soon, and there was nothing, *nothing* I could do to stop it or delay it. So I accepted it. I had no choice.

Neither did I have a choice in what flowed from that one thought: I must do all that I could to make her last days on Earth as good as I could; to love her and care for her and cherish her.

Because she deserved it.

Because it was the right thing to do.

Because I could and I *must*. Nothing less would do.

Anger and resentment surged within me; late to the stage but overwhelming me anyway. *Too much . . . I can't . . .!*

"Why *me*?" I shouted at the implacable blue sky overhead and nothing, no One answered. "Couldn't You have chosen someone else to do this? Is there no one else? Please?"

I sat down, tears pouring down my cheeks and rubbed the grass, trying to reassure myself that I wasn't imagining this. It was real: the grass, the sky, the beautiful day around me; all of this was real and there was no place I could run and hide.

It was *my* responsibility. Mine and mine alone.

I thought I knew how the Carpenter felt in that moment, that night on the hillside among the olive trees. He had no more choice in the matter than I. Did He? The alternatives were much worse.

The same was true for me.

After a while, I got up, wiping my eyes.

I went back to the house. There was work to do.

He got up to get me a glass of water. He was silent, watching me as I drank thirstily and dabbed at my eyes. I wouldn't swear to it but there was trace of suspicious moisture in his eyes, too.

But he was a cop. It was important to remember that. He was a cop and he was asking me questions to discover if I'd murdered my friend.

I could never forget that.

"Do you feel like continuing?" he asked. "We can finish this later."

"I think I should, don't you? Frankly, I'd rather not come back here." I drank some more water. "Am I boring you, Detective?"

He smiled. "No, not at all. I find this . . . fascinating." He settled back in his chair and laced his fingers together over his belly. "Please continue, Mrs. Alexander."

Mishelle at eighteen months

Mishelle on a tractor

Mishelle with Big 'un

Deep sea fishing in Florida

In Seattle

Mishelle in Seattle

Goin' out on the town in Kalispell.

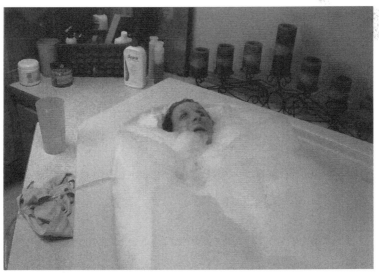

Mishelle in the jacuzzi the day before she passed away.

Happy Days in Seattle

Mishelle in Kalispell

Mishelle and her new puppy, Nicholas

Mishelle's Brailler

Mishelle's chess board.

Mishelle's 60th birthday and Gay Pride Weekend in Kalispell, Montana.

CHAPTER TEN

Directions

THE TOWN OF KALISPELL is a little less than two miles wide, west to east and about three miles long, from north to south. It really is a town and not a city. I've lived here for more than ten years, since almost two years after the birth of my eldest son Zach.

I thought I knew it by heart until I met Mishelle.

About five and a half square miles, Kalispell contains less than twenty thousand human beings and less than a hundred stoplights, most of which are scattered around the city center. It takes all of forty minutes to traverse the whole length of the center and that's if you hit every stoplight possible.

On my way to Mishelle's, I was certain I had. Every damn one.

Early that Tuesday morning, the experiences of the weekend still vivid in my mind and resonating throughout my whole body, I called her: "Hey, sweetie."

"Well, hello there! When are you coming over?"

"I'll be there in just a few minutes." I smiled at the excitement in her voice. Well, I was pretty excited, too. "I need to pick up a few things at the office."

"Ooh, don't take too long! I've missed you so."

"Hey, Mishelle?"

"What?"

"I've missed you, too."

I drove along Main Street, stopped at work to get my files and other incidentals then to City Brew to get her a caramel latte and a couple of the strawberry danishes she so adored. They have a drive-through: it's very convenient.

When I finally let myself in at her place, I realized that my hands were shaking, ever so slightly. It was beginning to dawn on me that what I'd said to Dave just last week was truer than I could have imagined: this was much more than just a job.

During the retreat, I'd picked up a few trinkets for her and I was a little anxious about them. Would she like them? Would they be appropriate?

My anxiety vanished when I opened the door and saw her in the recliner, grinning back at me.

"There you are," she murmured in my ear as I bent to hug and kiss her. "How was the weekend?"

"Better than I might have imagined," I responded. "Illuminating, in fact." Pulling back, I studied her face. Tired, yes, there were always signs of that in her face but today she looked pretty good, even though I knew most of that was due to the powerful antibiotics coursing throughout her system.

When those ran out again, there would be a change for the worse as always, but for now she was holding her own.

I handed her the latte and the bag with the danishes. "I got you some goodies."

She tore into one of the danishes as if she was starving. She probably was; her caregivers usually didn't arrive until the afternoon and her compromised breathing made an act as simple as fixing breakfast just too much effort. "Thanks," she mumbled around a mouthful of strawberries and cream cheese. "'Preciate it."

"No, not those. That's just because. I mean some things from the retreat."

Her face turned up to me. She swallowed; her Adam's apple bobbing up and down. "You didn't have to do that."

"I know. I wanted to."

She smiled like a little girl on Christmas morning: ear to ear and I swear, I think even her glass eye twinkled in delight. "Cool! Can I have them now?"

"No, we need to do some business first." I began my assessment while she munched the last of her danish and sipped her latte.

"You want the other one?" she murmured wistfully as I was taking her pulse.

"Split it with you," I replied absently, my fingertips feeling for the rhythm of her heart. There: strong as ever. "You take the strawberries. Hold still, your pulse is a bit choppy this morning."

She giggled. "I'm excited! I love getting presents."

There was a pang in my own heart as I looked up at her. How many had ever given this woman a present, much less the time of day? Even her family, her mom with her pies and her dad with his stern, emotionless expression and ramrod posture; had they ever given her something just because?

No, not lately. She was holding her own, though.

It may have been subjective. Maybe I wanted to believe she could beat this and live a good full life before her treacherous lungs brought her down for the final time. Beat this and win some kind of approval and acceptance through sheer determination and out-living her detractors.

I hoped so. Mishelle's breathing hadn't changed any, but she tolerated being short of breath better than any other patient I had ever cared for. Just about anyone I could name with a similar condition would have thrown in the towel long ago and headed off to the ER.

But not Mishelle. Her need to stay out of the hospital far outweighed her desire for comfort.

Out of sheer frustration, I sometimes wanted to smack her. Or hug her. I couldn't decide most of the time and so I let her make her own choices.

Finished, I stowed my things and got out her presents. "Ready?"

Mishelle nodded; grinning excitedly and set her latte aside. I knelt next to her recliner and placed the box containing her trinkets into her hands.

"This feels heart-shaped," she commented. "With a bow and beads."

"Open it." I was grinning, too.

She removed the top and set it aside. The first item to come out made her coo in delight: "This feels like a little angel."

"It's to remind you that you're never alone. That God is always with you. There's more."

"I know. I can feel it. Wow." Her long, strong fingers traced the next item carefully. "Wow, what *is* this? I can't figure it out."

Solemnly, I said: "That's a little white dove, to symbolize your freedom. It represents the freedom you felt when you finally decided to be true to your inner self and transition."

Her smile was shy and altogether charming. She removed the final item from the box and declared, "This is a heart."

"That represents God's love for you." Quietly I added: "And mine, too."

Her eyes welled with tears. Mine were about to. I patted her hand. "Wait, not yet. Don't get all mushy just yet. One more thing. Put out your hands."

Mishelle held out her hands, cupped. I slipped the last item into her palms, letting the end drape across her fingers.

"It's a cross! With beads," she added as she let them slip slowly through her fingers.

"The beads are in different shades of blue and tan, to set off your eyes and hair."

"Will you put it on me?"

"Of course." I got up and lifted it from her cupped hands, unhooked it and slipped it around her neck. She lifted her hair for me and I hooked it.

"Ooh, it's a choker! I love chokers!"

I swallowed a nervous giggle. It wasn't meant to be a choker. I'd forgotten about her neck size being larger than most women's, especially her Adam's apple. The cross hung barely below the prominent bulge. "Is it too tight? I don't want to really choke you!"

"It's perfect." Her long fingers traced the golden symbol with reverence. "I love it." I knew then that I had to ask her:

"Mishelle? Can I ask you something?"

Her fingers continued caressing the symbol of shared pain and grief. "Ask me anything."

"Do you believe in God?"

"Of course. He made me." It was said with such simple, complete confidence that I shivered.

"Do you have any anger toward God about the way you were made?"

She smiled. Her hand never left the cross at her throat. "There was a time; yes. Not anymore. I was very angry for too long, but I realized some time ago that He had his reasons."

Her smile was touched by something I could not name. "He doesn't make junk, you know. And He doesn't make mistakes. *We* do. And yet He loves us still."

I nodded and patted her hand. "Yes."

"I accepted Christ as my Savior long ago," she said in that matter-of-fact tone. "And in case you've forgotten, I know where I'm going when I die. I've seen it. Death holds no fear for me, Michelle."

I swallowed, blinking my stinging eyes. "I remember."

"Good. Don't ever forget." She took her hand away from the cross at her throat and covered mine. "So tell me why you gave me these things, Michelle."

"At the retreat, they gave us each a little box. Each day we were given a different item to put in the box to remind us of what we were learning. I . . . I wanted to give this to you."

Her hand squeezed mine gently. "And what did you learn, Michelle? No, don't give me a shopping list. Tell me the truth, *Reader's Digest* condensed version."

I swallowed again, harder this time. "That . . . That all life is precious. That all are Loved, even the least of all."

"Very good. I think you're getting it." She released my hand and reached for her latte. "And I think that's enough theology for today, Michelle. Would you do me a favor, please?"

I shook my head, feeling as if I was coming up from deep underwater. "Sure. Anything."

"I've been looking for this movie all over and I cannot find it any-where!"

"What's it called?"

She named a title I recognized. "It might be in the entertainment center or over there in the cabinet."

I went hunting and eventually found it under a pile of CDs and DVDs. I shook my head in distaste. Her library was in serious need of organization.

Fortunately, that's one of my strong points. I made a mental note to re-organize her disks, both CD and DVD and computer software on my next visit. I don't know much about computers, but I can file just as well as one.

"Here," I said, placing it in her hands. "Tell me, how the heck do you watch movies, anyway?"

She grinned. "I don't, silly. I listen to them. It takes my mind off my troubles, just like you and everyone else."

I squinted at her skeptically. "Yeah? And what about the silent parts? What then?"

"It's called imagination, Michelle," she said gently.

I turned red. "Oh. Yeah. Uh, *that* could be interesting, huh?"

She smirked a little. "Always. Thank you for finding this. My apart-ment is getting so cluttered and full of stuff. Lynn and Nicky don't seem to have the time to really deep clean this place and put things in order and it's really beginning to frustrate me. I need to be able to *find* stuff!"

Without thinking, I blurted: "I can help. Organization is my stron-gest trait. Really. I have tomorrow off and I could come over in the morning."

Her face turned toward me. "I couldn't ask you to do that," she said in the same gentle tone. "Not on your own time. That wouldn't be right."

Oh, no? I thought. *It's the rightest thing I'll ever do.* Aloud, I said: "You're not asking, I'm offering. I'd like to spend more time with you, to learn more about . . . This."

She chuckled. "Still having trouble with the words, Michelle?"

I shook my head, maybe just a little defiantly. "No. Not anymore. I just don't want to offend Nicky and Lynn."

Her hoarse cackle resonated through the room: "I doubt if they'll even notice, Michelle!"

"Okay, then." I faced her down, daring her to stop me. "I'll be here first thing tomorrow morning, right after I get my kids off to school. A little after eight?"

"Huh, you sound pretty determined. Okay, Miss Perky. See you then. And thanks for all my presents. I *loved* them!"

* * *

I called her that night. I couldn't resist. I was half asleep when I hit the speed dial: call it impulse dialing.

"Hi. What are you doing?"

"Shopping," she replied. "Aren't you up past your bedtime?"

"Maybe," I said sleepily.

I was lying on top of the bed in my sweat pants and hoody with thick socks on my feet. I felt sluggish, a bit chilly and I was thinking about a blanket in a half-hearted sort of way. I was right at the edge of the borderland of sleep, when everything takes on a slightly surreal quality: muzzy and very, very comfortable. "Shopping? At this hour? What's open?"

She chuckled. "The Home Shopping Network is twenty-four hours a day, sweetie. It's my one major vice since I gave up smoking."

"You mean on TV?" I envisioned it and at that time, in my state, it was a strange and wonderful sight indeed. "That's weird, Mishelle. How do you know what you're buying? What *are* you buying?"

"Nothing right now. Just browsing. The descriptions are pretty complete, though. You ever watch?"

"Once in a while. Couple times . . ." My voice was drifting away; an incoherent mumble.

"Why don't you get some sleep?" Her voice was gentle, altogether forgiving and very, very soothing. "Was there something you needed to tell me?"

"Nah . . . yeah. Love ya, tha's all . . ."

Quietly, almost as if she was right next to me: "I love you too, Michelle. See you tomorrow."

I shut off the phone and rolled over, fell fast asleep before the movement was complete.

* * *

I woke to see my husband looking down at me quizzically. "'Morning," he said. "Hold still, the phone's tangled in your hair." He gently extricated it. "How you feelin'?"

"Gah," I croaked. "Coffee."

"That's what I thought. Already started. Sorry about letting you sleep in your sweats but you were . . ."

I covered his mouth with one hand. He had serious morning breath. "Coffee," I croaked again. "Please."

He kissed my hand and moved it away. "Sure. Did you know you talk in your sleep?" His mouth was smiling but there was something in back of his eyes . . .

I froze, suddenly wide awake. "What did I say?"

His quizzical look deepened. "I don't know. I couldn't make it out."

"Mom!" It was Zach, my other early morning riser. His voice floated in from just down the hall. "We're out of toilet paper!"

Ah, life in the Alexander household. Never a dull moment.

I rolled out of bed.

* * *

The TV was blaring away when I arrived at her door. For a moment, I let my fingertips rest against the smooth lemon colored wood with my eyes closed: listening and feeling and imagining that this was what her life was like, every day, every minute, and every waking moment.

If nothing else, it had texture.

I opened the door and Nicholas began barking his head off. Just as well: she wouldn't have heard me otherwise, the TV was that loud. Her head turned up, away from the glories of the HSN and toward me. She smiled like sunshine and reached for her remote.

"Is that coffee I smell?" The TV volume fell to a conversational level, leaving me with a bit of a hum in my ears.

Might have been excitement, too. Maybe.

"Uh-huh: caramel latte, your favorite. Also a strawberry danish. You get any sleep last night?"

"Some. You don't have to do this, you know. I feel bad about it . . ."

"You'll get over it." I glanced at the TV. A pretty blonde was modeling a jade necklace that would have looked very chic on Mishelle. I looked back at her and noticed she was still wearing the choker I'd given her. "Well, did you buy anything?"

"No." There was real regret in her sigh. "I didn't hear anything good enough to tempt me."

I nodded. "I've had shopping days when nothing appealed to me. So what do you want me to do first?"

She waved a hand in the general direction of the entertainment center. "Alphabetize my CDs and DVDs. That's the biggest chore, I think. If you could do that, it would help a lot."

"I can do that."

I started by moving all the DVDs from the cart in the hall and the entertainment center. There must have been over two hundred!

Each was labeled with Braille along the spine and the collection spanned all the popular genres: science-fiction, comedies, romances and classic black and white. (*Casablanca* caught my eye. One of my favorites.) Even a few war movies; which made me shudder a little. Mixed in with the movies were several empty CD cases; also labeled with Braille.

"Why are all these empty?" I asked.

She sipped her latte. "Oh, those are in my CD player. It holds two hundred CDs."

"Wow, mine only holds a measly six. How the heck do you keep track of them all?"

"There should be a spiral notebook on the entertainment center."

I found it on top of the CD player itself. As I thumbed through it, she continued: "I have them Brailled in numerical order and they should be like that in the player."

"You've got a great collection," I mused, flipping pages. Classic rock, jazz, compilations from the Seventies and Eighties and a whole lot of Beatles; everything they'd recorded, from what I could tell. She even had some country-western, some of the newer stuff and a bit of the outlaw material from Waylon and Willie and the boys.

"Thanks. I love music. Being blind, my hearing is enhanced, you know. That's one reason I enjoyed being a recording engineer so much. I don't know what I'd do without my ears."

I looked up at her and grinned. "That makes two of us. I love music, too. Do you have an I-Pod?"

"No. I've heard of them but I have no idea how they work."

"Well, hang on a minute. I'll show you! Mine's out in the car."

I darted outside, dodging a few raindrops, grabbed my I-Pod and came back, shaking out the earbuds. I don't like to use the buds; they never seem to fit properly.I have all the other gadgets that let me interface it with my home stereo and car stereo. I handed it to her.

"Ooh, it's so tiny."

"Yeah, which is why you can take it anywhere. Here's how it works." I took her index finger in my hand and demonstrated. "Wanna listen to it?"

"Sure. Got any Pink Floyd in there?"

"Of course. *Dark Side of the Moon* okay?"

"My favorite."

She put down her latte and I helped her put the earbuds in place. I dialed up *Money* and watched her expression.

She frowned. That's all. I felt a bit disappointed. She listened for a few moments and then pulled the earbuds out.

"Great acoustics, but things in my ears bother me." She handed the I-Pod back to me. David Gilmour's screamin' guitar sounded very tinny. I shut it off. "No offense, but my ears are like my eyes. I need to hear what's going on around me."

"Okay." I coiled the wires and tucked it into my purse. "You can hook it up to your stereo, too."

A low chuckle rumbled out of her chest, accompanied by a cough she managed to control. "I'm not sure I could figure out how to operate it."

"What?" I looked at her, trying to decide if she was kidding. "If you can operate a computer and all those other gadgets then you ought to be able to figure this out."

"If you say so." Her smile was a little wry. "Technology is pretty amazing, isn't it?"

"Yeah." I went back to arranging her DVDs, mildly miffed and wondering. With her expertise in electronics and music, this should have been irresistible but she'd gently turned it (and me) down. *Odd.*

When I was done with the DVDs, I went into the kitchen to wash up. (The covers were pretty dusty.) Movement in the corner of my eye made me turn and I was startled to see Mishelle get out of her recliner and follow me over to the chair by her computer. When she got up, I realized that I hardly ever saw her out of her recliner and just how *tall* she was.

She wanted to talk, so we chatted while I reorganized her kitchen. We went through each cabinet and drawer while I described what was there and she would tell me if it needed to be kept or tossed out.

We didn't toss out very much. She was kind of a packrat, I think. During this, somehow the subject of our conversation drifted in the direction of high school. I told her of my being a bit of a hell-raiser too, gently correcting her impression that I had either been a cheerleader or class president. I tried out for the cheer squad once, but didn't make the cut. Politics gives me indigestion.

"Mishelle, what did you do after you graduated from high school?"

"Well, I lived with my Mom and Dad for awhile. I actually had a job for a while down at the post office. I sold candy and cigarettes at a little stand outside." That wry grin surfaced again. "I did that until they had to let me go, because people would steal things from my stand, and I wouldn't know about it."

I was shocked. "You've *got* to be kidding! People *stole* things from you?"

"Pretty bad, huh?" The grin had a slight edge to it, now.

"How could anyone steal something from a blind person? That's . . . that's . . ." I was speechless and it takes a lot for words to fail me.

"Michelle sweetie, I've had a lot of things stolen from me in my days." Her expression was resigned and her tone weary. "I've grown used to it. Anyway, after that, I went back to Kansas and spent some time with my extended family. That's when I had my eye surgery."

"Eye surgery?"

"Haven't you ever noticed that my left eye is fake?"

"Well, kind of." I had, but I wasn't going to make a big deal of it.

"My real eye almost exploded, so they removed it and put this one in."

"Ugh. What happened?"

"Excess intra-ocu . . . ockoo . . ."

"Intra-ocular eye pressure?"

"Yeah, that's it. Always had trouble pronouncing that. Come closer. See the little red lines in my fake eye?"

I walked over to her, bent and looked close. "Yeah?"

"Well, when I had it put in, I was really stoned and I told them to make it look as bloodshot as my other eye." She laughed.

"Are you serious?"

"Serious as a heart attack, darlin'. If you look really close, the blood-shot lines actually spell *I Love You.*"

I looked at her eye again. I couldn't see it. I shook my head in wonder. "You are something else, Mishelle."

"Yeah, I'm a piece of work, aren't I?" Her hoarse snicker was full of genuine mirth. "After I had my surgery, I hitchhiked to Florida."

I nodded. "Yeah, you told me that earlier. All by yourself, huh?"

"Yeah, just me and my cane. I got picked up by a trucker. He picked up another hitcher along the way and we wound up getting pulled over by the cops for speeding or something. Anyway, I guess the other guy was wanted for murder, so the cops hauled us all off to jail. They seemed to think we knew each other because we were traveling together. I spent the night in jail until the cops figured out that I had nothing to do with this guy."

My mouth was open again. It was becoming a habit around her. She continued: "I finally made it to Florida a few days later. While I was there, I worked in a dark room at a photo shop."

"A dark room? Processing pictures?" I was starting to wonder if she was pulling my leg.

"Yeah, I processed pictures. Kind of ironic, isn't it? A blind person processing pictures." Another hoarse laugh as she continued: "I was really good at it. And I really liked Florida. I love the ocean. I spent a lot of time swimming in the ocean and did a lot of deep sea fishing. I also spent a lot of time partying."

My voice was as dry as a good martini. "Well, imagine my surprise. Any memorable ones?"

Her grin was wide and Cheshire Cat-like. "Yeah! I used to party with Jimmy Buffet!"

My bullshit alarm went off. "Oh, come on, Mishelle! Jimmy Buffet? You expect me to believe that?"

Impossibly, her grin stretched wider. "Sure. He was a big time party animal, too. Nice guy. I spent many a night getting stoned with him."

"You're serious, aren't you?"

"Yep. Michelle, this was the Sixties. Sex and drugs and rock and roll." She snickered. "Well, maybe not a lot of sex on my part, but lots of drugs, that's for sure. Jimmy always hung out with musicians. There were jam sessions every night. I heard some great music at his place."

Mishelle sipped her latte, which must have been stone cold by then. "Florida is where I went skydiving." She vented another hoarse snicker that turned into a short but sincere coughing fit. I waited patiently until she'd caught her breath. Then she said:

"Two minutes."

"Huh?"

"That's how long I fell. Skydiving. I was supposed to pull the ripcord after ten seconds but I was in freefall for two minutes." She panted gently. "The instructor was so mad! I wanted to jump again but he wouldn't let me."

She giggled, the air squeaking painfully in and out of her compromised lungs. "He said I was crazy. He might've had a point there."

"I think I have to agree," I said quietly, my insides churning with conflicting emotions. "That was pretty crazy stuff. Can I ask you something?"

She was bent forward in her chair, elbows on her knees: panting. Her face turned up to mine. "Sure. You know you can."

"Thanks. What drugs did you do? Were you stoned that day?"

"Probably. I don't remember. Why? Is it important?"

I nodded and said: "Yes."

Mishelle shrugged. "Pot, mostly. I think I did 'most everything except the hard stuff like smack. Heroin." She grinned wryly. "Never did figure out how to shoot up, sweetie. You gotta be able to see the vein."

"I know," I said, my insides going cold.

"Yeah, you would, wouldn't you?" She shrugged. "I much preferred marijuana anyway. I still smoke it."

I stared at her. "*What*? With *your* lungs?"

"Hell, yeah! Shit, I wish I had some right now! It would make it easier to breathe."

I found myself kneeling in front of her, holding her hand. "Mishelle, *don't*. You have less than twenty percent lung capacity. That stuff can only make it worse."

"Huh. You've obviously never smoked any ganja, sweetie."

"Wrong," I snapped. "I used to smoke it in high school. I know what it's like."

Her other hand came up and stroked my hair. "Then you know it can make someone's breathing easier. I've put in an application for a medical marijuana card, too. C'mon, Michelle. You know the stuff helps more than it harms."

I bit my lip; training and experience and compassion all conducting a brief but spirited free-for-all within me. Reluctantly, I said, "Okay, I'll concede that it can help, a little. But promise me you won't smoke it anymore. Please? Your lungs are messed up enough as it is."

She shook her head. "Nope, sorry. Can't promise you that. I should be getting my card any day now."

I looked up into her face, realizing at last that she was being completely straight with me about all of it: her life, her experiences, her drug use then and now.

"Damn," I said, very sincerely.

She smiled. "Yeah. Anything else you wanna know, sweetie?"

"Why did you leave Florida if it was so enjoyable?"

"I had an opportunity to go to school." She paused to gasp for air. "In Eugene, Oregon. U of O." Another gasp. "I was a duck."

"A . . . duck?"

"That's the school mascot, hon. Ducks. OSU are beavers, U of O are ducks." She giggled again, air squeaking painfully in and out of her tortured lungs. "Ducks can fly, at least."

"Were you Mike or Mishelle then?"

"Mike. Oh, I had a stash of women's clothes and I dressed in the privacy of my own place, behind closed doors and no one, and I mean *no one*, knew."

She snorted and gasped for a few seconds. Then: "Although I think my parents were beginning to suspect something."

My knees were beginning to hurt but I stayed motionless. "What do you mean?"

"I flew home before I started school. Got off the plane wearing a pair of white go-go boots."

"Oh, God," I said and tried to stifle laughter without much success. "*That* must have been an interesting sight! What did your parents say?"

She laughed back, with me and not at me. "Not much. Just: 'Nice boots, Mike.' God, I must have looked like a complete dork."

"Maybe, maybe not." Behind her, the date and time robot chanted the time in its metallic voice and I realized that it was almost noon. "Jeez, the time! Lynn will be here soon and I gotta go."

"I know." She caressed my hair a final time. "It was nice having you here, Michelle."

I reached up and took her hand. "It's always nice to be with you, Mishelle. Even if you scare the hell out of me sometimes."

"Well, I don't mean to . . . it's just . . ." She struggled for air. "It's just me. The way I am. Sorry."

I came up out of my crouch and wrapped my arms around her. "Don't ever apologize for being yourself," I whispered in her ear. "Not to me, not to anyone. Okay?"

"Okay," she whispered back and I knew it was one promise to me she would always keep. "Okay."

* * *

Later that evening, sometime after dinner, Dave and I were talking and I recounted some of our conversation. He smirked when I got to the parts about Pink Floyd and the drugs.

"A real stoner chick, huh?"

I looked at him, trying to decide whether he was being sarcastic. "What's that supposed to mean?"

"Oh, you know. People who listen to Pink Floyd and smoke pot. Stoners." His grin turned wry and I remembered that my dear husband had done his own share of smoking pot when he was younger. "Hell, I was that way myself, y'know."

"I know," I said quietly, fighting down a sense of unease. If anything, my husband is even more conservative than myself. In the seventeen years of our marriage, I'd never seen him take anything harder than a double Scotch. "You approve, I take it?"

He shrugged. "I didn't say that. But it's her life, isn't it?"

I studied his face, seeing nothing more than amusement there. "Yeah. It is. And you're okay with this?"

He shrugged again. "Different strokes, I guess. Can't say that I approve but it's not up to me, is it?"

Choosing my words carefully, I said, "I don't think anything *anyone* says or does will change her. She's her own person. Always."

"You got that right, honey." He smiled. "Actually, she sounds like my kinda gal. Like you, you know? Maybe that's why you like each other so much. Neither of you two give a damn what others think."

I stared at him. "Is that how you think of me?"

"Sure." He looked me right in the eye. "It's the reason I married you, babe. Why I fell in love with you in the first place. You're your own person and you always will be." He looked resigned and a little regretful. "I've grown used to that. Had to, y'know?"

"Really?" We were sitting on the couch, the TV on, the movie we were watching ignored by both of us. "I never knew that."

He reached over and squeezed my hand. "Lots of things about me you don't know, Michelle. Lots of things."

He was right. People you know and people you don't.

Sometimes they're the same people.

CHAPTER ELEVEN

The Kids Are Alright

"I T'S BACK."

I already had my bag open and was rummaging around for things. "Let's not jump to conclusions, Mishelle. Have you been able to cough anything up?"

"Yeah." Her voice was a harsh rumble that fought to escape her chest. "I saved you some. Here." She held out a wadded piece of tissue cupped in both hands, as if she were a child offering a handmade gift.

I took it, one eyebrow warily raised, unfolded it and looked upon the contents, my lips pursed in concern: about twenty cc's worth and dark green. Yup, it was back. I checked her temperature and listened to her lungs. Her fever was back and her lungs sounded thoroughly swampy.

For the briefest moment, just a tick, I felt a surge of despair. But then I remembered . . .

So I said: "I need to call your doctor," and pulled out my cellphone and dialed his number.

Most nurses in a busy metropolitan setting can't just punch in the doctor's number and expect to get anything besides his answering service or the hospital switchboard or, at best: his office and his MA. But this is Kalispell, Montana and I work for Home Health and I had his cellphone number in my directory. And I knew he'd be at work.

In the big city, I think they call this *juice*. I call it getting results.

He picked up and I gave him an update in about five succinct sentences. There was silence on the other end of the line while he digested my report and then, sounding very weary, he ordered another antibiotic in a remarkably high dosage and longer duration than usual. It was at that point that I knew we were out of variations left to try and he knew I knew.

It was a depressing conversation. He ended it by telling me to inform my patient that she no longer had any options. When I clicked off, her head was turned toward me, chin down. She looked sad and determined, all at once.

"I'll go." She spoke before I could open my mouth.

"What?"

"The hospital. I'll go. If you'll take me. I'll go." Her words were short, her sentences equally abrupt and punctuated between each with a tiny gasp. "Can you tell them not to call me sir? Or mister?"

"Heck, yes. You had to ask? Of course."

She was silent, getting her breath. Finally she said: "This is what, the fifth round?"

I agreed.

"Maybe this one will kick its ass."

"You really believe that?"

She nodded. "Don't you?"

She had to ask.

* * *

Three days crawled by and not a word from her did I hear. I wanted to call but I deliberately kept busy and, wonder of wonders, stayed away from my e-mail for nearly that whole time.

Thinking about her: ah, non-stop. This is what happens when you receive a heavenly directive: it becomes as much a part of your life as breathing or sleeping. More: you sleep less, staring at the ceiling and wondering how in the world you'll ever again get a good night's sleep, knowing what you do.

Things have a way of working out: I sleep fine these days, thanks.

I showed up at her door the fourth day, bright and early, bag in hand and a resolute set to my chin. *Okay*, I thought. *We can do this, right?*

Nicholas did his happy dance around me as I settled down on the love-seat with my bag. I absent-mindedly scratched his back while I looked her over.

"Are you feeling any better?" It was a rhetorical question. She certainly looked better: the dark circles under her eyes had lessened considerably in three days and her color was much better, less pasty gray.

But there were deep lines on her face and she still looked tired, so tired. My heart ached for just the smallest tick of the clock.

"Yeah, a lot better," she said cheerfully. "I actually got some sleep last night." She saluted me with the latte I'd handed her on my way in. "Thank you. This really hits the spot! But where's my danish?"

"Greedy girl." I patted her arm. "You can have it when I finish my assessment. Now, hold still while I get your blood pressure and pulse, would you?"

"But I'm *hungry*."

I wrapped the cuff around her arm. "Just imagine my surprise. Did Nicky fix you any dinner last night?"

"Yeah, but . . ." She subsided as I pumped the cuff. "Wasn't much. Bacon and eggs. She had to leave early." She scowled. "Always doin' a deal, that one."

"Deals?" I released the valve and noted her blood pressure on the chart. "You don't mean a drug deal, do you?"

The scowl didn't quite go away. "I didn't say that."

I looked up at her and a sliver of ice seemed to slide down my back. "Mishelle, you think Nicky's involved in illegal activities? That's . . . that's not something a caregiver should be doing."

There was a set look to her movie idol jaw that told me this particular subject was closed to further discussion. "Ask me no questions and I'll tell you no lies, Michelle."

I paused, my fingers on her wrist and I could actually feel her pulse increase. "Girlfriend, I'm serious. If you think Nicky's doing something illegal, you should tell me. I have to report it."

She shrugged and I could feel her pulse jump again. "Nothing to report. I didn't say anything about drugs, did I?"

I gnawed my lower lip. "No, but . . ."

"No buts. I didn't say anything about drugs, okay?"

It was my turn to shrug. "Okay." I let it drop. There didn't seem to be much else to say and for a few minutes there was a distinctly uncomfortable silence. I finally filled it with a question:

"So, you have any plans for next weekend?"

"What's next weekend?"

I was a bit taken aback. "Memorial Day. Aren't you going anywhere for the weekend?"

Her smile was bitter. "What plans could *I* possibly have, Michelle? I don't go anywhere for holidays. I sit right here, like I always do."

I stared at her. "Your family?"

She shrugged. "My family always goes up to their cabin on Ashley Lake for Memorial Day and Labor Day. I never get invited. Haven't been for years."

"Well, for the love of . . ." For a moment, I wanted to pick up the phone and give Louise and Earl a piece of my mind. How could anyone leave their kin alone, to exclude a family member from a family gathering, especially one as sick as Mishelle?

"I haven't been invited since I transitioned twenty years ago," she said, her mouth twisting painfully. "Mom told me that if I put on a pair of slacks and a sweater, I'd be welcome but I swore I'd never wear pants again when I transitioned." She sipped her latte. "Now they don't even bother to ask me. I hope their boat sinks."

"Mishelle!"

"Well, how would *you* feel?" she said irritably. "Holidays are always the worst time for me. I get to sit here, feeling sorry for myself while . . . Oh, never mind. I just get really depressed around holidays." She sighed, congestion gurgling in the back of her throat. "I can't help but think about how most families spend their time together during the holidays. Christmas is about the worst, I think."

She sipped her latte. Briefly, her voice cleared: "It really sucks but I guess I should be used to it by now, don't you think?"

Carefully, I said: "No, I don't think I'd ever be used to it. Not even after twenty years."

"I haven't been invited out by them *anywhere* since I moved back here to Kalispell four years ago," she stated bleakly. Her head turned toward me and again I had the odd feeling she was somehow studying my expression. "What about you? What are *you* doing next weekend?"

I hesitated and in that moment, I think I might have hated myself almost as much as I hated Louise and Earl for abandoning their child. "Uh, nothing much. Ah, my brother is having a barbecue or something. Pretty low-key, actually. No big deal."

Her smile was hovering right on the edge of *gotcha*. "Oh, yeah? Your kids are going, aren't they?"

"Well, sure."

"Good. Uh, Zach is what, twelve? And Chris is . . . nine? Is that right?"

She knew it was right. That steel trap memory of hers retained everything, especially numbers. "That's right," I said quietly. "Twelve and nine. Why?"

"Oh, no reason. Just asking. What are they like?"

For some reason, I felt uncomfortable talking about my boys. "Oh, they're great kids. Completely different in personality, though." I laughed, perhaps a bit uneasily. "Dave always jokes that our little one is the ice cream man's."

"I'd love to meet your family sometime," she said quietly.

"Uh, maybe just Dave, for now," thinking back on his comments about her journal. My cheeks were bright red about then.

"Not your boys?"

"Um, I think my boys are . . . uh, that is, I don't think they'd understand about you. They're . . . a little young, I think."

"What's that have to do with meeting me?" Her voice was cool and unyielding.

"Well, Zach . . . He's just coming into his sexuality. Puberty, y'know? I don't want to confuse him."

Her tone was stern. I was reminded of an instructor I'd had in nursing school, an old battleaxe of a chemistry teacher who did not suffer fools gladly and invariably left comments on my exam papers like: *You can do better than this!*

"Children are the most open people in the world, Michelle. It's their parents who have closed minds." She sipped the last bitter dregs of her latte. "Isn't it weird how parents mold their children's thinking when it should be the other way around?"

I opened my mouth, closed it. I had no answer, none at all. What can you say when your prejudices bite you on the nose?

"Well . . . well, we'll see," was all I could manage right then. I was saved by her time and date robot when it announced that it was now nine-thirty. "Oh, jeez. I, ah . . ."

"Time to go?" Her voice was neutral, almost casual now, with no trace of that unyielding cool sternness.

"Yeah, I've got a full schedule today. Lots of patients. Busy day." I was perilously close to babbling. "I'll see you tomorrow, 'kay? Uh, call me if you feel, uh . . ."

"I will." There was nothing now but gentle forgiveness in her voice. "Hey, Michelle?"

I stopped halfway to the door, bag in hand. "What?"

"My danish?"

"Oh." Feeling foolish, I handed her the bag of goodies. "Sorry."

"It's okay. Really. 'Bye, dear."

"'Bye." I closed the door behind me on that final vowel and beat a hasty retreat to my car. Safely inside, I slumped back against the seat, staring blindly through the windshield.

"Well." I did not recognize my own voice. "*That* went really well, didn't it?" I started the Toyota and backed away.

I'd lied through my teeth: I had no other patients to see that day. On my way home, my eyes suddenly blurred with tears and I had to pull over and stop. I rested my forehead against the steering wheel and fought for control, her comment ringing in my ears: *parents mold their children's thinking.*

We sure do. Oh, we blame TV and peer pressure and things like that but the real truth, the real and present truth is that *we* are the ones responsible for the way our little ones grow up and *we* are the ones responsible for the people they become.

I thought about it and my stomach twisted. I wanted my boys to grow up free of the dangers of city life which was why I'd come here, to live in Kalispell. I wanted them to be safe, to be able to thrive in a place where there were no gangs, no crime or drugs or . . .

Or hatred.

Or prejudice.

I wiped my eyes and looked up again; out at a beautiful spring day in Montana; a big, beautiful blue sky almost free of clouds and a glorious mountain vista north of me that never failed to take my breath away.

I realized then that I'd done my kids a disservice; I'd raised them in a place where diversity was a rare commodity and bigotry came all too easily because everyone here was much like everyone else.

And the one exception to that had just poked me in a tender spot I'd thought I didn't have anymore.

I thought I'd learned something with Mishelle and the truth was; I hadn't learned much at all.

I put the car in gear and drove home.

* * *

"Dave, what do you think about the boys meeting Mishelle sometime?"

We were in the front room. The boys were in bed, I was curled up on the couch and Dave was in his armchair, reading the housing section of the want ads and circling likely prospects. He's a real estate agent and for him, it was homework.

He looked up at me over his glasses. "Why?"

"I think it would be a good learning experience for them." Perhaps I sounded defensive, but so did his response:

"Why in the world would you think it would be a good learning experience? How many transgender people besides Mishelle live here in Kalispell?"

"They won't be living here forever," I pointed out, reasonably enough, I thought.

"Why not?"

"Well, they *will* be going away to college eventually," I said. "It's a good learning experience, don't you think?"

He snorted. "And just how many of *those* are they going to find in Bozeman?"

"And what if they don't want to go to Montana State? Suppose they want to go to California? Or New York?"

He shuddered visibly. "God, I hope not!"

"It's a possibility, Dave. We should consider it."

He tossed the paper aside. "Okay, I've considered it. I still don't see the point. There's plenty of time for the boys to learn about this. Why right now?"

I may have looked relaxed, there on our couch but inside, I was trying to control my temper. My husband can be very stubborn sometimes. "It's a good lesson in diversity and it's always a good time for that. If you met her, you'd know that she's *not* . . . one sick puppy, as you so charmingly put it."

He studied me. "Well, maybe you're right. I can see that you feel pretty strongly about this though, don't you?"

I sighed. "I just feel really sorry for her, Dave. Her family is getting together for Memorial Day and she's not even invited."

I sat up and swung my legs over the edge of the couch, leaning forward, warming to the subject. "As a matter of fact, she's not been invited to any family gatherings since she moved back here to Kalispell four years ago." I looked him right in the eyes. "Tell me, how would *you* feel if you were her, hmm?"

His eyebrows went up. "Really? And *all* her family lives here, is that right?"

Family is a hot button for my husband. If anything, he's more passionate about the subject than me. "They do. And she sits in the dark, all by herself. You tell me: how right is that?"

I watched his expression change as he thought about it and my heart lifted when he said: "Well, what the hell would we tell the boys?"

"We needn't tell Chris anything. I think he's too young to understand." I smiled; thinking of Cee-Boo and his pure and perfect innocence.

"Maybe so, but we have to tell Zach *something*. He'll figure it out right away. Remember that transgender person we saw in Minneapolis three or four years ago during the Junior Olympics? Zach knew about her right away and he was only eight. I think we should tell him the truth."

I cocked my head to one side, studying his face. "You're actually considering this." It was not a question.

He nodded. "Yes. But I want to think about it some more."

My heart, ready to soar, fell. I was all primed to throw my arms around his neck and give him a hug and a kiss and thank him for being so open and fair.

But my husband is a cautious man, perhaps to a fault. He doesn't jump into anything.

I was left with a mixture of frustration and determination; a volatile combination as far as I'm concerned. I didn't want to nag him and it wouldn't have worked anyway. My husband can also be a very stubborn person.

For that matter; so can I.

In the following three days, I did manage to bring it up a time or two and Friday afternoon, he finally agreed.

I wanted to do the happy dance like Nicholas. But I bided my time until after dinner was done and the dishes put away then made a beeline to my computer to e-mail Mishelle.

Great news, I typed. *We're go for Sunday afternoon!*

Her reply came back almost immediately and that told me volumes right there. I imagined her sitting in front her computer; waiting for this, dreading the worst. My eyes momentarily misted over, thinking how awful it would be for her to sit in the dark by herself once more: alone, unloved and unwanted.

Cool! What time?

Rapidly, I typed: *How does two in the afternoon sound? Your place or mine?*

There was a longer pause and I knew she was thinking about it, hard. Then: *Mine. I'd feel more comfortable on my own turf if that's okay with you.*

I smiled and nodded, typed: *Sounds good. Can I call you? I want to hear your voice.*

Her response was quick and typically wry: *I'd hate to have your cell-phone bill, girlfriend.*

I laughed out loud. *It's okay. I get lots of free minutes.* I picked up my phone and dialed her number.

"Hi!"

"Hi." I could hear her little pants for breath between each short sentence. "Thanks, Michelle. Thank you more than I can say."

For some reason, my breathing was a little difficult as well. "You're very welcome, Mishelle. I'm looking forward to seeing you this Sunday."

"Me, too." There was a short pause filled only by the sound of her panting. "Hey, Michelle?"

"What?"

"Do you think your family will like me?"

A thousand answers came to me, all at once, but I simply said, very sincerely: "Of course."

"Did you tell Zach and Chris?"

I bit my lip. "Not yet. Probably tomorrow."

"You *are* going to tell them, aren't you?"

"Yes." My lip was beginning to hurt, so I stopped gnawing at it. "I wouldn't . . . wouldn't . . ."

She chuckled hoarsely. "Surprise them with a dude in a dress?"

Blood surged to my temples. "Don't say that. It's not true."

She sighed and I could hear that damned congestion crackle over the phone like a bad case of static. "I hope not."

"Believe it, Mishelle. *It's not true.* What did you tell me about kids being more open than their parents?"

"Yeah." She sighed again. "Okay. Two o'clock."

"Right. Two o'clock. See you then."

"Okay. I love you."

"I love you, too." The phone went dead. I closed it and placed it carefully on my desk next to the computer, staring at it as if I expected it to give me more answers than was ever possible for a machine or a person. "I really do."

* * *

"Zach, I need to talk to you."

He looked up from his Gameboy, startled, his expression a little guilty. "Am I in trouble?"

I smiled at him. "No, nothing like that. Come with me please, sweetie." I held out my hand.

He put down his Gameboy and took my hand. I led him outside onto the deck at the south end of our house and indicated he should take a seat. I took a seat opposite him, drew a deep breath and started in:

"Zach, we're going to visit someone tomorrow. She's a patient of mine. More than that, she's a good friend, maybe my best friend." I hesitated. "She's . . . different. Special." I studied his face and saw only open curiosity. "She's transgender. You understand what that means?"

He looked back at me, his brow furrowed. "You mean like that girl we saw at the Junior Olympics?"

"Yes, exactly."

"Oh." He thought about it. "Wow."

I smiled ruefully, thinking: *You got* that *right, dear one.* "Do I have your promise you'll behave like a gentleman? You may not approve of her or even like her, but she's very nice and I want you to promise me you won't be rude to her."

He looked annoyed for a moment. "Well, sure, Mom. I wouldn't do that." His brow was still furrowed. "Is this the blind lady you've been taking care of? Mishelle?"

"Yes."

He shrugged. "Cool. I've never met a blind person before. Hey, does Chris know?"

"No, not yet and I don't want you to discuss her transgender condition with him, okay? Just treat her like anyone else, please."

He nodded. "Okay. I promise."

I sighed in relief. "Thanks, Zach. I knew I could count on you."

"Okay. Can I go back to my Gameboy? I'm up to level thirty on Pokemon."

I grinned at him. "Sure. Scoot. Send Chris out here, will you?"

He was up and out of his chair like a shot and disappeared inside. I sat for a moment, drinking in the sunshine and the birdsongs, musing: *If only it was always that easy.*

Inside, I could hear Zach yelling at Chris, telling him to get his butt outside, Mom wants to talk to you. A few moments later, my Cee-Boo poked his head out of the door.

"Mom?"

I beckoned to him. "Come here, baby."

He came to me and parked himself on my lap. I put my arms around him and mussed his hair. "Chris, we're going to meet one of my patients tomorrow. Would you like that?"

He bounced excitedly on my lap. "Sure! Who is it?"

"She's that lady you've heard your Dad and me talking about. Mishelle. She's blind, you know."

"I know. I heard you and Dad a *lot*." His brow furrowed, just like his brother's. "I wonder what that's like; to be blind all the time." He looked into my eyes. "What's she like, Mom? Is she sad because she can't see?"

"Well, tomorrow you'll find out." I hesitated again, thinking about that question: *Is she sad?* "No, she's not sad. In fact, she's one of the happiest people I know." I smiled. "But she *is* really tall."

His eyes grew big. "Taller than Dad?"

I laughed out loud. "Yes, taller than your Dad."

"Wow, she must be *really* tall. Does she play basketball?"

I laughed again. "No, that would be really hard to do because she's blind."

"Oh. Yeah." He shrugged. "Well, that's too bad." He squirmed off my lap. "Can I go watch Nickelodeon now?"

I sighed, maybe a little shakily. "Sure. Go ahead."

He went through the door like he was on roller skates. I sat for a few minutes, enjoying the fine spring afternoon; thinking.

The other way around.

"Yeah," I whispered. "It's weird, alright."

* * *

I called Mishelle as we were preparing to leave. "Hi! Are you ready for us to come over?"

Her voice was more breathless than usual. "Can you give me fifteen minutes or so? Nicky is just putting the finishing touches on my hair."

"You bet. See you soon!" I shut the phone, tried to visualize Mishelle all dolled up and smothered a nervous giggle.

Please, I thought. *Not like Darcelle's. Not like that.* Anything *but that.*

Dave came in and eyed me. "You still want to do this?"

I turned quickly, too quickly and I really didn't mean to snap at him. "Of course! You?"

He shrugged, but there was a wary glint in his eye. "I told you that I would, didn't I?"

I closed my eyes and nodded. "Yes. You did." I opened my eyes and looked at him. "I'm sorry, Dave. I didn't mean to bark at you."

He nodded. "You're nervous. Well, so am I." He grinned and I felt a sudden surge of affection for my husband. "Let's do this, honey."

"Okay."

We stopped at Norm's on the way over and I dithered a bit over which kind of pie to bring along. I finally settled on banana-cream, Mishelle's favorite and mine, too. When I got back in the car, I realized that my heart was hammering hard enough to burst. Dave glanced curiously at me, but didn't say a word, bless him.

As I knocked at her door, he leaned past me to tap at the *Elvis Fans Only* sign. He grinned sidelong at me and I grinned back and shrugged, using just my eyebrows.

The door opened and Nicky stood there, a sullen look on her face. For a moment, only a moment, nervousness gripped my throat like a steel fist but then I saw Mishelle sitting in her chair and it vanished: a chip of dry ice on a hot sidewalk.

She looked *wonderful*. She was wearing a burgundy blouse and a black skirt that flowed almost to her ankles in a smooth, midnight-colored waterfall. Her face was carefully made-up and nothing at all like a drag queen's, just like . . .

A woman's face. Foundation that nicely smoothed out her complexion, eye color in a rich cinnamon shade and not too much eyeliner or mascara, a touch of blush on her prominent cheekbones and some color on her lips; a subdued coral tint that defined her mouth very well without looking garish.

Her hair was beautifully done: a smooth wave up across one side of her forehead and loose, open curls that cascaded around her shoulders.

Nicky had done a good job. I looked at her and mouthed *thanks* but she responded with a half-hearted glare, took the pie I offered and disappeared into the kitchen.

I shrugged and put her out of my mind. I made introductions, including Nicholas who was dancing around our ankles, barking and wagging his tail. Chris wanted to play with him but Nicholas kept his distance. Blue, on the other hand, loved all the extra attention and moved from lap to lap with dignified abandon.

I took the opportunity to lean down and give Mishelle a hug.

"You look beautiful," I whispered in her ear.

"Thanks," she whispered back.

Chris grew bored with trying to get Nicholas to play with him and found Mishelle's mesh bag of remotes almost immediately. He pulled out something blocky and metallic that I instantly recognized and stared at it with intense curiosity: "What's this, Mishelle?"

She reached out her hand and smiled from ear to ear as her long, strong fingers caressed the object in my son's hands. "That's my Brailler," she announced cheerfully. "It's how I change words into little raised dots called Braille that I can read."

"Cool! Show me how it works!"

And they were off and running. My Cee-Boo loves gadgets and Mishelle had a whole room-full of them. The ice was broken, between the two of them at least, but I could still sense a core of reluctance within my friend; an air of reservation that reminded me of our first meeting.

I still don't know to this day if what I sensed that day was Mishelle's wariness among strangers or simply my own anxieties. I wanted so much for her to like my family and for them to like her that my senses were hyper-acute.

I do know one thing though: Chris and Mishelle hit it off like brother and sister, two peas in a pod, friends for life. She had him from hello and I think we *all* sensed it. I glanced at Dave, who was watching them with an air of gentle bemusement and I began to relax a little.

Even Nicky couldn't manage to spoil it when she leaned around the corner between the kitchen and front room, her expression still sullen.

"Who wants pie?" She didn't quite snarl. She was met with a chorus of "I do," and withdrew to rattle the dishes.

We had pie. We watched Chris and Mishelle become fast friends and it was very, very good. Somewhere after the second or third bite, I realized that I was very happy and proud of my family, especially my youngest son.

Much sooner than I wanted, it was time to go. We each gave her a hug, even my big, conservative husband who had once called her a name I think he regretted right then.

When it was my turn, I whispered in her ear, "I'll e-mail you later, okay?"

"Okay," she whispered back.

When I stood, I saw Nicky staring at us, her expression similar to that of a speeder getting a ticket from an unsympathetic cop. I smiled and gave her a little wave, but she turned her back on me; on us all and disappeared again into the kitchen.

It didn't matter, right then. I felt buoyant, like I was walking on air.

Mishelle had a little surprise gift for us all though, just before we trooped out the door: an index card with a short explanation of the Braille system and a line of Braille at the bottom of the card.

Her expression was pure *gotcha*. "Chris," she said, "Try to figure out that sentence using the guide. 'Bye, everybody. It was nice having you here."

I followed my family out to the car. Chris had the sentence figured out before we got home, of course.

Sometime after dinner, I stuck my head in Zach's bedroom. "So what did you think of her?"

He looked up at me from his Gameboy. "She's really nice." He looked down, paused his game and looked up at me again, his expression perfectly serious. "Mom, I don't think it matters what's on the outside. It's what's inside that counts."

My eyes welled with tears and behind me, I heard Chris: "Yeah, she's really cool! When can we go see her again?"

I turned and pulled him close and beckoned to Zach. He came off the bed and I held him too, held them both; my two good boys.

I knew in that moment that they would grow to be the kind of men this world so desperately needs: free of the prejudice within myself I was so afraid of, unencumbered by hatred and untainted by the arrogance that comes from believing any human being can possibly be better than another.

I held them close and for a long, sweet moment, I was very much at peace.

Dave was out on the deck, sipping a beer and placidly watching the sunset. I sat down next to him. We didn't speak for several minutes, just watched the salmon-colored clouds of the long Montana twilight.

The silence between us was very fine and comfortable.

"Thanks," I said quietly when the light had all but gone.

"You're welcome." He finished his beer. "She looks like a guy but acts like a girl."

I hadn't asked, but he knew what I was thinking, oh yes. He shook his head, the air of gentle bemusement still draped about him like a priest's stole. "Amazing. She's not at all what I expected."

My husband turned his head to me. I could barely make out his features in the gloom of evening. "Go e-mail her. I know you want to. Go on, it's okay."

I rose wordlessly and kissed him on the cheek, touched his face gently, my heart full.

"Michelle?"

I stopped at the door and turned.

"I'm glad we went."

I managed a nod. I couldn't speak; my throat was too tight with emotion.

I went inside. My laptop and my best friend were waiting for me.

They like you, I typed. *They really like you. Zach said it's what's on the inside that counts and Chris wants to see you again as soon as he can. I'm very proud of them both.*

Her reply zipped back to me at the speed of light: *Your family is so very kind. Tears are rolling down my cheeks as I write this.*

Mine were wet, too. I typed: *I think Dave likes you, too. He's just too uptight to admit it.*

Her reply came back within seconds: *Thank you so much for introducing me to your wonderful family. Have fun tomorrow at your brother's. I'll be thinking of you, always.*

I typed with some difficulty because I couldn't see the keys very well: *Thanks. Sleep well, Mishelle. I love you.*

I love you too, Michelle. Thanks.

I shut down my laptop and wiped the tears from my eyes. "Thanks," I whispered, to my friend, to the day, to Anyone who happened to be listening. "Thanks."

CHAPTER TWELVE
Family Matters

I TOOK A DEEP BREATH and a dozen different smells assaulted my nose: wood smoke, the aromas of half a dozen kinds of cooking meat, bark dust, perfume, baking odors from the open kitchen door behind me and cutting through it like Nature's own incense; the winey, piney odor of evergreens swaying in the warm spring breeze just upwind of Margie's place.

It was a warm, lovely Memorial Day there in the woods, just a few miles north of Kalispell. Margie and my brother held this little shindig every year and every year she went all out:

Sports? There was badminton and volleyball for the active types, horseshoes and croquet for the more sedate folks.

Food? Hotdogs, hamburgers, steaks, lamb, a dozen different salads, chips of every hue and texture; we could have easily fed a medium-sized village in any Third World country.

Booze! Her wine selections were to die for, but that year was my Cosmopolitan period. I dunno; I guess I thought they were . . . elegant.

If you felt really bored and antisocial, there was always the state of the art home-theatre in their basement; a seriously expensive piece of high-tech that made Mishelle's system look like an antique.

Kids roamed, romped and generally raised hell across the lawn and all the way out to the tree-line. An unwritten roster system I've yet to fully understand and I suspect is imparted telepathically serves to rotate adult attention on this unruly mob so that no one gets cut, bruised or otherwise eaten by a bear, a distant but real possibility this far out in the woods.

I tilted my head to one side, gazing out at the lawn full of kids and picnic tables and badminton nets and good folks chatting, drinking, eating and having a pretty good time, myself included.

It was nice to be in the moment, even if for just a little while.

"Hey, Michelle?"

I sighed. So much for the moment . . . "Yes, Margie?"

"Can you help cart the salads out to the tables? I've gotta get the cookies out of the oven!"

"Coming!" I turned and dodged a pack of laughing, running rug rats on my way. "Slow *down*, you guys!" Inside, Margie waved an oven-mitted hand at the prep table loaded with a dozen different salads.

"Be a dear, would you, dear?" She looked happily flustered; a loose curl floating over her left eye and a smudge of cookie dough on her lip. "Oh, Anne, *hi!* Could you help Michelle with the salads? Oh, dear . . ." as the timer went off and we lost her in the depths of her brand-new GE range.

I grinned at Anne, one of Margie's best friends, a doll-like blonde even tinier than I and, like me and Margie; a nurse. She's also head nurse for Mishelle's pulmonologist. "Hi, how are things at the office?"

She smiled right back at me. Anne is shy but very sweet. "Busy. How 'bout you?"She cradled a bowl of bean salad in each arm and headed for the door. I grabbed a couple as well and followed her.

"The same here," I admitted. "Hey, you know we have a patient in common?"

Anne set the bowls down and looked up, her brow furrowed. "We do?"

"Yeah, Mishelle Woodring?"

Her expression cleared and she rolled her eyes. "Oh, *her.*"

I kept the edges of my mouth curved up. "Yes, she's quite a character." We strolled back to the house, swerving to avoid the horde descending on the food. "Anne, I'm really concerned about her inability to cough up enough to clear her lungs. She's at about twenty percent capacity with her COPD and anything that might help her at this point would be so very welcome."

Her brow furrowed again as she balanced a huge nacho over her left forearm. "Well, there's the IPV but I would have thought Brent would have tried that by now. Is she still on antibiotics?"

Brent is Michelle's pulmonologist. "A what?" I picked up a bowl of Spanish rice with one hand and some guacamole with the other. "Yeah, her fifth round. She's had a course of IV too, but her condition only seems to improve while she's on the meds. When she goes off them, she's right back where she was."

"Well, of course, that goop in her lungs is a prime breeding ground for bacteria." We went back outside. "Yeah, the IPV would be the way to go. I wonder why he hasn't tried that."

"My thoughts exactly," I muttered under my breath.

"Pardon me?"

"Uh, we need more napkins. What's an IPV?"

"Intrapulmonary percussive ventilation. It's a gadget that beats on the patient's back while they inhale on a nebulizer with special meds to loosen the goop. Works like a charm in most cases."

I frowned. "I don't know. Mishelle has fractured thoracic vertebrae."

"No problem." She waved a hand dismissively. "They can adjust for that. It's more like a massage for most patients. Did you see if we have enough plastic forks?"

"They could always use some more." I grabbed two boxes and picked up a plate full of fragrant, freshly-baked cookies. "Can you ask Brent if he'll consider that for Mishelle?"

"Even better." We went again into the warm sunshine. "I can set up Mishelle for a series of treatments. She can go as often as she wants. We can also give her a flutter valve to take home."

She saw my puzzled expression and added, "That's a gadget the patient breathes into. It has a valve that flutters regularly as the patient inhales and causes the lungs to resonate and break up the mucous. Home maintenance item. Medicare covers it."

I wanted to hug her and did. "Anne, that's great news! This is just what Mishelle's been needing. Yes, set her up and I'll tell her about it. This is an outpatient procedure, I take it?"

She was a little befuddled at my excitement. "Sure, it only takes about an hour or so. Works right away."

"Super." I caught sight of Zach and Chris. "Hey, you two! Did you wash your hands?"

"Aw, Mom . . ." But they headed off in the direction of the garden hose where a few other more fastidious children were rinsing away the residue of some serious play.

I saw Dave standing out on the deck, drinking a beer and chatting with the rest of the guys. The brave hunters were clustered around a massive black barbecue cooker the size of a hotel water heater. I waved.

He waved back and nudged my brother Stan who was in full regalia: apron, daffy hat, spatula and tongs firmly gripped in each hand. Stan the Man looked up and waved the spatula at me. I waved again.

The day had taken a quantum leap into something very fine indeed.

* * *

It was the first thing out of my mouth when I called her that evening: "Well, what do you think?"

She still sounded doubtful. Who can blame her? "I dunno, I guess I'm willing to try anything at this point."

"Does going into the hospital make you nervous?" I rolled over on the bed, hugging my pillow.

"Hell, yes! The first time anyone calls me sir or by *that* name, I . . . I'm *out* of there. I mean it."

"I believe you," and I did. "Who's going to take you?"

"I'll have Lynn do it. Nicky's been . . . unreliable, lately."

"You're a trouper," I said quietly.

She snorted and coughed. "Hah! Just scared, sweetie. I'm not done yet, Michelle."

"Neither am I." I rolled again. Somehow the pillow seemed inadequate. "Neither am I."

* * *

My cellphone rang in mid-afternoon the next day. I was driving and didn't recognize the number when I flipped it open. "This is Michelle."

"*You are my sunshine/my only sunshine/you make me happy/when skies are grey . . .*" Her hoarse voice broke on the upper notes. I giggled.

"Don't quit your day job, sweetie." I slowed behind a truck. "I take it things went well?"

"Oh God, yes! I can *breathe!* I feel like I just coughed up a small bus!"

I laughed. "Interesting image, that."

"And a few schoolchildren, too!"

"Did they treat you well?"

"Oh, they were wonderful. Nobody mis-gendered me and everyone was very polite. Oh, Michelle, I feel so much better!"

"I can tell." The truck lumbered along but I controlled myself. "I'm very happy for you, Mishelle."

She giggled. "I *love* that machine! I asked them if they could hook up a bong to it."

"You *didn't.* Oh, Mishelle . . ." That damn truck was beginning to get on my nerves. It slowed for a stop sign and I pulled up behind it. "I hope they could tell you were kidding."

"Well, I wasn't, but I let them think I was. I'm going back tomorrow for another treatment."

"Wonderful!" That frickin' truck finally made a right turn. "Hey, speaking of tomorrow: I've got it off. Mind if I drop by and listen to your lungs?"

"Well, of course you can!" She sang again, the dear idiot: "*You'll never know dear/how much I love you/please don't take/my sunshine away.*"

"And I thought *I* was a bad singer. See you tomorrow, girlfriend."

* * *

I took the stethoscope out of my ears. "Much better," I announced. "It's still too early to tell if the infection is present, but it's quite an improvement." I stowed my things and smiled at her. "You look good, too."

She smiled back at me. "I actually got some sleep last night." For a moment, I wondered if she could feel my smile as strongly as I felt hers and decided that she probably could. "I'm really glad you heard about this. I feel so much better."

I shrugged and patted her hand. "This was exactly what you've needed, Mishelle. I still don't know why they didn't do it earlier but I'm glad, too."

I stood and stretched. It was Wednesday, my day off and a whole list of chores at home to do: laundry, yard work, vacuuming and two bedrooms occupied by my sons I was reluctant to approach without a pitchfork.

But I didn't care, somehow. I knew I'd have to go eventually, but for now, I was visiting a patient on my day off; without a scheduled appointment; without authorization: enjoying myself.

Another day, another barrier crossed.

She read my thoughts: "You enjoy coming here, don't you?"

I looked down. "Yes. As a matter of fact, I do. Is it that obvious?"

"Uh-huh." She smiled. "But you have to leave soon, don't you?"

I felt a pang. "Unfortunately. Can I get you anything before I go?"

"No, I'm fine. But I have something for Dave before you go." She held up a package of men's toiletries: face balm and shaving cream and cologne. "I know it was his birthday last week. Tell him Happy Birthday for me, would you?"

I took it. "Mishelle, you didn't have to do that." I felt another pang; a different sort. "Jeez, you can't afford this."

She looked a bit smug. "Sure I can. I had a little windfall this week."

I stared at her. "What, did you win the lottery or something?"

The smug look didn't quite disappear. "Something like that."

I kept staring. *Ask me no questions* . . . A sliver of ice slid down my back.

I looked around at her stuffed apartment and for the first time wondered how a person on Social Security disability could afford all this stuff.

She spoke again, neatly derailing that train of thought: "I know I didn't have to, Michelle. I *wanted* to."

My friend took a deep breath that, at last, was not strangled by a cough. "I really like your family, Michelle. I'd like to see them again sometime, especially Chris. He's a good one, that boy."

"Well, I know he wants to come over again." I smiled, thinking of my littlest. "Did I tell you he figured out that Braille sentence on the way home?"

"I'm not surprised. Kid's got a mind like a steel trap."

"Like yours, you mean. He said you promised him a game of chess." I shook my head. "Okay, I'll bite: how does a blind person play chess?"

"Feel and memorization." She dimpled. "I also have a special board on order that might give me a certain advantage."

I couldn't stop smiling. "I gotta *see* this."

* * *

She had two more visits with Brent and his magic machine. With each, her lungs cleared further and they finally declared her free of that accursed infection.

But her COPD had worsened. The smallest exertion tired her out and caused her distress which aggravated her breathing which caused even further distress . . .

I didn't want to bring up Hospice again, not yet. I didn't want to consider it until it was necessary, until it was unavoidable. COPD patients can stabilize, even at really compromised levels, sometimes for years.

I still had hope and that's one thing I refuse to apologize for.

* * *

"She sent these over for you," I said as neutrally as possible. I handed the package of toiletries to Dave. He looked at them, a slight frown creasing his forehead. "You don't like them?"

He looked up and shook his head. "No, not at all. I mean: yeah, I think they're great. *She's* great. Tell her thanks, would you?" He hefted the package, eying the contents. "She doesn't get a lot of money on disability, does she?"

"Not as far as I can tell."

He looked up again, his gaze keen. "What's that supposed to mean?"

I chewed my lip and stopped, shrugged. "I don't know . . . no, I really don't. Don't ask me to speculate, Dave. I really don't know how she affords all this on disability."

His eyes never left my face. "But you've got an idea, don't you?"

I nodded. "Credit cards. I don't know how many she has, exactly, but I'll bet she's close to maxing them out."

His eyes narrowed. "I see."

* * *

She was even more improved on my next visit. I actually had to listen carefully to hear congestion past her usual COPD symptoms. Her vitals were right on, her color good, interactivity fine and her appetite was normal; two danishes and a latte that morning.

But her respiration was still impaired and the least little stressors worsened it. That morning, she was fidgety and predictably short-winded.

"What's eatin' you?" I finally asked.

She continued to shift around then said, in a breathless rush that ended with a whoop for air: "Nicky can't make it this Saturday and Lynn can't cover for her 'cause she's got something to do and Saturday's bath day and I can smell my pits and I don't know what to *do! Ooop!*"

Sternly, I repressed giggles. "Don't *do* that. You'll pass out. I'll cover for them Saturday."

She turned her head to me. "You will?"

I sighed. "Oh, jeez. You had to ask? Of course. I'll have to clear it with Dave first, but I don't think he'll mind. Oh, by the way, he really liked his birthday present. He says thanks."

"Tell him he's welcome. You'll really come over Saturday? You'll help me with my bath?"

I patted her arm. "Love to." I let my hand rest for a moment on her upper arm and noticed she was trembling, ever so slightly. "What's wrong?"

She was silent and her brow was furrowed. I squeezed her arm. I waited, cultivating patience.

She burst out: "Will you hate me after you've seen my body?"

It took a few moments to get my own breathing under control. "No. Why? What . . . you ought to know by now that I couldn't care less what your outside looks like."

"You might think a lot differently when you see me," she grumbled.

Gently, I touched her cheek. "I won't. I can tell this is really important to you. Tell me why."

There was more fidgeting. Then: "I hate my male parts. I *do!* I hate being a, a . . . a chick with dick! I hate it! If I could castrate myself, I'd do it with a rusty set of garden shears! I would!"

I slipped my arm around her shoulders. "Calm down. You're going to pass out from lack of air. Take a deep breath. Hold it. Let it out. Again."

Under my arm, I could feel the trembling in her shoulders lessen as she inhaled deeply and regularly. I didn't have to use my stethoscope to know that her heart; her Tinker-toy heart with the clickety-clack valve was pounding away like the Little Engine That Could.

So I held her and stroked her shoulders and her hair and soothed her; trying to imagine what it must be like to be so horribly at odds within.

I still do: try to imagine and I always fail. But I know pain when I see it.

After a while, I said: "Well, I could always close my eyes, y'know."

She laughed and the tension was broken. "Oh, great. The blind leading the blind."

I gave her a quick peck on the cheek. "See you Saturday."

* * *

Saturday dawned bright and clear. I sat and drank coffee at the kitchen table, thinking about the conversation with Dave that night after my visit:

"You're going to *what?*"

"Be her caretaker for a day. It's not hard."

My husband took a deep, careful breath. "Nor is it permitted. You're doing this *pro bono*, I take it?"

"Well, she can't afford to pay me, you know."

"I *know*. What the hell are you *doing?* Do you *want* to be fired?"

When my husband starts using emphasis a lot, it means he's about to lose his temper. I folded my arms and tried to look stubborn. "Dave, she needs a bath. It's not like I'm taking her to the spa or anything like that."

He sighed and ran a hand through his silvery brush cut. "I give up. I visited her with you and I admit, she wasn't what I expected but I never expected you to violate your oath."

"I haven't," I said quietly.

"Then what do *you* call it?"

I shrugged; a dismissive gesture I instantly regretted. "Being a friend. Helping someone who needs it. Reaching out. It's on my own time . . ."

"Which is part of the problem, isn't it?"

"And it's a time of need." I said, simply: "I'm needed."

He looked back at me and I hope I never again see eyes that sad. "Yes, you are."

My husband turned as if to go and then said, in a gentle voice that barely managed to cover his hurt: "I hope she's worth it."

Sitting at my kitchen table, drinking coffee, I thought about that. I thought about why I was doing this and what it really meant.

It had been only two short months since I'd met Mishelle; met her and had my comfortable, complacent, day to day routine of nurse, mother and housewife turned upside down and inside out.

I'd been challenged, shaken and jolted out of that rut, that predictable routine. Long-held beliefs that once served me well now seemed . . . obsolete.

I'd grown up.

It was one answer but then, right then, my fingers wrapped around a warm coffee cup, the warmth of my kitchen wrapped around me; it seemed the only answer to that question:

Is she worth it?

Is *anyone* worth it?

Shoe on the other foot, then: what if it was *you* in that chair, Michelle?

Or Dave?

Or Chris? Or Zach?

Oh, the answer's easy then. Too easy. Blood's thicker than water, isn't it?

I had always thought so, until I met Earl and Louise. I didn't hate them, I realized, looking into my coffee cup. I just didn't understand them.

How could they *do* that, leave their own alone and in the dark?

Mishelle had asked me how I'd feel if Chris or Zach turned out to be trans and I'd told her that I'd try to understand, to love them regardless of what they might be inside.

It came to me then and I sipped my coffee, thinking about it, the corner of my mouth tipped up in a wry smile that was very much like her smile:

I loved her.

It wasn't a shocking revelation: to realize that I loved her. Rather, it was like remembering something familiar, as if I'd heard an old song that had once made me cry or seeing a favorite old movie with a plot I knew by heart. Of course I loved her: not because she was unloved or that she needed to be loved, but simply because she was worth it.

I loved her because she was lovable.

Looking up from my coffee, I saw a bird alight on the windowsill. It fluttered about for a moment and then stopped. I swear it seemed to be looking into my eyes for a second.

It flew away.

I sighed and finished my coffee. I've never liked omens; it gives away the plot.

* * *

Omens or none, I said a prayer on my way to her place:

Dear God, please give me the words she needs to hear. Please let my hands do Your work and convey compassion and love to my friend. Use me as You see fit for I am Your faithful servant. Amen.

Since the Crusillo, prayer had become a daily part of my life. That seemed perfectly natural, too. At that moment though, I was rather glad she couldn't see my reddened eyes and drippy mascara.

I parked the Toyota, got out and banged on the door. Nicholas began barking and I let myself in. "Hey, sunshine!"

"Hi, sweetie."

The radio was on and she was tapping her foot along to an old Sly and the Family Stone tune but the tension in her body language was immediately apparent. "Thanks again for doing this." She turned her face toward me. "You still want to?"

I sat on the edge of the recliner. "Yes. I do. Are you okay with this?"

She reached up to take my hand. "I still don't want you to see me naked, but I'm okay with it, I guess."

I squeezed her hand. "I'm okay with it, too. Really and truly. But you don't have to take a bath if you don't want to, Mishelle." I leaned down and sniffed. "And no, I don't think your pits smell."

She giggled. "Thanks! But a bath always feels so good on my back. It helps relax me."

I gave her hand another reassuring squeeze. "It's your call either way. But how about we get you some breakfast first? Scrambled eggs okay with you?"

"Sounds great!"

I made her ham and eggs and toast. When I set the plate before her, I said: "The eggs are at the noon position, ham is at six o'clock and the toast is at three."

She grinned and picked up her fork. "Good job, Michelle. You did that perfectly." She dug in and I was struck by how she managed to eat without losing even a crumb into her lap.

It didn't take her long to clean her plate. When the last scrap was gone, I said, "Well, ready for your bath?"

She shifted uncomfortably. "Yeah, I guess. Are you sure . . . ?"

"I'm sure," I said firmly. "No more asking that question. Tell me what you need."

"Okay." She took two puffs off her inhaler and leaned forward. "First, fill the tub with fairly hot water and then add some bubbles."

"Can do!" I got up and went into the bathroom, Nicholas trailing at my heels. When I began filling the tub, he started barking again and racing up and down the hall. I went back into the front room.

"What's up with him?"

She smiled. "Bath time is play time for Nick. You'll see." She took off her watch and sat for a minute, catching her breath. "Okay. Let's do it."

She pulled herself up with the pole and headed for the bathroom, arms outstretched. I followed her, watching as she hiked up her skirt and sat down on the potty. "Ah! 'Scuse me."

I sat down on the edge of the tub. "No problem, sweetie." I waited patiently while she caught her breath. "Tell me what you need me to do, Mishelle."

Still panting slightly, she said: "I need help getting my shirt off. I can't lift my arms without a lot of pain in my back."

"I understand." I helped her slide the shirt off, one arm at a time, but she still winced a few times and I winced in sympathy. I knew how bad those fractures were; I'd seen the X-rays. Frankly, it was remarkable she could lift her arms at all. "What else?"

"Could you wash my hair?"

"Certainly!"

"Thanks. After that, I can do the rest myself." She panted, then: "What are you thinking?"

"Nothing," I said. "Nothing at all."

That wry smile again: "Liar." She stood and dropped her skirt and panties. I helped undo her bra strap.

I couldn't help it. When I saw them, all I could think was: *Jeez, she's seventeen years older than me and her breasts are firmer than mine.*

Envy? I chuckle about it now, thinking back, but that's what I felt. I nursed two big, healthy baby boys and my breasts show it. I'm not ashamed of the way they look; I earned every wrinkle and sag line but right then, I would have cheerfully traded mine for hers.

And I suspect she might have agreed to that trade if it meant having children of her own.

Again, I waited for her to catch her breath. When she held out her hand, I helped her stand and then I saw her naked for the first time.

I was ashamed then of my reaction and I'm still ashamed.

For a moment, just a brief tick of the clock, I was back at Darcelle's with my Mom, hearing that introduction: "Here she is; that chick with a dick, the Venus with a penis, the broad with a rod! It's Darcelle, ladies and gentlemen!"

No. Not that: a chick with a dick. Never *that.*

All at once, a wave of empathy and sadness welled up in me and I truly saw and felt for the first time how she must have felt about the terrible incongruity of her existence; the shame and pain of having a body that wasn't hers.

The courage and strength she must have had to endure that, day after day, every moment of her life! Again, my eyes stung with tears.

"Are you okay?"

Somehow, I managed to keep what I felt in that moment out of my voice. "I'm *fine.* Will you stop worrying?"

"Okay." She settled down into the tub with an audible sigh, felt along the back edge and tossed a squeaky toy out into the hall. Nicholas went scampering after it and ran back with it in his mouth. He tossed his head and the squeaky toy plopped into the water. She threw it again and Nicholas went after it like it was a rabbit disappearing down a burrow.

"See? Bath time is play time." She threw it again and barely missed me.

"Oops! Hey, watch it. You almost took my head off." I stood. "You soak while I go do the dishes. Holler if you need anything."

My nerves steadied a bit while I was rinsing the dishes and placing them into the dishwasher. Some years before, I'd stopped smoking but I *needed* a cigarette right then. Instead, I busied myself with domestic things until I calmed down.

Dishes done, I went back into the bathroom and stopped dead in my tracks.

Dumfounded, I watched her lift her oxygen tube off, soap her face and shave with quick, smooth strokes. She completed the whole procedure in less than a minute. I know; I glanced at my watch and timed her.

I found my voice: "Holy cow, Mishelle. How can you *do* that without cutting yourself a dozen times?"

Her face turned toward me. "Pretty quick, aren't I?"

"I should say so!"

"Can't do without my Oh-two," she sighed, sing-song. "What are you thinking, Michelle?"

"Will you please stop saying that?" I perched on the edge of the tub and found the shampoo. "Let's wash your hair, girlfriend."

I washed my girlfriend's hair. Do I need to mention that it was as enjoyable for me as it was for her? I didn't think so.

When we were done, I helped her stand and wrapped a nice long towel around her: above her breasts to afford her some measure of dignity and low enough to cover that which she hated most. She sat on the toilet again to catch her breath, so I took that opportunity to duck into her bedroom and pick out some clean clothes for her.

She didn't have a single pair of trousers or slacks. Not one. I wasn't particularly surprised.

While I was rubbing lotion on her back, she asked me that damned question again: "What are you thinking?"

I smiled. "I'm thinking that I feel very privileged to do this for you. That I'm privileged that you trust me." I leaned over and kissed the top of her damp head. "I'm thinking that I'm privileged to be your friend. *Now* are you done fretting?"

She smiled like the sunshine just outside her door. "Yeah, I guess I am."

I helped her get dressed and held her hand as she went back to her recliner.

She sat down, sighing with pleasure. I'd never seen her look so relaxed. But the satisfaction I felt in a job well done was tempered in knowing that she really was a prime candidate for Hospice. After watching her struggle with bathing and shaving, I knew that she couldn't maintain that much longer.

Sooner than either of us cared to admit, she'd have to accept that.

But I couldn't say anything. She wanted to live. She didn't want to die. I couldn't talk about it after seeing that look of deep peace and content-ment on her ravaged face.

So we chatted about inconsequential things and it was very nice. Her head began bobbing, rather like Chris when he was up past his bedtime, so I suggested she take a nap. It didn't take much convincing and soon she was sound asleep.

I took the time to do a little cleaning in the kitchen while she snoozed. I was scrubbing out the microwave when she called to me. I came out of the kitchen, wiping my hands on a clean towel. "What is it, sweetie?"

"I smell cleaning products."

"Guilty as charged: I'm cleaning."

"Well, take a break and come here."

I saluted. "Yes, ma'am." I giggled, forgetting for the moment that she couldn't see me and perched on the edge of her chair. "What else can I do for you, Miss Woodring?"

Almost timidly, she asked, "Can I feel your face?"

"Huh? Sure. I'm kind of surprised you haven't asked me sooner."

I knelt next to the recliner and turned my face up to her. She reached out and gently touched the sides of my face with her fingertips, then lightly ran her long, strong fingers across my brow and nose; touched my eyes and my cheekbones, down to my lips, where they lingered for a long moment; then down to my chin.

"You're beautiful," she whispered.

I was embarrassed. "How can you tell? I could be homely for all you know."

"I can tell," she said softly but with complete confidence. Her hands continued down to my neck and shoulders, stroking and caressing.

It should have been creepy but it wasn't, not at all. I closed my eyes and let her touch me.

"God really did make males and females different, didn't He?"

I opened my eyes. "Hmm?"

"You're so little . . . so petite." There was a look on her face that I'd never seen before on anyone: a kind of gentle ecstasy. "And so very beautiful."

I reached up and took her hands in mine. "So are you."

She snorted but there was real mirth there, not like the humorless noise she so often made. "Sure I am."

"You are," I insisted. "You are. And besides, you have nicer boobs and softer skin." I stuck out my tongue at her and added, "So there. You're two up on me, girlfriend."

She smiled, sadly this time. "I kind of doubt that."

"I'm serious! After nursing two kids, mine look like a pair of banana peels."

She chortled. "Better that than a pair of poached eggs like mine!"

I squeezed her hands. "Enough. Stop beating yourself up or I'll do it for you. Want some lunch?"

She nodded. "Yes. And then you have to go, don't you?"

Sadness welled out from the center of my chest. "Yup." I glanced at the clock. It was past two. "I'll make you some dinner, too. You can heat it up in the microwave later. Can you manage that?"

She closed her eyes and nodded. "I think so. After today, I think I can manage almost anything."

Our hands were still joined. I looked down and carefully, reverently; I kissed the back of hers. "Yes, you can."

CHAPTER THIRTEEN

Pieces of the Puzzle

T HE PHONE RANG. I flipped it open one-handed because the other was holding a tuna fish sandwich.

"Hur-roh?" I said around a mouthful of white albacore, lettuce and mayo on wheat.

"I got a package!" Mishelle said, sounding as if she would burst.

I swallowed. "That's nice. Hello to you, too."

She giggled. "Sorry. Hello! I'm just so excited! I couldn't wait to tell you: UPS delivered my chess board!"

"Uh, good. Remember to breathe, girlfriend."

"Okay." I could hear her panting, trying to catch up. Then she said: "I was hoping you could bring Chris over for a game."

I chewed some more tuna and considered it. "We could do that. He's outside right now, playing with friends. I'll ask him when he comes in for dinner, okay?"

"Call me later?"

"Sure. Promise." I snapped the phone closed and gazed out the window; not seeing a thing beyond the glass and homemade curtains, ruminating like Bessie the cow.

With Chris, it wasn't a question of *if* but rather *when*. No, it was his father that posed a bit of a problem but he hadn't said no, not yet.

I had hopes he wouldn't. I didn't want to have to defy him.

I finished the sandwich. It was delicious. Once you've had the good stuff, you'll never go back.

* * *

The chess board was simple in design: clever and cute. I wished I'd thought of it myself.

The black squares were slightly raised and could be felt with finger-tips. Each square had a tiny hole in the center and the pieces all had little pegs on the bottom that fit into the holes. The black pieces were slightly flattened on top so she could feel the difference between her pieces and her opponent's.

I sat down, propped my chin on my cupped hands and watched them. Nicholas parked himself next to my right ankle and thumped his tail on the carpet, so I scratched his back.

My son was grinning like a thief. "Ready to get your butt whupped?" he asked.

My friend grinned back at him. "Bring it on, little dude," she responded cheerfully and battle was joined.

It was fascinating. Mishelle's fingers fluttered above the board like butterflies: delicate and landing on each piece, her arm bracelets jangling in counterpoint.

At first, I was confused. "Hey," I protested. "Those aren't your pieces, Mishelle."

"Mom, she's feeling which ones *are* hers," my son said in that bored, superior tone so well developed by pre-adolescent boys.

I shut up and let them play, noticing finally that whenever he moved, she had to touch the pieces again to re-fix the new positions in her mind.

She beat him. It took less than a half-hour and she checkmated him in less than thirty moves. They whooped and cackled at each other like old friends as the pieces crawled across the board. I think I had as much fun as they did just watching them play.

I lost track of how many moves, exactly; bemused by the sight of my son and my friend; their heads down over a chessboard, two peas in a pod; communicating on a level I could barely sense.

Brother and sister, I decided. They had a friendly rivalry that was nothing like what my little Cee-Boo had with his older brother. Zach is such a gentle soul that I don't think pulling rank on his little brother had ever occurred to him.

I think Chris enjoyed being with someone who was cool enough to tease him gently, in a way that made him laugh.

His heart and mind were opened as wide as hers and it was a joy to watch.

"Not bad, kid." She smiled as her long fingers claimed his king. "Maybe next time I'll wear a blindfold and give you an advantage."

My son snickered. "Hey, yeah! I wonder if *I* could play blindfolded?" He covered his eyes with one hand and tried to navigate the board with the other. "No *way*!" he declared after a few moments.

Mishelle's smile turned impish. "Maybe you need to learn the basics, Chris. You want to learn Braille?"

He squirmed like an over-excited puppy. "Sure! Only . . . uh . . . can I use your bathroom first?"

She pointed unerringly. "Right down the hall, little buddy. Remember to wash your hands when you're done."

As he disappeared down the hall, she leaned over and whispered: "Can you believe that they charged me forty-five dollars for that piece of shit chessboard? I'm gonna send it back!"

"Oh, *that's* ladylike, Mishelle."

"I don't care! They ripped me off! I could build a better one myself."

I opened my mouth to retort, but Chris came back into the room, so I closed it. I don't argue with another adult before children; it's bad form.

"I washed my hands," he announced. "Can we learn Braille now?"

"See that box over by the computer? Bring it to me, please."

Chris went to her computer and brought her the box. Inside was a silver object that looked a bit like a small typewriter with only six keys, three to a side. She loaded it with paper, all the while keeping a running commentary on what she was doing. My son listened with rapt attention.

Myself, I was lost within seconds. I've never been mechanically inclined. Certainly my nursing skills include a lot of mechanical abilities (like putting an IV into an eighty year old patient with pipe-cleaner veins) but I was baffled by what they discussed that day.

My son adores gadgets that *do* things and one that made a secret language only he and his new friend could share was right down his alley.

She typed out something and gave it to him. "Try to figure this out on the way home. When you do, give me a call and tell me what you think it says."

My son nodded, folded it and placed it carefully in his pocket. I made a mental note to make sure I removed it before laundry the next day.

I put in my only two cents: "Mishelle, why don't you show Chris your Braille embosser?"

He went to her workstation again and touched the piano-like machine. "This thing?"

"That one."

Following her careful instructions, he loaded the embosser with paper and typed something out. He gave it to Mishelle and she smiled, her long, tapering fingers gliding across the bumps.

"Thanks, Chris."

"You're welcome," he responded, grinning.

I looked back and forth between them. "What did you say?" I demanded. "Tell me!"

But they wouldn't. It was their secret and they didn't want to share.

On the way home, Chris was silent until we were almost out of town then he burst out: "I wanted to stay! I was kinda hopin' to play her another game and get my revenge."

I patted his shoulder. "You'll get another chance. We'll see her again."

"Okay." He sank back in his seat. "She's so cool. I really like her."

"Well, if it's any consolation, she thinks you're really cool, too."

"Really?" He squinted up at me. The clear Montana sunlight spilled around him and he looked so very young, so very open. "I'm really . . . happy."

"Me too, Cee-Boo."

* * *

If only that was all it took . . .

She was taken off our service the tenth of July, 2006. I had mixed feelings. On one hand, I was happy she was no longer a patient. I could just relax and be her friend.

It was something I very much wanted: to be her friend. I wanted to see her bloom, like a flower, and I did in those last weeks. I saw the color return to her cheeks and a zest for life appear where there had been nothing before but despair and gray depression, spurred on by that damned persistent cough she'd carried around for over a year.

I found myself making almost any excuse to stop by before work, during my lunch period or after work, just to say hi and bask in the warmth of her smile, to watch her flower and grow.

She was my best friend and the finest memories I'll ever have of her were those few weeks when anything seemed possible.

I didn't want to take away her hope right then. I couldn't, so I let her talk to me about her life and her dreams and her hopes and yes, I told her mine, too.

On the other hand, I knew what was in store for her and that we would have to talk about it fairly soon.

And make some decisions.

* * *

"And then the flying saucer landed and the aliens came out and took Mishelle along with them to Uranus where they circled a black hole, looking for Klingons," I concluded, and sneaked a peek at her.

"Ha-ha."She cracked an eyelid. "Smartass. I wasn't asleep."

"I was just testing you," I said innocently. I dog-eared the well-worn copy of *Confessions of a Shopaholic*, one of her favorite books (for obvious reasons) and set it aside. "Do you need to take a nap?"

She stirred and shifted to her usual position: slightly forward, elbows on her knees. "No, it's just that your voice is so soothing. It relaxes me. Can we talk for a while instead?"

I was a bit taken aback. "Sure. 'Bout what?"

Her voice was very quiet: "You know."

"Yeah. Okay." The ball was now in my court and I had no one to pass it to. "Why do you think I'm in your life, Mishelle?"

"So you can help me while I'm dying." Her voice was perfectly matter-of-fact.

I was silent for a while. I remember blinking a lot. "Do you think you're dying? Now?"

"Maybe not now. But soon. Am I right?"

I shrugged helplessly and didn't care she couldn't see it. "I don't know."

"Frankly, I wonder if I'll make it through another winter." That casual, matter-of-fact tone wouldn't go away. "I'm not bouncing back from this infection like I used to. Even with the new meds you got me, it's hard to breathe almost all the time now."

It was pretty hard to breathe, myself. "So you think you're getting worse?"

She smiled wryly. "I can't tell. Sometimes yes, sometimes no. I know I don't have much lung capacity left. What do *you* think?"

I shrugged again and this time I laid my palm on her knee so she could feel it. "Same here. I see some improvement, but I agree that you're in a much compromised state right now. Twenty percent isn't much."

She put her hand over mine. "Will you let me know if you think I'm getting worse?"

I tried with limited success to swallow a big lump in my throat. "Sure. As long as you're truthful about how hard it is to breathe."

"How will I know?"

"Well, the best benchmark seems to be everyday tasks like bathing and walking, even for short distances. Eventually, these things are going to become harder for you. Your shortness of breath will increase, you understand?"

"Yes."

"Eventually you'll be unable to do even the simplest tasks, like bathing."

"Ah." In a very small voice: "That would not be good."

I sighed. "Look, can we just cross that bridge when we come to it? As far as I can tell, your condition would be considered guarded, not serious. You shouldn't worry about this; it won't do you a bit of good." I added: "And I'm not going anywhere, girlfriend. You're stuck with me."

"I can't think of anyone else I'd rather be stuck with." Then she added: "But I can tell this upsets you, doesn't it?"

For some reason, I was standing now, my palms sweaty. "Well, *of course.* I just met you. I think it's a little early to be saying goodbye, don't you?"

That damned matter-of-fact tone . . . "I hope so. But if you have any more questions to ask teacher, you'd better do it soon."

I stared at her, my palms still sweaty, like a schoolgirl's. *Soon.* "Mishelle? Do you think there's a reason we met?"

"So I could educate you about transgender people," she replied. "What else?"

"That's it? That's all?"

"What else do you want? An engraved invitation? Hello, that's pretty damned monumental, Michelle. And you're the perfect student."

I sputtered: "*Me?* Why me?"

"Because you don't know shit about it, that's why. Because you're naive and completely clueless and you have absolutely no idea how it feels."

Mishelle paused to pant while I gaped at her, and then added: "But you're curious. And you have an open heart." She panted some more. "And an open mind. Perfect."

I managed to squeak something out: "I sure wasn't open at first!"

My friend grinned ear to ear. "No, you sure weren't, were you? I could tell."

"Well, I *tried.*"

"I know. And you did a pretty good job. I could still tell you thought I was weird, though."

I sighed; sat down; closed my eyes. "You're right. I did."

Her smile was pure *gotcha*. "Thought so. But I grew on you, didn't I?"

I laughed and she joined in, a little raggedly. "Yeah, you're just fine with me now." I found a tissue and wiped my eyes. "Damn, you'll say *anything*, won't you? I've never understood how you can be so open with me. After all you've been through; I would have thought your heart would be nothing but callous and scar tissue."

"Well, there's a lot of scar tissue on my heart, that's true enough," she answered soberly. "But I had to let that anger go, to forget about it. Otherwise I'd have never made it through transition. I wanted that part of me to die; to go away but then I realized that I had to learn to forgive all the ones who bruised me and left scars on me, real and otherwise."

She panted and turned her face toward me. "An angry heart can kill you, Michelle. Trust me, I know."

"I wish I'd known you then."

"No, you don't."

"Well, I could have helped . . ."

"No, you *don't*, Michelle. I was a very angry person. I was destructive and suicidal." She took a deep breath, visibly trying to calm down.

"Have you had a Lorazepam today?"

"No, I was saving it."

"Well, for heaven's sake . . . It won't don't do you any good if you don't take one."

I got up to get her one from her pill box. She was running low on the Oxycodone, I noted. I gave her a Lorazepam and she washed it down with cold coffee.

I looked back at the meds box. *Low?*

"Hey. Didn't you have a meds delivery yesterday? The Oxycodone?"

"Uh-huh," she panted.

"Well, you're almost out. What's up with that?"

Her brow furrowed. "Out? It should be full!"

I felt cold all over. "Mishelle? There aren't but a few in here. Four, in fact."

She was motionless. "Then . . . then someone took them."

"Oh, boy." I looked at the door that she never locked. "Who's been here?"

"Uh, Nicky and Lynn. You. A few others."

"Which others?"

She shifted in discomfort. "Friends. You know." Her panting was beginning to set off alarm bells in my head.

"Take deep breaths, sweetie. Let's try to figure this out." I looked at the door again. "You don't ever lock that door, is that right?"

Mishelle shifted again; embarrassed. "Well, yeah."

"Okay. Why don't I have the locks changed and you give a copy of the new keys to just me, Nicky, Lynn and . . .?" I thought fast. "Your mom. That way we know someone won't come in and rip you off. But you have to promise me to keep the door locked. Will you do that?"

She squirmed like Chris when I would asked him if he'd done his homework. "Okay. I promise."

"And you should keep these meds locked up in a box, too."

My friend looked none too pleased but she muttered, "Okay."

"Good. Then we're on the same page. Take some slow, deep breaths," I advised. "Try to relax."

"Oh, like I don't all the time," she panted. "This isn't so hard, really. Before I transitioned, now *that* was hard."

"After your divorce, when you moved back here from Eugene?"

Mishelle shook her head. "I moved back here in '75, the first time anyway. I didn't transition until about twelve years later." Her face puckered and for a minute it seemed as though she might spit. "Twelve years of a charade, of dressing in my apartment and being the mistress of presto-change-o."

"Excuse me?"

"There's a knock on my door, you know? And in *seconds* I could change from Mishelle to Michael. Cross my heart bra."

I giggled quite involuntarily, suddenly remembering that scene in *Tootsie* when Dustin Hoffman dashes back and forth, tearing off the girl things while Terri Garr waits outside, a puzzled look on her face.

"Did your parents know?"

"Ah." She sighed. "I certainly dropped enough hints! I used to send them some of the things I got in the mail: pamphlets and stuff like that. It did a better job of explaining matters than I ever could." She snorted. "Dad called me a faggot and a closet queen. My brothers used to call me Klinger."

"What did your mom think?"

Mishelle laughed. There was genuine humor in it this time. "I think she was most puzzled by never finding any underwear when she did my laundry. I hand washed my panties, you see."

She sipped at her water jug and the effort made her pant some more. "She doesn't change, really. She still brings me leftovers and pies, like you saw last week when they busted in on our chess game."

"I remember." Earl and Louise had worn the most peculiar expressions when they beheld us: a nine-year old boy playing chess with their daughter and the boy's mother placidly curled up on the loveseat, reading. "I was just glad they didn't slip and call you Mike in front of Chris. How the hell would I ever explain that?"

She made a face. "I think you worry too much. You want to know the truth? I think he's already figured it out."

I sat up straight. "Really? No! I mean . . ."

"Now, *you* relax, Michelle. What difference does it make? I'm going to die soon, anyway."

I drew my knees up to my chin and regarded her somberly. "I wish you wouldn't say that."

"It's true, though."

"No," I said wearily. "No. it's not. It's not time. I'd know. And so would you."

She didn't answer, so we sat for a few minutes, thinking about it in our own way. Something else occurred to me:

"You let him win that night, didn't you? When your parents were here."

"Who, Chris?"

"Who else? You let him win. Why?"

"Because if I beat him all the time, then he'll lose interest and won't want to play me," she said, that matter-of-fact tone returning to her voice and this time I knew she was right: my son likes to win. He won't play unless he thinks he has a chance but give him that chance . . .

So I changed the subject: "Does *anybody* in your family deal well with this? What about your sister?"

"Oh, she knows. I doubt if she understands it any better than Mom and Dad, though. She was, let me think, about eighteen when I began transition and in the mid-eighties, nobody knew much about being transsexual, least of all my teenaged sister here in Kalispell."

She giggled hoarsely. "Although, she did feel my bra one day when she gave me a goodbye hug. 'What's with the bra, Mike?' she said."

"What did you say?"

"Oh, I just winked and said: 'I should have been your sister.'"

"Mishelle, why didn't you just *tell* them? 'Hey, I'm trans and it's not the end of the world.'"

"Because I didn't know! I thought I was crazy and so did my family! The first clue I had that I *wasn't* crazy was when I heard that transsexual on *Geraldo*. I couldn't relate at all to the way she behaved but it was my first clue that I wasn't alone!"

"*Easy,*" I said, alarmed. "Give that Lorazepam time to kick in, will you?"

"You started this," she said, accusingly.

"No, *you* did with all that talk of dying. And then you told me to ask questions."

Her smile was rueful. "Okay, you got me there. Huh, so you want the dirt again, do ya? How it felt, what it was like?"

"I can't imagine for a moment how it felt," I said very sincerely. "I just want to know how you survived."

"Why?"

I sat back on my heels, considering that. There it was: *why.*

Slowly, carefully, as if seeing it for the first time, I said: "Because it might help someone else someday. Because you're not alone; you never were." I took a deep breath. "Because it's *important.*"

Mishelle was silent, eyes closed and I wondered if she'd drifted off. But no: "I wrote letters, asking for more information, at first to *Geraldo* and then to other places I stumbled onto through pure luck."

"And they wrote back?"

"Sure, in *print.* There was lots of information out there but nothing in Braille or audio cassettes, even though I requested it. The rest of the world isn't set up for blind people any more that it is for trans people."

She sighed and sipped her cold coffee. "Talk about frustration. I had all this stuff that could have told me what was going on and I couldn't *read* it. And I couldn't give it to someone else to read it for me."

"You were still . . . in the closet."

"Half in and half out. At home, I was Mishelle, mistress of the presto-change-o. In public, I was Mike, audio engineer and charity case."

My lip curled. "Sounds like you're having a pity party. Am I invited?"

"Oh, *phht* . . ." She blew disgustedly in my direction. "I was *good* at it, but my boss never saw fit to pay me. I had the best ears in town, hell, in the entire state of Montana, but did I ever get a dime for my hours behind the console? *Nooo!*"

"Did he know about Mishelle?"

"Sure. I never hid anything from him. He'd listen and then say: 'I know you'll be healed, Mike.'" She snorted. "Being healed doesn't pay the bills, honey."

"And then?"

"Then? I showed up to work one day in a dress, right after I began transition and suddenly he didn't need me anymore."

"He fired you?"

"He asked me not to come back if I was wearing a dress. I guess that means I was fired, right?"

"Yeah, that's usually what it means. What the hell did you do then?"

"Well, the vocational department of the school I went to was always trying to find me a job. I think they got funding from the government and it was part of their contract or something. But Kalispell was only about seven thousand rednecks back then and there weren't many jobs to go around, especially for a blink."

She gulped some water and I waited for her to catch her breath.

"I finally got a job in a thrift store. You'll never guess."

I sighed. "Okay, I give up."

"Girl, you are too easy. Tagging clothes." She giggled suddenly and I joined her. "Can you imagine? A blind person tagging clothes? I worked for eleven hours and got this measly check for eleven bucks."

I gasped. "You're kidding, right?"

"Nope. Eleven dollars. They were paying me by the piece and naturally I didn't tag a whole lot of pieces. When my case worker saw the check, she told me she'd try to find me something else."

"Did they?"

"Not until some time later. In the meantime, I was out of control for a while. Over a year." She held up her coffee cup. "Buy me another, sweetie?"

"I'll make a fresh pot."

While I was rummaging in her kitchen for the filters, it finally sank in: *out of control.* I froze with one hand on the filter basket and the other with a measuring spoon full of dark, finely-ground aromatic powder.

For exactly one breath, I was a little bit afraid of what might be coming.

Reflexes let me finish what I was doing and start the pot. Slowly, I walked back into the front room. I perched myself on the arm of her chair and took her hand.

"So tell me what you meant."

She just squeezed my hand. I gave her some time. It didn't take long, really.

"I felt smothered."

I waited.

"Every time I dressed. Every time I had to go back to . . . to being . . . Mike." She struggled with that name, poor thing, and I stroked her hair. "I . . . I really lost it one day. I was still Mike. In public, I mean. I don't even remember what it was that set me off. But I blew up, right there in Norm's News and, and. . ."

"And?"

She shrugged. "They hauled me off and stuck me in the loony bin for a while. Medicated me and made sure I didn't hurt myself. Good drugs, but I still prefer ganja."

"I know. How many times?"

"I lost count. Not many times here in Kalispell. A few times in Seattle." She grinned suddenly. "Actually, I kinda liked being locked up in the loony bin. They had pretty good food, even the one here in Flathead County. And I was assigned a counselor, finally."

"Did she do any good?"

"He. No, he didn't have any experience with transgender people." Mishelle shrugged, fatigue starting to creep along the lines of her shoulders. "I brought him all the stuff I'd received in the mail and he read it to me so at least I had that. And we talked. It was a relief to finally talk openly, you know?"

"What did you talk about?"

She drank some water. "Me. This and that. Being trans and how lonely it is. You know something? In the twenty years I've been trying to learn about myself and people like me, I've never come across another blind transgender."

I studied the lines on her face. She was tired but I knew she wanted to talk; needed to talk. "You're kidding. Not one?"

"Nope. Not one." She smiled and reached for my hand. "I guess that makes me a minority's minority, huh?"

I chuckled. "So you're famous, huh? Can I have your autograph?"

She made a face. "Huh. You'd think with all the attempts I've made to educate people about this, I'd be some kind of famous but no, not really."

My ears pricked up. "I'm not your first pupil, then?"

"Oh hell, no. I even went on a radio talk show here in Kalispell a few years ago to talk about it. I invited all callers to ask me *anything*."

Mishelle looked sad and disgusted and annoyed all at once. It was not a pretty sight. "You wouldn't *believe* what some of those rednecks had to say to me."

"Yes, I would."

"Guess you would, at that. Is the coffee done yet?"

"I'll check." It was, so I poured her a fresh cup, added milk and sugar and went back into the front room. I glanced automatically at my watch when her time robot announced the hour: three pm. I handed her the cup. She took it and sipped cautiously.

"Perfect. Thanks, Michelle."

"You're welcome. I'm going to have to leave pretty soon."

"I know."

"Who's coming in to make dinner?"

"Lynn. Nicky's been taking a lot of time off recently." Her expression indicated a displeasure she didn't want to discuss so I tried another tack:

"Do you mind if we skip ahead a little? To when you were in Seattle? What was that like?"

"Better than here, that's for sure. I couldn't even find a doctor here to prescribe hormones, so I got some street hormones. I was getting pretty desperate."

"Street hormones?"

"Yeah. Premarin, mostly."

"Okay, but *six times* the usual dose? Jeez Mishelle, if you weren't on the blood thinners, you'd be full of clots."

She smirked. "Yeah, funny how that worked out, isn't it?" She swigged her coffee. "I'd still do it, even without the blood thinners. It was worth it."

I eyed her bosom. "How long did they take to grow?"

"About seven years. I started feeling the effects the first few weeks."

"Did they hurt?"

"Did they! If I bumped one, it would hurt worse than getting kicked you-know-where. But the thing I noticed right off is how much calmer I was, how relaxed I felt."

"Let's not forget the soft skin and total lack of hair," I said, not without some asperity. "Most women, including me, would kill to have skin like yours."

Mishelle looked smug but I suppose she was entitled. "Well, there are some advantages to being trans, I guess."

I was beginning to think she had a very good point. "Were there *any* people here in Kalispell who supported you when you first began transition?"

"I did have a few friends here who knew me as Mishelle. Some of them used to hang out at Norm's with me. They helped me with my makeup and hair, although I know I stuck out like a sore thumb when I first started dressing as myself." She sipped her coffee. "I have to say that the more counseling I got, the harder it was to go back to being . . . Mike . . . on a regular basis."

Her face turned toward me. "It was tearing me apart, you know? I couldn't go on being two people. It's hard enough to be just one person."

"When did you go to Seattle?"

"Spring of '91. I *loved* it. The vocational rehab center flew me out there to check things out and the first thing I did was sign up for a transgender support group."

I patted her shoulder. "Felt right at home, did you?"

"You know it! The girls all made me feel so welcome!" Enthusiasm rose in her voice, wiping away the fatigue. "I'd never had a chance to talk to some of my own people before and it was wonderful!"

"So you jumped at the chance to move there?"

"Sure. The job opportunity was pretty good, too. I had an offer to work at a place called The Lighthouse for the Blind. We made parts for Boeing. I found a doctor who was willing to prescribe hormones. I started going to that support group on a weekly basis. I was assigned a counselor through the Seattle Support Center and let me tell you, they have some great counselors! I even was able to save some money toward my SRS."

"Was it a hard decision, to leave your family and friends here in Kalispell?"

"Of course." She closed her eyes for a minute. "I didn't know a single soul in Seattle and everyone I knew was here, in the armpit of Montana."

"No," I interjected, grinning. "Butte's the armpit of Montana. We've worked hard for it and we deserve it."

Her eyes popped open and she cackled like Janis Joplin. "Okay! I'll give ya that one. But it was still a difficult decision, even though I was eager to leave after that first trip." She took another sip of coffee. "The deciding factor was that I could be *me*, Mishelle, all the time."

"Where did you live?"

"Downtown, at a subsidized housing apartment complex. A lot of disabled people lived there. Not a good part of town, unfortunately."

"Why do you say that?"

"I was walking home from a store on Rainbow Drive with a jug of milk in one hand and my cane in the other when someone took a shot at me." She said that as casually as I might say: "Nice weather, isn't it?"

My mouth opened, but nothing came out.

"Oh, don't worry. I dropped the milk and ran which must have looked pretty silly, what with my cane and all. It didn't happen again and there were some nice moments." She smiled suddenly. "I got whistled at more than once, actually. I had a great swish, you know?"

"I'll have to take your word for it," I said shakily. "Did you make any friends?"

"Oh, sure! Lots of friends. Renee and Charles. Arlene, my counselor. Just about everyone in my apartment complex was my friend. I used to cook a lot, back when I could still get around without help and when I had something tasty going; everybody in the complex could smell it and would drop in for dinner."

"I've heard you mention Charles, but who's Renee?"

"Oh, she's just about my best friend. Besides *you*," she added hastily, patting my hand.

"Tell me about her?"

Mishelle giggled. "Oh, she's a hoot! We met in the support group. I made some smartass joke using the n-word and she nailed me on it right away. 'Excuse me, but what color do you think *I* am?' she said. I didn't know she was black, you see."

"Oops."

"Yeah. It was pretty stupid. But I apologized as sincerely as I could and she forgave me. Renee has a very forgiving heart if you're sincere and she's pretty good at figuring out if you mean it or you're just a phony."

"So she's a transgender woman, like you?"

"Well, not exactly like me, no. For one thing, she's never had the SRS and has no intention of doing so. She doesn't need it to feel complete, unlike me." She made a wry face.

"Well, but . . . does that mean . . .?" I struggled to put it into words.

"She's gay, sweetie, so stop chasing your tail. She likes guys. She's had two long-term relationships with men and if they weren't marriages, then I don't know what else to call them, license or no license."

"You two are still pretty close?"

"Oh, sure. We call each other all the time." She giggled and almost dropped her coffee. "I remember coming into the support group meeting one night, clutching my purse so tightly that Renee leaned over to me and asked me why I was squeezing it so hard. I told her it was because I had a gun."

I gasped again. "A *gun*? Where did you get a gun?"

"You don't want to know. Anyway, she said: 'Uh, Mishelle? You can't see, remember?' And I told her: 'Yes, but I can *hear*.'" Her laugh was loud and long and apparently very satisfying.

I joined in but my eyes were a little wide; imagining a blind person with a loaded handgun and very acute hearing, taking potshots at anything that made a noise.

When she finally stopped laughing and had caught her breath, I said, "So tell me about Charles."

She sighed. "Such a sweet old man. He's the one that gave me this sapphire ring." She held out her hand. "We met at my apartment complex. He's ninety years old and you've never met a truer gentleman. He took me to lunch at MacDonald's every Sunday. We keep in touch, too."

"Was he . . . a boyfriend?"

"Who, Charles? Heavens, no!" She fell silent and then whispered: "Paul."

"Who?"

"Paul. He was my boyfriend." She sighed and fell silent again. I waited patiently because I knew she wasn't done, not yet.

"We were going to be married after I had my SRS," she said finally.

"Did you . . . have sex with him?"

"Oh, no. I'm not gay, you see, not like Renee. I wanted to wait until the SRS but . . ." She fell silent again, longer this time. I had to prompt her:

"What happened? Did you two break up?"

"He was murdered."

I wanted to bite my tongue. Instead, I waited.

"He was found beaten to death. The police labeled it a hate crime but they never arrested anyone for it." Mishelle shrugged tiredly, the years settling across her broad shoulders like a thick, wet blanket. "And when I got the diagnosis for my mitral valve not long after that, nothing seemed to matter any more."

"You went into depression again?"

Wryly: "You have a real gift for understatement, sweetie. Yeah, I had my heart surgery and went into a tailspin. I was down to a hundred and fifty pounds, drinking that awful stuff; Ensure, and just wasting away."

"How long did that last?"

My friend sighed and sipped her coffee. "Long enough. I tried suicide a couple of times but I wasn't very good at it, obviously. Didn't take enough pills, I suppose. So they locked me up, thirty days at a stretch. It wasn't too bad. Good food, nice counselors and they even let me teach a few classes about transgender stuff and GID to University of Washington med school students. That was a lot of fun!"

"Fun?" I shook my head. "You have an odd definition of fun, Mishelle."

"It *was*," she insisted. "They asked me smart questions, the first time anyone had done that. And they were polite. Respectful."

"What did you do when you finally got out?"

"Tried to put my life back together. Started my own business, converting text into Braille for Microsoft at first, then for a blind lawyer. Did an entire law book for him. He was very pleased." She looked sour. "He should have been: I underbid the job. That damned Braille embosser! You know that stupid thing cost me over ten thousand dollars?"

"Oh, my *God*!"

"Yeah! *Everything* that blind people have to buy is expensive. And we have to have it, whatever it is, otherwise we're cut off from the world and we can't make a living or learn anything." A glum expression hung lopsided across her face. "I had to put it on a credit card and I'm still paying for it, damn it."

I was almost speechless. I looked at the piano-like device across the room and it seemed as though my mouth moved of its own will: "But you came back here. To Kalispell. Why?"

Again, she fell silent while the years and fatigue settled once more across her broad shoulders. For a long moment, I feared that I had finally probed too deep, too hard but she answered me, as she always had and would always until the end:

"Unfinished business, Michelle. There were some other people I wanted to educate. My family. If I'd spent more time educating them, maybe my life would have turned out differently."

She turned her blind eyes in my direction and I was struck dumb.

"I love them, Michelle," she said quietly. "Even my dad, who beat me and called me a faggot. My mom, who never understood but loved me as much as she could. My sister, who deserved an explanation. Even my dumb-ass redneck brothers who thought I was nothing but a freak and a bad joke. I love them and they're my family and they deserve to know, even if they can't understand it."

She sighed and leaned against me. I put my arms around her. "I *owe* them. They're my family."

My throat tight, I said: "I understand."

CHAPTER FOURTEEN
Come on Home

"WELL, HOW DID IT GO?" I asked.

Mishelle chuckled. "He beat me."

I was shocked. "You're kidding! Just like that?"

Another chuckle, sounding like static on my cellphone: "Well no, not exactly. I gave him a good fight. It took about an hour, but I was forced to concede. He took both my knights and my queen. That's what I get for leaving my flanks open."

"Good grief. Did you two get along okay?"

"Sure." She sounded mildly surprised. "Why not?"

"Well, you've never been comfortable around men, Mishelle."

"Yeah, but he's your husband, sweetie. He's also a very nice guy. You should feel lucky to have him."

I was a bit flummoxed. "I *do*. What else?"

"Oh, we listened to some records. Talked." She giggled. "Got high."

I sat up straight on the couch. "*What?*"

"I had a little ganja. So did he." She giggled again. "Sorry. Was I corrupting him?"

"Something like that," I said grimly. "Do me a favor and don't do that again, okay?"

"Well, it's not like I twisted his arm or anything." She sounded distressed now. "Are you mad at me?"

I sighed. "No, not you. Him, maybe. He knows better."

"And I don't?"

"That's not what I meant. I . . ." The front door slammed and I could hear his footsteps in the foyer. "Hold on, he's home. Look, we can talk about this later, okay?"

"Okay. Call me tomorrow?"

"Of course. G'night, Mishelle."

"'Night."

Dave came into the front room as I snapped the phone closed. I looked at him. "Well, how was it?"

"Nice," he said calmly. "She's a helluva good chess player."

"But you beat her."

He smiled. "You just get off the phone with her?"

"Uh-huh. What else did you do?"

He flopped into a chair across from me. "Talked. I had the feeling that she wanted to discuss trans stuff, but I didn't go there."

"Why not?"

He shrugged. "No need. It's obvious that she thinks and feels like a female which is just fine with me." He studied me quizzically. "Did you expect me to act any different?"

"No." I shook my head. "No, I guess not. How did she look?"

"Okay. Why?"

"I mean, what was she wearing?"

"Women." A grin played at the edges of his mouth. "Uh, a yellow dress. She looked cute."

"Cute? Was she wearing any makeup?"

His eyebrow rose. "A little. I really didn't notice."

"What else did you do?"

He shrugged. "Listened to some of her CD's. She's got a really terrific collection."

"I know," I said. I got up, went to him and leaned close. I sniffed.

He looked up at me. "What's wrong, honey?"

I looked him in the eye. "First off, I'm very proud that you treated her with respect and that you two got along so well."

"But?"

"No more ganja. Not here, never in front of the kids and don't you ever come home stoned again or I'll kick your ass, understood?"

His eyes were very big. He nodded.

"Don't get me wrong. I think marijuana has its uses. But you aren't sick and you have responsibilities to your family. Do I need to remind you that THC can remain in the tissues for up to a month?"

He shook his head.

"I didn't think so." Our faces were very close. I leaned in and kissed him firmly on the mouth. "Thanks for being a gentleman. Just remember that you have a family to consider."

There was a glint of something 'way back in his eyes. "I've never forgotten."

"Okay." I went back to the couch, drew my legs under me and regarded him soberly. "I have another favor to ask."

Dave sighed. "What now?"

"Her fifty-seventh birthday is next week. I want her to celebrate it here. Do you have any problems with that?"

My husband sighed again. "No, of course not."

"Good. I'll go over to her place that morning and help her get ready. When we're ready to go, I'll give you a call and you can come over."

"Why? I mean, what do you need me for?"

"That damned oxygen concentrator. It's too heavy for me to lift. And we'll have a bunch of other things that need a strong male back. Okay?"

He looked a bit glum. "Sounds like a logistical nightmare if you ask me."

"I didn't." I grinned at him. "Just leave the planning to me, dear."

* * *

June twenty-second arrived and found me standing in front of the lemon-yellow door with determination in my heart and a list of necessities clutched in my left hand. I rapped just under the Elvis sign with my right and Nicholas barked a welcome within.

I let myself in. "Hi! Ready to go?"

She sat up in her recliner, looking more worried than I'd seen her in quite a while. "Are you sure this isn't too much trouble?"

"Don't be silly. Of course not." I looked around and then down at the list in my hand. It was pretty long:

> *portable Oh-two tanks*
> *concentrator*
> *wheelchair*
> *change of clothing*
> *makeup*
> *meds*
> *nebulizer*
> *water jug/glass & straw*
> *chessboard*
> *liters of Pepsi*
> *dinner tray*
> *Nicholas/food/toys/leash*

"Jesus, I hope I haven't forgotten anything," I muttered, more to myself than anyone.

"I'm such a burden," she said in a small voice. "It's too much work."

"Knock it off, Mishelle," I said absently. "I *want* to do this. Where's your overnight bag?"

"In my bedroom. Are you sure?" she asked, timid as a mouse.

I looked up at her. "Very sure." I suddenly realized that I hadn't given her a hello kiss, so I fixed that first and added a long hug to reassure her. I felt her trembling. "Are you nervous?"

She nodded silently.

"How's your breathing?"

"Okay," she said, not quite wheezing.

"No, it's not. Did you take a Lorazepam?"

She nodded.

"How long ago?"

"About an hour," she gasped.

"Well, let's get you another. I don't want you passing out from lack of air." I got her the pill and set about packing her things into her bag.

When I was done, I carried it into the front room and went to her computer.

"What are you doing?" she asked.

"You'll see." I grinned at her, even though I knew she couldn't see it. "Hang on a minute, sweetie."

I typed rapidly, referring to another sheet of paper from my purse and then clicked *print*. The piano-like Braille embosser grunted mechanically and disgorged a sheet of stiff paper covered with raised dots. I handed it to her.

"When did you learn to do this?" she asked, astonished.

"A few days ago." I perched on the arm of her chair. "I wanted to do something special for you. Go on, read it."

She did: "Dearest Mishelle. Happy, Happy Birthday, beautiful lady! Today is the day to celebrate the day that you were born. I know that you have questioned your existence and place here on Earth for a very long time. But I have not. I am so glad that you are here with me to celebrate another year lived. You are a survivor. You are strong, courageous, kind, patient, loving and gentle. You have a great sense of humor that I love. I thank you from the bottom of my heart for opening your heart and soul to me. I cherish the time that we spend together. I promise to always keep my promises to you and never make a promise that I can not keep. I will never hurt you or betray you. You mean the world to me and I love you. Happy Birthday, Mishelle!"

She tilted her face up to me, grinned from ear to ear and quietly said, "Thank you."

"You're welcome." I gave her another kiss. "Hold on, let me get you your presents."

Sandalwood sugar scrub for her bath and a charm necklace she'd dropped hints about many times. The necklace had three charms: a dangling beaded blue one, a music note and a triangle with an inscription. *I Love You.* She ooh-ed and ah-ed over them, running her fingertips over the charms repeatedly, the smile never leaving her face.

"Time to fix your face and hair, Mishelle."

"Are you still going to let me use your Jacuzzi?" she asked anxiously, "Because I don't want to ruin my makeup."

"Of course you can use it! Don't fret: I packed your makeup. We'll re-do it after you're done with your bath."

Her hair and makeup didn't take long. I didn't do quite the job Nicky had for our Memorial Day visit, but when we were done, I thought she looked very nice.

I glanced down at Nicholas, who had been alternating between trotting around eagerly to sitting on his rump, staring disconsolately at us with his big brown eyes. "Don't you think Mommy looks pretty, Nick?"

He woofed; approvingly, I thought.

I did a final walk-through her apartment, checking off everything on the list. It was complete, so I flipped open my phone and called Dave.

"Honey? We're ready to go. Okay, see you soon." I closed it, perched on the arm of her recliner and took her hand. I could see her panting gently; clearly agitated.

"Relax." I rubbed her back with my other hand. "It's going to be fine. *You'll* be fine. Take a deep breath. One. Hold it. Breath out through your mouth with your lips puckered. In through your nose so you pick up more Oh-two. Again. Better?"

"A little," she gasped. "Can you make sure my cellphone is in my purse? I don't want to leave it behind; it's my link to the outside world."

"Sure. Where is it?"

"Next to my computer."

I got up, found it where she'd said, put it in her purse and put the purse in her lap. "Okay. Dave will be here soon."

I resumed rubbing her back. "Relax."

And he was: in less than ten minutes. (Ran a few stop signs, did you, dear?) He knocked and came in on the heels of the echo with a cheerful smile on his face and a hug for our guest.

Nicholas started yapping and dancing around madly as I hooked up her portable oxygen. Dave carried that cumbersome and heavy concentrator out to his truck; grunting, his face red with effort.

"Time to go, sweetie!" And we were off. About halfway there, she asked where we were. I told her and she grinned.

"There used to be a bar here," she said. "On the southwest corner. It was my hangout, back when I was a drinker."

"And you don't? Drink, I mean?"

"Not like I used to. And I was a mean drunk, sweetie."

"Just imagine my surprise. Hey, I want you to listen to something."

My I-Pod was already plugged in so I dialed up *I Want to Know What Love Is*; Wynona Judd's cover. That gorgeous melody poured from the car speakers like thick honey, impelled by Wynona's rich voice. When it was done, my friend smiled wistfully.

"Now I know. Thank you." Our hands linked. I confess to a slight lump in my throat at that moment.

I parked in our driveway and got her wheelchair out of the back. It was only twenty feet to our door, but I wanted her to conserve her strength. Getting her through the door was another matter:

"Mishelle, we're going to go up two steps, turn right and then about five steps to the front door. It's a few feet past the door to the living room, perhaps ten steps, and then a jog to the right and into your chair. Okay?"

She nodded; her expression intent. I helped her stand, took her hand and supported her by the elbow as we went up the steps.

Her oxygen bottle was slung over her left shoulder, adding just a bit of wobble to her gait. But she let me lead her and it worked out fine.

We got her settled. Dave hooked up her concentrator and stood; his expression rueful. "Ladies, I have to head back to work. Two houses to show this afternoon. I'll be in time for dinner."

He blew me a kiss, which I caught, and left.

Zach and Chris trooped in and said their hellos. My boys were very polite, but Chris's eyes suddenly grew big and he pointed:

"*Mom.*"

I looked. Nicholas! That damned dog had been trotting around, sniffing things and was lifting his leg against the corner of our couch!

The little stinker was marking his territory. I sighed and motioned to Chris. He came close. I whispered in his ear. "You and Zach clean that up and keep an eye on him. No more accidents! Take him outside if you have to."

He nodded solemnly. I went to unpack her things.

When I returned to the front room, Mishelle and Zach were already heads down over a chess game. I watched them for awhile, smiling slightly.

She kidded with him, much as she'd kidded Chris and my eldest blushed and grinned and generally had a swell time as she beat the pants off him in less than twenty moves.

I think he was having trouble concentrating. Mishelle took the sting out of his loss by remarking: "Playing with you boys irons out all the wrinkles in my brain." She reached for his hand and gave it a squeeze. "Thanks, Zach. Good game."

My eldest stammered his thanks. For myself, I very much wanted to give him a hug and a kiss. But he was at that fragile age when young men are loath to be pawed by their parents, so I just smiled at him as he slouched past me with a sheepish grin hanging awkwardly on his face.

"Ready for your bath, sweetie?"

The birthday girl turned her face up to me. "*This* is what I've been waiting for, Michelle!"

I patted her shoulder. "I know. Zach, why don't you and Chris take Nicholas for a walk while I get Mishelle into the Jacuzzi?"

Behind me, I could hear the fridge close and he sidled past again, a pop can in his fist. His ears were still a bit pink. "Okay, Mom."

In the bathroom, I ran it medium hot, the way she liked it and added a handful of foaming bath beads. With the bathroom door securely locked, I helped her undress, leaving her Oh-two cannula in place, and eased her into the tub. Her expression turned blissful, almost beatific.

"*Ah*," she breathed. "I could live in this thing. It's the first time I've ever been able to stretch out all the way."

"Like that, do ya?"

"Just throw me a bone once in a while."

I snickered. "Ha. Just wait 'till you taste the feast we've got ready. Kiss your diet goodbye, sweetie, at least for today."

"Diet? Was that a diet? *Now* she tells me."

"Ha-ha. Are you going to be okay? I need to go check on Chris and Nicholas."

"He'll be along soon." Her eyes slowly closed. "I'll be fine."

"Who? Nicholas?"

"You'll see." She sighed again in bliss as I got up and went out to the front room, leaving the door slightly ajar in case she hollered for help.

I opened the front door and stared. Here came Nicholas, little legs blurred beneath him as he sprinted down the street, Chris in hot pursuit. The damned dog zipped past my legs, a furry brown bullet, and disappeared into the house.

I spun and gave chase, thinking: *If that little shit pisses on my couch again, he's going to be a* dead *little shit!*

Behind me, Chris yelled, "Mom, he got away from me! He started running and knew where exactly where to go!"

I ran into the living room just in time to see Nicholas scoot down the hallway to the bathroom and bump the door open with his pointy little nose. I went after him and peered in.

Nicholas was scampering back and forth across the bathroom floor, yapping his head off. Mishelle was sitting up in the tub, suds fetchingly arrayed across her bosom, smiling in my direction.

"Did you bring his toys? It's playtime."

I gaped. "How did he know?"

Her smile grew dimples. "He just knows. Get the froggy. He likes the way it squeaks."

Shaking my head in disbelief, I went to get the froggy. I dropped it in the tub and got out of the way, knowing what was coming.

Mishelle found it and tossed it out the doorway. Nicholas went after it with a manic intensity, his nails skittering on the hardwood floor.

Mishelle chuckled. "You see? Playtime. I'll be fine, Michelle. Go be with your kids and let me turn into a prune, okay?"

"Okay."

* * *

"I can't believe you're doing all this for me. I feel utterly spoiled."

I took the last roller out and started styling her hair. "Why not? I mean, why not feel spoiled? What's wrong with that?"

"Nothing wrong with it. I'm just not used to it."

I glanced down at her. Her true eye looked suspiciously wet. "Now, now. None of that, sweetie. I just spent a half-hour on that make-up. If I have to re-do your eyes, we'll be late to dinner and you don't want that."

She smiled and sniffled. "No, I guess not. What's on the menu?"

"You'll see." I rubbed her shoulder. "First, we get you into a dress. I packed that long one with the flower print from Newport News."

"Oh, that's one of my favorites!"

"I know."

When she was finally ready, I helped her into her chair and rolled her through our family room on the way to the deck. She held up her hand and said: "Listen."

I stopped and tilted my head. I didn't hear anything. "What am I supposed to hear?"

"This room. The acoustics." She clapped her hands together abruptly and it sounded like a gunshot. "Hear that echo? Perfect for vocals." Her head tilted back and I could almost see her ears prick up. "This room has a nice high ceiling, almost twelve feet. It's vaulted, especially around those windows *there*." She pointed. "And the shape is roughly octagonal. The standing waves cancel out."

I looked at her, astonished. She'd perfectly described the size and shape of our family room ceiling. I looked around, seeing the room as if for the first time.

"You *do* have good ears."

She looked a bit smug and rightfully so. "Tol' ya."

I brought her out to the deck and made her comfortable in a patio lounge chair, the sort that rocks. It needed a pad for the metal back, so I fetched her one and slipped it into place behind her poor, fractured spine.

Though the cause was never officially diagnosed, I'd often suspected that osteoporosis from the enormous hormone load she was taking was the culprit. Whatever the reason, her back was as fragile as a ninety year old woman's. Despite the advantages there might be in hormone replacement, I can't agree that a disability like that would always be worth it.

Mishelle sighed and relaxed, her head turning to catch the many sounds that made up her world: the tinkle of Nicholas's collar as he ran back and forth, playing with my sons, the squeals and laughter of other children playing nearby, a lawn mower in the distance and the chirp of birds.

My backyard is full of birdsong. They like my garden and the trees that surround our house. I watched Mishelle's head turn to and fro, listening to the sweet music.

While I was trying to hear things her way, I recognized the familiar sound of my husband's pickup at the foot of the driveway. He soon joined us on the deck, greeting us each with a hug and a kiss, bless him.

"I don't know about you ladies, but I need a drink." He turned to our guest and touched her on the shoulder to let her know he meant her: "Mishelle, what can I get you to drink?"

She thought it over. "I believe I would like a gin and tonic," she declared. Dave busied himself inside, returning with a tall one for her and a glass of white wine for me. He knows me well.

Mishelle sipped. "Oh my," she sighed. "I haven't had one of these in years. Thank you, Dave."

"You're welcome." My husband signaled me with his brows, so I got up and followed him inside.

"Time to start dinner?"

"It's mostly ready." I started pulling things out of the fridge. "Go entertain our guest while I do this. Talk music or something. Pretty please?"

The menu was shrimp and fettuccine alfredo with spinach, her favorites. Strawberry shortcake for dessert. I warmed things, microwaved some others and had it on the table in record time.

We feasted.

It was beautiful. The day; the occasion; the respectful way my family treated her all came together to make a day that was as special for me as it was for her.

But the best part, the absolute best part was watching her relax completely for the first time since I'd met her. The little grunts and gasps for air that punctuated nearly all her sentences grew less pronounced as the day progressed. Her features took on that uncanny aura of serenity and repose that had fascinated me so much when we'd first met. She seemed less angular somehow, more rounded and soft, the most feminine I'd ever seen her. Even her voice took on a softer, hushed quality.

It was *beautiful*.

We took her home around ten, the last amber and salmon streaks of Montana's long summer twilight still painting the midnight blue sky. Stars were beginning to twinkle overhead as I walked her into her apartment and put her to bed.

Dave wrestled her concentrator back into its usual place. He hooked it up, kissed us goodbye and left.

We sat for a while, just holding hands. Then she said: "This was the best birthday I've ever had."

"You're welcome."

"And the best day I've had in years."

"Good."

I didn't want to leave. We sat some more. Then:

"Why, oh why are you all so nice to me?"

I squeezed her hand. "Because we all love you and we want you to feel special."

She smiled. "Well, it worked."

Then her eyes teared up, even the glass one and she was sobbing softly on my shoulder. I held her and stroked her hair until the tears went away as if they'd never visited, kissed her goodnight and left.

That was the last birthday she would ever have.

"You're avoiding some things," he said.

"I am?"

"Yes. Inviting her to your home wasn't the worst of it. You should have told your supervisors." He studied me, face impassive. "Tell me something, Mrs. Alexander. If you had to do this all over again, would you still *not* tell them? Would you cross those lines, violate the rules again?"

"No," I said immediately, lying through my teeth.

"Is that so?" He smiled pleasantly. "Please continue, ma'am."

CHAPTER FIFTEEN
Breathe

IT WAS A SCORCHING THIRD OF JULY. The forest fire season was literally cookin' and Flathead Valley was a hazy, nearly opaque blue from Whitefish to Polson and from Marion to Big Fork. You couldn't see the mountains at all. Visibility was down to a few hundred feet and everywhere was the campfire stink of old growth timber going up in flames.

Not one window was open, anywhere you cared to look.

She wasn't going anywhere this holiday: Nicky was back on the job and the plan was for her to spend the long weekend with Mishelle while Lynn and I caught up on some much-needed family time, each to our own.

Mine involved a lot of shopping and prep. I did a brief inventory of my kitchen and realized I'd let a few basic supplies slip. We needed snacks and tons of soft drinks for the kids too, so I hopped in the Toyota and headed off to Target.

I did the shopping in record time. I was loading some diet cola from the cart into my car when I happened to look up and see Anne. She turned and saw me at about the same time. She waved. I waved back.

"Hi, Anne!"

"Well, hi! How are you?"

"Good. How's Mishelle?"

"Well, honestly, I'm a little worried about her breathing in this nasty haze. She was wheezing when I spoke to her last night."

Anne frowned, an expression that didn't belong there. "Yes, I would have expected that. She's still on the Lorazepam?"

I nodded. "It works, as long as she remembers to stay calm and concentrate on her breathing. I've been showing her some exercises to slow her respirations." I hesitated and then took the plunge: "Anne, in your opinion, do you think Mishelle's a candidate for Hospice?"

She nodded back at me, her pretty face uncommonly solemn. "Oh yes, absolutely. I've read the notes Brent dictated at her last visit and she's definitely end stage."

I blinked. "Did he say how long?"

Anne shrugged, her mouth still turned down. "No. It's a difficult call. The respiratory therapy might extend her life three or four months."

"That's *all*?"

She nodded and bit her lower lip. The look on my face must have given me away because she said, hesitantly: "Is there anything I can do to help?"

I shook myself. "Uh, sure. Just . . . Keep me in the loop if something comes up." I pinched myself on the thigh where she couldn't see, to make sure I wasn't dreaming.

It hurt, so I said: "Thanks, Anne. I was expecting this but you understand that I don't want to tell Mishelle this right now? Not a good time, you know?"

Anne nodded again, her expression sad.

"She's been doing pretty well for her, up until these forest fires, I mean. I don't want to burst her bubble."

Very quietly, she said, "I understand. You'll keep me in the loop too, I hope?"

I nodded. She patted me on the shoulder and left me standing there. I found myself looking up at the sun glaring through the murk like a fiery brass coin and wondering: *what now?*

Three or four months.

And then she would probably die.

Unpleasantly, despite what I'd told her. Slow suffocation is not what I'd recommend for a final exit, even with the nice drugs they have for that sort of thing. It's not that you can't feel yourself suffocating; it's just that you don't *care*.

I rested my forehead against the edge of the trunk lid, the stink of burning forest tarring my nose, coating my tongue with a taste like turpentine.

If it was this bad for me, I could only imagine how bad it must be for her, even with her air conditioning going full blast.

My head lifted from the hot metal. Time to go: people were waiting on me.

* * *

It was cool in my bathroom. The Jacuzzi was full of tepid water and chest deep bubbles. I started to peel off my running shorts, changed my mind and picked up the cell phone.

"Hi!"

"Hi. How's your weekend so far?"

"Great!" She sounded enthusiastic, if a bit more raspy than usual. "We're having a big ol' slumber party. We ordered pizza, watched a ton of movies and Nicky even took me shopping earlier." She coughed. "Hard to get my breath, though. God, it stinks out there!"

"Yeah, it does." I was trying to keep my voice even, not so much cheerful. "Did you get anything?"

"Sure did! Three new skirts and some of that bath stuff you got me for my birthday. It felt great to get out of here." She coughed abruptly and my hair stood on end. It sounded like wood shredding.

When she got her wind back, she added dryly, "We would have stayed out longer, but it's *terrible* out there."

"Yeah, I know," and I could not keep the dullness from my voice.

"Hey, what's wrong?"

"Wrong? Nothing, nothing at all."

"Like hell. Out with it, Michelle."

I sighed. "I'm just tired, is all. I've been running my legs off all day, doing errands for tomorrow."

She chuckled. "This is supposed to be a holiday, remember? Why don't you take a long, cool soak and get your beauty sleep for tomorrow?"

I looked at the suds. "My thoughts exactly."

"Good. Talk to you tomorrow?"

"Love to. Love you."

"Love you, too. G'night, Michelle."

"'Night." I closed the phone, placed it carefully in my lap and covered my face with my hands.

I don't know how long I sat there on the edge of the tub, but Chris's voice brought my head up.

"Mom? Are you crying?"

I sniffled. "No . . . yes, honey, I am."

"Why?" He stood stock-still in the doorway, apprehension on his face. I motioned to him and he came to me, hesitantly. I wrapped him in a hug and the tears poured anew.

"Because," I sobbed into my youngest son's shoulder. "Because she's going to die and I'm *sad*, that's why!"

His body was rigid in shock and I wanted to die myself, telling him like that, but it all came out at once and I couldn't stop it.

"How do you know?"

I lifted my tear-smeared face from his shoulder. "Oh, Chris. You know that she has a fatal disease. We've discussed it enough. I just *know*. She's getting worse with each passing day and I know what's going to happen but I don't know what to *do*!"

I buried my face again in his shoulder. He put his arms around me.

"I'm sad, too," he said, with a moment's hesitation. I sniffled noisily into the next silence and then he said: "What can I do?"

I lifted my head and touched his cheek. A child's eyes should never be that tragic.

"Same as me. Focus on whatever time we have left and help her as best as we can. Okay?"

He nodded. "Okay."

I hugged him. I felt something in that moment that could have been sadness but it wasn't, not at all.

* * *

I waited until Nicky had left Mishelle's to drop in the next day. The uncomfortable feelings I'd had around her were beginning to bloom into full-blown distrust and I suspected it was mutual.

So I waited until just afternoon and drove over. I picked up a latte and danish for her and an apple for me.

I gave her a hug after I set down my bag and the goodies. She felt it immediately, damn it.

"Hey, what's wrong?"

"Nothing. Nothing at all." My voice cracked on *all*.

"C'mon, Michelle." Her voice was nothing if not amused. "I've known you long enough to be able to tell when something's bothering you. Out with it."

I was silent.

"Huh, must be important." She was curiously calm. "Do you want to tell me or do we play Twenty Questions? Animal, Vegetable, Mineral?" Her head tilted in my direction, brow furrowed. "I'll play; I've got nothing else to do this afternoon."

"Okay, I'm worried about you," I muttered. "Satisfied?"

"Now we're getting somewhere. Why? I feel fine."

"Even with all the fires?"

"It's a problem," she admitted. "Sometimes I feel like I can't get my breath, no matter what I do and then it passes and I'm okay. I feel pretty good right now." She sipped her latte, the danish by her elbow; untouched. "What do *you* think?"

"The same." I fell silent again. She sighed.

"Jesus, this is like pulling teeth. Will you *please* tell me what's on your mind? Or do I have to spank you?"

I smiled feebly. "You'll have to catch me first, girlfriend. Okay, I think we need to talk about your code status."

"My what?"

"Your code status. If you should go into cardiac or respiratory arrest, what kind of measures do you want taken to resuscitate you?"

It was her turn to fall silent, to think it over. "What are my choices?"

"A full code means we do everything in our power to revive you, including intubating you and shocking you."

She thought about it. "And if I . . . arrested? That means die, doesn't it?"

The words came out of me like they were covered in glue. "Yes, that's one way to put it."

Her tone was gentle, almost dreamy. "And if you brought me back again, would I be okay? Still me?"

Glue and fishhooks: "In my professional opinion, no. You would most likely be on a ventilator for the rest of your life. In bed, with round the clock care."

"Helpless."

"That's about the size of it, yes."

The dreamy tone was still in her voice and I thought I recognized it now. "And if I don't want that? To be revived? How do I go about making sure that doesn't happen?"

I stared at her. "Is that what you want?"

She smiled crookedly and sipped her latte. Her free hand felt for the danish on the side table, slipped it out of the bag and broke off a corner. She popped the morsel into her mouth and chewed before answering. "Hell, no. I've never felt happier these past few weeks. I've been welcomed into your family, made to feel like I'm a person and not a freak."

She nibbled another piece. "It's all your fault, you know," she said, mostly joking, I think. "You and that boy of yours."

I was kind of proud my voice was steady. "Chris would miss you terribly."

"I know." She nibbled some more danish. "I should probably get this in writing, don't you think?"

"We should, yes. Do you want me to set it up with your doctor?"

She nodded. "Please."

"No code?"

"That means don't revive me?"

"Yes. DNR for short."

"Okay, that's what I want."

I wrapped my arms around myself. I really wanted to wrap them around her. "You're sure?"

"Michelle." Her voice was very gentle beneath the smoke-induced rasp. "I think you know me. Do you believe for a minute that I'd want to spend the remainder of my life hooked up to tubes, lying in bed like a useless lump, unable even to get up and pee? Does that sound like something I'd want?"

"No."

"Okay, then. Set it up." Then she hit me with another body blow: "What's it like to die that way? The other way?"

I swallowed. "If you didn't arrest, you mean?"

"Like that, yeah."

I was sitting on the edge of the loveseat, my usual spot. I wanted to perch on the arm of her chair and take her hand, stroke her hair, hug her; anything but have this conversation.

"Not as bad as you might think. If you follow the usual course of the disease, you'll get weaker and weaker. Your breathing will become more difficult. Eventually you'll be bed-bound, unable to move on your own."

"Sounds just as bad."

"No, they can give you drugs to ease your breathing and make you comfortable."

She chuckled. "Oh, goody. A free high."

"After a while, you won't need them anymore. You'll be in a comatose state, unconscious."

"But not aware?"

"There will probably be a period when you'll still be able to sense your surroundings but unable to respond."

"A vegetable?"

I winced. "We don't use that word. It's cruel."

"But accurate, right?"

"Yeah. More or less."

"What if I get sick again? Another infection?"

"The process would be much faster, especially if you elected not to have us treat it. Without treatment, you'd . . . die much more quickly. Do you want that? To not be treated?"

Very quietly, she said, "I am *done* with taking antibiotics. Okay?"

"Got it." I studied her. She looked a lot calmer than I felt. "I hope I haven't scared you, Mishelle."

The danish was almost gone. She popped another morsel into her mouth. "I'm not scared. I just want to know what I'm facing. Thank you for being honest with me."

I went to her and hugged her, finally. "You're welcome. I just want you to know that you won't be alone. I *promise*. I promise you won't be in discomfort, either. I'll make sure of it."

Her grin was again wry. "Oh, I'm not worried about you, Michelle. It's Chris I'm worried about."

"What do you mean?"

She reached up to pat my cheek. "I don't want him to see me as a vegetable. I don't want him to remember me that way. Promise me that you won't let him see me like that? Promise?"

"I promise."

"Okay, then. I also want to be buried in a wedding dress."

I pulled back and looked at her mischievous expression. "*What?*"

"A wedding dress! Y'know, the real reason I moved back to Kalispell is that I didn't want to die in Seattle. Promise me one more thing?"

"What now?"

"Make sure my family doesn't bury me as Michael. I swear, if they do that, I'm gonna come back and haunt the whole lot of them!"

I half-believed her. "You've been thinking about this, haven't you?"

Her grin was all dimples and elvish glee. "Sure. It's not a conversation you can have with just anybody, you know. Thanks again for being so open with me. Not many people can do that."

"Just call me the angel of death," I said and wondered briefly if it was true. "I take it you want an open casket?"

"Uh, with the lid open, you mean? So everybody can see me?"

"That's the kind, yeah."

"Yup! Make sure I look pretty." She sighed. "Maybe the wedding dress *is* a bit much. What do you think?"

"It would certainly cause talk," I observed. "Perhaps one of your nice frocks instead?"

She pouted. "That's so ordinary. Okay, you pick it out for me. Do you want to do my makeup, too?"

Carefully, I said: "I think Nicky should do it. She's a little better at the beautician thing than I am."

"Okay." She finished her latte. "I knew I wouldn't make it through another winter," she said wistfully. "It's too bad. I really wanted to spend Christmas with my new family."

That did it. The tears welled up in my eyes and I sat mute; immobile.

She went on: "I knew when I was sick the last time, that if I got another infection, I'd be toast." She shrugged.

I sniffled.

"You okay?"

The dam broke. I leaned over, put my arms around her again. "*No!* No, I'm *not* okay! I don't want you to die!"

Her long, strong arms held me close. "Hey, hey. I'm not going anywhere anytime soon. I know that much." She rubbed my back, soothing me. "And I'll be waiting for you in Heaven. I'll be the one to hand you your wings when it's *your* time. So why don't we just enjoy the time we have together for now, okay?"

I sat up and wiped my eyes with the back of my hand. "God, you're strong. I couldn't do this."

The gentle tone returned. "But you *are*, Michelle. You're strong, too. I knew that from the moment we met. You have to be, to do this."

"Yeah, but I don't love every patient I have, either."

She chuckled. "I'm flattered, then."

I wiped my eyes again with the heel of my hand, heedless of my mascara. I probably looked like Alice Cooper about then. "I'll never forget you as long as I live."

"What a coincidence." Her grin was ear to ear. "Me neither."

CHAPTER SIXTEEN

Breathe (a slight return)

THE GUIDELINES SAID she was recovered from the lung infection, at least as well as could be expected under the circumstances.

But I knew: summer heat, forest fires, and the continual stress of simply not being able to breathe; all were taking a toll on her. I watched her flower and grow and wilt all in the space of about two months.

Her air conditioner was on its last legs and kept popping the circuit breakers in her apartment. Getting up to reset them took about all she had in reserve and sometimes it was easier for her to sit and swelter in the dark.

Some folks might have trouble grasping that notion. I tried this once, just to see how she felt: I held my breath for about a minute. Then I let all of it out in one big rush. Without taking another breath, I walked across the room, turned on the TV, changed the channels for about fifteen seconds, tottered back to my chair and sat down.

Then I took a breath.

I almost passed out.

That's what it was like for her, every single day. Imagine: the air blue with smoke from burning timber upwind of Flathead Valley, no air conditioning, the interior of her apartment a toasty ninety-eight degrees plus.

Alone, in the dark.

I tried to look on the positive side. (Don't I always?)

I didn't have to worry about crossing boundaries anymore. She was officially no longer my patient. I could visit her; help her; even pamper her as I chose; whenever I chose.

But that did nothing to relieve her skepticism and stubbornness.

I don't know why she felt that way. Not always, of course. I suppose I felt at the time it was a natural suspicion, a reflex that had kept her alive for many years, but really didn't suit her anymore.

But it still *hurt*:

"Hi."

"Hi! Hey, are you okay?"

"Uh, sure. It's kinda hot, isn't it?" She took a moment to pant noisily.

"You sure?"

More panting: "Yeah. It's just . . ." Her voice sounded hollow and I suddenly knew why.

"You're on speaker phone, aren't you?"

"No . . ."

"Yes, you are. You don't want me to hear how bad your breathing is, do you?"

"I'm fine," she insisted.

"Like hell you are." I felt a flash of irritation. What was so bloody hard about telling me the truth? "Did you take a Lorazepam?"

"Just one." *Pant-pant.*

"Take another. I'll call you in a half an hour."

She sounded doubtful. "You're sure?"

"Yes. Take it! Call you in half an hour."

I bounced around my bedroom; picking up things, throwing them in the general direction of an overnight bag that had somehow found its way to the head of my bed. I wasn't packing, exactly, just getting ready to pack.

I wasn't going anywhere; that would be pushing the envelope here at home. I was trying to split myself equally between my family and Mishelle, knowing on some level that she didn't have much time left on the clock; a level I dared not go, not yet.

For the most part, it was working, but tonight was not a good night for a house call.

At twenty-nine minutes, I called back.

"Are you sitting down?"

Her tone was dust-dry between pants. "No, I'm doing handstands in the kitchen. Want to join me?"

"Sheesh. Okay, breathe with me. Take a deep breath, hold it for three seconds. Pucker up and blow out for five seconds. Again."

I could hear her struggling. My heart blistered with an icy heat. "Keep going! Nice and slow. In. Hold it for a count of three. Pucker up for a kiss, sweetie! Blow!"

She giggled abruptly and I knew it was working. I could hear her breathing slow. "Are you feeling better?"

"Some. Your voice is so soothing to me."

I grinned in relief. "Glad you like it. I wish I could do more, though." I hesitated, nibbling my lower lip. "I don't suppose you'd consider going into the ER? Just for tonight? They can give you meds to ease your breathing."

I shifted the phone from one sweaty hand to the other. "I promise I'll go with you, stay with you if you want me to."

"No."

It was like a door closing. That single word was steel-clad, vacuum-sealed and utterly bombproof.She stood behind that word and nothing and no one, not even me, would ever get past it.

It didn't stop me from trying though: "But you said . . ."

"I know what I said." Her voice was much calmer and I suddenly knew that *this* was what gave her the strength she needed to endure all that she'd been through, all that she had experienced.

Another might see it as simple obstinacy, but I knew in that moment what it meant. "I said I'd go if it was time." She paused to pant, then: "It's not time, Michelle."

I wanted to throw the phone at the wall in sheer frustration. I wanted to scream at her: *What are you* doing? *You could* die, *you darling idiot!*

Instead, I said: "Okay. Is there anything else I can do for you?"

She chuckled. "Sure. You've got tomorrow off, right?"

"Yeah." She knew my schedule almost as well as I. "Want me to come over?"

"Of course. Any chance you could bring Chris with you?"

Smiling felt pretty strange, right then. "He'd love that. He's headed off to summer camp at the end of the week, you know. Four days."

"I know." Her voice still held that supernatural calm and a part of me marveled at it even as I hated it; longed to tear it down. "I wanted to see him again before he left. There are a few tricks with the Brailler I want to show him. It'll make it easier for him."

"Your secret language?"

"Not so secret, if you want to learn." She was relaxed now. I wondered if the meds had finally kicked in and then wondered if it really mattered. "Good night, Michelle. See you tomorrow. Call me when you're coming over, okay?"

"Sure. 'Night." I shut off the phone and tossed it on the bed. I turned.

Dave was leaning against the door jamb, arms crossed, his expression somewhere between sullen and sour; an uncomfortable place. He eyed the bag on the bed and looked at me. "Going somewhere?"

"No. Not tonight, anyway." I brushed past him and headed for the kitchen, pausing only to grab my purse.

I went outside and sat down, took out a pack of cigarettes and lit up.

The air was so foul, I could barely taste the cigarette; not that it mattered. I sat there in the hazy blue twilight: smoking, seething inside; frustration climbing up my throat like the world's worst case of indigestion.

Stupid? Self-destructive? Guilty as charged.

Caring too much? That, too.

* * *

"Mom, can we stop at the Dairy Queen and get something cool for Mishelle to drink?"

I looked over at him as I finished backing out of the driveway. "And pick up something for you, too? Didn't you get enough breakfast?"

He scowled at me. "No, *her*. I don't want anything, thanks."

It took a second or two for me to find my voice. "Sorry, Cee-Boo. Okay, what do you want to get her?"

"She told me she likes banana blizzards. Can we get her one?"

"Of course."

We stopped at the DQ and while the drive-up person was mixing it, I said as casually as I was able: "Mishelle told me she wants to give you a hug. To see what you feel like. Are you okay with that?"

He nodded. "Sure. I'll give her a hug. I think she needs one."

My eyes blurred. I covered it by turning to the attendant for my change. I handed him the drink, rather proud that my eyes were still dry, even more proud of my son. "Yes, Chris. She needs one. Thanks."

He shrugged and my eyes blurred again. It passed.

The blizzard was half-melted by the time we arrived at her apartment. I opened the door and gasped as a wave of wet, rank heat rolled out like a smelly miniature tsunami.

"Oh, my God," I muttered. I looked at her. Mishelle was bent over in her chair, limp hair cascaded around her face. She raised her head and seemed to look in my direction.

"Hi," she managed. "Thought you'd never get here."

Chris went to her and handed her the blizzard. "We brought you something cool to drink, Mishelle. A banana blizzard. Your favorite."

"Thanks, little buddy." I noticed how she fumbled at the drink, so unlike her usual sureness of movement. God, she looked *exhausted*!

Chris looked around at me. "Mom, can we open the windows or something? It's awfully hot in here."

"Too much smoke outside, honey." I went to the circuit breaker panel and flipped the open breaker back to the *on* position. Her air conditioner thumped and kicked in. Warm, stinky air began flowing from it.

"Don't bother," Mishelle murmured. She slurped at the blizzard. "I've already reset them twice." As if to underscore her point, the breaker popped open again. I slammed the panel shut with a silent curse and turned.

"Where are your fans?"

"One in the bathroom. The other's in the kitchen."

I looked around. "Where's Nicholas?"

"In the bathroom," she mumbled, still working on the blizzard. She brushed a lock of sweaty gray hair from her forehead and I was shocked at the sheer size of the dark circles under her eyes. "It's cooler in there."

"There he is!" Chris pointed. I glanced over my shoulder and saw the poor little guy standing in the entrance to the hallway.

Nicholas didn't look so good either: tongue hanging out like a sloppy pink necktie and panting even harder than his mistress. He wagged his tail in a half-hearted fashion as Chris went to him and scratched his back.

"Chris, move that fan from the kitchen over there." I pointed at her computer table. "Mishelle, do you have a spray bottle? One that has only water in it and no cleaners?"

"Under the sink, behind the garbage can." She slurped at her blizzard. "Boy, this is good. Thanks, Chris."

"You're welcome," he grunted, busy with the fan. "Where do I plug it in, Mishelle?"

"Uh, all the power strips are full, I think. That's why I had Nicky plug it in there."

"Extension cords?" I called out, my head under the sink. I was starting to sweat, too. It had to be nearly a hundred degrees inside her apartment!

"Should be some on the hall rack where my Oh-two bottles are stored."

I found the spray bottle and went back to her. "Close your eyes, sweetie."

"Oh, like it matters if my eye gets wet," she grumbled, slurping the last of the blizzard. "Ah," as I misted her face. "That's better."

"When was your last Lorazepam?" Her refill should have been delivered the day before.

"About twenty minutes before you got here." She panted and for a moment her tongue hung out like Nick's. "Two. Like you said."

"One every hour. The worst that will happen is you'll get sleepy. And if you get sleepy, you won't be feeling short of breath. Okay?"

"Well, I'm not sleepy now."

"You will be. Before you do though, we need to discuss what to do about your air conditioner. It's about due for the junk pile."

She brushed lank gray hair back from her furrowed brow. "Well, Nicky borrowed my other one."

"You have another?"

She nodded silently, panting.

"Deep breaths," I advised. "Count three before you exhale, like we practiced. C'mon, girlfriend." I placed my hands on her shoulders. "Slowly."

"Hey, Mishelle," Chris piped up. "I brought you a note in Braille. You wanna read it?"

She'd given him a brand spanking new Brailler about two weeks before. When I asked how she could afford to spend almost seven hundred dollars on another of the heavy, clunky six key typewriters; that damned Madonna-like mysterious smile had surfaced again:

"Ask me no questions . . . ," she'd said. I wanted to spank her skinny bottom right on the spot. Another credit card? *The little stinker* . . .

"Sure, Chris. Let me have it." She held out her hand and my son placed the stiff sheet of paper in it. Her slender fingers danced across the page and she smiled broadly. "You're right: it *is* fun."

She read a bit further. "Well, I can't give away *all* my secrets, but I'll tell you how I did the telephone thing sometime," Her grin was impish. "If you promise not to try it yourself."

"Just don't teach him to pick locks," I warned. "You promised."

"*Mom.*"

"No, Chris. I won't have a budding career criminal in my home. Mishelle, stop trying to corrupt my son."

"Listen to your mother," she said, her words starting to slur a bit. "Don't be a bad girl, uh, boy . . . Whatever. Like me."

I looked carefully at her. Her breathing had definitely eased. My fingers found her wrist and it was immediately evident her pulse had slowed, too. "How are you feeling?"

"Be'er." Her right hand went down next to her chair. She came up with a sheet of the stiff, white Braille paper. She handed it to Chris. "Your turn, li'l buddy."

Chris took it and peered at the array of raised dots. His lips moved silently. His eyes widened.

"You made a mistake!" he blurted. "You misspelled guitar. And Hendrix is spelled with an *x*, not a *ch*."

Mishelle's grin flickered like her eyelids. "Good . . . job . . . kid. Anythin' . . . Anything else?"

"No, uh . . . Wait! Love only has one oh."

"You got 'em . . . got 'em all." Her eyelids drooped.

"Chris," I said, gently. "I think it's time to go. Why don't you take a nap, Mishelle?"

Her head came up. "Wanna hug," she managed. My son wrapped his arms around her and she held him for a long moment, her face blissful even though glistening with perspiration.

"See you next week," he said, releasing her. She held onto his arm for a long moment.

"Have fun . . . at summer camp. Be, be careful."

"I will," he promised. He looked at me, his cherubic face uncommonly solemn. I nodded. I took Mishelle's hand again.

"You get some sleep, girlfriend." She nodded jerkily, her head drooping.

I took a final look around. Nicholas had retreated to the coolness of the bathroom. I let go of her hand and went back to the circuit breaker panel, determined to try one more time. With a silent prayer, I flipped the switch and, miracle of miracles; this time it held.

"See you later, Mishelle," I said softly.

I was answered by a snore. I motioned to Chris and we quietly let ourselves out.

* * *

"You asked him to hug me, didn't you?"

I rolled over and looked at the clock: it was ten past ten. It wasn't that late, but the day had seemed endless after we'd left that morning. Supplies shopping for Chris had turned into the Safari from Hell, Dave had been in one of his moods at dinner and wasn't talking to me and Zach was engrossed in his own preparations for camp.

I felt drained and didn't really want to talk, but I called her anyway; still in denial; still fighting it.

"Who, Chris?"

"Who else?"

I rolled away from the clock, hugging my pillow, relishing the coolness of my darkened bedroom.

Feeling more than a little guilty: "No, I didn't. He did that all by himself."

She snorted gently. "I don't believe you but it felt nice, anyway. Tell him thanks. He's a stocky little bugger, isn't he?"

I smiled into the dark. "Yeah, he's pretty solidly built. He'll be a big fella when he's grown."

"I predict football and massive manual labor for him," she declared. "But the football ought to be good for a scholarship. Where you planning on sending him?"

"Bozeman. Montana State."

She made a small, disgusted noise and I could just imagine her expression. "Football, yeah. What does he want to do?"

I shrugged; an odd feeling while flat on my back. It felt like exercise. "Even he doesn't know yet. Isn't it a bit early to be deciding this?"

"Depends on how you define *early*. It's never too early to find out who you are and what you want to do." There was silence for a moment that she ended with a small sigh. "I sure love that funny little guy."

For some reason, my eyes were stinging. "He loves you too, Mishelle."

"I know. I wish . . ." The pause was longer this time. "Never mind."

I filled the aching hollow that followed with the only thing I could think of, right then: "Hey, I have Wednesday and Thursday off. Why don't you ask Lynn if she wants Wednesday off and I'll look after you?"

She sounded doubtful: "You will?"

"Sure! Even better, I'll ask Dave if you can come over Thursday. How's that?"

Her tone was wry. "Jeez, two whole days with you. You're gonna get sick of me, girlfriend."

"Somehow I doubt that," and I meant every word. "Check with Lynn and let me know tomorrow, will you?"

"Okay. Say hi to Dave, huh? Give him a big wet one for me."

I chuckled softly; sleep beginning to blur my thoughts. "I'll do that. Anything else?"

I could hear the faint rasp of her breathing; still there; still unconquered. "You have such a beautiful family, Michelle. You should feel lucky."

"I do." I meant that, too. "Goodnight, Mishelle."

"'Night, sweetie."

* * *

I called her Tuesday, between patients.

"Nicky's not here yet!"

"Calm down. Don't shout. You'll pass out. You take a Lorazepam?"

"I may have to take the whole goddamn bottle after this! I bought both of them cellphones and I pay the goddamn bills on them but does she ever answer hers when I call? *Nooo!*" I'd never heard her so angry. "Maybe they should just put my butt in a nursing home!"

I was getting a little angry myself. "Stop it! You don't belong in a nursing home. What time was she supposed to be there?"

"Noon. It's past one."

A reflexive glance at my watch confirmed that it was one fifteen. "Have you eaten yet?"

"Stupid question. Of course not!"

I ignored her comment. She was mad and rightfully so. Also hungry, the poor dear. "Okay, here's what you're going to do. Order yourself a pizza. Eat and get your blood sugar up. When Nicky finally arrives, I think you should have a talk with her about her sense of responsibility."

"Damn right I will! This kind of shit is happening way too much!"

"Will you calm *down*? Take some deep breaths."

"I'm fine," she insisted, wheezing.

"Sure you are. C'mon, work with me, girl. In. Hold it for a count of three. Out through your mouth. In through the nose. Let that Oh-two work for you."

I could hear her breathing slow after a minute or two of that. We'd practiced these breathing exercises, endlessly it seemed, weeks ago before the air in Flathead Valley had become foul and blue with smoke from the forest fires. It was finally paying off.

"Feel better?" I asked after a while.

"Some," she admitted.

"Good." I pulled up to my next patient's home: a dilapidated double-wide surrounded by low chain-link a few miles south of Kalispell. Three rusted-out pickup trucks sat on blocks in the yard (if you could call the weedy, refuse-strewn lot a yard) and a large, mangy dog with a worn leather collar eyed me suspiciously from the other side of the fence.

"Listen, I'd come over and make you something to eat if I could, but I'm at work and I can't get away. I really think you need to have a talk with Nicky about this tardiness of hers. Be firm."

Cellphone still pressed against my ear, I grabbed my bag with my free hand and got out, kicking the door shut with a heel. The dog immediately began barking.

"I will."

"I sure hope so. You said it yourself, Mishelle: you're a lousy boss. It's time you cracked down on her. You've let her get away with this too long."

Cautiously, I approached the chain-link fence and the dog went into full defense mode: bounding back and forth, barking his head off. A face appeared at the window of the doublewide.

I set my bag down and waved. The face vanished. "Listen, I really need to go. I'll call in a few hours and see how you're doing. Okay?"

She sighed. "Okay. Thanks, Michelle. Love you."

"You're welcome. Love you, too." I snapped the phone closed as the doublewide's door opened. A little old lady poked her head out and eyed me in much the same way the dog had.

"Yes?"

"Hi! I'm Michelle from Home Health."

Typical little old lady voice; thin and querulous: "Can't you read the sign?" Her head withdrew and the door slammed with a rickety finality.

The dog was about to have hysterics. I looked down and saw a sign wired to the fence with rusty bits of coat hangers: *No Trespassers. No Salesmen.*

I sighed, but a smile found its way to my face. I love my job, really.

* * *

Later, around three o'clock, I called her again:

"Did Nicky show up?"

She sounded depressed. "Yeah. She just got here."

"Did you eat yet?"

"Yeah, I ordered a pizza, like you suggested."

"What kind?" I slowed the Toyota, negotiating a tricky curve in the road. This far out of town, it wasn't too unusual to see deer or other forest critters. I had no wish to turn Bambi or his mom into road kill. Our freezer was stocked well enough, thanks.

"The usual: pepperoni and black olives."

"Hmm, sounds yummy. Listen, I have one more patient this afternoon then I'll call you when I get home, okay?"

"Okay." She hung up, out of breath and dead tired; stressed.

Suppressing how I felt about it took a lot out of me, too.

* * *

I called her right after dinner, a damp dish towel still draped across my shoulder:

"Is Nicky still there?"

She still sounded depressed and even more tired, if that was possible. "Nope. Stayed a couple of hours, then left." She took in a hoarse, rattling breath. "When you come over tomorrow, would you check how many hours she wrote down? I have a feeling she, ah . . ."

"Padded it a bit?"

"Yeah. Like that."

I was twisting the end of the towel, hard, with my free hand. "You say anything to her about what we discussed?"

"Well, kind of . . ."

I snorted. "You sound like Chris. Y'know, if she were my employee, I'd have fired her ass long ago or at least written her up. But you do what you think is best."

There was dead silence on the phone for a long moment. I was about to ask if she was still there when she said, "Are you mad at me?" in a very small voice that trembled on the verge of tears.

"No," I sighed. "No, I'm not mad at you. Never. I'm just mad at the way some people walk all over you."

"Really?"

"Really."

It was her turn to sigh. "Me, too. I *hate* being dependent on others. I hate not being able to *say* anything."

"Because you don't want to go through the hassle of hiring another caregiver?" I guessed.

"Well, sure! Do you know how long it took to find Nicky and Lynn? How many people laughed at me or were . . . grossed out?"

I winced. "Don't say that, please."

"It's true! One old bat left after less than a minute, screaming Scripture at me." There were definitely tears in her voice now.

"Okay, calm down. Do we need to do the breathing exercises?"

"No." She panted briefly. "No, I'll be okay. And I took a pill about twenty minutes ago."

"Should kick in any minute." I had the end of that dish towel pretty well frayed by then, but I had one more thing to say to her: "Mishelle, as I see it, you have two options. One: look for a new caregiver and be prepared for the ridicule and discrimination that will come from it. Two: accept things as they are and learn to put up with it. Either way, you have to accept some unpleasant things and getting worked up about it is, frankly, going to shorten your life expectancy somewhat. You understand what I'm saying?"

I could almost hear the gears turning in her head. "You might be right. I'll think about it, I promise."

I let go of the towel. "Okay, then. On a lighter note: I love you and I'll see you tomorrow. Okay?"

She sounded almost cheerful. "Okay! What time?"

"About nine. I have to pick up some things first."

"Okay. Love you."

"You, too." I clicked off the phone and turned. Dave stood in the doorway to the kitchen, an uneasy expression on his face.

"Tomorrow?" he said.

"That's right."

"I need to take the truck in for some work. In the morning."

"I'm not stopping you."

"But I need someone to come pick me up."

I snorted, thinking: *What am I, your mother?* Instead, I said, "I'm sure the shop has someone who can bring you home." I hung the towel on the fridge and brushed past him, went into my office. He followed me.

"Michelle, I have to do some errands. I need to use the Toyota."

I looked up. "No. Sorry. I'll have it until early afternoon and then I'm picking up Chris and Zach from school."

He set his jaw or tried to. "I really, really need to use the Toyota tomor-row. In the morning."

I sighed. "Dave, it's late and I'm tired. I don't want to argue about this. I need my car most of the day tomorrow. I'm sorry you need to run errands with my car. Perhaps you can call your mother and have her drive you."

I shuffled some papers around. After a moment, I looked up and he was gone. I resumed sorting and filing, my mind elsewhere.

Life in the Alexander household. Never a dull moment.

Damn it.

CHAPTER SEVENTEEN

Under the Skin

*C*ARAMEL LATTE *and a strawberry danish.*
The short drive to her house.

That anticipation when I lifted my fist to rap on the lemon-colored wood beneath the Elvis sign, my other hand already turning the doorknob.

Others have their morning routine and I had mine for a while and now mine's much like everyone else's.

They say you never know what you have until it's gone.

I disagree.

* * *

"You look cute," I commented, shifting things in my hands, kicking the door shut with my heel. Ecstatic, Nicholas started barking. "Is that a new dress?"

She smiled as she put her face up to be kissed. "Yeah. Nicky and I went shopping."

"Yesterday?" My eyebrows rose. "In *this* heat? Mishelle . . ."

Her laugh was a little hoarse, but not bad, really. "No, silly. Home Shopping Network; my obsession and eventual downfall. It was weekend of the Fourth when I bought this. Just got it today."

"Oh, my." I had to laugh too, but I was wincing a little. "I'm thinking we should block that channel off from you, sweetie. Your spending is getting out of control. It's like Christmas every day around here! You must be a regular stop on the UPS guy's route."

Her smile became placid. "Don't worry, Michelle. My credit cards aren't anywhere neared maxed out." Now an edge of *gotcha*: "And a little extra money came in last week."

Parrying, I let a little exasperation show in my voice: "Do me a favor? If you won't talk about it, then don't talk about it. Or tell me everything. One or the other, please."

She nodded. "Maybe I will, someday."

"Jeez." But I looked her over appreciatively. "That really *is* a cute dress. You have good taste."

"Nicky picked this one out. What color is it?"

"Khaki."

"What's khaki?"

"Uh." I had to think. "It's kind of sand-colored. A very light brown." I watched her brow furrow. She thought about it. She said:

"Like what soldiers wear?"

"Sort of. That's close. I guess I never really thought about it before."

"That doesn't sound very attractive. I don't want to look like a soldier." She said it with such perfect seriousness that I laughed.

"Don't worry, Mishelle. You look *nothing* like a soldier!"

"I better not!"

I patted her cheek, still smothering giggles and I know she felt it. But she just patted my hand in return, smiling. "So, what needs to be done today?"

"Probably a lot," she admitted. "Nicky was only here for about an hour."

I looked around, nodding. It was certainly an understatement. Things were in disarray: the CD rack was a disaster area, the laundry basket was overflowing and dust lay everywhere. I was going to have to take a damp towel to every flat surface in sight.

Another sigh and I got busy.

It didn't take that long, fortunately. Our conversation helped pass the time. She was in better spirits that morning; her breathing easier and speech more animated than my last visit.

The air conditioner was working pretty well, although noisy. I had to raise my voice once in a while for her to hear me over its rattling whoosh. I decided to speak to Nicky about the one that she'd borrowed and suppressed a slight shudder. Conversations with *her* had grown less pleasant, while mine with Mishelle had become more familiar and personal the more I came to know her.

The irony hadn't escaped me and yes; I thought I knew just how excluded Nicky felt.

I'd known Mishelle for about three months and yet I'd become as much a fixture in her life as Nicholas or her voice robots. Nicky had been her caretaker for over three *years*. I wasn't surprised that she was resentful of me.

Sad, yes, but not surprised.

"Hey," she called. "Are you done yet? I want my bath!"

I came out of the kitchenette, wiping the platter from the microwave. Someone had nuked a bowl of chili without a cover and the interior of the unit was a repulsive mess. "My, don't you sound like a pampered little rich girl. I suppose you want me to wash your hair, too?"

She snickered hoarsely. "Of course. Aren't you supposed to be a full-service nurse?"

"Not anymore," I said. "Today, I'm just your friend. Want to try that again?"

"You're right." She was instantly contrite. "Michelle, would you give me my bath, please?"

"Love to," I said, meaning it. "I'll go run a tub."

I helped her into the tub and Nicholas did his usual wacko imperson-ation of a mighty rabbit hunter. We talked some more while I scrubbed her back and washed her hair:

"How new is that a/c unit Nicky borrowed?"

"I dunno. Newer than the one that's in the window right now."

"Why did you lend it to her?"

"She needed one. Her kids didn't have one in their room and she told me it was incredibly hot because their room doesn't have any cross drafts."

"Hmm." I soaped her back, noting the lack of tension this time; relieved that she no longer experienced the body shyness with me she'd once had. "Y'know, Home Health's regulations say we're not supposed to borrow things from a patient, even if offered."

"Uh-huh." Mishelle splashed a palm full of water on her face. "And?"

"Well, did she ask you for it or did you just offer?"

"I can't remember."

I suppressed a snort of disbelief. "Right. Okay, I can take a hint. But I think you should ask her to return it. You need it more than she does."

She was silent. I could feel the muscles tensing again in her back. I scrubbed and waited. She said finally: "I'll think about it."

"Okay."

We finished, I helped towel her off and finger-combed her graying hair; still amazingly thick and full. While I was helping her into a clean dress, I noticed the elbow-shaped depressions above each knee and real-ized that constantly leaning forward and resting her arms there had left permanent imprints.

It made my heart ache for just a moment; less than three breaths.

I settled her back into her armchair and began to read *Confessions of a Shopaholic* to her. Soon her eyes had closed and her head was nodding. I got a little playful:

"Then Mishelle realized her life's dream: to be turned loose in Neiman-Marcus with an unlimited credit card. 'Whatever shall I do?' she said."

"You are so weird," Mishelle said without opening her eyes. "And it wouldn't be Neiman-Marcus, anyway. Saks for me, sweetie. They have tall gal fashions that make me drool."

"Sounds good to me, too," I agreed. "Really, if you could shop anywhere, where would you go? Top three."

"Only three? Oh, that's so . . . limited. Uh, okay: Coldwater Creek, Newport News and Saks."

"There's a Coldwater Creek outlet in Missoula," I offered. "Kind of a long drive, though. And isn't Newport News strictly online? Mail order only?"

"Whatever. This is *my* fantasy, okay?"

"Fire away, sweetie." I had her left foot in my lap, rubbing it. For all that she rarely wore shoes; her feet were surprisingly free of callus or rough spots. Like her legs, they were smooth and supple-skinned, although certainly the largest feet I'd ever rubbed.

"Do I get to add more to my list?"

"All you want."

"Hmm, Lane Bryant. Nordstrom's. Macy's. Gimme a minute to think of some more."

"No Victoria's Secret?"

Mishelle made a face. "They don't have clothes for real women. I have yet to find a bra from them that actually fits. I have better luck with Sears and Lane Bryant."

"I should take you to Sears for their next lingerie sale, assuming there's anything left on your card."

"You let me worry about that. Oh, speaking of which, I need to make a payment online soon. Will you take a deposit to the bank for me? Nicky will probably be late tomorrow and I want it posted before noon."

"I'll do it today on the way home," I assured her, glancing at my watch. It was three-thirty; plenty of time.

"Thanks, sweetie." She leaned sideways and picked up her lockbox, never far from her since the incident of the missing meds. She wore the key around her neck and the only time I'd ever seen her take it off was during a bath.

She opened the box and removed her wallet, opened that and began removing bills folded differently to indicate their respective denominations. I could see her lips move as she silently counted, then she handed me the money.

"Here's one hundred. You can give me the receipt next time you come over."

Brow furrowed, I counted the thin stack of bills. "Mishelle, I hate to be the one to tell you this but there's not even close to a hundred dollars here. More like thirty."

"*What*? There should be a twenty, seven tens and two fives!"

"Not even close. Let's see." I counted again: "One ten, two fives and the rest are ones. Twenty seven bucks. Are you sure you counted these right?"

She looked outraged. "Of course I'm sure! Damn it, someone stole my money!"

I was frowning so hard; my forehead ached. Absently, I rubbed it. "Calm down. Let's think about this. Who's been here since you put the money in there?"

"You, my mom, Lynn and Nicky."

"That's all?"

"Yes!"

I considered the fact that she still did not lock her front door despite the change of keys. A sigh: "Oh-*kay*. I know you leave that key around your neck except when you take a bath. When was your last bath before today?"

"One on Saturday and one on Monday."

"Where did you put the key then?"

Her face went unnaturally blank. "Oh, shit," she said quietly.

"Yes?"

"On the table. Here." She patted the side table between her inhaler and keys.

"How long did you leave it there? When did you put it on again?"

"The next day," she said in the same quiet tone.

I glanced at the door. "You still aren't locking your front door, Mishelle. I walked right in here today. So anyone could have come in here and taken that money."

"But Nicholas would have barked!" she protested. On cue, Nick jumped into her lap and tried to lick her face. "No lick, Nick. I would have heard it!"

My shoulders wanted to slump. "Or maybe it was hot and he was sleeping in the bathroom. And you might have gone to the potty too, and someone could have come in and opened it, took the money."

I rubbed my forehead again, stopped when I realized it wasn't doing me any good. I was suddenly very tired. "Mishelle, we can't say *anyone's* guilty of this. But you're going to have to be more diligent about keeping that key with you. And will you please for God's sake start locking your front door!"

"I will," she said in a small voice. Nicholas, anxious, was still trying to lick her face, silly boy. She pushed his pointy muzzle aside. "No *lick*, Nick. What'll I do?"

I folded the bills. "I'll make up the difference. Don't worry; your payment will be covered."

Putting her bills into my purse next to mine, I silently counted my own cash: a fifty, two twenties, three fives and a crumpled cluster of ones. I'd been intending to go grocery shopping, but it would have to wait.

"You can't do that," she protested feebly.

"Sure I can. I'm not your nurse anymore, remember? Just a friend. Can't a friend loan a friend some money once in a while?"

"Thanks." Her voice, although still small, was steady and crystal clear. "I love you."

"I love . . ." My answer was drowned out by the phone ringing. Krystal the robot announced the number in her flat mechanical voice.

It was Nicky. Even I could recognize her number now. We both sat there, the phone ringing, and then it cut off before the message machine kicked in. Her cellphone, on the table next to her with her keys, suddenly rang.

She let it. I remained silent, not really watching her, barely breathing. The cell stopped ringing and then the landline rang again.

This time there was a message. I listened, my mouth hanging open in shock.

"Mishelle, pick up. I know you're there!" *Seething*; that's what I first thought. Like a brimming pot of water about to hit full boil. "I know that Michelle's there, too. Listen, if you want your stupid video camera back, just say so, would you? Oh, and Michelle Number Two? Huh, maybe I should just call Home Health and tell them what you've been doing 'cause that's crossing boundaries and I *know* they've got policies about that!"

She hung up. Mishelle looked furious. I just sat there, mouth open.

"She does that and I'll kill her." She turned her face to me. "I mean it."

"I didn't know she borrowed your video camera, too," I said. It sounded inane in my ears. "What else did she borrow?"

"Never mind. That's *my* problem, not yours."

"Uh, if you say so. Uh, you're not on Home Health anymore, you know?" My tongue seemed thick and sluggish. "I'm not acting as your nurse. I'm just your *friend.*"

Ooh, that sounded lame, too.

"*Don't worry about it.*" She was seething as well. Her breathing was becoming visibly erratic and labored. "I think I might mention her name to the cops when I report that my money was stolen."

Alarmed, I said, "Calm down, please. And I wouldn't blame anyone unless you're *sure*, Mishelle. Promise me."

Muscles stood out along the line of her lean, finely-formed jaw. Sweat dotted her brow and her curls hung limp. "I better take a pill. Could you get my coffee, please?"

"Sure." I filled her mug and brought it back, watched as she washed down a Lorazepam. "You want to go through some breathing exercises?"

"I'll be alright." She put her cup down and flipped open her watch. "It's past four. You better get that deposit down to the bank."

I started. "Oh. Yeah." I packed up my things in a hurry, gave Nicholas a brief but vigorous back scratching and bent to kiss her cheek.

"You'll be in a better mood tomorrow," I whispered. "Bath in my Jacuzzi! Two days in a row! You'll be the cleanest lady in town."

She reached up to pat my cheek and I took her hand. "I'm really look-ing forward to it. Will Chris be home?"

"Still at camp." I gave her hand a squeeze. "Which you know perfectly well, young lady."

"Yes." Her voice was subdued. "Just . . . Hoped. See you tomorrow."

"'Bye, sweetie." I kissed her cheek again and beat a hasty retreat.

On the way home, I considered my options. There weren't many.

I could pre-empt Nicky and tell my employers that I was visiting Mishelle on my own time, but warning bells rang in the back of my head when I thought about that. I could talk to Nicky directly and try to straighten this out, but I had a sick feeling it would only make things worse.

I pulled into the driveway and sat for a moment, listening to the engine tick as it cooled; trying to think. Had I truly been over the line here?

Perhaps I had before Mishelle was discharged, but not now. Home Health did not have a policy regarding visiting discharged patients on one's own time. I'd never heard of anyone else doing that.

So far as I knew, it wasn't a problem.

But I still didn't like the idea of Nicky talking to Jodie about my relationship with Mishelle because I didn't want to be seething about this either.

Someone had to keep a clear head in this mess. It might as well be me.

I dumped my things in the foyer and changed clothes. I glanced at the clock, went back to the foyer and dug out my cellphone.

"Did you call Nicky?"

"I did." She wasn't seething anymore but she still sounded pretty pissed.

"Well?"

"I told her someone stole money out of my purse and that I was considering calling the police to report it." Her tone was laced with an icy anger unlike anything I'd ever heard from her. I shivered. "That shut her up pretty quick."

"I'll bet. Is she going to give your things back?"

"She can keep the video camera. I won't be needing it."

I let that one go by without comment. Instead, I said: "I think she and I need to talk. I'll tell you about it tomorrow."

"Okay." She sounded dubious. "You okay?"

"Sure!" I said brightly. "I'm fine. See you tomorrow, sweetie!"

"Uh-huh." She still sounded doubtful. "Okay. Nine-ish?"

"Around there. 'Bye, Mishelle!"

I clicked off, my hands shaking and immediately dialed Nicky's number before I had a chance to change my mind. Caller ID: she picked up immediately.

"Hello?"

"Nicky, this is Michelle. We need to talk."

She was silent for a moment. "Yeah, I guess so."

"I was there when you called today. Mishelle and I were having a conversation and we didn't want to be interrupted. So we weren't trying to be rude and I'm sorry if it looked that way."

Cautiously, she said: "Okay."

"But I overheard your message. Tell me why you'd want to call my employers."

It was her turn to sound a little lame: "Well, I'm not going to do that."

"That's good." I suddenly realized that the fingernails on my free hand were cutting into my palm. I keep them clipped pretty short for my job.

Carefully, I unclenched my hand. "I mean, I don't know why you'd want to do that anyway, considering I've done nothing that would warrant that."

I really think she was trying to keep the whine out her voice. For the most part, she was successful: "Well, I just know that the agency I used to work for had a policy of not visiting former patients for at least six months, that's all."

"Not at Home Health," I said firmly.

"Oh. Okay. Uh, so I guess someone stole some money from Mishelle, huh? I just talked to her."

I had to admire her slippery way with a subject. "Yeah, pretty sick, huh? Someone who'd steal money from a blind person has got to be the lowest of the low."

There was dead silence for the space of four heartbeats. "I did not steal money from her, Michelle."

"I never said you did. And frankly, I don't think you're that stupid. You'd be the first one they'd suspect, wouldn't you? I mean, if she went to the police, that is."

Subdued: "You think she's going to talk to the police?"

"I have no idea what she's going to do. All I know is that I'm staying out of it. My only concern is keeping Mishelle comfortable and happy until it's her time to go."

There was another dead silence, shorter this time. "You think she's going to die?"

"I didn't say that. But she's functioning on only twenty percent lung capacity and almost anything can happen." I sighed and closed my eyes. "I'm thinking of talking to her about Hospice, but I don't want to destroy her last hope, Nicky."

"She told me last week that she didn't think she'd make it through another winter." There was a funny catch in her voice and I realized that she felt just as rotten about it as me. "And she *gave* me that video camera, you know. On the Fourth. She said she wouldn't be needing it anymore."

Wouldn't be needing it . . .

I stood stock still, the phone spot-welded to my ear. "She said that to me, too. The awful thing is, Nicky, when terminal patients say things like that, they're usually right."

Silence hung like a curtain between us; thick and black and absorbing everything.

For the life of me, I couldn't tell you what she was thinking.

I broke through the curtain: "Well, look. I've gotta go and fix dinner for my kids." I think my voice sounded properly brisk and pleasant if not exactly cheerful. "I'm glad we had this talk, aren't you?"

"Me, too. Yeah, I'm glad we talked. Thanks for filling me in, Michelle."

"Anytime, Nicky." *Anytime*, I thought and suddenly longed to take a bath myself; full of bubbles and soothing warm water, a glass of chilled chardonnay balanced on the edge of my Jacuzzi. "See you later."

"'Bye." She hung up.

I closed the phone, staring at the floor, feeling my stomach churn. "Damn."

* * *

As I was packing her things the next day, almost ready to call Dave, I saw her cellphone on the side table. "Hey, don't you want your phone?"

"Not today," she said firmly.

"No?" I was astonished, to put it mildly. That little device was her link, her lifeline to the outside world and she was ready to relinquish it just to spend uninterrupted time with me? I stared at her. "Really? Are you sure?"

Mishelle nodded. "Today is an *us* day and nobody else's," she declared, already in her wheelchair and visibly eager to leave. "No stress for me, thanks."

Nicholas was standing on her lap, tail vibrating madly, eyes bright with excitement. He knew that *go for ride* also meant *good things to eat*.

I was deeply touched. "Jeez, Mishelle . . ." There seemed to be something in my eye. Both of them.

"And you don't have to take my makeup kit, either."

She'd refused any when I'd arrived earlier and I assumed she was merely anticipating her bath. "Why not?"

She shrugged. "I'd rather you didn't spend a half hour putting makeup on me. I want to relax."

I grinned. "You don't care if Dave sees your naked face?"

She grinned right back at me. "Why not? You're family, aren't you? Neither of you cares what I look like, right?"

"That's true." I flipped my phone open and punched speed dial. "Honey? We're ready. Don't run any stop signs this time, okay?" I closed the phone. "Okay! Did I miss anything?"

"Yeah, like you've ever done that."

"It's been known to happen." I looked around, itemizing without a written list this time. I couldn't think of anything.

We chatted until Dave rapped on the door. He wore a pleasant smile and was entirely friendly, but I watched him with barely narrowed eyes, wondering what was going through his head, too.

Aw, jeez, I thought to myself and I still remember how it felt. *I'm turning into a complete paranoid over all this. Relax, Michelle.* I resolved to follow my girlfriend's example: today was not a day for stressful thoughts.

Less than a minute from turning into my street, she casually remarked, "Okay, there're three speed bumps on your street. Remember my back."

"How could I forget?" I looked at her with barely concealed astonishment. Steel trap memory. "Don't fret, I'll be careful."

I was. I slowed for them and she smiled a *gotcha* smile with each bump. We pulled into our driveway and Dave pulled in behind me, got out and assisted me getting her into her chair. He set up her oxygen generator, kissed us both goodbye and headed back to work.

Nicholas, bless his nasty little heart, immediately ran inside and peed on my couch! I glowered at him and he slunk away into the kitchen, eyes downcast and tail between his legs. I wasn't impressed; I knew he'd do it again and again . . .

"Mishelle, I've got an idea. Nick just peed on my couch again. Since I don't have Chris or Zach here to keep an eye on him, I'm going to put a peri-pad on him and wrap it with an ace bandage. I won't let it get too tight. Okay?"

She looked wry. "Well, he'll just have to suffer, won't he? Sorry, Michelle."

"It's okay. I just don't want my furniture ruined."

"I know. Neither do I."

Nicholas looked so sorrowful (and utterly ridiculous) when I was done; I had to give him a doggie treat. I left him happily crunching a milk bone and went back to his mistress.

"How would you," I asked. "Like a complete pedicure, foot soak and massage?"

"Ooh, I'm all yours, dearie."

I did a bang-up job, I think. I soaked her feet for about a half hour in one of those vibrating heated footbaths which drew little groans and sighs of pleasure from her.

When her toenails were nice and soft, I brought out clippers, nail files, cuticle scissors and the like and set to work. I painted them and while they dried, I did her fingernails, both in a nice light baby pink. Her toenails were dry when I finished so I massaged a little moisturizer into them.

"Girlfriend, you weren't kiddin'." Her eyes were closed in bliss. "Why are you being so nice to my feet, though? Just curious."

"Well, I was thinking." I rubbed her heels, one in each hand. "Your feet are almost like hands for you, y'know? Except you walk on them and that's gotta be tough. So I decided to treat your feet."

She giggled. "That ought to be a shoe company's slogan: 'Treat Your Feet'."

"Might be." I stood up, wiping my hands on a towel. "Hungry?"

"Ravenous."

I made sandwiches and took them outside to the patio. It was raining but still warm without much breeze. I rolled Mishelle out to our table, seated myself and we ate lunch while the warm rain streamed down, pattering on the roof above our heads.

It was so very Zen; wonderfully, exquisitely calm and relaxing. I'll remember that day forever: the sound of the rain and her quiet voice; the solitude that was composed of just us and no others; a perfect sense of being in the moment.

You don't get those very often and when you do, it's a good idea to stay there for as long as you can.

You never know when the next one will come by.

"Bath time?"

"Bath time," she agreed. Nicholas eyed me from under the dining room table, sulking as I rolled his mistress back inside. His peri-pad looked like it might be wet but he could wait until I had Mishelle in her bath.

Full of bubbles and blood-warm; it was just right, or so she said when I helped her in. I left her with my I-Pod playing a set of nice meditation music and went to find Nicholas.

He was still under the dining room table, looking like the most mournful dog in the world. We had a little conversation, he and I. His side of it was mostly rolling eyes and sorrowful expressions but mine went something like this:

"Listen to me, you little stinker. I know what you're doing. You make messes around here because you can get away with it at your Mommy's." I unwrapped the ace bandage as I spoke to him. He endured it stoically with only his eyes telling me anything. "You could make your life so much easier by just being a good boy and doing that outside, where it belongs."

I finished unwrapping him and kissed his little head. "But I love you anyway, you little shit. Now, go to Mommy! It's play time!"

Ecstatic, the dachshund scampered down the hall in search of his mistress and the magic froggy, barking his silly little head off.

The Color of Sunlight

Smiling, I rose and began rolling the ace bandage up into a neat ball. I froze when I heard a lady-like shriek from Mishelle:

"Michelle!"

Scared out of my wits, I dropped the bandage, clattered down the hall and burst into the bathroom. I gaped and then began laughing.

Mishelle was laughing too. Nicholas wasn't doing his wacko rabbit hunter impersonation; instead he was doing a pretty fair cover of *Dog at Sea*.

He'd fallen into the tub! The poor mutt was frantically paddling and pawing at the edge, realizing too late that he'd made a serious error in judgment.

"What *happened*?" I choked out between gales of laughter. Mishelle was leaning against the side of the tub, giggling helplessly.

"He jumped up on the tub to get the froggy and fell in!" she gasped between giggles. "I don't think he was ready to go swimming."

I got myself under control. "I've got lots of extra towels. C'mon, Nick." I fished the soaked little dog out of the tub and grabbed a used towel from the rack. "Are you okay, sweetie?"

"Never better," she giggled. "That was fun!"

"Sheesh. And you think *I'm* weird."

I let her soak for as long as she wanted, about an hour, then helped her out and began putting her hair in rollers. When I started in on her face with some of my makeup, she protested, but I said firmly, "No buts. Dave may be your bong buddy and chess partner but I won't let him see you without your face, not for dinner, anyway."

"But . . ."

"He's also my husband."

She smiled, shrugged, sighed. "Okay. Go ahead." Suddenly, she yawned.

"Sleepy?"

"A little," she admitted. "I'm really relaxed." She tittered and said, "Listen."

I cocked my head and could hear faint strains of Pink Floyd coming from the I-Pod, still playing in the bathroom. "That's . . ."

"Uh-huh. *Comfortably Numb.* That's what I am right now."

"Why don't you take a nap?" I suggested. "I'm all finished with your face. I'll style your hair when you wake up."

"You talked me into it."

I rolled her into the front room, put a pillow across her poor, dimpled knees and read to her until she drifted off.

I studied her while she slept, her face smoothed out, the ravages of time and pain and care softened finally; enough to let the person beneath the years come forward into the light.

The rollers pulled much of her hair back from her face so that I was finally able to really study her bone structure and the character that lay behind it:

I saw a woman peacefully sleeping; a truly remarkable woman who had survived everything thrown at her; a strong, willful woman who had bootstrapped herself into a life-changing transition with almost no help, few resources and nothing but her own carefully nurtured self-image to guide her. She'd never swerved from her path, never faltered, even when locked up and she knew herself as no one else I'd ever known.

I saw my friend, my best friend and she was dying.

For some reason, my eyes remained dry. Zen? I don't know. Perhaps I was finally reaching some level of acceptance within myself. It was nothing like the moment in my garden; my epiphany.

No, this was much more immediate, more . . .

More human.

She opened her eyes. For a brief, eerie moment, I could almost believe she was looking back at me. "Hi."

"Hi."

"How long have I been asleep?"

I glanced at my wristwatch and saw with mild surprise that over an hour had passed. "About an hour."

She sat up. "Mm, that was lovely." She stretched her arms out before her and yawned delicately. "I feel very refreshed."

"You should be."

"Did I snore?"

I chortled. "No. But you slept like a log. I could have marched an army through here and you wouldn't have twitched. Do your hair now?"

"Yes, please."

We went into the bathroom and I turned the I-Pod down a bit. When I started taking the rollers out, she said: "I've been thinking."

"Good. Maybe it'll become a habit."

"Smartass. No, what I meant was, about the caretaker thing. About maybe hiring a new one for when Nicky can't make it. And I think Lynn's getting burned out. Nicky says she isn't keeping up with her end of the housework."

I froze but my hands kept moving on their own, fortunately. "Is that so?"

"Yeah. She says she wouldn't mind picking up a few extra hours too, which I'm thinking might not be such a bad idea until I hire a new one." She turned her head to me. "What do you think?"

"You don't want to know what I think."

"Yes, I do."

Picking my words carefully, I said, "Why in the world would you want to give Nicky more hours when she doesn't even put in the ones she's supposed to work?"

She didn't answer, so I went on: "Look, sometimes she just wants to stir the pot, y'know?" It was a real struggle to remain diplomatic on this subject. "And it stirs you up too, and I think she knows that, uses it even. Maybe. Possibly." I drew a breath. "Lynn doesn't have that effect on you, Mishelle."

"Really?"

"Really. On the days she's been there when I drop in, your breathing is much easier. You're not as riled up."

"So what should I do, then?"

I shrugged, my fingers buried in her hair, a hair clip in my mouth. "Ah nunno. Hah-are ah new cahre-taker?" I took the clip out of my mouth. "I would have fired her long ago, but you two have a history and I can understand why you're reluctant to do that. I'd hire a new person and cut Nicky's hours. She obviously can't handle as many as she has now."

She was silent for a long moment while I picked out a curl and spritzed it. "You may be right," she said finally. "Should I put an ad in the newspaper?"

"Might be a good idea. A back-up plan, you know?"

"Okay."

Our front door thudded shut and I heard Dave's distinctive footsteps. "Hello, ladies!" he called out.

"Just a minute, dear!" With a few last touches to her hair, I rolled her out to the front room. He gave us a cheery smile that morphed into bemused pleasure when I greeted him with a kiss.

"For once," I whispered in his ear, "You have perfect timing. Thanks." I added another kiss to the one still warm on his cheek and moved out of the way so he could greet our guest. She got kissed, too.

"Well," and his manner was so completely affable and relaxed, I was beginning to wonder if it was contagious. "How was your day, ladies?"

I opened my mouth but Mishelle beat me to it. "We had a perfectly wonderful day," she stated most firmly. "Your wife should be a professional foot masseuse. Look at these tootsies!" She held her feet out for Dave to admire.

He looked down at them, then up at me; an amused glint in his eye. "Nice color. Hey, I could use one of those massages myself someday. I'll pass on the polish, though. If you don't mind."

"Let me check my calendar. Why don't you two play some chess while I get dinner started? I believe our guest has a score to settle with you, dear."

He beat her but not by much. By the time he finally took her queen, dinner was ready. The rain had lifted and most of the clouds had drifted away but enough were left to provide a splendid backdrop to the beginning of one of Montana's beautiful sunsets.

We ate chicken and rice by torchlight on the patio, the early evening breeze fresh and clean about us, the setting sun spraying red and gold and pink against the fluffy gray clouds above and beyond us. The conversation among the three of us was quiet and reflective and it seemed a perfect end to a perfect day.

Dave excused himself as the last of the colors faded from the sky and went back inside to catch up on some overdue paperwork. Mishelle and I sat: at peace, silent for a long time.

"I wish Chris were here," she finally said, dreamily.

"Two days. He'll want to see you."

"I know. I wish he was my little brother, sometimes."

"Well, he might as well be, you know." I shifted in my chair and tried to stifle a burp. Despite my efforts, it escaped and I wished it well. "Besides, that would make me your mother."

"His aunt, then."

"Then I'd be your sister."

She turned her face to me, her blind eyes seeking mine in the twilight. "Well, aren't you?"

"Yeah. I guess I am."

CHAPTER EIGHTEEN
"If it ain't broke . . ."

THE PHONE RANG. Rolling, I groped for it and then realized it had cut off in mid-ring. I heard my husband whisper: "Shh. You shouldn't be calling, honey. She might find out about us."

I smiled into the dim coolness of the bedroom and held out my hand. Dave rolled toward me and placed the phone in it, wearing a sly grin as he kissed my cheek. I winked back.

The bed bounced a little as he rolled out and padded toward the kitchen, giving us some privacy.

"Hi. Is there something I should know about you two?"

There was a brief but sincere laugh, damaged at the end by a hoarse cough. "Yeah. We're running away to a tropical island next week. Borrow your car?"

"Only if I get to come along." I stretched, feeling muscles unwind and come online. "Jeez, what time is it?" I tried to see the clock.

"Just a moment." I knew she was touching the hands of her watch. "Seven-fifteen. Time to get up, lazybones."

"Don't rush me. Today's my day off."

"Planning on sleeping in?"

"Well, I already did. Actually, I have to clean this swamp of a house today. I've let too many things pile up here and that's not like me." I yawned. "To what do I owe the pleasure of your call, Miss Woodring?"

Another chuckle; unmarred by a cough this time, thank Heaven. "I just wanted to tell you that I took your advice and placed an ad in the paper for a new caregiver. Lynn helped me with the wording."

"That's wonderful, Mishelle." I flipped the covers back and sat up. Dave came in as I was finding my slippers and put a warm cup of coffee in my hand. He made sign language that seemed to indicate that he was going to start some breakfast and went out. I sipped: *ah*. "I'll be happy to help you with the interview process if you'd like."

"You would? Really?"

"Sure." I took another sip and wandered toward the potty. "I promised, didn't I?"

"Yeah, but . . ." She sounded doubtful. "It won't be too much trouble, will it?"

"Nah." I dropped my drawers, settled down and relaxed. *Ah*, again. "I'll come up with some questions for you to ask. You have any plans for today?"

"Not really. Lynn is going to take me up to the hospital for a treatment but that's about it. Why? You want to come over?"

"Sorry, I really need to attend to things here." I looked around with distaste. "Starting with this bathroom."

Mishelle chuckled. "I could tell where you were by the echo. Okay, tomorrow then?"

"Yeah, that could work." I flushed and went back into the bedroom. "On my lunch break. Sound good?"

"Sure! Uh, did Chris come home yet?"

"Day after tomorrow." The kitchen beckoned with the heavenly aroma of sizzling sausage. Dave was cracking eggs for omelets into a bowl. His glance featured a raised eyebrow. "Zach gets to stay there for a few more days 'cause he's older."

"That'll be nice, having Chris all to yourselves for a day or two." I could hear the barely restrained eagerness in her voice. "When do you think I'll get a chance to see him again?"

"I'll come up with something. Trust me; he's itchin' to see you, too. " I poured myself more coffee and looked at the time. "I'm burning daylight here. I'll give you a call later, okay?"

"Okay." She didn't sound too sulky. I clicked off and arched an eyebrow right back at him.

"*Honey?*"

He grinned at me while flipping an omelet onto my plate. "Well, she *is* sweet, despite all the spare time she's been monopolizing."

"Huh." I dug in, unsure of why I felt a twinge right then. "I think you're just happy to get some clean underpants, is what I think."

"There's that," he admitted. "Pass the salt, would you?"

* * *

She called me while I was in the middle of scrubbing out the Jacuzzi, but I was glad for the break. I peeled off a disposable glove, made a long arm and snatched the phone off the end of the sink.

"Hi. What's up?"

"We got an appointment for the first interview!"

"Okay, that's good. When?"

"Noon tomorrow. I'm really nervous!"

"I can tell. Calmly, now. Take some deep breaths. Did you talk to her?"

"No, Lynn did."

In her words, this was like pulling teeth. "Tell me more."

"Like what?"

"Like what kind of experience she has! Jeez." I peeled off the other glove. My hand was sweating. "Do you know *anything* about this person? What did Lynn ask her about her background?"

"I dunno. All she said was that she has caretaker experience."

"That's *it*? Oh, boy." I rubbed my forehead with the back of my hand. "Does she know you're blind?"

"I dunno. I don't think Lynn told her that, no." Her breathing was starting to sound erratic.

"Easy. Slow your breathing, like I showed you. In. Hold it. Out. Hold it. In. Hold. Out. Better?"

"Yeah," she panted, but gently now. "Much. Should Lynn have told her I'm blind?"

It was like speaking to Chris. Exactly like Chris, in fact. "Yes, she should have. Also your trans status."

"But we don't want to scare anyone off, do we?"

"Calmly, now. No, and we don't want to surprise anyone either, do we?"

"I guess not."

"I can see that I'm going to have to draw up some guidelines along with those questions. Look, let me finish mucking out the stables here and I'll call you right after dinner, okay?"

"Okay. Michelle?"

"Hmm?"

"Did we screw up?"

"No, I don't think so. But this is just the first interview, so don't place too much importance on it, 'kay?"

"'Kay. Love you."

"Love you too." I clicked off and went back to scrubbing the tub, muttering to myself. I might have used a swear word or two.

* * *

This time, I called her. "Hey!"

"Hi." Her voice was subdued and there was something funny about the sound of the phone. I didn't immediately put my finger on it. "How was dinner?"

"Good," I said cautiously. "Whatcha doin'?"

"Just sitting here rocking."

"All by yourself?"

"Nick and Blue and me." The background sounded odd and then I had it: there wasn't any background. Normally when I called, there would be the sound of the TV or the stereo and the many sounds of her robots.

Now: nothing; the presence of absence.

"Why's it so quiet?"

"Nicky told me that she talked to the apartment assistant manager and that there were complaints about my place being too noisy, like something out of a science fiction movie."

"Nicky told you this?"

"Yeah. She said I had to keep it down or I'd be evicted."

I snorted. "Mishelle, you live in senior citizen's housing. Most of your neighbors are as deaf as a post. And they can't evict you just for that unless you're really loud all the time, which you aren't."

"I'm not going to be evicted?"

"No, you're not going to be evicted."

"But they're going to inspect my apartment next week." There was a note of real concern in her tone. Not panic; not yet.

Great, something else for her to worry about. Aloud, I said, "Relax. Apartment inspections happen all the time. Maybe they're going to put in new carpets or something."

"I hope not," she said, a bit grimly. "'Cause they'll have to pull the old ones up and I'm pretty sure *those* stink to high heaven."

"Your place isn't that stinky."

"You sure?"

"Of course." I thought about it. No, even when I'd first visited, it didn't smell that bad, but still . . . "Okay, I agree that your carpets could probably use a good cleaning. We might be able to help you there. But I have to ask: did Nicky talk to the actual manager of your place or just the assistant?"

"She said the assistant."

"Well, then we should wait to talk to the manager."

"Nicky says he'll be gone for a few days on vacation. But I really need to get this place cleaned up for the inspection. She offered to help clean

the carpets, too. You think you can help her? It's a big job, Michelle."
She sounded so tired.

"Sheesh. Of course I'll help. You know, what you really need to do
is stop worrying so much. Remember our talk about how it aggravates
your breathing?"

"Uh-huh." So help me, there was a catch in her voice and I knew suddenly that this might very well be the straw that broke the proverbial
camel's back. "Michelle, I'm such a failure."

"*What?* You're kiddin', right? *You?* Look at all that you've accom-
plished. Skydiving? Deep sea fishing? Driving a *car?*"

"No, I mean like being successful at something, like a job. Saving
money, too." Her voice broke and so did my heart, a little. "I've just
never been successful at those kinds of things."

"Huh," I said. "I guess it kind of depends on how you define successful. If you think money and prestige is important . . . Well, *I* don't, not
at all."

My ear was getting hot. My palms were sweaty. I shifted the phone to
the other ear. No improvement there. "What about your transition? I'd
say that was quite an accomplishment."

"I *had* to do that," Mishelle said. Her voice was steady. "Or I'd have
died."

"Yes, and you're still alive, aren't you?"

"Ya got me there," she admitted. "For a little while longer, anyway."

I waited, knowing what was coming.

"Michelle, how much time do you think I have?"

I tried to keep my own voice confident and steady and it worked,
mostly. Even with sweaty palms and a feeling of walking a tightrope on
a windy day. "I have no idea. And neither does anyone else. Only God
knows that and He's not talking so let's not worry about it, okay?"

I paused to take a deep breath and felt the imaginary wind subside.
"Did you look at that list of questions I gave you?"

"About the caretaker?"

"No, the ones I gave you in Braille. The ones about how to redirect
your thinking if you start feeling depressed and negative."

"Just a second. They're in my pouch." I could hear her shifting around.
"Okay, got it."

"Read them." My voice was firm and in control. "What's number
one?"

"'What am I happy about right now?'"

"Okay, answer that for me, please."

Her voice was just as firm. "I'm happy you're in my life and that you care for me."

Me, too. "What's number two?"

"'What am I excited about in my life right now?' Oh, that's an easy one." She cackled. "I'm excited about seeing Chris this weekend!"

"Good. Keep going. What's three?"

"'What am I proud about right now?'"

"And?"

She was silent. Then: "I don't know."

"Sure you do. Think about it."

The pause was longer, her breathing calm though, and I knew she was as contemplative as she'd ever be. "I guess I'd have to say that I'm proud that I've been fairly independent all of my life, considering that I'm blind."

"And you have every reason to be proud of yourself. It's a long list of accomplishments. That's why I think this talk of success is pretty silly. How 'bout four?"

"'What am I grateful for?'"

"Tell me, please."

"You had to ask? You and your family, of course. You're the best thing that's ever happened to me."

I swallowed a big lump. "Thanks. But there must be others."

"Nicholas and Blue. They're my friends, too."

I let it pass. "Okay. Five?"

"'What am I enjoying in my life right now?' Huh, the time I spend with you and your family. Playing chess. Teaching Chris Braille." She chuckled. "A no-brainer, sweetie."

I didn't sigh, quite. "I'm flattered, Mishelle. Honestly. Six?"

"'What am I joyful about?'" She snickered. "You. Your family. Big surprise, huh?"

"You have a one-track mind." I smiled, despite myself. "Seven."

"'What are you committed to doing in your life right now?' Well, I guess I should say that I should worry less, huh?"

"Something like that," I agreed. "Eight."

"'Who loves you and who do you love?' 'Baby, who do you love?' " she half-sang, all scratchy and ending with a cough. I tried not to let the wince show in my voice.

"C'mon, this is the last one. It's the most important, too. Who do you love?"

"You and your family. Nick and Blue." Somehow her voice sounded shy, the scratch faded into the grain of her words. "My family; all of them. Lynn and Nicky; bless her anyway. Renee and Charles. I miss them a lot."

"And who loves you, Mishelle?"

Her voice came back clear and steady; full of certainty: "*You* do. Your family loves me." She paused. "Everyone that I love; loves me. *Yes.*"

Her breathing had returned to normal, as normal as it would ever be. "Okay, I feel a little better." With a chuckle: "But you're just avoiding my question, you know."

"I told you. Honestly, I don't know. But you know that I'd tell you if I thought it was time, don't you?"

"Yep." There was not a tremor to be heard in her voice. I had to marvel for a moment, listening to her. "I'd expect it. And who knows? I might get another two or three years. Wouldn't that be great?"

"Well, *yeah.* Jeez, you might as well move in with us if you hang on that long, y'know?"

A short giggle, almost a hiccup: "Deal. But first let's get this one cleaned up, okay? Still coming over for the interview tomorrow?"

"Yes to both. I'll be there about eleven-thirty. We'll go over the questions; the other questions about the caretaker's background, alright?"

Mishelle sighed finally and it was a nice sigh: relaxed and relaxing. "Wonderful, Michelle. See you tomorrow."

"Hey, Mishelle?"

"What?"

"Turn on your stereo. Or your TV. You're not going to be evicted, okay? Enjoy yourself. It's not against the law."

Her giggle was very rewarding. "Okay. Thanks. I love you."

"Love you, too. 'Night." I clicked off, racked the phone on the charger and looked at it for a while, smiling. "Wouldn't it be nice?" I whispered to it. "Wouldn't it?"

* * *

I showed up on time: about a half an hour before the interview; eleven-thirty Sunday morning. While Nicholas barked and did his happy dance, she put her face up for a kiss.

"Hey, you." I stood, looking her over. "Another new dress? Where's this one from?"

"Newport News. I love their selections."

"Yeah, I guess, but it's a bit too risqué for an interview. If you're going to wear a halter dress, you should make sure you don't show too much cleavage. Let me adjust those ties." I put down my bag, bent over her again and re-tied the straps. She giggled.

"*What* cleavage?"

I fussed with the front a bit. "Trust me, you've got cleavage. True, you ain't no Dolly Parton, but if you were to bend over, a boob might pop out and that would not be cute."

More giggles: "No, that would definitely end the interview in a hurry!"

I stopped fussing and stood. "Well, you don't seem nervous and that's a good sign."

Mishelle shook her head. "Nope, I'm not nervous at all 'cause *you're* here." She reached out for my hand. Our fingers linked. "Thanks for coming."

I squeezed gently, again feeling that strength flowing from her; comforting and reassuring. "Of course, sweetie. Where's . . .?"

"Hi!"

I looked up. Lynn had poked her head around the corner from the hallway. Her smile was infectious. "Hi, there! I didn't know you were here. Good, you should ask some questions, too. Sometimes three heads are better than two. What's this lady's name?"

"Annette." Lynn came into the room, wiping her hands on a towel. She'd obviously been cleaning the bathroom. "She seems really nice."

Inwardly, I groaned a little. "That's, um, that's good. How much does she know about Mishelle?"

Her smile grew uneasy. "Well, nothing, actually. I've always found it best to just wait and see how they act around Mishelle before deciding."

Uh-oh. I tried to put my best face on it: "Well! Alright, then. We'll just have to wing it, I guess. Let's go over these questions, shall we . . .?"

It could have been an utter disaster. Instead, it went pretty well and I found myself breathing more than few sighs of relief, there and again during the process.

Annette was a small, pleasantly plump woman; middle-aged with a comforting, relaxed manner and not once did she even blink at Mishelle's appearance. She addressed Mishelle in her proper gender and answered all of the questions in a straight-forward, professional manner. Mishelle's trans status was never directly addressed, mostly because I didn't consider it relevant by the end of the interview.

Neither did Annette, apparently.

I noticed that I was the only one asking questions, though. Throughout it all, Mishelle and Lynn remained silent, uttering nary a peep.

When she left, I sat for a moment, looking down at the list in my lap with my scribbled notes in the margins; pondering things.

"Well, what do you think?"

I looked up. Lynn and Mishelle were both looking at me expectantly. That is: Mishelle had her head tilted in my direction; down and slightly to the left as she did when she was listening intently. It was Lynn who had spoken.

"Hmm." I cleared my throat. "Well, I think she's very nice. She's quite professional. What do you two think?"

"Oh, I think she's really nice," from Lynn, whose expression was showing a vast relief. "Me, too," from Mishelle, who was wearing the tiniest hint of a *gotcha* smile. I doubt if anyone else might have noticed.

But I sure did.

"Okay. Then let's give her a shot at it. I suggest that you have her come over when Lynn is here to get her accustomed to the routine and observe how you two get along. Lynn, you can show her the ropes: meds and so forth." I paused, tapping my pen on the list, frowning at it.

"Well, I wouldn't feel comfortable alone with her," Mishelle commented. "I'd rather Lynn or Nicky was here while she's here."

I nodded. "Well, sure. I suggest you start her out at about two or three hours a week and see how things develop. I'm confident she'll integrate just fine into everybody's schedules. By the way, where's Nicky? I thought she'd be here for this."

Lynn glanced at Mishelle before replying. "She called me and said she'd be late. It's my day off but I just wanted to be here for the interview."

"Well, thanks. It was awfully nice . . . ."

The door opened and the subject of our discussion breezed in like we'd been waiting for her. "Hi, everybody! Hey, Mishelle! You're wearing that dress!" To Lynn: "Thanks for filling in for me, hon. I'll pay ya back." To me: "Well, how did it go?"

I shrugged, opening my mouth. *Better late than never . . .* But Mishelle beat me to it:

"We all think it went well. We're going to give her a try." Her chin tilted up with just the merest hint of defiance. "Sorry you couldn't be here."

Nicky shrugged and opened her mouth, but Lynn rose and said, rather wryly, 'Thanks, Michelle. I appreciate you keeping me in the loop on this. Will you excuse me? I have some things to do at home. 'Bye, everybody."

She nodded to me, at Nicky, patted Mishelle's shoulder and left.

Short and sweet, I said to myself. While I was wondering what to say to fill the sudden silence, Michelle piped up:

"She sounds really flexible, Nicky. She can fill in when you're sick or unable to make it for . . . whatever reason."

Nicky shrugged. "Cool. Sounds good to me." She smiled at my friend. "Hey, that dress really looks cute." She turned to me. "*I* picked that dress out for her. What do you think?"

She was smiling but there was a belligerent glint deep in her eyes.

I gave her my best Hollywood smile in return. "I *love* it! I think you have great taste, Nicky." *Take that, young lady.* "Everything you've picked out for Mishelle looks really nice on her."

Maybe I shouldn't have encouraged her. "Oh, yeah? Well, I know that Mishelle likes things that she can *feel*, you know? Touch. Beads 'n stuff. Not like Lynn. I swear, I think Lynn must think that Mishelle wants to dress like an old lady or something. Have you *seen* the hideous shit she's picked out for Mishelle to wear? Huh!" She snorted. "Maybe she just picked them out hoping Mishelle wouldn't like them and give them to her."

I opened my mouth. Closed it. Tried again: "Well, we all have our strengths and weaknesses, Nicky. You do a really good job picking out Mishelle's clothes and she always looks well dressed while Lynn . . . well, Lynn has . . . other strengths," I finished, sounding absurdly lame.

I glanced at Mishelle and didn't like what I saw: she had a set to her jaw that told me she was trying really hard to remain silent. She was beginning to pant, too.

So I feinted: "Ah, Nicky? What's this situation with the assistant manager? The noise problem?"

To her credit, she kept cool and didn't even blink. "Yeah, she says she's had complaints about her TV being too loud and all the robots keeping people awake after midnight, you know? Also, there's too many people coming and going at all hours, she says. They may have to move her."

I almost came up out of my chair. *Like hell they will!* Instead, I kept my seat and said as casually as possible, "Well, this is the *assistant* manager, right? The second in command?"

She glared at me. "Right. So?"

"Well, the *assistant* manager doesn't have that kind of authority." I stressed that word ever so lightly. "I think we should wait until the manager, what's his name?"

Her glare went up a notch in intensity. "Curtis."

"I think we should ask Curtis what options are available right now," I said smoothly. "When does he come back from vacation?"

"I'm not sure." Her mother should have told her that scowling like that would leave wrinkles.

"Well, let's not stress Mishelle about this, okay?" I gave her a sweet smile. "I've noticed it tends to affect her breathing and we don't want *that*, do we? I understand that you're thinking of cleaning Mishelle's carpets for the inspection next week?"

Quickly changing the subject on certain people is sometimes better than a kick in the pants. Her expression was bewildered. "Uh, yeah. Yeah, I was, like maybe Wednesday?"

I gave my smile a few more watts and she blinked at me. "Nicky, that is certainly above and beyond the call! You should be commended for that. Good on ya!"

"Thanks," she muttered, looking a bit stunned.

"Don't mention it. Please." I looked at Mishelle and there was the merest ghost of a *gotcha* grin tugging at the edge of her mouth.

Back to Nicky: "I was just thinking: some area rugs over the top of the clean carpets would go a long way toward extending their life. It makes it easier to clean just one area at a time, too. What do you think?"

Nicky was starting to look a little glassy-eyed. "Uh, sure. I guess I could pick some up tomorrow or something. But I gotta go to the store right now and pick up dinner stuff." She shook herself. "Yeah. Groceries. Mishelle, you want anything special?"

In a quiet voice, my friend said, "No, not really."

"Okay." Nicky looked at me, a hint of that cocksure edge still deep in her brown eyes. "I'll see ya later, Michelle. Carpet Day."

"Carpet Day!" I said cheerfully. "Sounds good. See you!"

"'Bye." And she was out the door. It slammed but I don't think she intended it.

We sat for a minute in blessed silence; then Mishelle said in the same quiet voice: "Don't say it."

"I don't think I should have to."

She sighed. "Okay, she's a problem child. But it's *my* problem, isn't it?"

I shifted forward, leaning toward her. "Mishelle, she's a grown woman. She can make her own mistakes and deal with them. But she doesn't need to make you part of them, too."

She shifted too and I think I saw her wince. "Oh, I know. But I care about her, Michelle. I really do."

"I know. I respect that. I'd never come between you two." She shifted again and I *did* see her wince. "I just hate to see you get so agitated when she gets chatty like that. Hey, do you need a backrub?"

"Wouldn't hurt," she grunted.

"Okay." I got up, perched on the arm of her chair and dug in; thumbing her shoulders and neck muscles and smoothing out the kinks. She moaned softly at the tender spots, so I kept it low key until she relaxed and her breathing had eased.

"I think we should call Curtis."

"And if he's not home?"

"Then we leave a message."

She nodded. "Okay, that sounds like a plan."

I dialed the number she had programmed on her landline and got him immediately; to Mishelle's surprise but not to mine, not really. After introducing myself, I handed her the phone.

"Hi, Curtis? This is Mishelle Woodring. Yeah, good, how are you? Uh, Curtis, I heard from one of my caregivers that your assistant manager told her that there have been complaints about my TV and stereo being too loud." She took a second or two to pant gently. "And my electronic aids, you know, the voice programs? Really? Well, she says I might be evicted. Yes, that's right, I said evicted." Pant-pant. "You don't? Huh, how 'bout that." She put a hand over the phone. "He says he doesn't know where she got that idea. What? Uh, she told me your assistant manager told her. Yeah, that's what I thought, too. Okay, thanks for looking into it for me. Sure, call me if you hear any complaints, okay?"

She handed me the phone and I hung it up. I looked at her; smiling, knowing that she could feel it like sunshine.

"Another crisis solved?" I inquired.

"I guess so." She panted, but there was little urgency behind it now. Long speeches like that were always difficult for her. "He says just what you said: the assistant manager doesn't have that kind of authority. He told me he'd check it out, but he hasn't heard any complaints." She smiled back at me. "So, yeah. Emergency over. Thanks."

"Good." I got up, went over and kissed her cheek. "Okay, I've gotta go pick up Chris. Dave has a school board meeting tonight so how about if we just order a pizza or something? I don't have the time to pick up dinner stuff."

"Pepperoni . . ."

"And black olive. I know. Be back around six. Nicky's not planning to stay, is she?" I asked with mock alarm.

"No, no. She's just going shopping for me. She'll drop it off and then leave." She panted and then added, "Thanks, Michelle."

"You're welcome, girlfriend." I gave her another kiss and left.

* * *

"So, are you excited to see her?"

My son bounced up and down in his seat. "*Am* I? You bet! I beat some guys in chess at camp but they showed me some cool new moves and I want to try them out."

"Well, we'll see how she's feeling and you just might get a chance." I parked the Toyota in front her place and we got out, the pizza balanced in my hand, Chris with the bag holding the sodas.

Her door swung open and I gasped. The wave of heat that rolled out at me might have been from an oven, it was *that* hot. All I could think was: *oh, no!*

Chris pushed past me, went to Mishelle and gave her a hug. She returned it. I could see the beads of sweat dotting her brow as her face tipped up over his shoulder.

He released her and looked over his shoulder at me. "*Mom.* Can we *do* something? It's like an oven in here!"

I was already at the air conditioner and opening the control panel. "I know, Cee-Boo. Give me a moment." I looked in the water compartment: it was empty. Hurrying; I filled it and tried the switch. No luck. I plugged it into a different outlet with the same result.

It was completely dead. I rose.

"We need to get a cross draft in here, right now." I started opening windows.

Chris was still crouched by Mishelle. "How can you stand it?" he asked softly.

"I can't," she panted. "But I'm glad to see you, little buddy."

He mopped the sweat from her face with a tissue. "Me, too. I missed you."

Her hand found his cheek. "Same here. You have fun?"

"Yeah, but I thought about you a lot."

"Well, that goes double for me."

Chris looked up at me. I was staring in disbelief at the thermometer on the wall near her computer station. It read one hundred and four degrees. "Mom, do you need any help?"

I snapped out of it. "Yes! Get that portable fan from the bathroom and bring it into the kitchen. Then you can help Mishelle outside. It's cooler out there than it is in here."

When Chris brought me the fan, I opened the freezer door and placed the fan in front of it, putting a finger to my lips when he realized what I was doing. I didn't want her to worry about her frozen foods melting.

My son got it immediately. He nodded and went outside to set up a folding chair for Mishelle and then helped her into it while I set up another fan in front of the opened front door.

Nicholas bolted for freedom once he realized the door was wide open. He raced around the parking lot, barking his pointy little head off while I set up the last fan in her bedroom window.

When I joined my son and our friend on the front porch, I could see that she was already feeling better. Nicholas wandered close when he smelled the pizza and plunked his butt down, watching us with great expectations, the little mooch.

"Hungry?"

Her smile was sincere if somewhat wan. "Starvin'."

"Then let's chow down."

It wasn't the most elegant dinner I've ever had but outdoor dining does have its good points; especially if the alternative is a snack in a sauna. We were peacefully feeding our faces when I looked up and noticed a woman striding across the parking lot toward us, an expression remarkably like an irritable eagle's plastered across her face. It didn't suit her very well.

Chris saw my frown and tilted his head to one side, trying to see more. "Trouble?"

"I don't know. Let me handle it." I stood, wiping my hands with a paper towel. "Hi!"

"Hello." She halted and looked us over, the grumpy expression dominating her features. "What's going on here?"

I offered her my hand; still a bit greasy, I'm afraid. "I'm Michelle Alexander, a friend of Mishelle's. This is my son Chris."

My son waved at her with a big slab of pizza clutched in his fist. "Hi!"

"Uh, hi." She took my hand. "I'm Anne, the assistant manager. What are you folks doing out here?"

Oh ho, said I to myself. "Well, we're just trying to cool Mishelle's apartment down. It's over a hundred degrees in there! Much cooler out here. Want some pizza? Pepperoni and black olive."

She waved it away, her expression changing to vague distaste. "No. Thanks. Why's her apartment so hot? Mine isn't."

Somehow, I just *knew* that this woman didn't receive many invitations to play gin rummy in the recreation hall. "Air conditioner broke down. We'll replace it in a day or two. In the meantime, you won't mind if she keeps the doors and windows open, will you? Until her place cools down?"

Reluctantly, as if it hurt to say it: "I guess not. But put that screen back in the window when you leave, okay?"

Brightly: "Of course! Promise. Sure you won't have a snack with us?"

Anne shuddered visibly. "No, thanks. Really. I have stuff to do." She turned and stalked away, presumably to find a can to kick.

Not once did she acknowledge Mishelle's presence.

"Well." I looked down at the two of them: my friend and my son. "She's a jolly sort. Maybe we should move back inside if it's cool enough."

My son was grinning proudly at me and I want to smack his bottom and kiss him; both. My best friend was also wearing a smile quite like his.

"You," she said cheerfully. "Are a motivational genius, you know that?"

"So I've been told. Let me help you."

We moved back inside and it was much cooler. I checked the thermometer. It had dropped to a reasonable eighty-two degrees. The contents of her freezer were still good and hard, so I closed the door and aimed the fan more or less in the direction of the front room, hoping the residual cool air would flow that way.

"Wow, it's a *lot* cooler in here," Mishelle commented. "How did you do that?"

I winked at Chris. He winked back. "Oh, the fans just blew some of the cool air in from outside, that's all."

"Well, whatever you did, it's much nicer in here. I might be able to get some sleep tonight."

"Sleep would be good," Chris said solemnly. I could tell he was fighting down a laugh, though. "Is it too late to play some chess?"

I glanced out the door at the setting sun. "'Fraid so, sweetie. I have to get you home and then pick up your Dad."

"Truck in the shop again?"

"Yup." I bent over to kiss Mishelle. "See you tomorrow, girlfriend."

"Hey," Chris protested. "Can't I come, too?"

I smiled fondly at him. "Sorry, Cee-Boo, but I'm just swinging by on my lunch hour. I won't have time to pick you up."

"Aw . . . that's not fair." He frowned. I think he wanted to do a little can-kicking himself, but Mishelle spoke up, that wicked little grin tugging at the corners of her mouth:

"How 'bout next weekend, little buddy?"

I wanted to smack her bottom, too. Yes and kiss her, which I did. "Okay. I have to check with Dave and see if he has any plans, but I think I can make it work."

My best friend grinned up at me. "I think you can make *anything* work," she said cheerfully.

"Not everything," I said. "C'mon, Chris."

CHAPTER NINETEEN

A Light in Your Life

THE DAY'S SCHEDULE WAS A LIGHT ONE, so naturally I was looking forward to seeing her at lunch time. I could hang out for a while, chat and generally goof off a little bit; one of the nicer aspects of my job I've been careful not to abuse.

She was still in a good mood; always a positive sign. The more she remained in a positive space, the longer she might have a chance, or so I told myself every day; usually in front of the bathroom mirror that has my power words posted on it as well as a dozen other mantras I find useful.

Oh, and prayer, too. Let's not forget that.

"Hey, you." I gave her a hug and almost jumped out of my shoes when I saw there was somebody else present: a trim-looking fellow sitting behind her computer who looked up at me, nodded and went back to peering at the screen. His fingers flew across the keys nearly as nimbly as hers.

"Hi?" I said tentatively. He waved a hand in my direction, never taking his eyes from what he was doing. If I'd seen him on the street, I would have taken him for a soccer coach; too athletic to be parked behind a terminal, pounding keys all day. Never judge a book by its cover, though.

My friend said, "Oh, I'm sorry! Michelle, this is Mike, my computer guru. He's troubleshooting some problems I have with my machine."

"Oh? What's the problem?" I should have kept my mouth shut . . .

Without looking up, Mike the computer guru said, "In DOS, she's got an at-fault switch stuck open, which tells me there's a bug in the source code. I can do a stack dump to make absolutely sure but it won't tell me *why*. At least, it'll tell me *where* exactly it's occurring but I might have to go into the BIOS, too and make sure that's not corrupted as well. Then re-format the whole shebang."

"Yeah, but if you do that, I'd have to reload the whole program and customize it all over again," Mishelle protested. "That took *days* last time."

"I can save the root files and append those," he grunted, his long, bony fingers stabbing at the keys. "Question is: is that what caused it in the first place?"

He glanced up at her from under shaggy eyebrows, looking like a disapproving Papa Bear. "If you didn't have so many bells and whistles on this thing, it'd run a lot faster, Mishelle. You need a bigger hard drive, too. Even with two hundred gig, you're running out of room. Some extra side RAM would be nice, y'know? Every time you boot up the Weather Channel, this thing has a shit fit."

Well, I think I understood the last sentence but the rest could have been Greek, for all I knew. They chatted back and forth, using a lot of acronyms and words that meant something important, I'm sure, but were largely wasted on me.

I sat; hands folded in my lap, thinking that I hadn't quite expected to spend my lunch hour this way and wondering if I should have brought a book to read.

He packed up his tools finally (I think they were tools. He might have borrowed them from the set of *Star Trek*.), said goodbye with a mumble and another wave of his hand and left; not quite jogging.

"Whew!" Mishelle commented. "Glad he's gone. He tires me out. When he gets started, I have a hard time following him. I'm not sure I completely understood what he was trying to tell me to do."

I had to smile. "No kiddin'? Why didn't you just ask him?"

"I didn't want to look like a complete idiot," she said, deadpan and then we both cracked up, giggling like lunatics.

The doorbell rang, abbreviating our giggles. Nicholas started barking.

"Now what?" I said, annoyed. So much for a few quiet minutes with my best friend!

"UPS, I think," said Mishelle. "Be a dear and let him in, would you?"

I did and it was. He had a smallish package for her, politely touched his brown cap to me and her when she signed for it and hot-footed it back to his truck; busy fellow. I watched with curiosity as she opened it.

"What's that?"

"Ah, it's my new money scanner!" Mishelle exclaimed. "I've been waiting for this ever since that cash went missing." She reached down and picked up her lockbox from next to the chair and opened it, removed a wad of bills thick enough to choke a horse and fiddled with the scanner. She fed a bill into it and it said in a flat mechanical voice:

"Ten dollars."

"It talks!"

"Yep." She grinned. "Cool, huh? Now I can tell exactly how much I have on hand and no one can cheat me by handing me a dollar and telling me it's a ten."

"Who," I asked, very cautiously, "Did that? And why? And what are you doing with all that money?"

"Ask me no questions . . ."

"And I'll tell you no lies. Right." I sighed. "I assume this has something to do with that street pot you buy? Look, why don't you just stick with the medicinal marijuana? Why do you spend your money on the other stuff?"

She looked smug. "Variety."

I shrugged. "Okay, I see your point, even if I don't agree. But you shouldn't leave money lying around. Do you want me to deposit it for you?"

"Please." When I took the roll of bills, she caught at my wrist with her other hand. "Michelle, do you know how much this scanner cost?"

"No, but I can guess."

"And you'd probably be off by at least half. I'm paying my bills, Michelle." Her voice was low and urgent. "I'm paying off those cards. One by one. In a few months, I could have them almost done and then maybe they'll raise my limit and I can . . . I can . . ."

I stared at her. "Pay for the SRS with them."

She nodded.

"You never give up, do you?"

She shook her head.

My staring was rude and I knew she could feel it but I couldn't take my eyes off her. "Even now? When you . . .?"

Mishelle smiled. "I told you that I would, even if I died on the table. At least I'd be female. Not . . . this." Her smile turned sly. "If I did manage to, you know, somehow survive it, would you be my nurse?"

I found myself smiling foolishly in return; bobbing my head up and down, feeling strangely giddy. "Sure. I'll be your private duty nurse."

"Thanks." She squeezed my wrist and released it.

"Can I ask you a very personal question?"

"As if you haven't already. What?"

"The SRS. Is it . . . I mean, will it be, y'know, functional? Will you be able to . . .?"

"Do the horizontal bop?" She grinned. "Well, I would hope so! Yeah, the truth is; you keep most if not all the sensation and after you heal, even an experienced gynecologist can't tell the difference."

I was awed. "No shit." (I seldom employ expletives for emphasis.) "How much will this cost?"

"About twenty thousand here in the States. Maybe twelve in Thailand. You rike Thai foo', missy?" she asked in an atrocious Asian accent.

My blue eyes were wide open. "Sure," I said faintly. *Twenty? Twelve?* Actually, when I thought about it; that didn't seem too unreasonable a cost. "Love it. The hotter: the better."

"Sushi?"

"Sushi's good."

"Mm, I love wasabi and ginger," she purred. "Shrimp! Hey, I was thinking . . ."

"Again?"

"Smartass. No, about this power of attorney stuff. Since we're talking about me dying or becoming incapacitated, I think I'd like to have you with POA. What do you think?"

I sat as if I'd been nailed to the chair. "I can't do that, Mishelle."

"Why not?"

"Because you're a former patient of mine. It's a conflict of interest. And I can tell you that it would look damned peculiar to all concerned, from the cops to the insurance company. You do have insurance, don't you?"

"Yeah, but it's a little bitty policy, like ten grand or something."

"Doesn't matter if it's ten cents. It's a conflict of interest and I can't help you there. Do you know any lawyers?"

Mishelle shook her head. "Nope. Just that one guy I did the work for a few years ago and I'd rather not talk to him. Huh, maybe I can ask Arlene, my counselor in Seattle. The resource center up there ought to have a few numbers I can call. Nuts," and now she looked annoyed. "I kind of wanted *you* to do it. It would have made things so much simpler. It seems like everybody wants my stuff when I'm gone, like Nicky and Lynn. And I'm not even in the ground yet."

She held out her hand and I took it, the wad of bills still in my other. "You seem to be the only one who *doesn't* want anything."

The only thing I want, I can't have . . . My voice was steady: "So you think you might be dying, then?"

"I know I probably won't make it through another winter. And I want my stuff to go to the right people."

"Like what? Who?"

"Well, Nicky and Lynn want my computers and Lynn wants Blue and Nicky wants Nicholas." She added hastily: "I wanted you to take Nicholas, but since he's not house-trained, I know you can't."

"No," I said, a bit numb. "I can't. What do *you* want?"

"Well, I want Nina, that little blind girl down at the Center for the Blind to have all my aids: my Brailler and my voice robots. This." She held up the money scanner and grinned impishly. "She's such a sweet little girl and I think it would help her a lot."

"She *is* sweet." She'd told me about Nina before and even showed me a picture of a gap-toothed little girl with brown hair in pigtails and an engaging grin.

"And I really do want Nicky to have my old computer, you know. She wants to go back to college and finish her nursing degree . . ."

Oh, dear, I thought.

"And I think it would really help her. Oh, and Dave can have my stereo and CD collection. I think he'd like that."

I put a hand to my forehead. "Stop right there."

"If he could take Blue; that would be really nice because he's an inside cat and Lynn may want to let him out at night. Chris can have one of my Brailllers, too."

"Please stop." It was getting to be too much.

"Hey."

I took my hand down and looked up at her.

"I don't want to upset you. I just want this done right, you know? And if I make it through to Christmas, I'm going to spoil you rotten! *All* of you," she added, as if it were necessary.

I forced myself to laugh. "I have no doubt, girlfriend. We plan to spoil you, too."

"Good. Then it's settled. I'm not going anywhere soon. Can we talk about something else?"

Swallow the lump, square my shoulders, take a deep breath . . . doing all that was just a loosely connected series of reflexes I'd learned in the last three months. It didn't make me feel any better, just more prepared.

"Best idea I've heard all day." I glanced at my watch as her time robot announced the hour. "Let's discuss Carpet Day before I leave. I have a patient scheduled at one thirty."

"Okay, I talked to Nicky and she wants to clean carpets on Friday. She wants to put down some area rugs, like you suggested, before the inspection."

"And when's the inspection?"

"I don't know. I think it's a week from Friday. Nicky said she'd find out for me."

"Hope so," I muttered.

"Oh, relax. She *wants* to help, Michelle."

"I know. I'm just . . . never mind. Okay, how 'bout all of us coming over to help?"

"*All* of you?"

"The whole gang. It'll make things go faster, speed up the process so you aren't so stressed. Chris can keep you company while the rest of us tote things outside and clean. If it's a week from Friday, then we have plenty of time to get this place ship-shape."

"I hope so," Mishelle said, rather anxiously. "I don't want to have to move."

"You won't have to move! Really." I kissed her cheek. "Okay, Friday then and expect us nice and early, like eight."

"Sure." She put a thick envelope into my hand. "This is for Chris."

I looked at it, hefted it. "More secret messages? One of these days, I'm going to learn your little code, girlfriend. And then you're *both* busted."

She smirked: *gotcha!* "I'll believe it when I see it. And since I'm blind, that might take a while, huh?"

"Oh, you . . ." I patted her on the arm and hurried out the door.

* * *

Nicky kept her word. She was there, bright and early on Friday morning when we arrived. Parked next to the porch were two carpet steamers, a big, industrial size shop-vac and a huge roll of dark green indoor/outdoor carpeting. She gestured at it.

"I got this instead of the area rugs 'cause it was lots cheaper. I figure we can cut it to fit and just put it down over the existing carpet in each room."

I sized it up. It would work, even if the color was a bit bland and lifeless. "Yeah, good idea, Nicky. Shall we get started?"

Our crew swung into action.

Dave started hauling out the big furniture, including Michelle's recliner, followed by our hostess herself who appeared unreasonably pleased to be carried bodily by a big strong man. Her arms wrapped comfortably around his neck as he carried her through the door; the two of them looking rather like newlyweds for a moment and it made me smile. He deposited her neatly into her chair in the parking lot and she sighed; relaxing into her temporary role as sidewalk supervisor.

Nicholas hopped up into Mishelle's lap when Dave set her down; wagging his tail and looking absurdly pleased himself about the proceedings. Chris planted his rear on an overturned milk crate next to her chair and they began conversing in low tones.

I grabbed my measuring tape and clipboard, started jotting numbers and sketching the shape of the carpet sections we would soon be cutting.

Nicky attacked the walls and baseboards with spray cleaner and a pile of towels, a single-minded gleam in her eyes as she scrubbed away years of dust and smoke and things better left unsaid.

I caught myself watching her while Dave and I took measurements, musing that she had a rather pleasant air about her when she was concentrating on a task; the-girl-next-door in a rough 'n tumble sort of way.

I snorted. And who was *I* to talk? Me: a country bumpkin from Butte, Montana, a clueless small-town girl who just happened to go to nursing school and make good?

I sighed and helped my husband unroll the carpet. It had occurred to me just then that Nicky was someone I might have been myself, somewhere, sometime and maybe the reason I didn't like her much really had nothing to do with her at all.

On my way out to the truck to get some tools, I saw Chris sitting with Mishelle, still conversing in quiet tones. I smiled at them as I passed, thinking that this was one assignment my son would really enjoy. They truly were like brother and sister, even to the shortcuts in their conversation:

"You see anything different with your eyes closed?"

"'Stead of open?"

My son nodded. "Yeah."

"Really, really dark."

"That's black, I think."

"I figured."

"Open?"

"Like thick fog."

"That's gray. Now put sparkles on the fog and that's silver."

"Cool. What about gold?"

Chris thought. "Like yellow, only shiny."

She smiled. "Sunlight."

"Yeah. Sunlight that's shiny."

"Cool."

"Yeah. Hey."

"Huh?"

"You had a choice, would you rather be deaf or blind?"

"Blind. Deaf, I couldn't hear music."

"Oh." My son thought about that. "Yeah. Me too."

I went back inside.

The organized bedlam was beginning to show results. Nicky was done with the walls and baseboards in the front room and had started in on the carpets, that mad gleam still afire in her eyes. Her hair was pulled back, she had smudges on both cheeks and I'd never seen her look so content.

Dave and I had completed cutting the bedroom and bathroom carpet so I went looking under the sink for some cleaner for the baseboards. I found some and next to it was a spray bottle of dog repellent. I took that too and showed it to Dave.

"We should spray some of this along the baseboards and furniture."

He took it, squinted at it and gave it a shake. Liquid sloshed. "Hmm, not much left. Was there any more?"

"I'll look," Nicky offered. She ducked into the kitchen and came back with different bottle and handed it to my husband. He took it, did a double-take and began laughing.

"Did any of you actually *use* this?" he chortled.

Nicky looked puzzled. "Well, yeah, I think Lynn bought it and used it when she first started caretaking for Mishelle. Right after she moved in here. Why?"

My husband was on the verge of losing it entirely. "Ohmy*god*! Look at it . . .!" He showed us the label: *Dog Scent*. There was a cartoon of a dog lifting his leg on a bush, a dopey grin on the mutt's face.

Nicky let out a whoop and slapped her thigh. I just stared. My husband laughed like a loon: "Well, at least now we know why that dog pees everywhere! Did she spray this on *everything*?"

"As far as I know." Nicky's face was bright red and she was giggling between hiccups. I said:

"Well, yeah, that would explain it alright."

"Oh, man." Nicky was about to pop from alternating giggles and hiccups. "Wait'll I tell Lynn! She'll be mortified!"

I was developing a pretty good case of the giggles myself. "Oh, no! Oh Nicky, that would be awful! Don't!"

"Why not? Wouldn't *you* wanna know?"

"Okay, but I think she may as well forget about a refund!"

We finished around three that afternoon and moved Mishelle back into her place. She sniffed, taking in the clean aromas. "Nice job, everyone. Thanks." She held out her hand and Chris put her coffee in it. She took a sip before continuing: "I wish I could have helped."

"You did fine," said Dave. "You kept Chris occupied . . ."

"And supervised," Nicky pointed out.

"And kept Nicholas from underfoot," I commented. "That's a big one right there."

"So now you're ready for the inspection next week and there should be no problems, right?" Dave said cheerfully.

"Uh-huh."

"What's that, Dad?" Chris pointed at the bottle Dave held. There were sudden grins all around.

"Uh, just something this place definitely doesn't need," said my husband, obviously struggling to contain his laughter.

"Like what?" Mishelle asked.

It was Nicky's sudden attack of the Hiccups That Wouldn't Quit that did it. We all cracked up.

Chris stared at us in turn like we'd collectively lost our marbles and they were even now rolling around on the new carpet underfoot. Mishelle waited patiently, a long-suffering expression on her face.

When the three of us had run down enough, she inquired: "I assume you're going to let me in on the joke some day?"

That set us off again. "Dog repellant!" Dave gasped, leaning against the fridge and holding his sides.

"Dog *attract*-ant!" Nicky giggled between hiccups. Her face was bright red again. I was feeling kind of giddy myself.

"Lynn . . ." I stopped, started over again: "Lynn bought some spray she thought was dog repellent." I wiped my eyes, feeling like an idiot. My sides hurt, too. "Only it was dog attractant. That's why . . ." I couldn't go on.

Understanding dawned on my friend's face like that morning's sunrise. "Oh! I get it! That's why Nicholas . . ." Abruptly, she started cackling like a crazed chicken. "No wonder he pees everywhere! Oh, that poor little guy!"

The subject of our collective mirth was staring at us just like Chris. Both of them cocked their heads and then looked at each other, which set us all off again.

Dave finally wiped his eyes and said, "Ladies, it's been a lot of fun. Really. Let's do it again soon." Another snicker escaped him as he hoisted his tools and headed out the door.

Nicky hugged us both and departed. Her hiccups sounded as though they might be with her for a while. I gave Mishelle a kiss on the cheek and took Chris's hand.

"See you Monday, girlfriend. I'll drop by for a few minutes between patients, okay?"

She beamed up at me. "You guys are awesome," she declared. "Thanks, Michelle."

I had that weird double glow that comes from the satisfaction of a job well-done and a massive release of laughter-induced endorphins to go with it. "The pleasure was all mine, sweetie. C'mon, Chris."

"I still don't get it," he grumbled.

"I'll explain it to you on the way home."

* * *

Monday rolled around and I arrived at her place just in time to see the UPS truck pull away. Shaking my head, I went in.

"Okay, what did you order this time? And how much did it cost, dare I ask?"

"I was going to ask *you* where it's from. I forgot to ask the UPS guy."

I looked at it. "Home Shopping Network."

She squealed in delight and clapped her hands together. "Oh, goody! It's your birthday present!"

"My birthday?" I looked at the box again and back at her. "Mishelle, my birthday isn't until the seventh. And you didn't have to get me anything either."

"I know that. I *wanted* to."

"Oh, jeez." I looked at the box again. It showed a picture of a Tiffany lamp, a very nice one, apparently. "Well, I can hardly wait to see what's inside this great big box."

She smirked. "Well, you'll just to have to wait a couple weeks, won't you?"

"I can handle it. I'm all grown up."

She laughed. We chatted for a while longer, my glance occasionally straying to the box, but I managed to keep my mouth shut, fortunately. It didn't do me much good.

When I got home that evening, she called:

"Why didn't you tell me there was a picture of the lamp on the side of the box?"

Oops. "I, ah, didn't want to spoil the surprise. Who told you?"

"Lynn." Her tone was only mildly reproachful.

"Aw, nuts." I couldn't think of anything to say except: "Sorry, sweetie. I didn't want to hurt your feelings."

"I think I'm more hurt you kept me in the dark about it. I feel pretty silly."

"You have a point. I'm really sorry," and I was, truly.

She sighed. "That's okay. You can open it next time you come over."

"You're not going to make me wait?"

She giggled. "No, I won't make you wait. When?"

It took me off guard. "Uh, Wednesday evening?" I stammered. "That okay?"

She sounded puzzled. "Sure. Something wrong?"

"Uh, no! No, not at all. I'll see you Wednesday, okay?"

"Okay. You gonna be here for the inspection?"

"Ah, we'll talk about it Wednesday," I babbled. "I'll order some take-out for us. Okay?"

I could almost see her puzzled shrug. "Okay. Wednesday, then. 'Night."

"G'night, Mishelle." I snapped my phone closed and looked up. Dave was in the doorway, frowning slightly.

"You haven't told her yet?"

"I will Wednesday." I shuffled papers around on my desk.

"That's kind of short notice. Doesn't she expect you to be there for the inspection?"

I didn't quite glare at him. "Dave, this is *your* family we're visiting for four days. Are you suggesting I stay home and look after her?"

"Not at all," he said mildly. "I'm glad you're going. It's the first time we've taken a road trip as a family all summer."

I looked away, nodding, trying to cover my embarrassment. "Yes. Which is why I should go. Sorry. I'm just . . ."

He nodded back at me. "Worried about her."

I didn't say anything.

He closed his eyes and sighed. "I appreciate it, Michelle. I really do. But I can see that this is really tearing you apart, too."

"Dave, I'm *trying*, I really am." I gestured helplessly. "I know how much I've been neglecting things here and this is the only thing I can think of . . ."

"Stop." He crossed the room and wrapped me in a hug. For a moment, I could almost relax. Almost . . . "Stop beating yourself up. I know how much her friendship means to you and so do the boys. If you want to stay here and look after her, we'll understand. I mean that."

"I know," I mumbled, my voice muffled somewhat by his broad chest. "But I should go. I really should."

He patted my back and released me. "Okay. I respect your decision. Thanks." He looked down at me soberly. "Just don't let it affect you, okay?"

I tried out a smile and it didn't feel quite right, but I did it anyway. "Okay. Maybe Chris can teach me how to Braille while we're on the road."

He sighed. "Great. Just what I need: a couple of merry pranksters passing notes back and forth."

"Oh." My smile grew a little more at home. "You'll get used to it."

* * *

But I didn't get away clean. She called me later that evening, gasping for breath: "Hi."

"Hi. Hey, are you okay?"

"Uh no, not really. I feel like I'm suffocating." She was wheezing. I could feel the little hairs up and down my arms prickle in response. "I can't seem to catch my breath."

Now? I thought *Now?* "Did you take a Lorazepam?"

"Three."

"Oh, *dear*. Mishelle, do you need to go to the ER? Be honest."

"No, not yet. Just talk to me. Read to me or something."

So I did. I spoke quietly and gently and I can't remember anything I said that night, less than a month from the morning she finally breathed her last.

I remember the fear that clutched at me though, and how my palms sweated and how my heart hammered in my chest; wondering if I would hear the peculiar choking sound of Cheyne-Stokes breathing that means: *this is it.*

But it passed and her breathing slowed and she came back to me, one more time and if I'd known that evening . . .

Maybe I would have stayed. Maybe.

*   *   *

The deli delivery boy almost beat me into my usual parking space in front of her door. I got out, waving a twenty. "Hey, I'll pay for those!"

He shrugged and handed over a couple of big subs with everything, fished around in his bag and gave me my change. I went in.

"Hey, you!" I gave her a kiss and checked her color. Not bad but not especially good either. "Wait a minute before we eat. I want to get your vitals."

Her blood pressure was good and pulse steady, but her lungs sounded raspy. Not congested, as when she'd had her infection, just hoarse and wheezy. I didn't have enough knowledge of pulmonary diseases to interpret what I was hearing, but I knew we'd have to have a talk, soon.

I wasn't looking forward to it. There was enough on the menu for that night already.

The sandwiches were delicious, but I didn't have much appetite. Nervous, I guess. I finally put mine down, less than half-eaten and cleared my throat. "Hey, I have something to tell you."

"Mrmph?"

"Don't talk with your mouth full. Here, hold still." I leaned forward and dabbed a glob of mayo off her upper lip with a paper napkin. "Okay. I'm, ah, well, I'll be gone for a few days this weekend. Family stuff." I sat and sweated, watching her expression.

Mishelle froze; the sandwich halfway to her open mouth. Slowly, she put it down and closed her mouth. She was perfectly quiet and still for the space of three breaths. I watched her prominent Adam's apple bob up and down as she swallowed.

"How long?"

"Four days."

"That's an eternity."

"I know. I'm sorry. I'll have my cellphone with me in case you need to call. But I gotta go."

"Where are you going?"

"Helena. To visit Dave's sister."

"Oh." She closed her eyes and nodded. "Yes. You have to go. I've been using up all your free time, haven't I? Time that you should spend with your family."

"No." To my utter astonishment, my hands were shaking. "Mishelle, *we're* your family. We . . ."

"Michelle." Her voice was clear as a bell and not in the least loud. "I *have* a family. Father, mother, brothers and a sister." She smiled placidly and took a big bite of her sandwich, chewed and swallowed. "See? I'm just like you, aren't I?"

I couldn't think of anything to say. She went on:

"So why should I be upset if you want to spend time with your family? I'm not *that* self-centered, am I?"

"Damn." My hands were knotted into tight little balls in my lap.

"Oh, c'mon," she said cheerfully. "What did you say? 'I'm all grown up.' Hey, me too. I'm a big girl, y'know. When will you be back?"

I unknotted my fists. "Sunday."

"Well, it sounds like fun. Helena's what, four hours, more or less?"

"About that, yeah."

"Well, you'll have lots of time to catch up on things with Dave and the boys."

Cautiously, I said, "Well, I was kind of planning on having Chris teach me how to Braille."

Mishelle clapped her hands together. "Cool! Then we can pass notes back and forth, too! That'll be a blast." She grinned wickedly. "We can tell jokes and pull some tricks on Dave. He'll never figure out what we're up to."

I said, "You might be surprised."

She looked smug. "Maybe. Hey, you want your present?"

I started. "I completely forgot about that. Where is it?" I glanced around quickly, noting that her apartment was still quite neat and tidy from Carpet Day.

"In the bedroom. You want it or do I have to send it back?"

"Don't be silly." I got up and went to the bedroom, returned with the box. It was heavy.

"Open it."

I did, carefully. The lamp looked even better than the picture on the outside of the box. It was solid antique brass in the shape of a tree trunk, a little less than two feet in height. A limb jutted out halfway up the length and two birds in stained glass that matched the shade were perched on it.

It was beautiful.

"Thanks, sweetie." I looked up and couldn't see her too well: blurry eyes. "I love it."

Her smile was gentle and loving. "I'm very glad. Happy Birthday, dear Michelle."

I got up to give her a kiss. As I pulled back from her cheek, Mishelle whispered, "When I'm gone, every time you turn that on, think of me shining a little light into your world."

My palm found her cheek and the kiss there, still warm beneath my hand. "You already do." I whispered.

CHAPTER TWENTY

Hospice

L EARNING BRAILLE WASN'T AS HARD as I thought it would be. Each of the six keys produces a bump in a particular position within the rectangular space for each character and with only a maximum of six dots for each, all that's needed is a little bit of memorization.

Once I understood the pattern, it went quickly after that. Chris and I were soon passing notes back and forth, much to Dave's amusement, but not so much Zach's. We passed the time on the way to Helena swapping bad jokes, goofy comments and silly one-liners.

Zach and my husband endured it patiently, occasionally communicating via shrugs and lifted eyebrows: their own secret language, I think.

The four days passed. I called her every day, sometimes twice and each time I could hear her struggling to breathe. I'd hang up each time with the sense that my back teeth were trying to lock into a grimace somewhere between a smile and a wince.

I might have seemed a little distracted to Dave's sister. If I was, she didn't mention it. Thanks, Ruth.

The trip home seemed to take forever. I spent a lot of time looking out the window at the Montana countryside; scenery I'd enjoyed dozens of times in the past but now seemed unreasonably vast and empty; time and space stretched beyond comprehension as the intervening distance puckered like a poorly healed wound; scarring me in ways I didn't want to think about then and certainly not now.

There is absence and then there is emptiness. I sometimes wonder which is worse.

We finally rolled into our driveway that Sunday afternoon. I loaded myself down with luggage and started hauling things inside. Dave stopped me in the middle of my second trip.

"What are you doing?"

I looked up at him and blew a lock of hair out my eyes. "What? What does it *look* like I'm doing?"

"Put that stuff down," he said quietly.

"Well, if you'll *help* . . ."

"I am." He handed me my cellphone when I dropped my armload on the floor. "Here. You need to call her. You've been fretting all day."

"I have not! I've been . . ."

"Distracted," he finished. "Daydreaming. Spaced-out." He held up his hand as I opened my mouth to retort. "Save it. I'll get the rest."

"I need to get dinner started . . ."

"I'll get that, too." He cocked an eyebrow at me. "Call her. Then get your tail over there so you can at least get some sleep tonight. Don't think I didn't notice that you didn't sleep more than twenty minutes at a stretch while we were gone."

I wanted to glare at him, but he kissed me and picked up the junk off the floor, so I missed my opportunity. I went back outside and flipped open the phone.

"Hi."

"Hi! You're back!"

"Uh-huh. How you feelin'?"

"Okay." She coughed suddenly, the little liar. It sounded like Nicholas, only lower-pitched. "Maybe a little tired."

"Want some company?"

She brightened. "Yeah? Sure! Did you bring me anything?"

I had to laugh. "No, but I will. Latte and danish?"

She chuckled hoarsely. "One danish, if you please. I'm trying to lose weight."

"Like you really need to. See you in a bit."

I closed the phone, went back inside, gave each of my guys a kiss, grabbed my purse and beat it.

I didn't run any stop signs but I didn't waste any time, either. I made it to the drive-in before they closed down the espresso maker, snagged her a goody and was on her porch inside of thirty minutes.

Not a record, quite.

I'd left my medical bag in the car on our trip; old habits are hard to break. I dragged it in with me, took her vitals and listened to her lungs.

No change? I couldn't be sure and that bothered me. I had no idea of what, exactly, I should be listening *for*. I spent extra time just listening to the wind flowing sluggishly in and out of her lungs and I think that might have alerted her.

"There's something you're not telling me," she said quietly.

Startled, I took the earpieces out and covered it while stowing my gear. "No, just concerned, that's all."

"So am I." She sipped her latte. "Out with it, girlfriend."

I sat down, hands in my lap and took a deep breath. "Okay. I think it's time to talk about . . . what we agreed we'd talk about, before. Every time I've talked to you in the past two weeks, your breathing has gotten slightly worse. Are you feeling this too or am I all wrong here?"

"No." Her voice was calm and steady. "No, you're not wrong. The fires and hot weather have made it really hard for me to breathe." She sipped, a thoughtful expression knitting her brows. "Your turn. Do *you* think I'm getting worse?"

I nodded, not caring that she couldn't see me. She knew. "Honestly, yes, Mishelle. I do. I think it's time we talked about Hospice. You remember me mentioning it?"

"Yes." Her head was tilted slightly down and to the left; listening intently; her expression now solemn. "Explain it to me again, would you?"

I cleared my throat. "Uh. Well, it's a program designed for patients who have a terminal condition, like yours. It's all about system management, you understand? To make you comfortable so that the quality of your life increases, if even just a little bit."

"I understand that part. Do I have to go into the hospital?" Her question held a glimmer of warning; a tiny glimpse of that steel resolve deep within.

"No! No way. Well, I suppose you could if you *wanted* to . . ."

"I don't."

"I know. And nobody will make you go. It's an at-home program. You'll have a nurse who works with your doctor on the best treatment program to make your remaining time more comfortable."

Her mouth turned down, just a little. "And how much time do you think I have left?" she asked wryly. "Six months? A year?"

I sat very still. "Mishelle, I really don't know. COPD is a difficult disease to treat and predict. I mean, it's not like you have terminal cancer."

"Well, hooray for *that*," she muttered.

I nodded. "Yeah. It could be worse. But a doctor has to be sure that the patient has six months or less before approving a Hospice application."

"So I have six months or less left to live." She sipped. When the cup came down, her mouth was a thin horizontal slot. "Wonderful."

"I did *not* say that. I've heard of Hospice patients who were on the program for over a year before they passed away. Six months is just a

Medicare guideline. It varies for each individual and how much will to live they have, what resources they have left to continue living."

I put out my hand and so did she, just as if she could see my gesture. Our fingers linked. "Mishelle, the program provides spiritual counselors as well, people who have extensive experience in social work and counseling and can meet you emotionally at whatever stage you may be in this."

Her mouth quirked: the hint of an almost-smile. "Do I get a personal trainer, too? In case I want to take up rock-climbing or something?"

I giggled, quite involuntarily. "Well, they *do* have physical therapists. Even at-home aides who can give you bed baths and such."

"No, thanks," she said; quietly again, the steel returned to her voice.

"Okay, we don't have to go there. I know how you feel about that."

"What does Brent think? Have you talked to him?"

Another deep breath from me: "I know he thinks you'd be approved for this under the Medicare guidelines. I do, too."

"I don't know if I'm ready to say goodbye." Her voice was wistful.

I wanted to gesture helplessly, but I didn't want to let go of her hand either. "Neither am I, Mishelle! I just want you to be comfortable. The medication program is different for Hospice patients. The nurses and doctors who administer the meds are experts in the field. The rules are a little more liberal on what kinds of meds are available, too."

Her ears pricked up at that. "Really? What kind?"

"Nothing like *that*." I squeezed her fingers. "Low doses of morphine in your nebulizer, for example. It might help your breathing a lot." I thought about the steroids that usually accompanied such treatments and decided not to share that bit, not just yet. "There are a lot more options available on Hospice. Options that will make your life easier and not the constant struggle it is now."

"I dunno." She didn't quite smile. "Morphine sounds pretty intense."

"Not at the super low doses they use. All it does is relax the bronchi so you can breathe easier. There's no systemic effect." I put my other hand on hers and she followed suit, linking all four of our hands. "Mishelle, does this conversation scare you?"

"You had to ask? Hell, yes!" She sighed. "But I knew I'd have to talk with you about it, sooner or later."

Suddenly, as if she'd shrugged off a heavy blanket, she shook herself and brightened. Our four-way grasp broke. "Okay, let me think about it tonight and I'll call you tomorrow morning. Did you have a chance to learn Braille while you were gone?"

I blinked at her. "Uh, yeah. Yes, I did."

"Well, show me!"

I dug around in my bag and pulled out the stiff, construction paper-like sheets I'd done under Chris's tutelage. She ran her fingertips across the patterns of raised dots, a half-smile on her face.

"Wow, you did a good job, Michelle." Her fingertips glided effortlessly across the pages. "I can see that I'll have to teach you some of those shortcuts I showed Chris. You're kind of wordy, girlfriend."

"Aren't I always?" I laughed. "I just wish I could read it with my fingers, like you. It takes forever to read a sentence!"

"Practice makes perfect. Would you get me my Brailler? I want to send some homework along with you."

I fetched the bulky machine, loaded it and set it in her lap. Mishelle typed for a bit, smiled to herself and added something else. She pulled the sheet out of the machine and gave it to me.

"Here you go. See if you can figure this out."

"I need my cheat sheet," I confessed. "I left it at home."

She laughed. "Thought as much. Okay, you're still a newbie, so I'll cut you some slack. Tell me tomorrow when I call you."

"Thanks." I put the Brailler back into its case. "How did the inspection go?"

"Aw, it was a joke! Curtis came in, looked around for about two minutes, said, 'Thanks, Mishelle,' and left. Nothing to it."

"So you're not going to be thrown into the streets, then?"

She stuck her tongue out at me. "Smartass. No, I'm not going to be thrown out. At least not this week." She grinned. "But I got a clean apartment, didn't I?"

"That you did," I said ruefully.

"Okay, then," and the rest of the visit passed very pleasantly. When I left, I gave her a hug and she whispered, "Thanks for being honest."

"You're welcome," I whispered back. "But why are we whispering?"

Her cackles followed me out the door as I left, smiling.

* * *

The phone rang while I was pouring my second cup of coffee. I put down a half-eaten banana and the carafe and plucked the phone from its charging cradle.

"Hi! You're up early."

She sounded rested and relaxed. "So are you. Busy day ahead of you?"

"Six patients." I blew on my coffee and sipped. "I still haven't figured out my homework yet. Sorry."

"Okay. Tomorrow, then. That's not why I called, though."

"Hmm? What's up?"

"I thought about Hospice and I decided that I'm ready." She coughed. I waited, feeling my heart skip a beat. "I have an appointment with Doctor J this Thursday. Can you be there to discuss this with us? I need you to make sure I don't forget anything."

"Sure." I blew again; the coffee was taking forever to cool. "You need me to pick you up?"

"No, Lynn will take me. Ten o'clock?"

"Yes, I'm off Thursday. I'll be there, Mishelle."

"Thanks, sweetie." She clicked off.

"Mom?"

I looked up, the banana halfway to my mouth. "'Morning, Chris."

He seemed worried. "Is Mishelle going to be okay?"

I motioned to him and he came into my arms. I finished the banana before answering my son, which gave me a little time to think about it.

"Yeah, I think she's going to be better. As to *okay*? I don't know. I'm going to see her Thursday and we'll see what her doctor has to say."

"Is she still going to die?" He lifted his head from under my arm to look at me.

I sighed. "Chris, I think that's inevitable. That means: yes, she will but probably not soon."

I looked into his blue eyes, like mine yet so not and smiled; rumpled his hair. "We're all going to die, honey. Because it's part of life: beginning, middle and end. Like a song or a book. But you can remember the song or the book or someone's life anytime you feel like it."

He shivered and burrowed his face into my tummy. "Scares me." he mumbled, his voice muffled.

"Me, too. Scares all of us." I reflected that it might be a good idea to contact a counselor for my son at his school; someone with experience in these matters. Zach, too. "It doesn't have to, though. It's not the end of everything; it's just one part of it."

Gently, I pried his face away from my stomach and looked into his eyes again. "And there's always Heaven to think about, you know."

He nodded.

"You want to see her again soon, don't you?"

He nodded.

"This weekend, I think. Sound good?"

He scowled. "If we go over there, I hope her house is cooler!" he grumbled.

"It will be. Nicky brought back the other air conditioner last week. But I think we'll have her over here so you two can beat each other's brains out at chess."

He grinned, all traces of worry gone. "Cool!"

I smiled back at him. "That's better, Cee-Boo. Now, tell me." I regarded him with mock astonishment. "What are *you* doing up so early?"

He had the grace to look faintly embarrassed. "Uh, I was wondering if you could take me shopping for stuff."

I sighed. "What stuff?"

"Football stuff."

"Already? Chris, it's still summer! You don't start fourth grade for at least another month!"

"Yeah, but signup is in two weeks and I need some cleats!" He hugged me tighter. "Please?"

"Oh, jeez." My son, the gridiron hero. "Football is very dangerous, you know. Kids have been hurt . . ."

"Aw, Mom . . ."

"Okay, let me discuss this with your dad. Did you talk to him about this already?"

He nodded, still looking sheepish.

"Well, there's a surprise." I shook my head. Men. "I'll talk to him. Now, let me go! I have to get to work."

He submitted to my kiss and I made it out the door on the stroke of the hour: eight o'clock straight up and thirty minutes until my first patient.

For me, work is often the best therapy.

* * *

Thursday, July twenty-seventh, 2006, I sat quietly with Lynn in the corner of the exam room as Doctor J did a thorough assessment of her condition. When he was done, he looked at us and smiled faintly.

"You have some questions, I presume?"

I nodded. "Only one, actually. Do you think Mishelle is a good candidate for Hospice, Doctor?"

Beside me, Lynn remained silent, but her expression and body language told me she was listening intently.

He glanced at his patient who was trying to put on a pair of shoes that she rarely wore. Nicholas was licking her face, so Lynn got up to lend a hand. While they were fussing ("No *lick*, Nick!"), Dr. J looked back at me with a raised eyebrow and that slight half-smile.

"It's okay, we've discussed this. Please speak freely, Doctor. I think she needs some transparency here."

He nodded. "Very well, then. Yes, I'd say she's a very good candidate. There are no gross abnormalities in her current condition, but I do note a slightly reduced lung capacity from the last assessment."

Doctor J ran a hand through his dishwater blonde hair, a mix of expressions on his boyish face: gentle regret, professional concern and a mild amusement that his exam room was crowded with three women and a dog. I had to admire his composure. "Not much change, in other words. But *that* could change very soon, too."

"How soon?"

"Ah, that's the big question, isn't it?" He shrugged. "You know as well as I that it's impossible to estimate. It varies too much to pin it down to any specific time-frame."

His eyebrows drew together. He put a hand on Mishelle's shoulder, "Six months? Perhaps a year?"

"Just get me through to Christmas," Mishelle grunted. Lynn looked up and nodded; her expression uncommonly solemn.

He patted her shoulder, reassurance radiating from his lanky frame. "That, my dear, is entirely up to you. But I think you've got a very good chance if you remain stable through Labor Day." Doctor J looked directly at me. "I assume you've contacted the Hospice program about this?"

I nodded. "Yes, I spoke with Robin yesterday. I'll be meeting with her later to hammer out the details and get the paperwork completed."

"Do you know who her nurse will be?"

"Well, I would prefer Lori."

He nodded. "Excellent. She's very good, especially with the medications. Best knowledge of pharmacology I've ever encountered in a nurse." That faint smile again. "I hear she's an expert at *kendo*. Don't annoy her; she'll mop the floor with you."

My returning smile was a bit wry. "I know. I used to work with her if you'll recall, Doctor. We bumped heads once. I don't care to repeat that."

"Oh? Personality clash?"

"Not really. Just a difference of opinion. Perspective, maybe. We settled it pretty quickly, though. I think we get along just fine now. But I agree that she doesn't suffer fools gladly."

"Quite true. And very devoted to her patients. She's a good choice."

"I hope she likes rock 'n roll," Mishelle commented. Nicholas was back on her lap. He resettled himself and yawned, probably from sheer boredom. "And dogs."

Doctor J laughed. "I think you'll find Lori to be a very accepting sort. Dogs and kitties, both." He folded his arms and looked at us in turn, even Nicholas. "Any more questions, ladies?"

Lynn and I shook our heads in tandem, but Mishelle lifted her hand to him, palm up. "My turn. What do you think of this perfume, Doctor?"

He bent and sniffed; his expression entirely serious. "Mm," he murmured. "What's this one called? Jungle Lust?"

Michelle giggled. "It's Georgio. You like it?"

"Delightful, Mishelle. It suits you." He winked at us. "You have exquisite taste. Now, if you ladies will excuse me . . ." He left, white lab coat swirling around his khaki cargo pants.

"He's so *cute*," Mishelle sighed.

"Girl, that's robbing the cradle." Lynn commented. "He's young enough to be your son, you know."

"And this is a problem?"

"Never mind." We were still laughing when we rolled her out to the parking lot. I helped Lynn put Mishelle into her seat, kissed her goodbye, added a thankful hug to Lynn and headed off to the office.

Robin's office is in the same building as Home Health; convenient for both patients and medical professionals. But Home Health is a private subcontractor and Robin works for the hospital so she has an actual office; with a door and a window, no less.

I have a cubicle. Rank hath its privileges, I guess.

She deserves it, though. Robin's been in the medical field in one capacity or another as an administrator for much longer than myself and she's *brilliant*, maybe even a little intimidating. I enjoyed working for her though, long ago when I was a Hospice nurse myself.

I really regretted leaving.

But it wasn't really a choice. It takes it out of you, it does.

I was finishing up some charting when someone put a take-out cup of coffee, grande-sized, on the desk next to my charts. I looked up.

Robin smiled down at me. "You take it black, right?"

"Uh-huh." I sipped. "Thanks, Robin. Have a seat."

"Thanks." She coiled gracefully into a chair and sipped with care at her own coffee. "How have you been?"

Wordlessly, I indicated my paperwork.

"I see." She fixed me with her luminous hazel eyes. Robin is a devastatingly handsome woman and her eyes are easily her most striking feature. "I hope you're taking some me time through all of this, Michelle."

I managed a weak smile. "Sure!" I said feebly. "Uh, I just got back from a trip to Dave's sister's in Helena. Had a very nice time."

"Good." Her eyes never left mine. "How are Dave and the boys?"

"Great. Just great. Chris is nine and he's all excited about football and Zach's growing like tree and Dave's . . ." My voice trailed off.

"Uh-huh." Her gaze softened. She rested her chin on a fist. "Bring me up to speed on this, will you?"

I hesitated. Mishelle's charts had already been transferred to her office so I knew it wasn't the bare bones she wanted.

"You know what transgender means, Robin?"

She nodded. "Yes. Gender identity disorder. Relatively common in urban settings. Not so much out here in Montana. Mishelle is a transgender woman?"

I nodded.

"Interesting. And her prognosis is six months or less? I saw no notation of her having had SRS."

I shook my head.

"Oh, dear. That's a shame. Does she want it?"

I found my voice: "More than anything."

"Has she come to terms with this?"

I shrugged, trying to keep my tone neutral. "I don't think she'll ever be happy she wasn't able to go through with it. Her mitral valve . . ."

"Yes, I read the note about her heart surgery." Her tone was kind. "What about her acceptance of her own mortality? Do you think she understands or is she in denial?"

"No, I wouldn't call it denial. Hope, maybe. She wants to live at least until Christmas. She's really looking forward to it."

"That's a very good sign. If a patient has a goal, a reason to keep on living, that can very often be the best thing for them."

She studied me carefully. Rather than feeling confronted by her direct gaze, I was finding it quite soothing. "I noted that you requested Lori. Didn't you two clash some time before you left? Something to do with a faulty medication pump?"

"We settled that," I said firmly. "I think she's the best choice for this case. I like her dedication and I'm in awe of her knowledge of pharmacology."

"Aren't we all? I agree: she's perfect for this case." She took off her glasses; a really cool, hip design I momentarily envied and adjusted a stray lock of spiky blonde hair.

She looked elegant and professional and so with it that her glasses weren't the only thing I envied in that moment. "Michelle, I can see that

Ms. Woodring is an unusual case. But I can promise you that Hospice will put every available resource into her final days with us. She has a good team, possibly the best team we have."

She put her glasses on and regarded me with approval. "That includes you, of course. We'll set her up for intake on Monday the thirty-first. Agreed?"

I agreed. We shook hands. Hers were soft and smooth and she had a really terrific manicure.

* * *

I called her the moment I got home, of course. The kitchen was a swirl of activity: Dave was trying to cook and Zach and Chris were verbally sparring over something in the newspaper, so I retreated to my office.

"Monday," I told her.

"Okay." She sounded dubious. "Michelle, do you think that Lori will accept me? I don't want to have to keep shuffling through Hospice workers like I did with caretakers."

"You won't have to," I said. "Lori is a very accepting person. The only thing she won't accept is less than the best effort from your support team. That includes me and Lynn and Nicky."

"Yeah?" Her tone was openly skeptical. "Does she know about trans people? Any experience with us?"

"Uh." I sat for a moment, staring blankly at the top of my desk. "Actually, no. Not that I'm aware of. How about if I call her tonight and fill her in?"

"Yeah, I think that might be a good idea," she said dryly.

"Okay, then." I took a deep breath. "I'll call you back when I talk to Lori. Don't worry, sweetie. I've known her for a long time and she's got a good heart. Why else do you think I requested her?"

"Okay." She panted for a moment. "Michelle? Thanks."

"You're welcome, sweetie." I glanced at the clock. Not quite dinner time. Like they say: do it *now*. "Talk to you in a few, Mishelle." I clicked off and immediately dialed Lori.

"Hello?"

"Hi! Lori, it's Michelle Alexander."

"Well, hi! How've you been? We haven't talked since you left Hospice."

"Yeah, it's been too long. Uh, Lori, I'll get right to it: you have a new patient coming on board this Monday. Mishelle Woodring. Blind, fifty-seven years, end stage COPD. Thoracic spinal fractures."

"Sounds like a handful," she responded cheerfully. "What's she on for the back pain?"

"Oxycontin and Oxycodone." I hesitated, nibbling my lip. "One more thing. Maybe the most important thing. Lori, do you know what transgender means?"

There was a slight but pregnant pause. "Uh, is that like transsexual?" she asked cautiously.

"In this case: yes. Pre-op."

"Hormones?"

"Estrogen: orally five to six milligrams daily for the last twenty years, thereabouts. Premarin, for the most part."

She whistled softly. "That's a damn high dose. Any thrombosis or circulatory problems?"

"No. She's on Coumadin for a mitral valve replacement about the same time she started hormones."

"Which explains why she's still pre-op."

"Right."

"The poor dear." There was nothing but sympathy in her voice. "It must break her heart."

My eyes suddenly filled with tears and it was all I could do to keep from letting them spill over into my voice. "Yes. It does. Especially now."

"I'm sure." She hesitated. "You were her home nurse, I assume."

"That's right. She was discharged a few weeks ago." I hesitated too, and was suddenly aware of how filled with silences this phone call was. "Lori, I have a . . . a confession."

"What?"

"I crossed a few boundaries with her."

"Such as?"

"She has my home phone numbers. Both of them. And my email address, too."

She waited.

I struggled for only a moment. "And I visited with her. On my off hours. She . . . she's my *friend*, Lori." For only a moment, I allowed the tears to show. "When you meet her, you'll understand why."

The silence was brief, but seemed to take forever. When Lori finally spoke, it was slowly and with great care:

"Michelle, sometimes those boundaries are meant to be crossed. It keeps the humanity in what we do."

The word rebounded in my mind like a vast, slow moving balloon; bouncing back and forth within the confines of my skull: *humanity*. When at last I could speak, my voice was firm and steady.

"Thanks, Lori. I knew I could count on you."

She chuckled. "Of course. You're a really wonderful nurse, Michelle. We all miss you on Hospice."

I swallowed. "Thanks. I miss you all, too."

"Anytime you want to come back, you'll have a job here, you know."

"I know. Sorry, it's just . . . too much, you know?"

"I know." Her voice held sympathy again. "You almost had a meltdown when you lost that patient a few years ago. What was her name?"

"Pam."

"That's right. You two had a very special bond. I could see then how hard it was for you not to care too deeply about your patients."

"It's a knack I never learned," I said with a laugh, the taste of lemon rind far back in my throat.

"And you need that so much on Hospice Service." She sighed. "Yes. Okay, Michelle. I'm really excited to meet your friend Mishelle. Huh, that's odd you two have the same name."

"She spells hers with an s," I said. "Thanks again, Lori. I'm going to give her a call and reassure her a little bit. She was worried."

"Oh, tell her she's got nothing to worry about. She's in very good hands."

"I know," I said. I hung up, my own hands trembling ever so slightly.

"Mom? Dinner's ready!"

"Be right there, Zach!"

I sat for a moment, feeling the tremors subside, feeling human once again.

Humanity.

Oh, *yes.*

* * *

I hate Mondays.

Which makes me no different than anyone else, I suppose. My job may be a bit different than most but I have the same reluctance to roll out of bed and face the day as anyone.

Even Miss Perky needs to sleep in, once in a while.

But that Monday, I bounced out of bed with fire in my eyes and a mental list of things to do blazing like neon in my mind: breakfast, domestic tasks and errands.

First on the list was Mishelle's intake session. I was off work that day; not that it made my schedule any less daunting. I knew Lori would be there around noon and I was determined to be present, if for no other reason than to thank Lori for her understanding.

I don't do that nearly enough, I think: thank people for understanding. Maybe I take it for granted too much.

I'm working on that.

Chris and Zach seemed to take it for granted that they would go with me that morning, so we all piled in the car and stopped by Wendy's for lunch. We picked up a burger for Michelle, a small order of fries for Nicholas and parked in front of her door some minutes before noon.

Nicholas went into joyful hysterics when he saw Chris and Zach. He probably thought Heaven had granted his fondest wish when both of my boys got down on their knees and alternated scratching his back and feeding him fries. Mishelle gave me a broad smile and a hug and eagerly tore into her burger.

"F'anks," she mumbled. "'Is is goo'."

"Did you have any breakfast?"

She chewed and swallowed. "No. Nicky left me something but I was too short of breath to get it." She looked abashed. "Sorry. I know I should be taking better care of myself, but . . ."

"Stop it. That's why Hospice is a good idea. Their scheduling will eliminate stuff like that. Lori will . . ." The door bell rang and Nicholas disregarded his own lunch long enough to bark a response.

"It's open!" I yelled.

Lori came through the door, a big smile on her face and a thick brief-case under one arm. "Well, hello there!" she exclaimed. "Didn't expect to see *you* here."

"Get used to it." I grinned as we hugged. "I'm here a *lot*. How are you?"

"Good. You?"

My grin wouldn't go away. Darn, but it was wonderful to see her again. "I'm okay. Working too much, I guess."

"Yeah, I heard. Hey, Chris! Hi, Zach!"

My sons looked up, waved and grunted and returned to their task of turning Nicholas into a miniature blimp. Lori studied me. "You lost some weight since I saw you last."

"Well, I was still heavy from carrying Chris."

"You look great. I like the new hair color."

"So do you." I looked her over. Lori is very petite, smaller than me or even Anne, with a gymnast's body: all smooth, taut muscle and corded tendons. Her hair is short dark curls and her dark brown eyes somehow reminded me of Nicholas: a sad puppy-dog.

A sad person she is most definitely not. She's a workaholic, like me; hyper-competent (unlike me) and fiercely devoted to her patients. She smiles a lot and it's hard not to return that smile of hers.

The verbal scuffle we'd had years ago involved a dispute over a medication pump that had run out in the middle of the night. Lori was called in and naturally she assumed I'd miscalculated the dosage. She went over my figures three times, concluded finally that I *hadn't* screwed up and we've been absolutely fine with each other ever since.

We found out later that the particular model of that pump had flaws and a recall was later issued.

But I'll say this about Lori: don't ever cross her when it comes to a patient's safety. Dr. J was perfectly correct: she'll mop the floor with you and she isn't likely to avoid the corners.

"Lori, I'd like you to meet my friend Mishelle. Mishelle, this is Lori. She'll be your Hospice nurse." I felt an inordinate amount of pride in being able to introduce them.

Lori knelt on one knee next to Mishelle's recliner. She took her hand. "It's a pleasure to finally meet you, Mishelle," she said gravely. "May I call you Mishelle?"

My friend cackled. "Sure! Just don't call me late to dinner!"

Lori looked up me and grinned. "I've heard so much about you . . ."

"I hope it was good!" she said. "If not, then it's all lies and the statute of limitations has expired, anyway!"

I could see Lori struggling to contain her laughter. "No, it was all good. But I'd like to hear more about you, just as soon as we get a bit of privacy." She glanced up at me again, a note of warning deep in her puppy-dog eyes.

I can take a hint. "Boys, it's time to go," I said briskly and picked up the lunch litter.

"Aw, Mom." From Chris; who was just starting to fool around with Mishelle's Brailler. "I wanted to try out some of those shortcuts Mishelle showed me!"

"You can do that later this week," I said with more than my usual firmness. "Let's move it, gentlemen. I have errands to run and I need your help carrying things. Say goodbye to Mishelle, now."

They gave her a hug and moved aside so I could do the same. I whispered in her ear. "I'll call you later and you can tell me how it went, okay?"

"Okay." We air kissed and I released her. When I stood, so did Lori. She beckoned to me and we hugged, too.

She was smiling. "Hugs are still a requirement, Michelle."

"I remember."

"It's really good to see you again."

I nodded and realized that my eyes were just a little blurry. It may have been only relief. My friend was in very good hands at last. Maybe the best hands imaginable. "Same here, Lori."

"Say hi to Dave for me, will you?"

"I will. Call me if you spot anything unusual or significant."

"Count on it, Michelle." Her smile was altogether warm and comforting.

* * *

Right after dinner, I called her as promised. "Well? What do you think of her?"

She sounded tired but I may have been projecting. It had been that kind of day. "Oh, she's really wonderful. I like her a lot."

"Good." I bent my head, wiggled it around, trying to loosen a knot between my shoulder blades. "Did you discuss your medications?"

"Oh, yeah. She called in an order for that morphine in my nebulizer. It's supposed to be here tomorrow."

"Good." The knot remained steadfast, no matter how I waggled my head and shoulders. "You'll have to load your own dosages, so listen carefully to what she says."

"I think I can handle my meds, Michelle." Her voice was quite dry. "I've only been doing it for over twenty years."

"Right." I felt my face growing warm. "Sorry. I just . . . *umph*!" The knot contracted and I felt the spasm clear down to my elbows. "Ouch."

"Something wrong?"

"Nah," I muttered. "Could use a neck rub, though."

"Poor baby. Come on over and I'll rub it for you."

"You've got that backwards, sweetie," I grunted, trying to find a more comfortable position in my office chair. "I rub *you*, remember? Besides, I have things to do here tonight. Sorry."

"Yeah, you always do, but who rubs *you*, Michelle?"

"Doesn't matter. I can always get a massage . . ."

"Sure. Cost much?"

For the life of me, I could not find a comfortable spot in that chair. "Not much. I'm fine, really."

"Uh-huh. Hey, girlfriend?"

"What?"

"I think you need some Michelle time, don't you?"

The room seemed unreasonably warm, though I knew the central air was working just fine. "What? No, I've got too much to do. And I just came back from four days of vacation."

"Some vacation," she murmured.

"Hey, Dave's family is really nice . . ."

"Yeah, I know. He's told me all about them."

"Is that so? When; during one of your smoke-outs?"

There was a pause. "We haven't done that in some time, Michelle. Really."

Rubbing the back of my neck wasn't doing any good either. "Okay. Sorry. Listen, I've got a lot to do tonight. I'll come by tomorrow. When's Lori coming?"

"Around noon, I think. Are you working tomorrow?"

"Of course." I flipped open my book and checked my schedule. A full plate: five patients. "Noon could work. I'll see you then."

"Okay." There was regret in her voice or something very much like it. "Sleep well tonight, Michelle."

"You, too. G'night." I closed my phone, closed my eyes and tried to relax, but it didn't seem to be working.

When I opened my eyes, I found myself staring at my day planner; seeing the busy days arrayed in front of me like a table-crushing banquet for a dozen people and myself the only guest.

I used a word I rarely use, even all by myself, but it didn't help either. I hate Mondays.

*   *   *

"Okay, I've drawn up five doses for you," Lori told Mishelle. "All you need to do is squirt them—carefully—into the nebulizer chamber. Remember: no more than one every two hours and only if you start to experience a pronounced shortage of breath."

"Mmph." I could tell my friend was listening intently: her head was tilted down and to the left. Mishelle removed the nebulizer mouthpiece. "How much morphine is in this stuff?"

"Keep that in your mouth for at least twenty minutes," Lori cautioned. "Very little, actually. It's mostly steroids, not so much morphine. But the morphine will relax the smooth muscles in your bronchial tubes so you can draw in more air."

"Steroids?" I could see her ears prick up, almost like Nicholas. "Will it make my boobs bigger?"

Lori snickered and glanced in my direction. I shrugged and spread my hands wide: don't look at *me.*

"No, it won't do that, Mishelle. Sorry." She gave my friend a hug and picked up her bag. "I'll be back tomorrow to see how you're doing."

"Mmph. G'bye."

I picked up my own bag a little reluctantly and gave her a hug, too. "See you tomorrow, sweetie." I planted a kiss on her cheek. "Be a good girl and do what she tells you, okay?"

"'Kay."

We left her there, placidly nursing on the plastic mouthpiece and as the door closed, the stereo went back up to full volume. Lori smiled at me.

"She likes her music, doesn't she?"

"That she does. She used to be a recording engineer, you know."

"I'm not surprised. She must have extraordinarily sensitive ears."

"Yup." I put my sunglasses on. "So what's her prognosis?"

Lori shrugged and donned her own shades, a nifty pair of Wayfarers. "Your guess is as good as mine. You know that COPD is a difficult disease to predict. But she seems to be responding well to the new meds and I'm thinking she just might make it through to the end of the year. Maybe even six months."

At that moment, it was all I could do to keep from going back inside. "I dunno, Lori. I've got a bad feeling about this."

I paused, trying to catch my breath. Scott studied me and then handed me a tissue. I didn't really need one but I took it anyway.

"I'm sorry," I said. "This is just so hard . . . There's so much to tell you, especially in that last week."

He nodded. "I expected that. Do you want to take a break?"

No, *I wanted to shout.* I want to go home! *Instead, I shook my head, wondering where to start among all the tangled threads of those last few days.*

"Well." He smiled; the first sign of real warmth I'd seen on his face since I walked though his door. "A week? Why don't you just take it one day at a time, then?"

PART THREE

Rubicon

CHAPTER TWENTY-ONE

Event Horizons: A Suite of Days

MONDAY, AUGUST SEVENTH

The phone rang.

Eyes carefully on the road, I fished around in my purse for it, keeping a death grip on the wheel with my left hand. The highway from Missoula to Kalispell isn't particularly winding or twisty, but it's only two lanes and there was enough traffic to make me cautious. There were semi-trucks, campers and fifth wheel trailers and vacationers all headed in the same direction as me: Flathead Valley.

Some of that traffic included a few Montana State Police cruisers. I'd spotted a few of them lurking in convenient off-road, tree-shaded nooks, radar guns drawn and aimed in anticipation. The Toyota seemed to slow all by itself each time I passed one. I haven't received a ticket since my teenage years and it didn't seem like a particularly good time to restart a bad habit.

As I flipped open the phone, I reflected that it also might be a good idea to invest in a hands-free rig for it someday, considering how much I used it while driving. I decided to ask Dave about it; he had a much better grasp of the tech stuff than me.

I held the phone in front of me and glanced at the display. It was her. I thumbed it on.

"Hey! How are you?"

"Hey, Birthday Girl!"

I smiled and shifted the phone to my other ear. "Thanks again. That was a really sweet e-mail this morning."

"You're welcome." She giggled. "You're gonna kill me, Michelle."

"Uh-oh. *Now* what did you do?"

She sounded wonderful: chipper and upbeat. "Uh, you promise not to kill me?"

"Sure, if you promise me that you didn't do anything silly." A semi lumbered by, rocking the Toyota in its wake. "Better 'fess up, sweetie."

"Uh, you know how I sometimes get up in the middle of the night for a brownie a la mode?"

"Yeah?" Another semi lumbered by.

"We-ell, I flipped on HSN . . ."

"Oh, God."

"And there was someone demonstrating a guitar! The description sounded so beautiful . . ."

"Let me guess. You ordered it, didn't you?" Yet another semi rumbled past me. I wondered if I was going to be caught in a convoy. *Wonderful.* "What kind of guitar?"

"An Esteban acoustic. It's handmade!"

"I thought you gave up playing guitar. Calluses and all that." I rolled down my window. It was hot in the car; the air conditioning had quit again just as I was leaving Missoula and I was sweating.

"Oh, it's not for me. It's for Chris!"

"What?" All three of the semis were in front of me now and I eased off the accelerator pedal. My blouse was beginning to feel like a damp towel. "For Chris?"

"Well, I know he wants to learn how to play. And Dave can learn, too. It comes with a hard-shell case and instructional DVD's."

I couldn't help smiling despite the perspiration rolling down the back of my neck. "Just how much did this cost, Mishelle?"

"Don't worry; it was on sale. Michelle, it sounded really beautiful! I couldn't help myself."

"I'll bet. When's it due?"

"The sixteenth." She sounded anxious now. "You aren't mad at me, are you?"

I couldn't bring myself to scold her. She sounded so happy about it. "Nah. It's your money, sweetie. Just don't shower us with gifts until Christmas, okay?"

"Okay." A giggle escaped her. "I had it shipped to your house. I hope you don't mind."

"Sheesh. No, it's okay. You want me to give it to Chris or wait for you to give it to him?"

"Uh, you can give it to him." There was a trace of embarrassment in her tone. "It's addressed to him anyway."

"Figures." I wiped my forehead with the back of my hand. Holy cow, but it was hot. More than anything else, I wanted to be home, under a nice cool shower. "How are things otherwise?"

"Pretty good." The cheerful tone returned. "I really like all the Hospice staff that's been visiting me. Robin's husband is really nice. Hey, when will you be home?"

"Soon." I glanced at the car clock. "About a half an hour, in fact. I'm about twenty miles out. But I can't come over tonight, sweetie. Can I call you later?"

"You can't?" Disappointment was plain in her voice, even though the reception was starting to break up. Cell coverage is pretty sporadic in the hills around Flathead Valley. She sighed and static mixed with the natural hoarseness of her voice. "I hate being alone at night, Michelle."

"I know." I negotiated a curve and the beginnings of another hill. The approach to the valley was coming up soon. "Mishelle, I took this whole week off to get a lot of things done at home so I can take care of you Thursday and Friday. Nicky and Lynn will be with you so you'll just have to wait a couple of days until I can get over to your place."

The hill grew steeper and the trucks ahead of me slowed, damn them. I rolled down the passenger window but it didn't help much. "Sorry, sweetie."

"Okay." She sighed again. "Two whole days. When will Chris and Zach be back from their grandma's?" Static crackled again, obscuring the tail end of her sentence.

"Saturday. Hey, I think I'm losing you. Call you tonight?"

"Okay. Love you." She hung up.

I closed the phone, tossed it in my purse as I reached the top of the hill. I started down the long incline into Flathead Valley, the lake glinting in the distance and that's when it happened.

Losing you . . .

Something like a steel hand wrapped itself around my throat and *squeezed*. The breath jammed in my lungs, my heart suddenly went berserk within my chest and for a brief, horrible moment; I couldn't see.

I almost slammed on the brakes, but my vision cleared enough for me to maintain control of the Toyota, even though my heart hammered away within me and my lungs ached.

It was like that moment in my garden but without the gentle implacability that had accompanied it. This was much worse. Glassy-eyed, I stared through the windshield; fighting for control, both the car and my emotions.

Tears started and I couldn't control them at all. Sweat ran like a waterfall down my forehead and mixed with the tears, stinging my eyes.

I could barely see the road.

Thank God there were no State Police on the road at the time. I suppose I should have pulled over and stopped but I didn't.

Somehow, I got home safely and pulled into our driveway, feeling a dull ache in my chest as my hammering heart finally subsided. My hair was plastered to my forehead. I felt like a used dish rag: soggy and wrung out.

I sat for a moment, trying to gather myself and finally got out; went inside; dragging my things behind me like a disconsolate child.

Dave glanced up at me as I came into the kitchen. He did a double-take and his eyebrows drew together. "What's wrong, hon?"

I dropped my things, went to him and let him hold me as the tears began again. "I . . . I had a . . . premonition. I . . . don't know what else to call it. I feel . . ."

I shut up and just sobbed into his chest while he patted my soggy back.

After a bit, he said very gently, "Is this about Mishelle?"

I nodded.

"Hey." I looked up into his face and his expression was reassuring. "Don't read too much into it. You've been working yourself into a frazzle lately. You're tired." He looked at his hand. "Sweaty, too. Air conditioning go out?"

I nodded.

"Damn. Why don't you pour yourself a glass of wine and take a long bath? That's a helluva drive from Missoula, especially with no a/c."

"Yeah." I looked at his shirt front. Mascara was smeared across it. "Sorry."

"Don't apologize. Maybe you should go over there . . .?"

"Nope." I held up my hand. "Nope, you're right. I shouldn't read too much into this." I rubbed at the mascara stain on his shirt. "I should run a load of laundry before I take a bath, though."

"That can wait. I have lots of clean underwear and the boys won't be back until the end of the week. Here: taste."

He half-turned, picked up a spoon and fed me a small mouthful.

I chewed. "Hmm, hamburger helper?"

He looked faintly embarrassed. "Yeah. Sorry I couldn't come up with something more elegant."

"Well, you ain't no Wolfgang Puck, but it tastes fine." In fact, it did and I realized I was hungry. "I think I'll wait on that bath. It's too hot right now."

"It is, isn't it? But it should be cool enough out on the deck for dinner."

"Yeah, that sounds nice."

He nodded. "Put your stuff away. I'll set the table."

* * *

Dinner done and the dishes cleared away, I relaxed at last; sipping wine after Dave had retreated inside to the coolness of the air conditioning and his realtor homework. It was still fairly warm but I wasn't thinking of that; that and the fact that I'd had better birthdays.

Instead, I thought about what had happened today above Flathead Valley and what it really meant.

A premonition? My own fears? Was I just projecting my own beliefs onto my friend again?

An anxiety attack, I decided. It had all the classic symptoms: impaired respiration, tachycardia, blurred vision, diaphoresis, a sense of impending doom. Textbook, almost.

And I couldn't possibly have heard a voice, could I?

Had I even heard one before? Was it only *my* inner voice?

Then and there, my tummy full of yummy hamburger helper (taco flavor!) and the aftertaste of a pretty fair chardonnay soothing my throat; I wasn't all that sure of anything.

Call it denial: I can't deny it.

For a while, ten whole minutes, I admired the sunset and then I took out my cellphone. "Hi. What are you doing?"

"Listening to the TV," she panted.

Uh-oh. "Are you having trouble breathing?"

"No more than usual, I think." Her tiny gasps between sentences had a rattling quality, as if her bronchi were slapping together; a horrifying image. I scowled at the gorgeous orange and salmon clouds far over the horizon.

"Did you take a Lorazepam?"

"Uh, Lori started me on that new stuff this morning." She coughed. I winced. It sounded worse than usual.

"Clonazepam? Did you have a nebulizer treatment today?"

"Uh-huh." Another hoarse breath: "Don't worry; she says I'm doing fine."

"I think we should do some breathing exercises."

"'Kay."

"In. Hold it. Out . . ." I walked her through it, listening to her wind slowly return; another small miracle for which to be grateful. I'd long since lost count of them. "How are you feeling now?"

"A lot better." Another cough and I could tell that something had come up because she paused, mumbled, "'Scuse me," and got rid of it in what was presumably a tissue. "Sorry. At least as well as we can expect, that is."

Ants with icy feet were marching up and down my back. "I'd better call Lori."

"Oh, hell." Now she sounded annoyed. "I'm *fine*, Michelle. Why don't you just relax and enjoy the sunset?"

The clouds were glowing like fire. "How did you . . .?"

"You're outside." It was not a question. "Weather Channel says sunset is at eight thirty-seven pm. It's . . . eight-sixteen." Her voice turned wistful. "I'll bet the clouds are real pretty."

"Uh-huh." I was beyond anything resembling surprise regarding her little quirks. "They are that. Okay. I'll come by tomorrow and check on you. Call me if it gets worse, okay? Then call Lori. *Immediately*."

A chuckle this time, full of gravel and gurgles: "I will. Don't worry, sweetie. See you tomorrow. Love you!"

"Love you, too." I closed the phone and watched the last light fade.

TUESDAY, AUGUST EIGHTH

The Elvis sign was tilted a bit to the left. I tilted it back to level, frowning at it and opened the door.

"Hey, girlfriend!"

"Hey."

Nicholas barked louder than usual. I squinted at him. His fur was erect but his tail was wagging. *What the hell?*

"How you doing, sweetie?"

"Okay," she said dreamily. "Hey, did I e-mail you last night?"

Cautiously, I approached them both. Nick seemed to be at full alert but his tail was wagging madly. With the same caution, I extended my hand and scratched his back. He wiggled, but there was something about his eyes . . .

"No, as a matter of fact. I wondered why." I shrugged, still scratching Nick. The little dachshund almost twisted himself into a U-shape to lick eagerly at my wrist. "I guess I figured you got a good night's sleep for once."

"Oh, no. I had the most horrible dreams last night. Really awful."

The hair on my neck prickled. "What kind of dreams?"

She didn't appear to hear me so I repeated myself.

"Oh, like not being able to wake up. Those kind of dreams."

I frowned. "Were you having trouble breathing?"

She nodded; sluggishly, it seemed to me. "Yeah. But in the dream, it seemed worse, you know? It felt like I couldn't wake up."

Her words were slow and deliberate, as if she were searching for the beginning of each to attach to the end of the one before it.

"And how do you feel now?" I perched on the arm of her recliner and felt her forehead. It was a bit damp but not unusually so.

She shrugged almost lazily. "Okay, now. Pretty good, actually."

I looked her over with some care. She appeared normal; utterly relaxed, in fact. Something in her posture reminded me of the times she'd had a long soak and a drink or two at my place. Her color was good, her respiration appeared normal but . . .

"Stay right there," and I wasn't remotely embarrassed at how ridiculous that sounded. I dashed out to the car, grabbed my bag and sprinted back in.

Her vitals were completely normal: pulse in the mid-fifties, blood pressure within normal limits and there were no outward manifestations of *anything* that I could find. Her lungs sounded just a touch more raspy than usual.

I decided to call Lori about it when I was back on the road.

"Hey." I had her hand in mine. "You seem okay. Do you feel dizzy or weak?"

"Hmm? No, not at all." She chuckled. "Jeez, you're such a worry-wart, you know that? I'm okay. Maybe a little sleepy. I *told* you I didn't sleep well last night."

"I heard that." I put a hand to her forehead again. I decided against taking her temperature; it didn't seem necessary.

A glance at my watch told me I had less than an hour to do two hours of shopping and then beat Dave home. I gritted my teeth. "Look, I've gotta get going. Who's on duty tonight? Nicky?"

"Lynn." Still in that dreamy, almost detached voice: "Hey, don't worry about Nicky. She's been a very good girl lately, Michelle."

"That's true." My erstwhile adversary seemed to be pulling her weight with as much dedication as any of us and I no longer felt any doubts where she was concerned. "What time?"

She flipped open her watch and touched the hands. "Any time now. Go on, sweetie. I'll be okay."

I stood, realizing that my legs were a bit shaky. "Okay. Have her call me if anything happens. You hear me? *Anything*."

She grinned up at me and Nicholas the protector joined her. "Worry-wart." She returned my kiss and relaxed back into her recliner. "I think I'll turn on HSN."

"Sheesh. No more presents!" Nicholas barked agreement as I shouldered my bag. "Love you. 'Bye."

She mumbled the same back at me as the door swung shut. I could hear the TV come up to full volume as I tossed my bag into the Toyota's front seat and followed it.

For a moment, for only a moment I gazed, blank-faced, at her door through the bug-splattered windshield, nibbling my lower lip.

Anxiety. Projection. *Yeah.*

I started the car.

* * *

Just as I was leaving Rosauer's, my favorite grocery store, the phone rang again. I slowed and pulled over, my heart accelerating in perfect inverse proportion; fumbled the damned thing out of my bag; expecting to see her number on the display and fearing the worst.

But it was Nicky. I thumbed the talk button, my heart still doing the Mexican Hat Dance.

"Hi, this is Michelle."

"Hi. It's . . ."

"Nicky. Hi. What's up?"

She was faintly puzzled. "Well, I just got off the phone with Mishelle and she sounded funny."

"Funny how?"

"Uh. Kind of groggy. Like she was really stoned or something. It didn't sound right, so I thought I should call you."

A quick glance at the car clock told me that just about three hours had passed since I'd seen her. "Huh, I was at her place this morning and she seemed fine."

"Not to me," Nicky declared. "She kept saying over and over: 'Nicky, I really love you.' I thought that was kind of weird. Did she take any meds?"

"Not that I know of." My heart had abandoned the hat in favor of enthusiastic break dancing. It wasn't as much fun as it sounds. "I'm going to call Lynn right now. I'll call you back in a few minutes."

"Yeah, do that, please." There was genuine anxiety in her voice. I was again reminded that this woman who I had once distrusted cared about my friend as much as I did.

"Be right back, Nicky." I hung up and speed-dialed Mishelle's number. Lynn picked up. I could hear the TV in the background.

"Hello?"

The hair on my neck was prickling: an unpleasant counterpoint to my heart's impromptu audition for *Dancing With The Stars*. "It's me: Michelle. How's she doing?"

"Oh, fine." She was puzzled. "Why?"

"She seemed kind of . . . I dunno. Sluggish, maybe. When I was there this morning. Nicky just called and said she seemed groggy and kept repeating, 'I love you', over and over."

Lynn laughed. "Oh, she just woke up from a nap. You know how she is when she's been snoozing for a while."

"Yeah." I gnawed at my lower lip, stopped myself. "Maybe. Listen; keep a close eye on her. If anything changes, call me and Lori immediately, got that?"

Lynn sounded just the least little bit offended. "Of course, Michelle. Don't worry, okay?"

Somehow, I managed to keep a snap out of my voice: "Lynn, I *always* worry about her."

"Well, so do I," she said, her voice cool. "You want to talk to her?"

I glanced at the car clock again. One more shopping stop this afternoon and then I was done for the day. But there was so much to do at home . . . "No. Tell her I'll be over tonight. When are you leaving?"

"Right after I fix her dinner." She sounded perfectly calm and for a moment, I hated her and in the next, hated myself for that.

"Tell her I'll be over tonight. Seven-thirty, maybe earlier if I can manage. 'Kay?"

"Okay. Shall I call Nicky and tell her everything's fine?"

"No, I'll do it. I promised." Another glance at the clock: "Gotta go. Thanks, Lynn."

"Of course, Michelle. Don't worry, she's *fine*."

Damned if she wasn't trying to soothe *me*. I wanted no part of it. I clicked off with a muttered, "G'bye," and put the car in gear.

* * *

The doorknob seemed to slither in my grip as I turned it. Self-consciously, I wiped my hand on the seat of my jeans as I entered her apartment. "Hey, you?"

"Hey." Her voice was subdued as her face turned toward me. We swapped smooches. Nicholas yapped once from his sentry pose on her knees so I gave him a quick scratch and rumpled his droopy ears.

His fur was still erect, I noticed.

I looked her over carefully. After you've come to know someone, their body language can tell you volumes in one brief glance. But I took my time and examined her with as much professional skill as I could muster in a visual examination.

Normal. Ordinary. The usual: a bit sallow, lines of fatigue around her mouth that were undoubtedly due to a lack of sleep and perhaps her bent posture was a trifle more strained than usual, but not unusually so.

I perched on the arm of her recliner and took her hand. I felt for her pulse and I doubt if she noticed. It too, was normal.

"So," I said, my voice cheery and utterly artificial, "How you doin', girlfriend?"

She smiled, stroking Nicholas. "I'm okay, Michelle. I'm glad you came over, though. I was hoping you'd have time to help me with a bath tonight. I'm having my hair done tomorrow."

I remembered. "Yeah, I could do that." Right on cue, her robot announced that it was seven thirty pm.

We both laughed. "I've got time. You're going to get pretty for your visit on Thursday, huh?"

She nodded, still smiling placidly. "I hope so. At least as pretty as she can make me."

I bent and kissed her cheek again. "Shouldn't be too hard. You're already beautiful, you know."

Her sudden grin was like sunshine. "Aw, you're just prejudiced 'cause you love me."

"Guilty as charged."

I helped her with her bath. Oddly, Nicholas didn't do his crazed rabbit hunter impersonation, but instead plunked his furry butt down in the doorway and watched us, tongue lolling out and eyes bright with interest.

I didn't pay much attention. I was focused mostly on her.

Another clue missed.

We didn't talk much while I was helping her bathe. I had an uneasy feeling that something was on her mind and I think she had the same feeling about me; body language and that unspoken communication that occurs between close friends.

I got her settled back into her recliner. She sighed. I took it for a sigh of contentment, but then she asked me:

"Do you think I'll ever need a bed-bath, Michelle?"

Her question took me by surprise. "Well, I suppose it's a possibility but I'll bet that Lynn and Nicky can both give a pretty mean bed-bath. So can I; for that matter."

To my complete astonishment, she started to cry. "Someone's not telling me something!"

I tried to catch my breath but it wouldn't hold still. "What? *Who?*" I put my arm around her shoulders. "What are you talking about, girlfriend?"

Her voice was raw with emotion. "When I got home from the therapy session today, there was a note on my door from the Hospice pastor." I'd never seen her blubber like a baby before. "I feel like they're keeping something from me!"

"Sssh." I stroked her weathered cheek with gentle fingertips; wiped away the tears. "Hey, Hospice always does stuff like that for a new patient. It's just part of their job: to make sure that everyone on the service has all the options available to them and to give you a chance to talk about your own situation."

I kissed the top of her still-damp head. "It's all routine, Mishelle. They just want to make sure that you're coping with this, that's all. If you need to discuss anything with them, that's what they're for: so you can talk about it no matter what it might be."

"Will they tell me the truth?"

I felt a chill even though her apartment was fairly warm. "Well, *of course.* Do you think they wouldn't?" I added, "I hope you know that *I'd* always tell you the truth, Mishelle. Always."

She was struggling to contain the tears. I could feel her shoulders quivering. "Okay. Tell me this: do you think I'm getting worse?"

I sighed, closed my eyes and chose my words with extreme care. "Sometimes yes, sometimes no. I know you're in a much compromised state right now, at least physically. Functionally, I'd say you're doing about the same."

I paused and then said as gently as I could: "What do *you* think?"

I held her, feeling her shoulders quiver. The words came from her as if they were being forced out, one painful syllable at a time: "Sometimes . . . sometimes I think I'm okay. Others . . . I feel *terrible.*"

The dam broke. Tears and words poured out of her in a torrent: "I don't want to die, Michelle! I'm not *ready*! I finally found some peace and happiness with you and your family and now I'm going to die and I don't want to *leave!*"

Stunned, all I could do was stroke her hair and hold her.

"There was so much I wanted to do! I wanted to, to . . . Go on a boat ride with you! I'll never be able to water ski again, but the feel of the wind in my hair, the smell of the water, just once more . . . And I wanted to go Christmas shopping with you!"

She sobbed like a child and it tore at my heart. "I wanted to hear Chris play his guitar! He's my little brother and I love him and I don't want to leave him!"

My mind was reeling. I was remembering a conversation I'd had with Dave last week about taking her out boating on Flathead Lake.

Friends of ours; Jim and Angela, had offered their boat and their dock at Big Fork was perfect for it: a nice flat approach with easy access for her wheelchair.

I'd been a bit dumfounded by their offer; it had never occurred to me that Angela would ever be so open about a trans person but again: it just shows that you can never judge anyone by their outside.

I wanted to tell her that but something held me back. Instead, I held her and soothed her, sliding so far over the arm of her recliner that I was practically in her lap and Nicholas was forced to scoot over to give me room.

The little dachshund was making anxious whining noises far back in his throat and doing his best to lick away the tears pouring down the ravaged cheeks of his mistress.

"Listen. Listen to me, dear one." I tried to keep my own tears under control without much success. "You're not going anywhere. *I'm* not going anywhere. No matter what happens, I'll always be here for you. I'll be at your side, come what may."

"I know." She turned her tear-streaked face up to me. "I don't know what I'd do without you, Michelle."

"I think you'd do just fine." I stretched out my arm, snagged a tissue out of the dispenser on the side table and dabbed at her face. "You did pretty darned well for twenty years before you met me, girlfriend."

"Yeah." A tremulous smile tried to surface. "I guess so."

"I know so." I shook my head, even though I knew she couldn't see the movement. She could feel it. She could feel *anything*, right then. "Jeez, what a life you've had, sweetie! And it's not over yet. I *know*."

"Okay." She leaned against me and I could feel her relaxing at last. Something unwound and smoothed out within me as well. "Can I call you tomorrow?"

"Oh, jeez. You had to ask? You'd *better* call me tomorrow. I'll be home all day, mucking out the stables for your visit on Thursday. Okay?"

Mishelle nodded. "I'm sorry to be such a baby, Michelle. I just had such a bad feeling about this weekend . . ."

"Well, you can tell that bad feeling to catch the next bus out of town," I said firmly. "And don't you *ever* apologize to me about your feelings or I'll give you *such* a smack."

I leaned over and kissed her to show I was teasing. "Now get some sleep and don't you worry about things like never waking up. You're a tough old broad, Mishelle. You don't give up. You've *never* given up."

I even managed a laugh, believe it or not. "Just like me. We don't quit, do we?"

"No." She sighed and seemed to relax, or perhaps it was only fatigue I saw clinging to her lanky, folded frame. "G'night, Michelle. I love you."

I kissed her again and rumpled Nick's floppy ears. The little dachshund had resettled into her lap and looked up for only a moment before relaxing as well.

His eyes closed as he vented a relieved sigh.

"Love you too, sweetie. See you Thursday."

WEDNESDAY, AUGUST NINTH

No e-mail.

I stared at the screen, feeling my forehead wrinkle. Two days in row. "But she *always* e-mails me," I muttered. "Every morning."

I sipped my coffee and made a face. It tasted like bleach. "Yuck." I looked back at the screen, noted that her last e-mail was Monday; two days ago. "Now *that's* just weird."

"You talkin' to yourself?"

I glanced up. "'Morning. Yeah, I guess I am. Don't tell me you've never done that?"

Dave yawned. "Sure, but I don't answer, usually." He scratched his sleep-tousled head. His silvery crew cut looked like a well-used cleaning brush. "At least, not out loud."

I shrugged. "Maybe it's early Alzheimer's." I looked back at the screen, still frowning. "Hmm."

"She didn't e-mail you, huh?"

I shook my head. "No." Another shrug and another sip of coffee: yuck, again. I made a face, looking down into the cup. "Did you put bleach in the dishwasher or something?"

He looked puzzled. "Why would I do that?"

"I dunno." I sighed. "Never mind."

"Y'know, you worry too much about her. She's got a busy day today, what with her hair appointment and all. Maybe she just forgot."

I looked up at him again. "Yeah, you're probably right. About the busy day, anyway. And so do I, for that matter. What's on your schedule?"

"Um, only two houses to show. But I've got a ton of paperwork at the office. Why? You need some help?"

I shook my head. "No, it's just as well you'll be out of my hair today. I have a lot of cleaning to do around here."

He smiled. "I don't know why. It's not as if she can *see* if it's a little messy, y'know."

I felt a flash of irritation. "*I* can, though."

In an instant, his look was wary. "Easy. I didn't mean anything."

"Okay. Yeah. You want breakfast?"

He shook his head. "No, I'll pick up something to eat on the way to the office. Mind if I use the shower first?"

"No, go ahead. Leave the towels on the floor. I'm doing laundry, too."

"Okay." He hesitated. "Hey, Michelle?"

"Hmm?" I was busy deleting the spam. "What?"

"Maybe you should just . . . I dunno, let it go for today. You said last night that she was scared?"

I looked up at him again. "Yeah. We talked about it, though. I think she's going to be alright."

"Why don't you call her?"

I shook my head. "No. She has to get ready for her hair appointment. Lynn will call me if anything serious happens."

"Then let it go for today," he said firmly. "Just for today, okay? Give yourself a break."

I snorted. "Sure, that's easy for you to say. *You* don't have to clean this pigsty."

"It's not that bad, Michelle," he said quietly. "Really."

I didn't answer. I was staring at an emptied e-box that still had no new message from her. When I looked up, Dave was gone and the sound of the shower filtered through the doorway.

I looked back at the screen, nibbling my lip.

Call her . . .

"Nuts," I muttered, picked up the phone and hit the speed dial for her number.

"Hi!" She sounded okay, if a bit wheezy. "You're up early."

"It's cleaning day, remember?"

"Oh, that's right. You really don't need to do that, you know. I don't care what your house looks like."

I bit down hard on what I almost said and replied, simply: "I need to, Mishelle. I can't stand a messy place, especially if I have a VIP visiting."

She giggled. "Oh, so I'm a VIP, am I? Ooh, I'm flattered."

A grin threatened to surface at the corners of my mouth, but I told it sternly to go away. "You are to me. Can I call you later? We'll set up a time for tomorrow."

"Sure!" she said cheerfully. There was a clatter in the background and I heard her say, "Thanks, Lynn." Then: "Uh, I've got breakfast in front of me. I should eat before my eggs get cold."

"Oh. Right. Okay. Talk to you later."

"'Kay." Her mouth was full. "Lurf ya. Shee ya."

"I love you, too." I closed the phone and laid it on my desk next to the keyboard; softly added a swear word I rarely use and got up.

There was work to be done, as always.

* * *

The phone rang about two that afternoon, startling me. I dropped the brush in the toilet and went flying through the house, trying to remember where I'd left the damn thing. Front room? Kitchen?

My office!

I flipped it open. It was Lori. "Hi, this is Michelle."

"Hi!" She sounded cheerful as ever. "Hope I didn't catch you in the middle of anything."

"Nah. Just cleaning." I peeled off the disposable gloves and dropped them in the wastebasket. "What's up?"

"Well, I just wanted to touch bases with you about Mishelle's medication status. Doctor J and I looked over her meds history and we both think that her Oxycontin dosage should be increased. She seems to have developed a certain amount of acclimation at her current levels and he wants to bump it up to two thirty milligram tabs every eight hours; one hundred eighty milligrams daily. Also, he thinks—and I agree—that she should be taking the Clonazepam three times daily. It should ease the anxiety she feels when she can't get enough air."

"Huh." My forehead wrinkled in thought. "One hundred eighty milligrams of Oxycontin is a pretty big dose, Lori."

"Oh, I agree. But she's become acclimated to the lower dose. It happens in these elderly folks, especially those with a history of chronic back pain."

She paused. "Y'know, Michelle, I'm concerned that she might not be keeping track of what she's actually taking. It's probably time to start with the pill boxes and timed dosages, maybe even a medication pump. I'm thinking we should also look into programming her computer to give her some voice prompts to help in that regard. Can her computer guy—what's his name?"

"Mike."

"Yeah, Mike. You think he can set that up for her?"

"I don't see why not."

"Got his number handy?"

"Sure." I flipped open my phone directory and read the number off to her.

"Okay, got it. I'll give him a call and set it up."

"I think Dave was going to assist on that. I'll tell him, too. Thanks, Lori."

"No problem," she said cheerfully. "That's what I'm here for, Michelle. Hey, when will you see her next?"

"Tomorrow. She's coming over here for a visit. Dinner and a bath. Maybe a chess game or two with Dave if she's up to it."

"Hmm, maybe we can get the two of them to do it then. I'd like to implement this before the weekend."

I had to admire her efficiency. I always did, though. "Sounds good to me. I'll be there around ten."

"Well, she doesn't have to be here for that. But I'll be there too; to explain it. I want you involved in this process in case she has any confusion about it."

"Thanks." *Confusion*, I thought. "Hey, Lori?"

"Yes?"

"Uh, I was over at her place last night and we had a long talk. About her status." *And other things*. "She's really worried that we're not telling her everything she needs to know about this."

Lori sighed. "Yeah, that's pretty commonplace, too. It comes from that feeling of helplessness and inevitability terminal patients have. Most of them want some feeling of control over their care and treatment."

I could almost see her shrug. "Can't blame her, really. If we can just reassure her that her input and feedback is every bit as important, then it can go a long way to relieving a lot of her anxiety."

"I hope you're right. Can we go over that with her tomorrow, too?"

"Of course. Anything else, Michelle?"

"No, that's it for now. I'll call you if I think of anything."

"Please do. Hey, Michelle?"

"Hmm?"

"Your input is important too, y'know." Her compassion and concern was evident and I was reminded again just how *good* this woman was at her job; how much she truly cared about her patients. "You're her best friend. She talks about you and Chris and your whole family all the time."

There was a tiny pause. "She really loves you and your family, Michelle."

My eyes stung. "Thanks, Lori. We all love her, especially Chris." My voice cracked for more reasons than I could say right then. "He's like her little brother."

"I know, Michelle." Her voice was infinitely gentle. "But don't thank me, my friend. Thank *her*. She's a very special lady. I'm honored to know her."

I was going to have to hang up very soon or I was in danger of making a complete fool of myself. "Me, too. Honored, I mean. But thank you, Lori. Listen, I've got to finish cleaning this dump for her visit. See you tomorrow."

"Okay. 'Bye, Michelle."

"'Bye." I closed the phone and carefully put it on my desk, took a few deep breaths and went back to work.

* * *

Dinner that night was homemade chicken enchiladas. It's a recipe I've polished to perfection over many years of trial and error. I actually enjoy making them, partly because the members of my family seem to find them so irresistible. Dave's eyes lit up when he came through the door.

"Oh, boy! Smells great, hon!"

I smiled at him and accepted his kiss. "Want to set the table and I'll load up our plates?"

"Sure."

We ate at the kitchen table since the boys were gone. I chattered away about my day while Dave silently forked in the food. I had reached the point where Lori and I discussed the change in Mishelle's meds when he stopped feeding his face and looked up, frowning.

"Say that again, please?"

I was puzzled. "Say what?"

"The part about the med pump."

"Oh. Well, it's just a gadget that automatically provides a metered drip of medication . . ."

"I know what med pump is, Michelle. What does this mean for her?"

His tone was harsh, almost demanding. Surprised, I looked at him. "Well, it just means she won't miss any of her pain meds. You know: not take enough or not on time. Why?"

His eyes were fixed on me. "How much of the meds? What level?"

Perplexed, I said, "Well, they want to raise it, like I said. She seems to be acclimated to the level she's at now . . ."

"How *much*?" he barked.

Surprised, I stuttered, "Uh, a hundred and eighty milligrams. About . . . about equal to another pill's worth, I think. *Why?*"

Until that moment, I had never seen my husband turn the color of a bleached bed sheet.

It's not a very flattering shade for him.

He swallowed. "I don't think that would be a good idea."

We stared at each other across the kitchen table. The silence grew. I'll give him this: he didn't look away.

"Dave," I said carefully, very slowly. "Is there something I should know?"

He nodded.

"I'm waiting."

He told me.

The enchiladas suddenly tasted like ashes. "Oh, dear God in Heaven," I said faintly. "How long have you known?"

He shrugged. "A long time. Couple months, maybe." He picked up his beer and took a long swallow. "Didn't you ever wonder how she could afford all that stuff she buys?"

"Credit . . . Credit cards . . ."

My husband's look was pitying. "You can't possibly be that naïve. Yeah, I guess *you* could."

My skin suddenly felt icy and I wanted to throw up. "She . . . She *sells* them? To *who*?"

He shook his head and took another swallow. His expression was grim. "Tell me!"

The beer bottle hit the table with a defiant thud. "I don't know." His voice was calm and unyielding. I wanted to pick up my plate of half-eaten enchiladas and throw it at him. "Probably lots of people. You know how they come and go at her place."

"And you've *seen* this?"

He shook his head. "I've never actually seen her sell them, no. I've seen the money she stashes and I've deposited some of it for her sometimes. But I've never actually seen money and meds exchanged." He added: "Pot, yeah. I've seen her buy that . . ."

"She's got a card!"

He shrugged and looked down, toyed with the food on his plate.

"Does Nicky know? Lynn?"

He looked up. "I really doubt it. She's very careful not to do it while they're present. They're usually around during the day and her buyers come around at night after they leave."

"So how come *you* know this and nobody else does?"

He shrugged again. "Maybe she trusts me. Bong buddies, y'know?"

I was beginning to feel really sick to my stomach. "And not *me*? Oh . . . *Shit*!" I wailed the word, tears springing to my eyes. "How could she . . .! How could you *do* this?"

My fists were clenched. "David Alexander, don't you realize what this could do my career? *You* . . . damn it, this is illegal!"

"Listen up, Michelle." There was steel in his voice. Another first: I'd never before heard my husband speak to me in that fashion. "You have any idea how much she makes on disability?"

Mute, I shook my head while the tears poured down my cheeks.

"Jack shit, that's what she makes. Barely enough to cover her expenses. Sure, the State covers her caregivers and Medicare covers her medical costs but that's *it*, baby. That's *all*. Nothing left over for those gadgets she needs."

His face was like stone. "And who's gonna pay for them?"

"The Foundation for the Blind . . ."

Now he looked disgusted. "Hah. They don't have the money, either. She's on her own, Michelle. Always has been. So she figured out a way to make ends meet and so what?"

"So what? It's *illegal*, that's what! And it puts me, my career as a nurse at risk!" I felt dizzy and wondered if I really was going to puke. "My God, if the police find out, she could go to jail!"

"So don't tell anyone."

I stared at him. "*Lie*? Oh yeah, add that to the list, too!"

"You're forgetting one thing," he said gently.

"What?"

"If Lori puts a med pump on her, she'll overdose."

Our eyes met. "I have to call her," I said finally. My tongue felt numb and funny.

"Yeah. Yeah, I think that would be a good idea."

I got up. My knees were wobbly. Heart pounding, I headed for the bedroom where I'd left my purse.

"One more thing," he called out.

"What *now*?" I was fumbling through my bag, looking for my cellphone.

He came to the door of the bedroom. "Don't tell her I told you this."

"*Why*?" I didn't quite snarl at him. "So she'll still be your bong buddy?"

"No." His voice was very quiet. "Because she's going downhill and she doesn't need to feel like we're betraying her. It might . . . it might . . ."

I stood, the phone gripped in my fist, staring at him. "Make it worse."

He nodded.

I closed my eyes and sighed. "Okay."

"Promise."

"Like you promised *her*?"

"I didn't promise her anything," he said in that same quiet tone. "I didn't have to."

I looked at him again. His eyes pleaded with me. I nodded. "Okay. I promise."

He nodded in return, turned as if to go, stopped and looked back at me. "You might want to give it a few minutes. To calm down, you know? Yelling at her won't do her any good, the shape she's in right now. Just a thought."

He paused. "I'll clean up the kitchen. You . . . You just relax."

I looked at the phone in my hand and then tossed it back in my purse. "No. No, I'll do it. Pour me a glass of wine, willya?" I laughed without any humor. "I have a feeling I'm going to need it."

He nodded and went back into the kitchen. I followed him and we both cleaned up the mess.

We had a lot of leftover enchiladas.

* * *

Cross-legged on my bed later that evening, surrounded by pillows, fortified by a second glass of chardonnay: I dialed her number. "Good evening, sweetie! How ya doin'?"

"Huh? Oh, jus' fine. How're you?" The TV was blaring in the background. It sounded like *Jeopardy.*

"Great. Hey, can you turn down the TV, please? It's awfully loud, dear."

"Sure, sure. Gimme a sec'. Where did . . .? Ah . . ." The volume dropped to less than deafening levels. "Whazzup?"

I took the phone away from my ear and stared at it, put it back. "Are you okay?"

"Sure, sure. Why?"

"Well, you sound funny." Something occurred to me. "Mishelle, have you been drinking?"

"Nah. Haven' . . . haven't touched . . . A drop. All day. Why?"

I laughed but I wasn't amused, for obvious reasons. "Because you sound *drunk*, that's why."

"Wish I *was*," she slurred. "Be a lot more fun than just sittin' here, all by myself."

"Where's Lynn?"

"Oh, she went home already. Long day for her."

The ants with icy little feet were back, marching double-time up and down my spine. "Did you take any meds? Oxycontin? How much did you take?"

"Just my usual."

"*How many?*"

"One."

"When?"

"Uh, jus' . . . after dinner. About two . . . Two hours ago. Really, I di'nt, didn't take more than that. Honest, Michelle."

"Well, you sound thoroughly baked," I said grimly. "Did you smoke any pot?"

There was a hoarse snicker. "Uh-huh. Wow, that medical marijuana is good shit."

"Jeez. Yeah, and it smells like a skunk died in your front room, too." I took a deep breath, suddenly aware of just how lucky I was to be able to do something as simple as that. "Did you take anything else besides the Oxycontin?"

"Just the new stuff. Clone . . . Clone-ah . . ."

"Clonazepam. Okay. *Don't* take any more until you talk to me and Lori tomorrow."

"'Kay," she wheezed. "Now that you mention it, I do feel kinda groggy."

"Yeah, I'll bet you do," I said with rather more sarcasm than I had intended. THC has this annoying tendency to turn otherwise bright, talkative people into mumbling idiots. But it seems to keep the convenience stores in business. "So, I talked to Lori today."

"Uh-huh. What about?"

"Oh, nothing much. Your pain meds, mostly. She wants to get you set up with pill boxes and constant monitoring of your dosages."

"Okay."

I could almost admire her calm. "So that means you won't be able to sell them anymore, Mishelle."

She didn't say a word. She didn't have to.

"You can't bullshit me anymore, Mishelle. I know what you've been doing with the extra meds and why you're always in pain from your back."

Cautiously, she said, "What do you mean?"

"You know darned well what I mean!"

"Did Dave tell you that?"

I gritted my teeth, but a promise is a promise. "No, I figured it out all by myself."

"I haven't . . ."

"She's also considering a pain pump, Mishelle." My voice was icy cold, as cold as those tiny feet marching up and down my back.

There was a short pause and I could hear Alex Trebek's calm, soothing voice in the background. It was utterly wasted on me. Still cautious, she said, "So?"

All my reserve melted, my control fled and I dropped all pretense. "Don't you *get* it?" I yelled. "They're going to give you the level of medication that you're *supposed* to be getting! And since you're only taking less than *half* of that, you'll be getting almost *three times* the usual dose!"

I was suddenly close to tears. "Jesus Christ in Heaven, Mishelle, you'll overdose! You'll die!"

In a very small voice, she said, "You're mad at me."

My eyes burned. "You're darned right I'm mad at you! You could have told me! I could have helped you do something about the money you needed for all your gadgets. But *nooo*, you had to play games with Schedule II medications which is a Federal crime, sweetie!"

"Michelle . . ."

"I *get* it! I understand *why* you're doing it, but it's not worth it!" I was openly crying now and I couldn't stop and I didn't even want to; much less did I care. "I *know* how hard it is to make ends meet on disability but for God's sake Mishelle, did you ever stop to think *where* those meds ended up? Maybe some junkie who goes out for a drive and wraps his car around an innocent family at eighty miles an hour? Maybe a nutcase with a passion for automatic weapons?"

I paused for breath and then said, steadily. "Maybe a schoolyard? Like Chris's school?"

There was a pause leavened only by her hoarse breathing and Alex Trebek. I resolved then and there never to watch *Jeopardy* again.

She said: "Isn't there anything you can do to stop it?"

I took a deep breath and wiped my face with the back of my hand. "Yeah, I can tell her the truth. And then we're *both* in serious trouble."

"Why would *you* be in trouble?"

"Because I should have known about it and I didn't!" I snapped. "I was stupid and I didn't notice the signs right in front of my nose because I love you, you idiot!"

I realized I was hugging myself with my free arm. I badly needed a hug, right then.

She sounded subdued and completely sober, thank God: "What should I do?"

"Stop selling your meds. Don't immediately start taking your usual dosage; cut the remaining pill in half and take that for a week. If you're still feeling back pain—which I doubt—then take the full dosage, but don't do it unless I'm with you and can stay with you for at least an hour. Got that?"

"Yes," she said meekly. "I got it."

I wiped sweaty palms on my pillow, switching the phone back and forth to do it. "Good. I'll try to talk Lori out of going to the pain pump anytime soon, but you have to be diligent about taking the meds. We'll try to figure something out for your, uh, reduced income."

I sighed and wiped my face again. "God, Mishelle, if she fits you with one of those things, you'll gork, sure as hell."

"I'll . . . what did you say?"

"Gork. *Die.*" I was trembling with a horrid after-reaction and suddenly all I wanted to do was collapse. "It's a nurse's term. What happens to a patient who doesn't tell us what they're taking and we give them the wrong dose. *Gork.* Like croak, only worse."

"Oh." There was silence for about half a dozen heartbeats, and then she said, "Are you still mad at me?"

I sighed again, suddenly aware how much my chest hurt. "No. No, I could never be mad at you. I love you. I'm just scared out of my wits for you, that's all. Scared for you, scared for us both. It's my fault, really."

I found myself longing for a smoke and another glass of chardonnay. The irony of that didn't escape me at all. "I was stupid. I let this go on too long. But it stops tonight. Okay?"

"Okay." She sounded utterly submissive and completely defenseless and my heart melted within me, leaving a void only she could fill. "I'll do what you want. I promise."

"Okay."I shot a glance at the bedside clock. It was just past eight. "Listen, I'll be there around ten tomorrow. Keep the phone close and if you feel really short of breath, call Lori immediately. She'll call me and we'll race each other to your place. Got that?"

"Got it. See you tomorrow, Michelle."

She sounded like a lost little girl. I wanted more than anything to jump in the Toyota and race over to her place *right now* to give her a hug.

"Yeah. Tomorrow. Get some sleep, sweetie. And don't worry, I won't let them gork you. I promise."

"'Kay. G'night. Love ya."

"Love you too, Mishelle." I clicked off, shut the phone and flopped back on the bed, staring at the ceiling.

"Aw, shit," I whispered.

THURSDAY, AUGUST TENTH

Again: no e-mail from her. I glared at a screen full of spam and no new messages and felt like dumping the damned thing in the lake.

It wasn't like her. I got up, went back into the bedroom, grabbed my phone off the nightstand and flipped it open. I started to dial her number.

Dave chose that moment to poke his head into the bedroom. "Hey."

I looked up, my finger poised over the buttons. Our eyes met and we acknowledged the night before and our mutual reluctance to talk about it in a single glance.

"Hey?"

"I'm going to pick up some breakfast on the way. I'll meet you at her place around ten-thirty. Mike should be online then and we'll do those updates we talked about yesterday."

"Oh, right. Her voice prompts."

"Yeah. It should take about an hour, hour and a half. Will you have her ready to go by then?"

"Sure. I'm just going to cook her some breakfast and then I'll pack up her stuff." I remembered something else: "Her bed will be delivered today. Can you help with that?"

He shrugged. "If I'm not at a critical point. When's the bed supposed to be there?"

"Around noon, I think."

"Cutting it close. I'll try. If nothing else, I'll load up her concentrator. How's her bottled air?"

"Should be fine, I think. I'll check. Look," I gestured with the phone. "Let me call her and find out."

"Right." He withdrew. I punched up the number. It rang three times. "Hello?"

A prickle, a mere prickle is all I felt. "Hey? Did I wake you up?"

"Uh-huh."

"Well, I hope you got a good night's sleep."

"Uh-huh, for once. I took that extra half-pill." She *did* sound rested. Relaxed. For some reason I was still uneasy, though. "You coming over?"

"Silly." I didn't want to talk about the night before. My own sleep had been less than restful. "Of course. In about an hour. Can you hold out that long?"

She cackled. "I think so." I could hear her grunt and stretch. "Ooh, I feel good. Hurry up, sweetie."

I did just that. I was at her place in less than an hour. I cast a critical eye on her the second I came through the door.

Normal, I thought. Only normal.

"How would you," I said, standing after our greeting kiss, "Like a pancake breakfast?"

She laughed while I looked her over, my professional persona still in charge. She seemed like herself: relaxed, cheerful, upbeat even if just a little bit tired. Her color was good and her breathing sounded fine.

She was almost lounging in the recliner instead of her usual slightly bent posture. Everything about her told me that she was in good shape.

Nicholas was bouncing around on the floor, yapping madly for attention so I rumpled his ears and rubbed his prominent chest while keeping my eyes on her.

Blue was in her usual spot, cuddled up next to her mistress. When I came in, the cat stood and stretched, staring at me with her startling eyes. She meowed once; a question and I answered it with a back scratch and head rub.

She ducked her head under my fingers and revved her motor for me.

Smiling, Mishelle said: "I was in a pancake-eating contest when I was young and I ate fifty-four pancakes, not a record for the contest but it sure was for *me*. I don't think I've had a pancake since then."

Such a wonderful smile, I thought, my insides unwinding themselves.

"I think enough time has passed that I could eat some more, huh?"

"Comin' right up," I said and got to it.

About the time I put the second stack of Texas flapjacks in front of her, there was brief knock on the door and Dave came in.

He kissed us both and made a beeline for the computer terminal, carefully stepping over Nicholas and his game of Intruder Alert, Round Two.

My husband was soon engrossed in his work, cellphone in one hand, the other on the mouse or keyboard, listening intently to Mike the computer guru. Occasionally, the computer would mutter something—the volume was turned way down, for once—and he would mutter back at it.

Mishelle and I chatted while she blissfully stuffed herself with pancakes. Nicholas scampered around her ankles, begging for scraps, so I fed the little dachshund tiny bits of bacon left over from a single strip I'd cooked for myself.

His fur was still oddly erect and he peered anxiously into my face as if seeking reassurance. I stroked his back, thinking: *Poor puppy, all this commotion is making you crazy.*

If only I'd known . . .

Earl and Louise put in an appearance shortly after eleven. I was glad to see both of them. My attitude toward Mishelle's parents had changed considerably in the past few weeks since they'd walked in on the first of the many chess tournaments between their daughter and my sons.

Earl had even showed up shortly after Carpet Day to help me disassemble and move Mishelle's bed so that new carpet could be laid beneath it. I found myself thinking that he wasn't all that different from many of the elderly male patients I saw on a daily basis: reserved, even tight-lipped and understandably wary of strangers.

I broke down his resistance that day, though. When I insisted on helping him haul the heavy mattress and box springs out the door and load it onto the back of his pickup truck, his comment that I'd make a good farm wife gave me a better insight into his thinking.

Yes, they cared about their daughter, in their own way and in their own time even if neither of them had anything resembling an understanding of the concept of transgender.

I doubted that they ever would.

But they tried to love her as best as they could. It was never a revelation for me to discover this; rather it was a slow understanding of two survivors who had endured much more than myself and would soon have to learn how to survive the loss of their first-born.

Personally, I thought Earl looked really cute in his overalls, kind of like Andy of Mayberry. And he had a nice laugh.

"Hey, you two!"

At our feet, Nicholas had advanced to Round Three and was torn between hysterical joy and the overwhelming urge to bite something, *anything.* He settled for punctuating the occasional human comment with a sharp yelp.

Earl nodded gravely at me. Louise said, bright as sunshine: "'Morning, Michelle! How's he doin'?" She held a plastic bag containing something that could only be Tupperware filled with leftovers.

I skipped over the jarring pronoun. "Good!" I had Mishelle's empty plate clutched in one hand and gestured with it. "Eight Texas flapjacks and four strips of bacon. And I think she's responding very well to the new nebulizer medication."

Louise chuckled. "Mike, did y'tell Michelle here 'bout that pancake-eatin' contest you entered?" Her eyes twinkled. "I swear, that boy laid on his bed all day, groanin'. Wouldn't even eat dinner."

My back teeth ached with the need to bite down hard, just like Nicholas. "Yes, she told me all about it, Louise."

I looked down at my friend whose expression was somewhere between that detached half-smile and embarrassment. "Do you want any more, Mishelle?"

She held up her hand. "Stuffed. Honest. Thanks for showing up today, Dad. You too, Mom. The bed should be here soon."

I raised an eyebrow at her and looked back at Mom and Dad. Good ol' Earl just shrugged. Louise smiled sweetly.

"When I called yesterday mornin', Mike told me his new bed would be here today. Ain't no room for the old one and he won't have no use for it anyways, so we'll take it."

She held up the bag containing the Tupperware. "I had some pot roast left over from last night, so it seemed like a good time to pay y'all a visit, maybe meet the rest of your kin?"

"Kin?"

Mishelle piped up: "I think she means Dave, Michelle."

"Uh." Flummoxed, I glanced at my husband. All this time and they'd never met!

I felt like an idiot. Dave rose and came over; courteously offered his hand while my cheeks flamed red and I stammered out introductions.

When Dave had retreated, I said, "Uh, *when* did you call yesterday, exactly?"

"Oh, I call Mike purt' near ev'ry morning, usually 'round eight. 'Long 'bout the time he gets up. Just to talk, see how he's doin'." Her smile was gentle and beyond reproach. "Reckon you do, too. He talks about you enough."

"Really." I realized that I was still waving the plate in front of their noses. "Uh, would you like some flapjacks, too?"

Louise smiled that serene little smile and it came to me then where Mishelle had gotten some of hers. "Naw, Earl an' me had breakfast already. But thank you, Michelle."

"Uh, you're welcome."

I was again saved by the bell. It was the bed and it was a whopper. Kalispell Medical Equipment had sent two strapping young fellows to unload it and set it up.

We got out of their way except for Dave, who was head down over the keyboard, typing and clicking with single-minded intensity.

I had to pick up Nicholas and deposit him on Mishelle's lap. The little dachshund was literally trembling on the verge of hysteria.

The computer had a developed a stutter of its own as well. Dave just scowled at it and typed faster.

Louise and Earl said their goodbyes—Louise did, anyway. Earl sort of grunted—and departed.

I realized that I hadn't even begun to pack up her stuff when the doorbell rang again, sending Nicholas into another attack of intruder alert hysterics.

He stood on Mishelle's knees, fur stiff and erect and protested in sharp, ringing yelps as Lori came in.

"Hi, everybody!" She took us all in with a big smile. "I saw the truck outside. Would that be Mishelle's new bed?"

I hooked a thumb over my shoulder. "They're setting it up now," I said. "Welcome to the circus, Lori. You just missed Mishelle's folks."

She appeared genuinely disappointed. "Oh, that's too bad. I've been wanting to talk to them."

"They're kind of hard to talk to. Actually, I need to talk to you, too. I'm a little concerned about her grogginess last night."

I gave her a thumbnail description of Mishelle's slurred speech and apparent confusion and concluded by saying: "I'm wondering if the Clonazepam is causing this. What do you think?"

I left out the other parts of the conversation, of course.

Lori's face creased momentarily in concentration and she stared off into space. I knew she was accessing her encyclopedic knowledge of pharmacology and I kept silent, waiting for her to process this new bit of data. Abruptly, she nodded.

"You could be right. Okay, let's reduce it. One half tab every eight hours and we'll see if that makes a difference. Mishelle?" She went down on one knee and took my friend's hand. "Tell me honestly: is your breathing more difficult? Do you seem like you have to work harder to get air?"

"No." My friend shook her head. "Not really. I've been fine these last two days. Just sleepy, that's all."

"How's your back pain?"

Mishelle shrugged and didn't quite wince. I saw it and wondered if Lori had, too. "About the same. It's okay for a couple hours after I take my pills, but then it comes back."

"Hmm." Lori stood and looked at me. "I know how you feel about medication pumps, but we may have to give that some consideration as well."

"I think the pill boxes are a good start," I said firmly. "Can we try that first before we stick her with a permanent catheter?"

I shrugged. "I really don't have anything against medication pumps, Lori. In fact, I think they're a godsend. I'm just concerned about limiting Mishelle's mobility at this time. Being blind, she might have some trouble maneuvering with all that."

Her forehead creased again. "Well, we've done med pumps on blind patients before, you know, and the results have been very good."

She looked back at Mishelle. "How do you feel about it, Mishelle?"

My friend cleared her throat. "Uh, I'd rather not be hooked up to a bunch of tubes if I can manage to avoid it. Maybe we should try the pill boxes first. I promise to be, uh, diligent about taking them."

"Okay." Lori stood up and looked at me. Her eyes twinkled briefly and something passed between us, accompanied by a pair of smiles. Mine was purely reflex as I vented a silent sigh.

I knew what she was thinking: that I'd already warned my friend about keeping to the medication schedule. She was so right and so utterly mistaken that I almost blurted out the truth, then and there.

Lori wasn't done, though. "There are some other things we can try, too. I was reading about a new ointment containing capsicum that seems to produce really positive results. Perhaps we can try that as well."

"Castration?" Mishelle pricked up her ears almost like Nicholas. "Where do I sign up?"

Lori rolled her eyes at me and we both laughed. Mine had a slightly hysterical edge that I hoped didn't show much.

"No, no. *Capsicum*. It's the stuff that makes hot peppers hot. It's supposed to generate soothing warmth when applied onto the skin. I'll look into it and order some for you, okay? By the way, how are your bowels? Have you been able to move them regularly?"

Dryly, Mishelle said, "My plumbing is working just fine, thanks."

"That's good. I was a bit concerned that the morphine might be causing some constipation." She smiled. "We don't want a case of the Triple-H."

"What's that?" Mishelle inquired.

"Hot, High and a Hell of a lot."

"Oh." My friend thought it over and then offered brightly: "Well, there's a sign back there that says *Do Not Enter*, so let's hope it stays that way!"

I think my laughter sounded much less forced that time.

About then, the two fellows from Kalispell Medical ambled back into the room. "We're all done, ladies," the taller of the two drawled. "Can we get a signature from, uh," he looked at his delivery manifest. "Mishelle Woodring?"

"That's me," Mishelle said and held out her hand.

He looked at her and his eyes widened. Perilously close to fumbling, he placed the metal clipboard in her hand. "Uh, just sign here, uh, ma'am?"

"Sure, but where's *here*? Need a little help, honey."

Lori and I watched with barely concealed grins as he guided her hand to the right spot. The tips of his ears were a bright pink.

He mumbled his thanks as he and his partner beat a hasty retreat. It occurred to me that he would have an interesting tale to tell the rest of the boys down at the warehouse that afternoon.

"Get over it," I muttered at his retreating back as the door closed behind them.

Lori spared me a wink as she gathered up her things and departed; giving us both a hug because after all; hugs were always a requirement whenever she was around.

I started packing up her things, finally. It didn't take long and as I passed Dave for perhaps the third time, I inquired as to his progress.

"Almost got it," he grunted. "What?" he said into the phone. "Yeah, I did that but it still . . . Oh, wait . . . I didn't . . ."

His face screwed up in concentration. "Uh, say again?"

I sighed and started hauling things out to the Toyota. Nicholas had finally figured out that we were going somewhere and was standing at attention on Mishelle's knees, watching me with avid interest.

His yelping had subsided, fortunately.

At last, I was done except for her concentrator. My timing was pretty good: Dave let out a "Yes!" and pumped his fist, gloating at the screen.

Apparently, things were working as they should because he closed his phone and looked up, beaming.

"I heard," I said. "Want to stretch your legs and give me a hand here?"

He looked a bit crestfallen. I trailed him to the truck as he lugged the concentrator out and when he turned around, I gave him a kiss.

"Thanks."

He grinned down at me. "You're welcome. How's she doing?"

I frowned and ran fingers through my hair; thinking. "Okay," I said. "She's tired but I'm hoping a bath and some dinner will perk her up some. What are your plans after you drop off her concentrator?"

"Work," he said gloomily. "I am so backed up on the quarterlies . . ."

"I'll bet."

My husband is not an office drone. There are few things he avoids as much as sitting down and actually doing paperwork. Sometimes I think he would cheerfully choose root canal without anesthesia over doing something as simple as our taxes.

"Okay, I'll see you at home in a few minutes. I have to stop at the pharmacy and pick up her meds." I made a face. "Time for the pill boxes, too."

He nodded. "Let me help you get her in the car," he offered.

"Please." We went back inside.

"Ready to hit the road, girlfriend?"

She giggled. "You know it!"

"Okay, then."

We helped her up and into her chair, ready and waiting outside the door. She was so wobbly that I was afraid any exertion might lead to a disaster. But Dave was smooth and sure in getting her into my Toyota.

He waved goodbye, hopped back into his truck and blasted off.

I took it slow. We stopped at the pharmacy and I went in to get her prescription.

I was gone no more than a handful of minutes but when I came back; she was asleep, her tousled head leaning against the window frame.

Perplexed, I gently rubbed her shoulder. "Hey, sleepyhead."

"Umf? Uh, oh . . . pardon me, I must have dozed off."

"Yeah." That warning tickle was at the back of my neck again, but I paid it no more attention than I had the last time. "You did. How many Oxycontin did you take this morning?"

Her voice was slurred. "None. My back felt fine, so I decided not to take any. I didn't want to doze off."

I stared at her. "Too late, I think."

I'd picked up a pill box with her meds, the seven compartment sort with the days in raised letters on the lid. When I got her settled at my place, I intended to do a full count; even though I was already convinced she was neither fibbing to me nor mistaken.

A shrug and I put the car in reverse, backed out of the parking spot. Home was only a few minutes away and once I had her in my Jacuzzi, I felt sure she would perk up and be her old self.

Dave was waiting for us at the front door and helped me guide her up the stairs and into her chair. If anything, she was even more wobbly.

He kissed us both goodbye after switching her over to her concentrator and departed, a sour look beginning to form on his face. I could tell he wasn't looking forward to his quarterly reports.

We had lunch: a simple salad and sandwich. I kept an eye on her, noting her sluggishness but her appetite seemed good and she wasn't slurring her words, so I shrugged it off again.

Her breathing treatment was due, so I set that up for her. She kept dozing off during the process. I tickled her feet, trying to make her stay awake. It worked and even elicited a few high-pitched giggles from her, but she still behaved as if she needed nothing so much as a good long nap.

Perhaps I should have been alarmed.

Perhaps I should have been more aware.

I have almost a quarter century of nursing experience and this should have rung alarm bells in my head but if they *did* ring, they were tiny bells and I didn't hear them.

In the end, the results were the same.

When I remember those last few days, all I can recall is that she felt fine, I felt more than fine about being with her and the only thing that comes to me is that I was too close to the problem to see it as one.

I don't know. I'll never know.

But I know I'll never forgive myself for not seeing it until it was all but done.

The treatment completed, I stowed the nebulizer rig and let her sleep. I studied her carefully, took her pulse without waking her and listened to her chest.

No change. A little wheezy, maybe.

I found her locked meds box, opened it and counted the pills very carefully. Not quite believing the tally sheet, I recounted them and got the same result.

I stared at my figures, the back of my neck prickling.

If anything, she'd been taking *less* than she should. All of them were accounted for: her Oxycontin, Oxycodone and Clonazepam. She'd told me the truth: she'd sold none nor were there any shortages.

I separated them into neat piles, loaded the pill box, closed it and set it aside.

I studied her most carefully this time, resisting the impulse to again take her vitals. She was sleeping peacefully and it seemed—to me, anyway—that she simply needed this nap.

The prickle faded away; became only a slight itch; then merely the distant memory of an itch.

Shrugging, I rose and cleared away the lunch dishes and tidied up the kitchen.

When I was done, it was mid-afternoon and she was still asleep. I went into the bathroom and started the Jacuzzi, added her favorite bath beads and went back into the front room.

I knelt next to her chair and stroked her face.

"Hey, sweetie."

She was unresponsive at first and for a brief moment, those tiny alarm bells grew louder and the prickle was back, along with erect hairs along my arms.

But she opened her eyes and stirred. "Um. Oh, did I doze off again?"

The alarm bells subsided, receded away into the distance. I chuckled as the hairs along my arms relaxed. "Yeah, you sure did. Feel like taking a nice soak?"

She stretched. "Ooh, that sounds *wonderful*. Love to."

"It should be ready. C'mon, girlfriend."

I helped her into her chair and wheeled her into the bathroom, undressed her in stages and helped her into the tub. She relaxed into the bubbles with a contented sigh.

"Gosh, I love this."

"I know." Something came to me. "Hey, hang onto the edges of the tub with both hands, Mishelle. I want to get my camera."

I dashed into my office, dodging Nicholas and snatched it off my desk. I was back in less than ten seconds. She was still hanging on to the edges of the tub, her trademark half-smile very much in evidence.

"Are you really going to take my picture?"

"Why not?" I fiddled with it and it clicked, whirred and the lens extruded. All the proper lights were on, so I took aim.

On that tiny screen, she looked like a mermaid surfacing.

"It better not be a naughty one!"

"Naw. Slide down a little so the bubbles cover your boobs, sweetie. Be careful," I cautioned her as she stretched out full-length with just her face showing out of the water. "I don't want to have to dive in there and rescue you!"

She giggled. "Are you my lifeguard, then?"

I grinned as I snapped the picture. "You bet. Also housekeeper, cook, chauffeur, masseuse, private nurse and your best friend."

"Yes," she said, so softly I had to strain a bit to hear her. "You *are* my best friend. I love you, Michelle."

My throat constricted and for a moment I couldn't answer. Instead, I looked at the picture.

It was a good one. I still have it.

"I love you too, Mishelle."

We chatted. I don't remember what we talked about. Girl stuff, mostly. Gossip and this 'n that. But I remember that she was full of smiles and gentle laughter and peace and contentment.

It was enough, more than enough for that last good day.

Her bath completed, I dressed her in clean clothes and got her into a comfy chair. It was almost dinner time and just as I was done switching her Oh-two supply back to the concentrator, Dave came home.

He greeted us both with a kiss and went into the kitchen to get a beer. I followed him.

"Hey."

"Hmm?" He eyed me down the length of the long neck. His Adam's apple bounced as he took a long, blissful swallow. "What?"

The words came haltingly: "I'm . . . I don't know. Maybe I'm being hypersensitive, but she's been acting funny all day."

He took another long swallow. "Funny how?"

I described some of what I'd seen. He frowned, went to the entrance to the dining room and peered around the edge of the door at her in the front room just beyond. "Huh. Now that you mention it, she doesn't look too good."

It was my turn to frown. "How's that?"

He shrugged, looking just as confused as me. "I dunno. Kinda . . . Spacey, I guess. Maybe droopy?" He rubbed the bottle against his forehead, leaving a trail of cold condensate above his eyes. "Hell, you know her better than anyone. What do *you* think?"

I looked around the edge of the doorway.

Nicholas was on her lap and she was stroking him and talking to him. I couldn't hear what she was saying to the little dachshund, but there was an uncommonly solemn look on her face as she whispered to him.

I looked back at my husband. "I don't know. Honestly. You think maybe my imagination is working overtime?"

He shrugged again and I suddenly realized how weary he was, too. "Honey, I don't know. I'm pretty beat. How soon is dinner?"

I realized with a start that I hadn't thawed anything. "Uh, soon. Why don't you play a game of chess with her? That might wake her up a bit."

"Okay." He went into the front room and asked her if she wanted a game. I could hear her cheerfully accept as I opened the fridge and started grabbing things almost at random.

Dinner was mostly freshened-up leftovers. We still had plenty of chicken enchiladas from the night before, so I added bits of this and that, another small salad and some banana cream pie for dessert.

While the enchiladas were warming in the microwave, I strolled back into the front room and watched the game progress.

It didn't, especially. In fact, it lasted less than ten minutes, not because Dave beat her but because she couldn't concentrate on it long enough.

She kept picking up the wrong pieces and making moves that made no sense. She finally conceded and to cover the awkward silence that seemed to spring from nowhere, I announced that dinner would be ready soon.

"Would Madame prefer dinner on the deck this evening?" I joked.

She turned her face up to me, a sweet if somewhat dazed smile there. "Sure! I love to eat outside. This is the only place I get to do that, you know."

I felt a pang in my heart that I sternly suppressed. "It will be my honor to serve you, Madame," and I wasn't joking, not at all, even though my tone was still light. "Dave, would you do the honors while I set the table?"

"Delighted to, my dear," he said gravely, every inch the gentleman.

My husband rolled her out onto the deck and chatted with her while I gathered up utensils and plates and napkins.

I served her, honored and grateful to have her break bread with me once more.

We ate, the setting sun casting tangerine and lemon shades against the back of our house and warming us with a gentle strength, a cool breeze wafting in from somewhere to leaven the heat and ruffle our hair.

As we were mopping up the last of the enchiladas, my cellphone rang. I'd brought it out with me, knowing that Chris or Zach would be calling to check in. I picked it up.

Dave and I spoke with each of our sons and Mishelle held out her hand as Dave finished.

"May I?" she inquired.

Dave handed her the phone. Quietly, I rose and started clearing away the dishes. My husband pitched in to help.

"Hi, Chris. Are you having fun? Well, that's good. I wanted to tell you that you'll be getting a little surprise in the mail next week. Well, if I told you, it wouldn't be a surprise then, would it? Be sure to call me when it arrives and tell me what you think."

Halfway to the door, my hands laden with dishes, I smiled to myself. But what I heard next stopped me in my tracks and wiped the smile from my face:

"Goodbye, little buddy." Her voice was soft, as caressing as the breeze that played with her long graying hair. I could barely hear her and I knew somehow that what she'd said was meant for his ears only. "I love you. Always remember that."

Eyes wide, I heard her close the phone and place it on the table.

I couldn't turn, couldn't move. I don't think I wanted to.

Somehow I managed to make myself put one foot in front of the other and go inside. I was trembling and the back of my throat felt sticky with dread.

Mechanically, I put the dishes in the sink and ran some hot water over them, rinsing the remainders into the disposal.

I was on autopilot again. It was only when I accidentally let some of the hot water splatter over my wrist that I snapped out of it.

No, I thought, numb all over and shaken to my core. *Not now. Not tonight. Please.*

Dave came into the kitchen with the rest of the dinner dishes. He glanced at me curiously. "You okay?"

I nodded. I smiled brightly, just like one of the many Barbie dolls from my childhood I keep stashed in dusty cardboard boxes in our garage. "Sure!" I replied, maybe a bit too eagerly. "Hey, let's give it a few minutes to let our dinner settle and then we'll have some dessert by candlelight. Can you help with the concentrator when I take her home?"

His right eyebrow lifted. "Well, of course. Are you sure you're okay?"

"I'm *fine*." I didn't quite snap at him.

I went back outside.

We had dessert. She didn't finish her pie. I kept glancing at her in the candlelight, expecting to see something and saw only her dear face, lined and careworn; full of pain and experiences I could only know from her own words, never inside where it counted the most.

We took her home about ten pm. I helped her into a nightie, sat with her for a few minutes; making her comfortable and just indulging in small talk.

I didn't want to leave her but I *had* to, even though the tiny bells were ringing in my head and that sick sense of dread clogged my throat.

Why did I leave her, then?

I don't know. Maybe I *did* know that it wasn't time, not then, not yet.

I was most of the way home and decided to call her. There was no answer.

I frowned at the display, saw that I hadn't hit the wrong speed-dial number and tried again. She picked up on the third ring.

"Uh, hi." She sounded breathless.

My stomach contracted. "Hi! Hey, are you okay? Where were you?"

She grunted. It sounded pain-filled. "Uh, let's not talk about it."

My stomach was tensed so tight you could have bounced a basketball off it. "*Huh-uh.* Let's. What's wrong?"

I finally recognized her tone. It was embarrassment: "I, uh . . . well, I fell. On my way to the bathroom."

I hit the brake pedal and the car screeched to a stop, tires smoking. My hands were shaking but my voice was calm and professional:

"Do you need an ambulance? Are you injured?"

"Oh, for . . . jeez, Michelle! I'm okay! Not even a scrape. I know how to take a fall, remember?"

"Well, what happened?"

Her voice, her breathing was returning to normal and now she sounded annoyed more than anything: "I got up too fast, that's all. Got a little light-headed and went down. Don't worry, I landed on the carpet."

"Do you need me to come back?" The Toyota was stopped in the middle of the road, but there was no one behind me and too bad if there was.

"No! I'm *fine*. Go on, go home and get some sleep." The annoyance leeched out of her voice and she said, more gently: "I had a wonderful time with you today. I'll see you again tomorrow, okay? In the morning?"

My tension had caught up with my voice. I ground out: "Keep . . . keep that phone close to you. I'll be right over. Call me first and I'll call Lori. *Promise.*"

She chuckled and there it was: her old sense of humor and self-reliance. "Jeez, you are such a worrywart. I'm fine. Just a little shook up, that's all."

Abruptly, she yawned. "Tired, too. Let me get some sleep, willya?"

I was strangling the wheel with one hand and the phone with the other. "Okay. I'll call you first thing in the morning. G'night, Mishelle."

"Good night, Michelle. Love ya!"

She hung up.

For ten seconds or ten years, I don't know; I sat there staring blindly through the windshield at nothing; feeling my heart slow to something like a normal rhythm.

I came back to myself and looked at the phone, closed it and drove home.

I didn't sleep well at all.

FRIDAY, AUGUST ELEVENTH

I was becoming very familiar with my ceiling; intimately so, in fact. I knew it like my tongue knows the inside of my mouth. Every nuance, every pore and bump in the textured paint eight feet above my head was as well-known to me as the skin on the backs of my hands.

I'd been awake for the last two hours, staring at it.

I rolled my head and looked at the clock for about the tenth time that morning. The big red LED's showed six-thirty, impudently leering at me as if to say: *Ha-ha! Did you really think you would get any sleep?*

"The hell with it," I muttered and rolled out of bed.

Dave snorted, soft and low, still deep in slumber. For a moment I resented him for his ability to snooze through nearly anything. "Stinker," I told him.

He grunted, rolled over and went back to snoring peacefully. I spared him a brief glare and padded into the bathroom to brush my teeth and splash some cold water on my face.

I lifted my face from the basin and caught sight of my reflection in the mirror. For a moment, I stared, transfixed.

"Oh my *God*," I mumbled.

I had bags under my eyes big enough for a cross-country flight and my hair looked like a minor hurricane had taken a short detour across my head. There were deep lines down either side of my nose and my skin had an unpleasant blotchy cast.

In short, I looked just as I felt: awesomely crappy and about six hours short of a decent night's sleep.

I shrugged, stuck out my tongue at that hideous reflection and went to start some coffee.

I parked myself in front of the computer and sipped: heavy caffeine, no bleach. The recipe was much improved this morning. I opened my e-mail. Nothing . . .

But that didn't mean anything, did it?

I looked at the screen clock: a bit past seven-thirty. It was too early to call her.

I sat back, scowling at the screen. *No.* I could wait and I did, for about two minutes.

Then I got up and did something else. I think it was laundry.

Dave wandered into the kitchen, scratching his chest and yawning. I was taking a bit of a break for breakfast: banana and a piece of toast. He eyed the banana as if it were a live grenade.

"Breakfast?"

I swallowed. "I'll pick something up on the way. Her morning special." I took another bite of banana. Mushily: "Shorry, dear. You're on your own thish morning."

He smiled. "I'll survive. You need the shower soon?"

I nodded; my mouth full of toast.

"Okay." He gave me a peck on the cheek; avoiding the crumbs. "Have a good day. Say hi to her for me."

I swallowed. "Will do,"

* * *

Fresh out of the shower, my hair still damp; I called her. It was about eight thirty.

"Her-ro?"

I laughed. "Did I wake you up again?"

"Uh-huh." She coughed and grunted. I felt that tiny prickle of alarm.

"Are you still sore from falling last night?"

"No, not really. Just woke up."

"Oh." I wanted to breathe a sigh of relief, but not yet. "Okay. I'm on my way over. The usual, ma'am?"

"Huh?"

Jeez, she *was* sleepy. "Danish and caramel latte?"

"Oh. Oh, yeah."

"On my way, sweetie."

I stopped and picked up two: one for her, one for me. I came through the Elvis door and there she was in her chair, smiling, cute as a bug in the silky pink nightgown I'd helped her don the previous evening.

Nicholas yapped excitedly from his perch on her knees as I bent to give her a kiss. The dachshund twisted like a living pretzel and pawed my arm as I straightened up. Affectionate little rascal.

I ruffled his ears and he yapped again.

His tail was vibrating like a tuning fork.

"How ya doin', sweetie?" I looked her over.

She looked relaxed but still tired. The bags beneath *her* eyes were big enough for an around the world cruise. But her breathing seemed relaxed and normal and so did her posture. I couldn't see any bruises from her fall, but I would soon find out if there were any. "You want your goody?"

"Yum," she responded with a lazy yawn. She stretched out her hand for the bag. Nicholas yapped again.

"You don't get any," I told him sternly as I pressed the bag into her hand. His ears drooped. He looked positively sorrowful, but dachshunds are especially good at that.

I glanced around. Nicky probably hadn't been in lately; the place was pretty messy. I could do that in a few minutes. "Let me see if you have any bruises, sweetie."

"Oh, I'm okay," she responded. "I'm sure I'd feel them."

"Yeah, but you can't *see* them, Mishelle."

I knelt next to her. Nothing on her knees or legs and a cursory examination of her arms showed no obvious trauma. Pulse was good, skin temperature normal and there was no sign of mottling which might indicate impaired circulation.

She looked as relaxed as she had the day before, if still somewhat sleepy.

"Everything normal?" she asked.

"I'd say so. You seem to have taken that fall pretty well."

She snickered. "Yeah, twice."

"*What?*" Stunned, I looked up.

"Yeah, I slipped and went down again in the kitchen this morning." She gave me a tired smile. "Just can't do those handstands anymore, I guess."

I didn't know whether to laugh or weep. "No, maybe you shouldn't do that. Uh, just stay in the chair, okay? I'll help you if you need something. How's your coffee?"

She lifted the cup in salute. "Perfect. Thanks."

I patted her knee and got up. "Finish your goody while I make you some real breakfast and clean this place up a little."

I glanced into the kitchenette. "I think I'll start with the dishes."

Breakfast was scrambled eggs, hash browns and toast. As always, she ate with exceptional tidiness, reminding me of a mouse alert for every crumb. "Yum," she said around her last bite. "I love the way you do scrambled eggs."

"A little milk and cook 'em on low," I responded. "'Scuse me. Dishes to do."

While I was midway through the pile, a motion out of the corner of my eye made me turn. Mishelle had gotten up and was weaving toward her computer. I opened my mouth to warn her to be careful and then shut it.

She found her way into the chair and began to tap away.

"Hey, there. Whatcha doin'?"

"Oh, I just wanted to visit with you for a while," she mumbled. "Hey, what's goin' on here? What did they *do* to this thing?"

"What do you mean?" Wiping my hands on a dish towel, I peered over her shoulder. "What are you trying to do?"

"Send an e-mail," she slurred. "This thing isn't working like it did before."

I laughed uneasily. "Well, no wonder. You've got the cursor in the subject line. Here, let me help . . ."

She pushed the mouse away and leaned back. "Never mind. I can do this later. I think I'll just go back to my chair. Help me up, please."

I glanced at her. She didn't seem upset.

She should have been, though. That computer was her voice, her eyes, her connection to the outside world and she didn't seem to mind that she couldn't get it to work.

Ants with icy feet were marching up and down my spine again. I helped her back to her chair.

When I got her settled, I asked gently: "Did you bump your head when you fell this morning? Or last night?"

"Hmm?" Her expression was entirely serene. "Nope. Landed on my butt the first time. On my side this morning."

"Let me check."

Carefully, I ran my fingertips through her hair and the base of her neck, feeling for bumps or swelling or even a contusion. I could find nothing unusual.

"Mm," she purred. "A scalp massage. You're gonna put me to sleep again."

"Want me to fix you some lunch later?"

"Sure. Wake me when it's ready." She yawned. So did Nicholas, already snuggled in next to her.

I let her nap.

A puzzled frown on my face, I finished the dishes and continued on to the rest of her place, wiping flat surfaces and putting things back where they belonged. I kept one eye on her, listening to her soft snore, alert for any change.

She was still sleeping when I was done cleaning. I looked at the clock and decided to start lunch. I made us sandwiches and took them back into the front room.

I woke her and we ate. Her appetite was good. We were about done when someone knocked at the door.

I opened it to the UPS guy. Today's delivery was a fairly small package. He tipped his brown cap to me when I signed for it and jogged back to his truck.

"Want me to open it for you, Mishelle?"

"Would you, please?" Her smile was rueful. "I'd probably mangle it."

I found a knife and cut it open, lifted out the plastic-wrapped gadget within and stared at it, perplexed. "What the heck did you buy this time?"

She held out both hands. "Give it here, sweetie."

I placed it into her hands and her fingers slid across it, sensing. Her face broke into a huge smile. "Ooh, it's that handwriting embosser. Check it out! Could you get me some paper out of the box it came in?"

I plucked a sheet of see-through, crinkly stuff that felt like thick cellophane and handed it to her. She fumbled a bit, but found the right way to load it and then used an attached stylus to scribble something across its face.

She pulled the paper out and handed it to me. "Look!"

It was handwriting, embossed like Braille only reversed; indented into the page so that the letters could be felt. *Her* handwriting.

I stared at it, astonished and looked up at her. "I didn't know you could write."

Her grin was pure *gotcha*. "You thought I could only do Braille, didn't ya? Or just type."

I nodded, feeling foolish. "Yeah. I don't know why, I just assumed . . ."

She waggled a finger at me. Again; I had the strangest feeling that she could actually see me. "Never assume anything about us blinks, Michelle. We can do stuff you sighted folks can only dream about."

"I won't," I said and I never have, not since that day. "Why don't you write something to Chris?"

"Good idea." I gave her another sheet of paper. She loaded the machine, wrote something carefully this time and handed it to me.

I read:

Dear Chris. Am I doing this right? You can help me to learn, too. Love, Mishelle.

I shook my head. "All this time I thought . . . You know; the only time I've ever seen you write anything is when you sign your name."

Her grin was smug but too weary for anything resembling *gotcha*. "Yeah. It's pretty cool though, isn't it?"

I had to admit that it was.

The phone rang. The voice robot recited the number and Mishelle's weary face lit up with delight. "Ooh, it's Renee! Hand me the phone, would you, sweetie?"

I found it on the computer workstation and slipped it into her hands. She thumbed it on.

"Hello? Renee? Hey, sweetie! How are you? Really? How's Andrew? Oh, good. Tell him I said hi, will you? Oh, not much. Michelle's here. Yeah, she just made me breakfast. Scrambled eggs and hash browns. Sure, you want to talk to her?"

She held out the phone to me. "She wants to say hi."

I took the phone. "Hello?"

A soft, pleasant drawl greeted me: "Well, hello there, Michelle."

"Hi! Nice to finally meet you, even if it's just on the phone. I've heard a lot about you."

Renee giggled. "Well, don't you believe ever'thing you hear. How's she doin'?"

"Pretty good today. She's relaxed and hasn't had any breathing problems. Her appetite's good and I think she's in a good space." I looked at my friend as she nodded in agreement.

"That's wonderful. I've been so worried about her lately. You think she's gonna get any better?"

My forehead creased. "Renee, I don't know. It's always a possibility."

She sighed. "That's what ever'body keeps tellin' me." She sounded sad. "I guess I should just be happy she's made it this far, huh?"

"Yes. *I* am."

"Yeah. Yeah, I guess you are, aren't ya?" I could hear the approval in her voice. "You take care of my friend, Michelle. There's nobody else here on God's green Earth like her. She's 'bout my best friend in this whole world, you hear?"

"Loud and clear, Renee."

"Okay. Let me talk to her again, would you? 'Bye, Michelle. Nice meetin' you."

"You too, Renee."

I put the phone back in Mishelle's hands. The two women chatted for a bit longer and then Mishelle hung up with a cheery, "Talk to you in a few days, sweetie!"

She handed the phone back to me. Her face was sagging with fatigue. "Michelle, I think I need a nap, okay?"

"Well, sure. You snooze and I'll find something to do, I'm sure."

She napped again and I filled and organized her DVD's and CD's. By mid-afternoon, I found myself glancing at her every five minutes.

The ants weren't marching, but I was getting a bit uneasy. It wasn't like her to sleep so much, but for the life of me I could *not* see anything wrong with her.

Vitals: normal.

Appetite: normal.

Appearance: normal.

Yes, she was sleepy, even a little euphoric; as if she were on meds but I knew from checking her pill boxes that she hadn't even taken her Oxycontin that morning. I thought about it without much in the way of results.

Finished cleaning finally, I came back into the front room and knelt next to her chair. Nicholas, who'd been glued to her side all morning and afternoon, cracked one eye and looked at me as I took her hand.

I leaned close to touch her face and then I smelled it: a sweet, almost fruity aroma.

I froze.

Another sniff and I recognized it: acetone. That's a byproduct of the insulin/sugar reaction during metabolism; usually broken down even further by the body.

The breath of a diabetic smells like that. But Mishelle wasn't a diabetic.

Gently, I stroked her cheek. "Mishelle? Wake up, honey."

"Mmf?" She stirred. "Wha' . . ." She stretched and put her hand out, touched my face. "Hi. How long have I been . . .?"

She stopped and said, almost timidly, "Why are you crying?"

I blinked. I didn't know I had been. "Uh, I'm . . . Mishelle, I'm *worried*. You've been sleeping so much and you're so groggy. I can't figure out what's wrong!"

Her hands were on my shoulders, rubbing me gently. "Ssh. I'm fine, sweetie. I feel fine. Just sleepy, that's all. Maybe that morphine is just relaxing me."

"No. It doesn't work that way." *And morphine doesn't affect your pancreas.* "I'm just worried!" Blinking back tears, I looked at my watch. "I have to go soon and I don't want to leave you!"

She chuckled: low and warm and utterly relaxed. "Such a worrywart." She pulled me close for a hug. "It's going to be okay," she said in my ear. "Don't worry. Nicky could come by later and check on me. You know she'll call if anything happens."

"She'd better," I muttered. "I'm going to call her now." I stood and went to my bag, looking for my phone.

My best friend sighed. "Okay. Just be nice. She's been . . ."

"I know, I know," I said, not without some irritation. "Hold on a minute." I punched in her speed-dial number. "Hey, Nicky. Yeah, it's Michelle. Listen, I need a favor."

My voice betrayed me on that last word and broke, crumbled like a freshly-baked cookie.

Nicky sounded faintly astonished and a bit fearful herself. "Hey, are you *crying*? What's wrong?"

"I . . . I . . ." I swallowed and got control of myself. "I have to leave soon, Nicky. Can I ask you to come by later and stay with Mishelle tonight?"

"Huh? What happened? Is she okay?"

"Yes . . . No! I don't know! She . . . fell. Last night and this morning. She's been groggy and she's been sleeping . . ."

I glanced at her and broke off, staring.

She was asleep again. Her snores had a wheezy quality that was making my arms and the back of my neck prickle with alarm.

The bells were ringing; impossible to ignore this time.

"Nicky, I think . . ." I stopped, swallowed hard and tried again in a quieter voice: "I think this may be the beginning of the end. Can you *please* come over and stay with her tonight?"

There was real distress in her voice. Distress and shock and barely contained fear: "She *fell*? For God's sake, is she hurt?"

"No. I checked her over thoroughly. No bruises. No head trauma. She says she's not hurt and I don't think she is. But something's not *right*, Nicky!"

There was a brief silence. "I can come over for a while, Michelle, but I can't *stay*. I can't get a sitter tonight and my littlest one hasn't been well lately."

"Your husband?"

"He leaves for work right after dinner. Gets home around three in the morning."

"Long drive, huh?"

"Yeah."

"Oh, God."

I kept staring at Mishelle, watching her shoulders move imperceptibly as she snored; listening to that faint wheeze which should not be there. "Okay, how soon can you be here?"

"About half an hour," she said immediately. "But I have to go home right after dinner."

"Okay. That'll have to do for now. Call me as soon as you get here, okay? Let me know how she's doing."

"Got it," she said; her voice crisp and completely professional. "Lori, too?"

"No, she's out of town for the weekend. Lynn's at a concert. She put in for the time-off weeks ago. It's just you 'n me, Nicky."

"Yeah." She sighed. There was a whole world of meaning in that sigh. "Yeah. Go on home, Michelle. I got it from here."

"'Bye." I closed the phone, took a pillow off the loveseat and gently woke her: "Hey, sleepyhead." I tucked the pillow across her poor, dented knees. "If you're gonna snooze, you might as well be comfortable."

"Thanks." Her smile reminded me somehow of Chris when I tucked him into bed. "You gotta go now?"

"Uh-huh." I put my head against hers. "Nicky's on her way. You'll be okay, won't you?"

Her nod was slow in coming. "Yup. I sure do love you, Michelle."

My chest hurt. "I sure love you, too. Call you later."

* * *

It was five-thirty when I walked in the door. Dave was rummaging through the fridge and glanced up at me as I came in to the kitchen.

He straightened, staring hard. "What *happened*? Is she . . .?"

"I don't know!" I bawled. I stood alone in the middle of my kitchen and I bawled like a scared child at my husband. "I don't know what's going on and I don't think she should be alone tonight and I don't know what to *do*! Will somebody *please* tell me what I can do?"

He spoke. With every word, I felt something terrible leave me, leaving room for something far greater and better than what I'd had when I walked in. For that moment, for that alone, I think I will always love him and always care for him, no matter what.

"Listen to me, Michelle. You've been a nurse for over twenty years. You have the best intuition of anyone I know. You follow your intuition better than anyone I know. So why aren't you listening to your intuition now?"

His expression was forgiving, his eyes wise and sad. "Why are you here? You know where you should be."

I gaped silently at him.

"Go to her." He closed the door of the fridge. "That's where you should be. Not here."

I said, "I'm going to pack a bag."

He said, "I'm going with you."

* * *

When we arrived, Nicky was still there. She nodded, almost as if she'd been expecting us. Nicholas danced at our feet as we came in, yapping enthusiastically

I raised an eyebrow at Nicky in silent request.

"She's had something to eat," she said quietly. A head jerk in the direction of the bedroom: "She asked me to make up her bed so I did that and then I took her vitals. Normal. Breath smells funny, though . . ."

"I know." I looked at my friend. "Surprise, girlfriend!"

"Hi," she said sleepily. "Hey, weren't you going home?"

"Well, I *was* but I decided to do something else. Guess what? I'm spending the night and we're going to have a slumber party!"

She giggled: a little one that sounded almost like a hiccup. "Oh, cool! Hey, Dave! Wanna bong out and listen to some tunes?"

Nicky looked horrified and clapped her hands over her mouth. My husband glanced at her, then at me, smiling. "I'll pass on the smoke, Mishelle. But we can still crank up the tunes. Feel like a game of chess?"

She smiled but still looked exhausted, the poor dear. "Not tonight, honey. Too tired."

Nicky motioned to me and I came close. "I gotta go," she said in that quiet, calm voice. She didn't mention Mishelle's comment, then or ever. "Will you call me if anything happens?"

"You know I will."

We looked into each other's eyes for a long moment.

I nodded. She nodded back, gave our friend a quick kiss and a hug and left.

It didn't go quite as planned.

Dave tried to chat with her, but her speech was so slurred and wandering that he was forced to abandon that in favor of switching CD's for her. When she started asking for the same disc she'd just heard, his eyebrows rose to mid-forehead. He looked at me and indicated the kitchenette with a jerk of his shoulder.

I got up and followed him.

Perhaps I could say what I didn't see in his face, but I'll never be sure what it was, exactly, I did see.

"I think you're right," he said; almost too quiet beneath the thumping bass of Sly and the Family Stone. "You should stay as long as you need to."

He looked down, obviously gathering his courage. He looked up and his eyes met mine. "I'll pick up the kids tomorrow. You stay. Attend to . . ."

He swallowed hard. I touched his arm. "You do what needs to be done. Call me when . . . when it's over."

He squeezed his eyes closed, shutting in his own grief, throttling it to a standstill.

In his family, men don't cry.

He looked at me again, his eyes bleak. "How long do you think?"

I shook my head, my eyes never leaving his face. "I can't tell."

"Not long, I think."

I nodded.

He wrapped me in a sudden bear hug and I returned it fiercely.

Letting go, he strode firmly into the front room and said his goodbyes to our friend; *his* friend and chess partner; a woman he had come to love in his own way and his own time.

Dry-eyed, I discreetly watched them, giving them their space, thanking God once more that I was fortunate enough to be married to one of the good guys.

My façade cracked for only a moment when I heard her say to him: "Goodbye, Dave."

Before, it had always been: "See you later, buddy."

But it was only a moment.

He left and I turned the music down to manageable levels. I knelt next to her chair. "Can I get you anything, sweetie?"

Her face turned to me. "Uh-huh. You could help me with a bath. I think it might help me to sleep."

I traced the lines along her cheeks; the furrows of time and trouble and pain. "I don't think you'll have any trouble sleeping, Mishelle."

Mishelle smiled. Her hand found my face. Long, still-strong fingers traced my own lines; the tips so soft and warm. "No. But it will feel good, especially my back."

She made a noise I realized was only a phlegm-curdled giggle. "I didn't take any pain meds today. Aren't you proud of me?"

"Yes," I said softly. "I'm very proud of you."

I got her bath ready and helped her into it. The tub seemed so tiny compared to mine. I momentarily yearned for our big, luxurious Jacuzzi but under the circumstances, her own hobbit-sized tub was the right place at the right time for the last time I would ever bathe her.

I bathed her: slowly, gently and with great care.

While shampooing her hair, I noticed that she needed a shave. "Would you like me to shave you, dear?"

She fingered her jaw and cheeks ruefully. "I guess so. I think I'm too tired to do it right. I'd probably cut myself."

"I promise not to cut you, Mishelle."

It might not have been the best job I ever did, but it was a task performed with nothing but love in my heart. I will always be grateful I had a chance to do that.

I cracked a little when I finished dressing her in a nightgown and helped her back into the recliner. My tears spilled over and dripped onto her as I settled her.

She felt it immediately. Her hand groped in the air until she found mine; gripped it with a surprising intensity.

"What's wrong, Michelle?"

"What?" Damn my voice, I could not keep it from cracking, even on words of only one syllable. "What do you mean?"

"You know what I mean," she slurred. "You're crying."

"It's . . . okay. I'm fine."

"No. No, you tell . . . Tell me the truth. You *promised*."

And here it was: the moment of truth and God, what an ugly thing it was.

"Okay. You're right. I promised. I promised you that I would tell you when it was time." Fat, oily tears leaked from my eyes and rolled down my cheeks. I made no move to brush them away. "I think this is the beginning of the end, Mishelle. It's time, girlfriend."

We held each other and I could feel her struggle just to breathe, just to stay with me a few more minutes.

"I think, think you're right. But I'm not . . . Not afraid. Not anymore." She squeezed me as hard as she was able. It was like being hugged by a toddler. "Thanks to you. Your family. All of you, Chris especially."

She wheezed. That horrible rattle was in there and I was beginning to suspect what it was. "Tell him . . . Love him. Always."

"I will."

"You know . . . You know I'm not really . . . Going. Anywhere. Right? I'll always . . . Always be here. In spirit. I'll stay . . . Stay until . . . Until I'm sure you're all . . . Okay. All of you."

She laughed and coughed together. "Guardian angel. Huh. Who'da thought?"

My tears leaked slowly, steadily from beneath my closed eyelids. "I know. And I promise to keep educating people for you in your place. I won't let them forget you. What you did."

"Good." Her breathing was becoming harsh. "My best student. Want your final grade, Michelle?"

"Sure."

"A plus."

We held each other for a long while. I could feel her breathing slow and I knew she was drifting off again.

I stroked her furrowed cheek. "Hey. You want to sleep here or in your brand-new bed?"

Her eyelids flickered. "Bed. Might as well try . . . Try it."

"Okay."

Getting her up and into the next room wasn't as difficult as one might think. She seemed light and airy to me; bones like a bird and insubstantial somehow.

I got her tucked into the bed; the head raised to what would be an uncomfortable position for anyone else but was just right for her. Blue levitated to the bedside, spared me an expressionless glance and settled herself next to her mistress.

I looked down to see Nicholas at my feet, his eyes bright with expectation, so I picked him up and placed him on the other side of her.

"Comfy, sweetie?"

"Uh-huh." Her eyes were already closed. "I'm fine."

"Okay." I rubbed at my sticky cheeks with the back of my hand. "I'm going to get an extra pillow and blanket. I'll sleep in here tonight with you so if you need anything, just call out. I'll be right here."

Her voice was a slowly receding mumble. "Me . . . too."

I found a blanket and pillow and stretched out on the floor next to her bed.

It was about eleven pm. I found myself dozing off at half-hour intervals, coming awake fast to look at her and listen to her breathing.

Around three thirty, I came awake with a prickling at the back of my neck and my own breath coming fast and short.

I flipped on the bedside table light and looked at her.

Her skin was mottled. Her breathing was hoarse and rattly. I could identify it now: Cheyne-Stokes breathing.

I sat on the edge of the bed and embraced her. Her eyelids flickered and her mouth moved as she tried to speak and failed.

"Well, hey there." Her good eye tried to track toward me but her lids would not stay open. "There you are."

I leaned in closer and discovered that she'd been incontinent; wet the bed. Her breath smelled both sweet and sour; an awful combination. "Okay, sweetie. We're going to have to get you cleaned up. Just relax and let me do this."

I gathered up a fresh nightie, a washcloth and towels with a basin of warm water and some liquid hand soap. With a pair of scissors from her computer desk, I carefully cut away her nightgown and cleaned her.

There were fresh sheets in the hallway closet and so I remade the bed with her still in it; a hard-won skill from nursing school you never forget once you've had to apply it to someone helpless or dying.

It's a respectful task; a gesture of humanity to the last moments of anyone's existence.

Most cultures make much of the body's final preparations for departure. That gives me great hope for the human species. I think it's when we forget or dismiss those things that we lose what has been granted to us by a merciful and loving God.

I cut the fresh nightgown down the back and draped it over her and tucked her in again. She smiled and kept trying to speak, but the words would not come.

Gently, I placed my finger on her lips.

"Hush. Don't try to talk. Save your strength, girlfriend. Let me do the talking, okay? I'm good at that."

I wanted to climb into bed with her, but Nicholas was cuddled against her and I didn't want to move him again. Changing the bed sheets had made him moan deep in his chest with distress. He hadn't liked being on the floor while I finished.

Instead, I held her hand and talked to her and the last few hours slipped by far too quickly.

"You know, when you said you wanted to spend twenty-four hours with me, this isn't quite what I'd had in mind. Shopping and manicures would have been a lot more fun."

Her mouth curved in a knowing smile. Her lips moved briefly.

"Yeah, we did waste a few opportunities. I'm sorry. Remember what you said about the boat-ride? I was going to set something up for next week. Did I tell you about Jim and Angela?"

It looked like a nod. I was pretty sure it was. "They have a boat and a nice place on the lake. Woulda been perfect."

I sighed and it turned into a sob. "Mishelle, don't be afraid!" and I knew I was speaking for myself too. "Remember what you told me about heaven? That you could see? You will! You'll be able to see again and you'll see your grandmother and Paul and all of your friends, even Big'un, your first dog. You'll be able to walk and dance and run and do anything you want!"

Her lids flickered. Her mouth moved silently. In her arms and hands, I could feel her struggle to say something, anything to reassure me in return.

I knew she could hear me. I knew she was still in there; within that poor, worn-out and battered body; fighting for those last few moments.

I couldn't bear it; watching her struggle.

"Please, baby. Don't struggle so. Relax. Let it happen. Your only job now is to let it all go. Let it go, Mishelle. Let all of the struggle and pain and heartache go. Please."

I can't say why I did not weep then, but I know that over twenty years of watching life ebb from so many people has left me with reflexes that are virtually unbreakable.

I've heard it said that funerals are only for the living. Let it be so, then. Let those who must leave us go in their own way, with as much dignity and love as we can give them. Let us not darken their passing with our own grief and regret.

I could not grieve for my beloved friend then because I knew how much she cared for me. I knew that it might force her to stay, long after her time was done; just to make sure I was happy and well.

She would have done for me what I did for her without hesitation. She would have held my hand until the last as I did for her, without hesitation.

I could not weep. And so I held her and prayed.

Around five am, she slipped into a comatose state, unable to move even her eyelids or mouth. But I knew somehow that she was still there: listening to me, hearing my voice, aware of where she was and what was happening.

I fetched my stethoscope and listened to her lungs. They were beginning to sound gurgly as the fluid from her failing systems built up in her pulmonary space; leaking across the fragile membranes into the places meant for air alone.

She was literally and slowly drowning in her own fluids.

It was a compressed version of what we'd discussed weeks before; a process that I was sure would take months, squeezed down into a period of a few hours.

I knew she would eventually lose consciousness and I prayed that God would take her soon.

Gently moving Nicholas aside, I finally climbed into bed with her and held her, stroking her hair.

I kept talking to her:

"Now, when you get to Heaven, make sure God makes you five foot seven so you can come raid my closet, okay?"

Was there a tiny catch in her breathing? Was that a smile wreathing her chapped lips?

Was there still a flame left flickering against the final darkness?

I wiped her forehead with the washcloth and moistened her lips. I prayed.

I talked:

"I promise you, Mishelle. You won't be buried as Michael. I promise. Everything will go as you want it to at your funeral. I swear to you, dear."

All I could hear was her slow, weakening breath; the tiny gasps coming farther and farther apart; shorter and shorter each time.

I held her and prayed.

She breathed her last at about seven am, Saturday morning, August twelfth, 2006.

* * *

For a long while I held her, my mind blank and without thoughts of any sort except one:

She's gone.

That was enough for a while. So I wept finally, holding her for longer than I care to admit.

Another thought came to me, much as one blade of grass is always accompanied by another:

I need to make some phone calls.

Given a task; my mind naturally started breaking the problem down and assigning priorities; a kind of post-mortem triage.

I'm a nurse: it's a reflex.

I gently disengaged myself from her still body; the Earthly form she'd worn like an ill-fitting suit of clothes no longer required.

I turned off her oxygen: the final act.

Dazed, I went into the front room in search of my phone, carefully placing my feet one in front of the other like a stroke victim.

My mind was slowly beginning to wake up.

Call Hospice first?

Lori was out of town and would her replacement raise an eyebrow at me; her former nurse the only one present at her passing?

No, it would have to be Nicky. She could call Hospice and make the final report.

I didn't have Earl and Louise's number and I couldn't have found it in Mishelle's computer anyway, but maybe Nicky would know it.

I dialed her number. It took only three attempts.

"Nicky. She's gone."

There was a tiny space filled only by the single hiccup of a sob. "Was it . . . Did she . . .?"

"No, it was very peaceful. She drifted off while I was holding her. It's over, Nicky."

"Oh, thank goodness." Her voice trembled. "I was afraid she might suffer."

"Not a bit. I need your help, Nicky."

"Of course. I'll be right there. You call her parents yet?"

"I can't find their number."

"I've got it here someplace. But her mom always calls in the morning."

"Hurry, Nicky."

"I'll be right there."

The next person I called was my husband: "Dave. It's over."

I heard only silence. Seventeen years of marriage told me that my big, strong husband was shocked speechless and probably fighting tears with all of his considerable strength.

Softly, he said: "Really?"

"Yeah. Really."

There was another silence. Then: "Good job, Michelle."

"Thanks." I did not feel grateful, merely exhausted. "I'll be home in a while. You tell the boys."

"Yeah. I will."

"Gotta go. Gotta make some more calls."

I clicked off.

The fog was slowly clearing, but my fingers still felt numb as I punched in Renee's number. It rang twice and I was afraid her message machine might get it, but she answered: "Hello?"

"Renee? This is Michelle. Mishelle died this morning."

Renee was silent for only a moment, and then vented a huge sigh. "Lord God, but she's been waitin' for this for such a long time." She burst into tears. "Oh my dear, what *happened*?"

"I don't know," I said, my voice quivering. "But I can tell you that she died comfortably."

"Sweet Jesus." Her voice held a quiet reverence that struck me dumb, even then. "I'm so glad. For both of you." Her voice sharpened: "My Lord, the ring!"

Dully: "The what?"

"The sapphire ring that Charles gave her! She wanted to make sure she was buried with it!"

"Okay." My tongue felt thick and I still couldn't understand what she was getting at. "So what do you want me to do?"

There was a note of exasperation in her voice. "Take the dang thing off her finger, Michelle! Otherwise someone might be stealin' it!"

"Uh, okay." I went back into the bedroom and put the phone down. Gently, as tenderly as I was able, I slid the lovely piece of jewelry from my friend's little finger.

I held it up and stared at it. I picked up the phone.

"I got it, Renee."

"Hide it," she advised. "Put it back on jus' 'fore the funeral."

"You sure about this?"

"Trust me," Renee snapped. "I know what she wanted, she must of tol' me a million times."

"Okay." It went into my pocket. Still dazed, I said: "Renee, I gotta go. Nicky will be here soon."

"Alright, girl." There was a deep sadness I could hear in her voice all the way from Seattle. "You take good care of my friend."

"I'll keep you posted."

I hung up and waited for Nicky, sitting on the loveseat, my mind utterly blank.

She's gone.

Nicky arrived about twenty minutes later. Together we cleaned Mishelle again, dressed her and Nicky carefully applied makeup to her face.

It appeared as if she were only sleeping, perhaps dreaming when Nicky was done.

Dry-eyed, arms folded, I stood at the end of the bed and contemplated my friend.

She's gone.

It didn't seem real, any of it, not at all.

The phone rang. Nicky picked up.

"Hello, Louise." She looked around at me, her eyes wide and a little lost. "No, Louise. She's gone. Yes ma'am, that's right. About an hour ago, I think. Michelle was with her. Do you want to come over now?"

Her eyebrows tilted up and now she looked annoyed. "*No?* Well, for . . . Okay, whatever you say, Louise. You'll tell Sue, though? Thanks. Yes, I'm sure she'd want to be here, too. Okay. Thank you, Louise. Goodbye."

Nicky's lips were compressed into a straight line as she hung up. "She doesn't want to come over," she said tonelessly. "Neither does Earl."

I said: "I'm not surprised."

"But she said she'd call Sue, Mishelle's little sister, and tell her immediately."

"Good. Do you want to call Hospice now?"

She held the phone out. "I think you should do it. I need to be with her for a moment."

I nodded and took the phone into the front room. I punched in the number with rock-steady hands. Amy, Lori's replacement for the weekend, picked up.

"Hello?"

Briefly, I delivered the last status report on my former patient.

Amy heard me out and said with a sigh, "Okay. I'll call the funeral home. Are you okay, Michelle?"

I asserted that I was, probably with more zeal than I actually felt.

"Okay. You want to handle the meds disposal or wait for me? I can't get away until about one or two."

"No." I cleared my throat. "No, I'll do it. I've done it before."

"I know. Did you find the logbook?"

"I know where it is. I can still sign for them, can't I?"

"You're a nurse. You can do it."

"Yes, I can. Thanks, Amy." I clicked off. "Nicky, we have something that needs doing right away."

With her as witness, I gathered up all of Mishelle's meds, counted them, tabulated them in her medication logbook and dumped every single one of them into the toilet.

There were a lot of Oxycontin pills, the Oxycodone and all of her old Lorazepam and not a few of her new Clonazepam.

It made for an impressive, multicolored little island floating in the bowl. I flushed and they all went away, never to be used for a lesser purpose.

We countersigned the logbook and that was the end of it, I thought.

The doorbell rang. Nicky went to open it and let Sue in.

Mishelle's sister is a taller, somewhat stockier version of her father; a big Midwestern farm girl transplanted to the Montana woods. Her straight dishwater blonde hair was pulled back into an efficient ponytail and her manner and gestures were just as unconsciously masculine as Mishelle's were feminine. I've never seen her in anything but jeans and flannel work shirts.

But she adores her three kids and she's been married to the same fellow for many years.

You never can tell a book by its cover. It's taken me a depressingly long time to understand that.

While Sue was sitting with her sister, holding her hand and whispering to her, there was another knock on the door; quite discreet. As I opened it, I found myself wondering if mortuary attendants are required to practice that knock as part of their training.

I don't particularly remember what either looked like and I suppose that's part of their training, too.

Sue came out of Mishelle's bedroom and faced them. For one brief, eerie moment, I could almost imagine her with a sword and armor; a warrior maid standing guard: *You may not pass.*

"Please listen carefully." Her voice was low and clear and altogether in control. I thanked her silently for that. "My sister is a transgender woman. She has not had the necessary surgery to change her body to the way it should have been. That means she still has her male parts. I want you to remember that it was through no fault of her own that she died this way. I expect you and your service to treat her respectfully, to refer to her as *she* and *her*. I warn you that there will be no jokes or crude remarks at her expense."

The look on her face reminded me of a picture of a Greek bust I'd once seen in art appreciation class: "Do I make myself clear, gentlemen?"

The older of the two, obviously the one in charge, cleared his throat. I swear, not a scrap of expression could be seen anywhere about his features.

"Yes, ma'am. We understand perfectly. We want to assure you that your sister will be treated with the utmost of respect while in our care."

Sue's eyes, deep brown and normally open and friendly, glittered with a steel resolve I admired from somewhere deep inside myself. I wondered how she could be so calm and in control and I envied her, I did.

"That applies to her funeral arrangements as well. My sister wanted to be buried as a woman. She will *not* be buried under her old name, is *that* clear?"

The older said, "Well, that's up to the terms of her will . . ."

"I have her will," Sue stated. Muscles bunched along the line of her jaw, reminding me of . . . someone else. "I'll have a copy of it to your office by this afternoon. It says quite clearly that she wanted to be buried as Mishelle Lynn Woodring, *not* Michael. Our parents may see it differently. You are instructed to ignore them and follow my sister's last wishes."

Her eyes flashed again. I half-expected a lightning bolt or two or at least a roll of thunder. "Are we clear on that, gentlemen?"

They both nodded.

"Quite clear, ma'am," the older one said diffidently.

Sue stood aside. "Then please attend to my sister."

I followed them into the bedroom. The younger one said, "Uh, can you do something about the dog, ma'am?"

Nicholas was standing on his mistress's chest, licking her face over and over. The poor little boy was trembling like a leaf as I picked him up, then it flashed through me like an electric shock and I almost dropped him:

All of his odd behavior, his refusal to leave her side, his yapping and mournful expressions, even his pawing at me; they were all part of a speechless animal's attempt to communicate the most basic of all concepts.

Danger.

And I'd missed it, every bit of it.

For a moment, I wanted to beg the little dachshund's forgiveness, that's how strange and disconnected I felt then. I think he might have understood it, too.

"Sorry, little guy," I whispered into his droopy ear. "I'm so sorry."

We watched them carry her out on a folding gurney; Sue and Nicky and Nicholas and myself.

The door closed. I sat down on the loveseat, still holding Nicholas.

I was so tired. So very, very tired. Sue studied me.

"You should go home," she remarked. "You look exhausted."

I nodded.

"Want me to drive you?"

I shook my head.

"You're sure? I don't mind."

I shook my head. "No." I was mildly astonished that I could still speak, much less speak in what sounded like a perfectly normal tone of voice. "No, I'm fine. But you're right, I need to sleep. Thank you, Sue."

I stood and carefully placed Nicholas in Mishelle's recliner. He looked so small and alone there.

"No, thank *you*." She studied me for another second and then held out arms. We hugged.

"You were good to her," she whispered to me. "I'll never forget that."

I nodded. I no longer had anything to say. Nicky and I hugged. Her embrace was quick, intense and entirely sincere.

Somehow, I found my purse and let myself out.

Bright sunlight blinded me momentarily. I fumbled my sunglasses out of my purse and slipped them on.

I found myself looking at the sky.

Broad and blue as always, flecked with high clouds. The same: yet not. Never again the same:

She's gone.

CHAPTER TWENTY-TWO
More . . . Or less

S HOCK. PAIN. GRIEF.
Saturate a mind with these and anyone might snap.

I retreated.

I don't know what else to call it. I curled up on my bed or the couch, eyes mostly closed; sometimes open but not seeing anything; hearing nothing; feeling emptied. I had no appetite. I didn't bathe and I didn't do a thing with my face or hair and I didn't give a damn what anyone might say.

Not even Chris.

When Dave brought the boys home early Saturday evening, I remember that I was on the couch, in a semi-conscious state and dressed in pajamas that I don't recall changing into. My eyes were open but I wasn't looking at anything in particular.

Chris entered my field of vision.

He looked worried. Or perhaps stunned. His eyes were big, I remember that. They filled my tiny, self-compressed world in that moment.

Somehow they managed to penetrate the fog that wrapped me like a thick blanket: *my Cee-Boo is unhappy.*

"Mom? Are you okay?"

It took me a few tries to re-start my voice. My throat felt as if I'd been gargling with battery acid and rusty razor blades. My voice was like ashes.

"What?"

"I said, are you okay?" He knelt by the couch and took my hand, peered into my eyes, filling my world. "Dad told us that Mishelle died. Is that . . . is that true?"

I nodded. He blinked slowly but that was all.

We were both silent for a long time. Finally he said, "When's the . . . you know . . ."

"Wednesday," I croaked.

"Okay." He looked down, thinking. Without looking up, he said quietly: "Did she, you know . . .?"

"No," I rasped. "No, she didn't suffer."

He sighed. I think he closed his eyes for a moment. I don't know. I was somewhere else again.

"Okay."

Then he was gone. He might have kissed me on the cheek before he left. I won't swear to it.

Somehow I made my way to my bedroom and curled up there. The ceiling and I were already far too familiar with each other so I stared at the wall instead.

Presently I became aware that Dave was sitting on the end of the bed, watching me. I rolled and looked at him.

No words passed between us and I doubt if our expressions were especially forthcoming, either. It was that kind of conversation.

At last I nodded at him and he slid toward me, embraced me as I wept, dried out and tearless, into his chest.

Stroking my hair, he said, "Chris told me the funeral is Wednesday."

I nodded.

"Okay. That gives me some time. I'd like to record some songs from her collection for the service. I think she'd like that."

I looked up at him. "Yes. She would."

"Okay. Let me know when you're going over there. Maybe I can meet you and pick out her favorites."

His calm, measured speech slowly penetrated my fog of grief and pain: a flashlight bobbing rhythmically toward me out of the murk. "Yeah, you'd know which ones, wouldn't you?"

He nodded, still stroking my hair.

"Okay. I'll let you know when I do."

"Good." He released me. "I'll get dinner. We're . . . me and the boys; we're pretty tired, too. Maybe we should all turn in early."

I nodded and ran my hand through my hair, wincing a little at the greasy texture. "'Kay. I'm not really hungry."

"I figured. Neither am I, really. But we should eat. Sandwiches. Something."

He rose and made his way to the door. "I'm very glad," he said. He wasn't looking at me, not really.

I waited, empty.

"Glad you were there."

I closed my eyes and retreated.

* * *

I managed to get it together long enough to eat some dinner and do the dishes. I went through it in a daze, of course, but enough of my senses had returned to note that all of my boys fled to their own hiding places the minute Dave pushed his plate back and rose from the table; retreated like me and stayed there.

I scraped plates and wiped countertops, half-heartedly wondering if this was the kind of example I should be setting.

When it was his bedtime, I went in search of Chris to tuck him in. As I brought the covers to his chest and bent to kiss him, he began to cry. God help me, he sounded like a lonesome puppy.

I held him and listened to him keen.

Through gulping sobs, he said: "Mom, I'm really gonna miss her!"

I said, "I know."

"She was so nice to me! An' . . . an' she taught me so much! 'Bout chess and Braille and music and electronics . . ." He paused to sniff and clear his throat.

I dabbed at his cheeks with a corner of the blanket. There wasn't much, really. Chris is far from a crybaby. "She was my best friend." Another sniff: "Or my sister."

"Sister," I said gently and kissed his forehead.

"Hey, you guys."

I looked over my shoulder, still holding Chris. Zach stood in the door, arms folded; his face sober in a concentrated effort to avoid adding to the waterworks. "Don't be sad."

We looked at him.

"Think about where she is now. Heaven. She can *see*. Run." He looked almost embarrassed. "*Dance*. She told me once that dancing was one of the things she'd always wanted to learn and never got a chance."

He bit his lip and looked down, then up again at us. His jaw was set. "Now she can. She can do anything she wants because she's in Heaven and she's looking down at us and she doesn't want us to be sad. I *know*."

I beckoned to him. He came to us and sat down on the bed. We wrapped ourselves in a three-way hug and remained silent for a long soothing moment.

Then my youngest said, almost to himself:

"She's probably shopping."

"Dresses and jewelry," Zach agreed.

"Purses," Chris muttered.

"Shoes."

"Naw, she hated wearing shoes. She'd go barefoot in the snow if you let her."

I listened to my two boys heal themselves and decided that I might do that too, in time.

* * *

Though I read the paper infrequently except for the grocery ads; that Sunday I took ours from the plastic cylinder outside our front door with something almost like eagerness.

I spread it out on the kitchen table, took a sip of coffee strong enough to straighten my hair and opened it to the obituaries.

There. My eyes blurred with relief. They had a good recent picture of her and the caption was Michelle L. Woodring, not Michael.

Not Michael. I read it carefully and yes, the obit referenced her as FKA Michael but only once at the beginning and that was enough. They even used the right pronouns.

I rubbed my eyes and sipped some more life-giving brew. Thank you, God. I'd been so worried . . .

The phone rang. I picked up. "Hello."

"Hi, Michelle? This here's Louise."

Speak of the . . . I punched that unworthy thought in the gut and it folded back into the darkness with nary a grunt. "Hi, Louise. What can I do for you?"

"Wey-ull, we've been goin' through Mike's stuff, tryin' to decide where it all goes and we was wonderin' if y'had any ideer 'bout that." Her flat, nasal Kansas twang was so at odds with the determinedly cheerful tone of her voice. "We could use your help, is what I'm sayin'."

I was touched. "Yes. She told me where she wanted most of it to go. I'll be happy to assist, Louise."

"Wey-ull, that's a relief, it is. We-all be goin' over t'his place today. You feel like joinin' us?"

"I'd love to."

* * *

Pulling up in front her apartment for what was to be the final time was beyond surreal, it was wrenching; like looking into your bathroom mirror one morning and belatedly discovering that someone has replaced it with a funhouse version.

I shut off the car and for a moment, I was afraid I was having another anxiety attack: blurred vision and accelerated pulse, difficulty breathing, dizziness. For about a minute, I stared unseeing through the windshield at the apartment, the last few weeks riffling past in my mind's eye like one of those illustrated flip books for children.

But I got my breathing under control, sternly commanded my runaway heart to cease and desist and the blurriness was only tears, after all.

Only tears.

I got out and went inside. The door was open and the Elvis sign was missing.

I placed a palm on the lemon-colored wood where it had hung and nearly made a fist. Instead, I stroked the smooth surface a final time.

I didn't say anything about the sign, then or later.

One step inside, I blinked. The front room was the brightest I'd ever seen it. All the windows were wide open.

It was pretty bare, too. Most of Mishelle's things were already packed up or dismantled. Louise was on the loveseat, placidly folding articles of Mishelle's clothing. She looked up and greeted me when I came in, but my gaze fell on the recliner and my bruised heart surged painfully within me.

Empty.

She's gone.

Somehow, that made it real; more than I'd been prepared for. I closed my eyes, shook my head just the tiniest bit and returned Louise's greeting, perhaps a little distantly.

I don't think she noticed. She started right in:

"So, d'you think y'might know where he wants his stuff t'go?"

I moved out of the way as Earl and Sue suddenly popped into the front room carrying the bedroom dresser. They grunted hellos at me as they lumbered past.

I acknowledged them and looked back at Louise.

"Yes. She wanted Chris to have her chessboard and she wanted her CD collection to go to Dave. Nicky was supposed to get the computer in the back bedroom and she wanted Nina, the little blind girl down at the School for the Blind to receive all her gadgets, like her Braille embosser and things like that."

Louise looked interested. "Well, 'magine that. Do y'know how to get ahold of her?"

I considered it. "I think so. I think her grandmother runs that bookstore across the street from Norm's News. I'll give her a call."

"Yeah, that's who you should call."

I turned my head. "Hi, Lynn. How are you, dear?"

She came to me and we hugged. "Okay," she said soberly. There were dark circles under her eyes. I realized that we all probably looked exhausted. "Just . . ." She gestured with the toiletry articles in her hand, a little helplessly. "You know."

"Yeah." I patted her shoulder. "She loved you too, Lynn."

She nodded back at me, her eyes suddenly full of tears.

Louise said into the sudden silence: "Michelle, is there anything of Mike's *you* want?"

I started to shake my head (*the only thing I want, I can't have . . .*) but my gaze fell on her stripper pole and the fluffy multicolored scarf that hung from it. "Yes. I'll take that scarf. And, and . . ."

I took a deep breath. "The necklace and little items I gave her from the Crusillo. Those. That's all."

"Wey-ull, we went an' packed up all her blind gadgets already. D'you mind takin' them to that little gal's grandma fo' us?"

"No. I'd be honored."

Earl and Sue loaded the gear into my trunk and said their goodbyes, leaving me staring down at the pile of items.

There was a lot of stuff.

"The only thing I want," I whispered. I slammed the lid and went home.

* * *

The phone rang while I was sorting laundry. (I think it's contagious.) For a moment, just enough time for my heart to bounce hard once within my chest, I forgot and I snatched the phone from its cradle.

But by the time I looked at the number, I'd remembered though, and a dull ache had replaced the lift of anticipation.

I didn't recognize the number. "Hello?"

"Michelle? This is Sue."

"Oh. Hi."

"How are you doing?"

"About as well as I can, I guess." I flipped a no-mate sock into a growing pile of other mismatches. "How are you?"

"The same. Uh," she cleared her throat with some difficulty. "I was wondering: would Dave like to be a pall bearer for Mishelle's funeral?"

"I'm pretty sure he would. Let me ask him. Hang on a minute, Sue."

I got up and went to the back bedroom; Dave's office. He was in front of the computer, disinterestedly tapping at the keys. He turned a haggard face to me when I spoke and I was shocked at how much this had affected him, too.

I don't know why. I shouldn't have been. It wasn't as if I owned it.

"Sue wants to know if you'd like to be a pall bearer."

He peered owlishly at me. His hair looked like he'd combed it with a garden rake. "Sure. I'd be honored."

I put the phone to my ear. "He says he'd be honored, Sue. Why don't the two of you talk . . .?"

"I want to tell you something first," she said quietly.

Uh-oh. "What's that, Sue?"

"Mom and Dad are going to let her be buried as Mishelle. I talked to them today. They don't like it much and we still haven't reached an agreement about the headstone, but it's a start."

I felt dizzy for a second. "That's . . . that's good news, Sue." My knees felt weak and I suddenly needed to sit down. "The service, too?"

"Especially that. If the minister calls her by that other name just once, I'm stopping it cold, right then and there."

Her voice had that touch of steel in it again and I shivered slightly. This was not a woman you'd want angry with you, for any reason.

"Okay." I was having trouble with my own voice. It kept cracking. "Thanks, Sue. Thank you with all my heart."

"It's for her, Michelle. I hope everybody remembers that. What we want doesn't matter."

Funerals are for the living . . . I'll come back and haunt them; I swear . . . I promise I won't let them forget . . .

"You're right, Sue. She earned it, didn't she?" I became aware that my husband was signaling me. "I think Dave wants to talk to you."

To him, I said, "The CD's?"

He nodded.

"Sue, I'll let you two talk. Thanks for letting me know." I handed the phone to my husband and left the room.

Outside, amidst birdsong and the warm, almost buttery sunshine of a balmy afternoon, I felt the cramped thing within me relax and un-kink itself.

So I looked at the sky and the flowers and listened to the world go on around me, trying to listen with her ears and trying to see the world as fundamentally no different than it had once been.

But it was. It would always be different.

I had changed and I could never go back to what I'd been or anything like the life I'd once led.

I knew too much.

I wouldn't have traded all that I'd gone through in the last four and a half months for anything in this world or in the next, for that matter.

I'd promised . . . and I keep my promises.

* * *

The doorbell rang while I was preparing dinner. Startled, I grabbed a towel, wiped my hands (meatloaf can be messy) and went to answer it. I opened it to a familiar face under a brown cap.

"Well, hi!"

"Howdy, Mrs. Alexander." He touched his cap in well-remembered fashion. "Package for Chris Alexander. I take it that'd be your boy?"

It brought a grin to my face and I could feel unused muscles creak. "Yes, he is. Can I sign for it?"

"Of course, ma'am." He lifted a long, rectangular object into the foyer and offered me the pad. "Right here, ma'am."

"I didn't order anything. For Chris? What the heck is it?"

He shrugged. "It's from a music company back East, ma'am."

"Oh, jeez." The guitar. I'd totally forgotten about it. I smiled at the driver. It still felt weird. "Thanks."

He touched his cap again, "Ma'am," and jogged back to his truck.

I took the package into the front room and set it on the couch. "Chris!" I shouted. "Package for you!"

He pounded down the hall and skidded to a halt. His eyes found it immediately. "What is it?"

I smiled at him. It was beginning to feel a little more natural. "I have no idea, but it's addressed to you. Open it, Cee-Boo."

He tore it open without bothering with the niceties. Cardboard and packing material flew left and right and at last he had the case exposed.

He opened it and gasped. I'd never heard him do that before.

"Who sent it?" he asked, awed. He caressed the burnished tobacco-colored wood of the body with suddenly gentle fingers.

"Mishelle," I replied. "She knew you loved music as much as she did and she heard this demonstrated on the Home Shopping Network. She ordered it for you just last week."

His head came up and he searched my face. "Before she . . ."

"Yes."

He looked down at it. It was a very beautiful guitar. "Wow."

My son lifted it from its case and a white envelope fell from it. "Hey, what's this?" He set the guitar back in the case and opened the envelope. His lips moved silently.

"Read it," I suggested.

"'To a very special little buddy: I hope you get years of enjoyment and good music from this.'"

His lips moved again as he softly repeated: "Special little buddy."

My son looked up at me. There were tears in his eyes. "That sure was nice of her."

I was choking back some of my own. "Sure was."

Chris touched the strings gently, reverently. Soft, subtle notes chimed from the instrument, tumbling into the air like bits of evaporating crystal, sweetly fading.

Slowly, my son closed the case and we held each other for a while; healing.

* * *

I hate Mondays.

I shut off the Toyota and got out, slinging my paperwork bag from my shoulder. I marched toward the office entrance. My head was up and my shoulders squared.

To hell with it, I was thinking. *If they're going to nail me for this, then let them take their best shot.*

I opened the door and strode in with a big smile plastered on my face, one I had spent some time practicing in the mirror that morning.

It still felt a little lopsided.

"Hi, Jodie!"

She looked up and nodded at me. "Hi, Michelle. Good to see you." She swept past; head down again over a stack of reports.

Stumped, I stood waiting for her to say . . . *something* but she kept going, briskly professional as always.

The rest of the morning went like that. Nobody said boo to me. A few people, mostly office personnel I knew well, stopped by to offer their condolences but that was it; that was all.

Rather than feeling relieved, it was giving me that surreal feeling again, as if this were a dream and I wasn't quite awake. In the meantime . . .

In the meantime, I had a medication log and a list of disposed meds to deliver to Robin.

I sighed, got the items from my bag and went down the hall to her office.

I knocked and her cheery tones invited me in. Silently, I placed the log and list on her desk and stood, hands folded; waiting.

She looked at them, did not touch them and looked up me. "I'm so very sorry," she said quietly.

I nodded.

Her gaze didn't change: gentle but unyielding. "Do you feel you crossed some boundaries, Michelle?"

"You spoke with Amy?"

It was her turn to nod.

I set my jaw. "Yes. Yes, I did. And you know something, Robin? I'd do it again in a heartbeat. Because it was worth it, all of it."

"Yes," she replied in that same quiet tone. "I rather thought that's what you would say." She continued to study me. "Was it a God thing, Michelle?"

I started to shrug and turned it into a nod. "Yeah. There's no other name for it."

Smiling, she rose, came around the desk and hugged me. "You gave her such a gift," she told me. "Such an incredible gift. From all that I've heard, you were both blessed to be with each other when she passed."

She embraced me again. "Bless you, Michelle."

I walked out of her office in a kind of daze. Surreal?

Oh, yes.

Mind on autopilot, it was actually pleasant to return to the minutiae of office work: reports, files, schedules. I didn't have any patients, just overdue paperwork so I did that, my thoughts . . . elsewhere.

When I got home, I found my husband seated in front of the big computer in Zach's room, an intent expression on his face. Stacks of compact discs were piled on the table and on the floor.

At first, he seemed oblivious and didn't even look around when I spoke: "Going well?"

He seemed to ignore me so I shrugged half-heartedly and turned to go. I stopped when he said, almost to himself:

"It's like she's helping me pick them out."

The hair on the back of my neck prickled. "Really?" I asked cautiously. "How so?"

He turned. There was an odd little smile on his face, as if he knew something I didn't. "Just a feeling."

He surveyed the stacks of discs, the smile ripening toward a grin. There might have been over two hundred albums there. "I'm almost done."

I stared. "That was fast."

His grin was entirely confident. "I think I had help."

Brow furrowed, I studied him. "You're serious," I said.

He nodded. I made a disbelieving face. He shrugged and returned to his work.

I put it out of my mind and went to start some dinner.

* * *

I was brushing my teeth when the phone rang. Still scrubbing away, I went into the bedroom, picked it up and looked at it; saw that it was Nicky. The screen informed me that it was past nine.

I went back to the bathroom and managed to spit before the machine picked up. "He-wo?" Discreetly, I spat again. "Nicky?"

"Hey, Michelle. Just wanted to talk. You busy?"

"Uh, well, I was headed to bed . . ."

"That's cool. Hey, I just wanted to ask about, you know, the way Mishelle died. Is that, like, normal for people with COPD?"

I wiped my mouth with the corner of a hand towel. "Well, now that you mention it; no, it's not. There must have been an event that we missed. Or was so small we wouldn't notice."

"An event. Like, what does that mean?"

"Well, possibly her heart. Or a blood clot. I really don't know, Nicky. Only an autopsy would tell us and even then the results might not be conclusive."

"Oh. Wow." I could almost hear her think. Or maybe it was just static on the line. "So, like, are you gonna be at the funeral home tomorrow?"

I smiled. "Of course."

I was glad we had all decided to meet the afternoon before her service and ensure that Mishelle was properly attired. A promise is a promise. "When we talked Sunday night, I think I made it pretty clear to you and Lynn that I had every intention of making sure her wishes were carried out."

"Oh, yeah. Me too, of course. Yeah. Uh, well, maybe it was a blessing, you know? Like, the way she died and all? Really fast, you know?"

I suddenly felt terribly weary. "I think so too, Nicky. Now, if you don't mind, I think I'm going to turn in. I have to work early tomorrow. I'll see you at the funeral home around one."

"'Kay. 'Night."

"Good night." I clicked off and racked it on the charger cradle, went to the bathroom to shut off the light.

Halfway back to my bed, the damned thing rang again. I looked at the tiny screen with some annoyance.

"Nicky? Now what?"

"Hey Michelle, I was just thinking, you know, that the way she died was just not *normal*, y'know? And my husband and Lynn keep telling me to just let it go and yeah, that would be cool if it wasn't so unusual, y'know? And Lynn says it doesn't matter *how* she died, like that wasn't important, which is really stupid in my opinion. You know?"

A twitch was gradually developing in my left eye. I rubbed it but it wouldn't go away. "Nicky, I'm not sure what you're asking me. Are you saying there was something suspicious about the way she died?"

"Well, I think maybe like an autopsy might not be such a bad idea, y'know. Like, it might show if she took too many Oxycontin or something the night before. Or something."

The twitch had developed a maddening consistency. "Nicky, you saw me count her meds and dump them. They were all accounted for. She didn't take any Oxycontin the night before, not for the whole day, in fact. It's in the logs."

Persistent, she said: "Yeah, but there could have been something else, you know?"

I rubbed gently at my eye. "Like what?"

She didn't answer the question. Instead, she said: "Hey, you know Julie?"

It caught me off-guard. "Julie? I only met her once, on my second visit to Mishelle's. Why?"

"Well, she thinks there's something really suspicious in the way that she, you know, died."

There was a tiny spark of irritation buried under all my fatigue. "Well, why don't you have her call me and I'll explain it to her, okay?"

"Well, I don't think she'd want to do that. Y'see, she kinda thinks that maybe it was a suicide and that maybe you helped her, y'know?"

"Oh, for God's sake!"

"Yeah, she's kind of upset, too."

The spark had turned into a blue-white jet of anger. "You tell her to call me," I said through clenched teeth. "And I'll set her straight. I can tell her *exactly* what I observed all week and I'll also tell her that I had *nothing* . . ."

"Uh, like I said, she's pretty upset." Nicky sounded almost apologetic. "She called the police station and asked them how they go about investigating stuff like this."

"*What?*"

"Oh, don't worry; she didn't give them your name or anything. She was just asking them questions about the procedure, how to go about reporting it and stuff like that."

I was suddenly wide awake and seriously pissed-off, but I bit down hard on it. "She called the police? Nicky, please tell her to call me immediately. Tomorrow, if possible. If she's not satisfied with my answers, she can talk to either Lori or Robin about this as well."

"Yeah. Yeah, I'll do that. Maybe she's just having a hard time with this, y'know? See ya tomorrow?"

"*Yes*," I growled. "I need to get to bed, Nicky."

"'Kay. 'Night." She hung up.

For a long moment I sat, the phone still in my hand, staring at nothing.

It occurred to me then that some people respond to grief with anger and that my coping skills were no better than Julie's or anyone else's, for that matter.

"Poor Julie," I whispered. I racked the phone in its cradle and crawled into bed; slept.

*   *   *

My cellphone rang the next morning, right between patients number two and number three. I flipped it open and saw that it was Lynn.

"Hi, this is Michelle."

"Michelle? We've got a problem. A big one."

Another? The high octane coffee I'd been slurping all morning was all that kept me from feeling that bone-deep weariness again.

"What now?"

"I'm down here at the funeral home and they dressed Mishelle in a pair of *Hanes boxer shorts*!" There was an edge of hysteria in her voice. "This is *not* acceptable. Can you go by the store and pick up something more appropriate for her?"

I didn't know whether to laugh or cry: *Enough!* "Okay, Lynn. Calm down. I'll stop by Wal-Mart and get something. Is there anything else you need?"

She drew a ragged breath. "No. No, that's all." She exhaled in one mighty gust. "After all she went through, to be buried like *that* . . .!"

"Don't worry," I soothed her. "I have one more patient and I'll meet you at the home by one, just like we agreed. Okay?"

"Okay. Thanks, Mishelle." Her voice was shaky with unshed tears. Well, I couldn't blame her one bit. "See you then."

She hung up.

I sighed, closed the phone and attended to my next patient. It was a simple case; a wound dressing, although it was a big wound and a small person, but it went quickly. I busied myself with the mechanics of the job; keeping my emotions at bay and the weariness at arm's length.

For a while, at any rate.

I dashed into Wal-Mart, grabbed the laciest pink panties I could find, paid for them and hurried back to my car.

I know everyone says this but it's true: funeral homes smell weird.

And why do they call them *homes*, anyway? There was nothing homey about the place. It was dark, dusty and that stink was everywhere; subtle and insidious.

The door creaked as I entered, just like a bad movie. Slowly, I approached the front counter and rang the bell. An elderly woman appeared out of the dim recesses toward the back, looking rather like a poor job of embalming herself.

She lacked an expression of any sort.

"May I help you?"

I was beginning to feel distinctly creepy, even though I've viewed quite a few dead bodies in my time. "Yes, my name is Michelle Alexander. I'm here to help prepare Mishelle Woodring for her service tomorrow."

"Ah, yes. Some of your party is already here."

My party. Somehow that didn't sound quite right but I let it go. "Uh, yes. I spoke to one of them, earlier. Where are they?"

An expression finally crossed her face and it took me a moment to register it as confusion. "Actually, I'm not sure where they are at this moment. Would you come with me, please?"

Well, sure. I've *always* wanted to follow a strange old person right into the depths of a mortuary.

Skin crawling, the icy-footed ants again marching up and down my spine, I followed the old woman.

We went down a long hallway, through a couple of empty rooms and came to an unmarked door. She opened it and gestured. "Mishelle is in here. I'll see if I can find the rest of your party."

"Don't forget the funny hats and noisemakers," I muttered.

"Pardon me?"

"Never mind." Cautiously, I entered.

It was creepy. There's no other way to put it.

Mishelle was lying atop a thing like a table, her hands clasped across her chest. She was wearing a black velour blouse and a black and white checkered skirt; not exactly what she'd wanted to be buried in, but it would have to do.

Feet dragging a little, I approached her.

But she wasn't there. Yes, I know her body was but *she* wasn't there. I could feel it. Or rather: I couldn't feel it. Her, I mean.

It was as if I was alone in the room and that which was before me was no more *her* than a pair of my old sneakers was actually me.

Looking at her, I shivered, even though I wasn't cold.

I put my hands on top of hers. *They* were cold; cold and stiff and none of the strength, none of that power and ability I'd felt so many times before was there anymore.

Hastily, I pulled my hands away; looking at her face. They'd applied most of her makeup and curled her hair. I was struck then at how few times I'd seen her with makeup.

It looked . . . odd.

I looked closely at her lips. They were coated with bubblegum pink lipstick and appeared badly chapped.

I frowned. *What the hell?*

"Mishelle," I said. "You have crusty lips. This just isn't going to work." I started carefully picking the crusts off her lips.

"What are you doing?"

I turned. Lynn and Nicky were in the doorway, staring at me.

"Picking the crusts off her lips." I suddenly realized how that sounded and pointed. "It looks awful!"

Lynn laughed without much humor. "Ah, that's *glue*, Michelle. They use it to keep the deceased's mouth closed."

"Oh." I looked down. Right on cue, Mishelle's mouth opened. "Oh, dear."

They joined me at the table. "They also use it on the eyelids," Lynn explained. She patted me on the shoulder. "Don't fret. You didn't know."

"Well, they got a little heavy-handed if you ask me," I muttered.

Nicky nodded at me and went back to work on the finishing touches of Mishelle's makeup. Lynn looked at Mishelle's folded hands and frowned.

"Where's the ring that Charles gave her?"

I was startled. "Oops. I've got it." I dug it out of my purse and started to put it back on my friend's finger.

I noticed Lynn's expression and stopped. "Renee told me to."

The dark clouds forming on Lynn's face blew away. She looked relieved. "Oh, okay. For a minute I thought . . . Sorry, Michelle."

I made sure the ring was back in place and nodded reassuringly at her. "It's okay, Lynn. I understand."

I looked over my shoulder as the door creaked.

The elderly lady stood in the doorway, expressionless still but surveying us all with sharp gray eyes. With eerie certainty, I knew in that moment that this woman had seen things most of us would only see in nightmares and in the next, I felt almost sorry for her.

Like a ghost, she drifted up next to us and began reapplying the glue to Mishelle's lips.

"Hey." I couldn't help it. "Could you do me a favor, please?"

Mute, she looked at me.

"Go easy on that stuff, willya? She doesn't like crusty lips."

She stared at me for a long moment. I really didn't want to know what was in her mind at that moment.

At last she was done. Slowly, like an old hurt long forgotten, she shuffled out of the room.

Lynn followed her to the door and when it was closed, she whispered, "Okay, let's hurry! Michelle, did you bring the panties?"

"Right here." I whipped them out of my bag and we swung into action.

Nicky waited by the door, listening for the old lady while Lynn produced a pair of scissors. We lifted Mishelle up and flipped her skirt back.

Yuck, white boxer shorts, just as she'd said. I held Mishelle's lower torso clear of the table while Lynn carefully cut away the offending garment.

We struggled for a bit to get the panties into place, but we were soon done and I lowered her back onto the table with a sigh of relief.

I smoothed down the material of the skirt and looked up at the two of them.

Lynn stashed the boxers and scissors in her purse. Nicky left the door and regarded our friend, her face working, holding back her tears.

"Done?" she asked; her voice husky with emotion.

"Done."

We all looked at each other. Suddenly, Lynn laughed and this time there was genuine humor in it. "Okay. Now the old girl can finally rest in peace."

CHAPTER TWENTY-THREE

"She's not there anymore . . ."

"**Y**OU SURE YOU WANT TO DO THIS?"

My youngest son's face was strained. He nodded.

"Are you scared?"

He didn't answer at first then nodded again.

"Well, it's okay if you are. Everybody is, a little. But there's nothing to be scared of, really."

We pulled up before the funeral home. "Chris, we don't have to do this, you know."

He grimaced. "I know. I *want* to, though. I have to . . . to . . ." He looked down at the envelope in his lap. "I don't want to with everybody watching."

I shut off the Toyota and patted his knee. "I totally understand, Cee-Boo." A deep breath, followed by a slow exhale: "Ready anytime you are, sweetie."

"Let's do it." He opened his door and got out. I followed him.

We went in the front door and it creaked again. Chris stopped. "Mom?" he whispered. "This place *stinks*!"

"I know." I tapped him on the shoulder. "Don't say that, honey. It's the chemicals they use to preserve dead people. C'mon, this way."

I led him into the chapel where Mishelle's casket was. He caught sight of it and stopped again. His eyes grew big.

I waited. After a moment, I asked softly, "Change your mind?"

His eyes were fixed on it. A moment of his own and he shook his head; walked toward it, his steps firm and steady. I had to hurry to catch up.

He paused at the side of the casket and looked down at her. He looked up when I came to stand beside him.

His expression was bewildered. "Mom, it's like she's not there anymore!"

"No," I said. "She's not. Her soul has left and all that remains is the body. It's like when you wear a pair of pants for so long that they wear out and then you have to throw them away."

"And her body wore out?"

"Just like the pants."

"But I got some new ones," he mumbled.

"So did she."

He squinted up at me. "That's why I can't feel her anymore, huh?"

My eyes blurred with sudden tears. "Yup. Guess so. Do you want to touch her?"

He looked shocked. "Heck, no!"

"Okay. Time to do what you came here for, then."

He nodded. Carefully, almost surgically, he placed the envelope near her hands. He'd labored for some time over the Braille machine, composing the note the envelope contained. I knew what it said because he let me read it before slipping it into the envelope.

Dear Mishelle,

I will miss you a lot. I will see you in heaven.

I miss playing chess with you. I miss going to your house.

Your Friend Always, I Love you,

Chris

When he was done, I took an envelope of my own out of my purse and slipped it down beneath one of her legs where it couldn't be seen.

I had also spent some time on my message and, no; I don't care to discuss the contents, thank you.

I took another deep breath, regretting it instantly. "Want some time alone with her?"

He shook his head. His eyes were sad. "No. She's not there anymore, Mom."

He walked away and I followed him, back into the sunshine and clean air.

We got into the car and I started it. "Good job, Chris." I glanced at him. My son's face was like stone. "I'm proud of you."

He nodded jerkily. We drove home.

We didn't talk.

* * *

"Zach?" I poked my head into his room. "Are you about ready? We should leave soon."

He looked up from tying his shoes. "I know, Mom. I'm almost done." He finished and stood. "Okay?"

I looked him over. The new dress shirt had softened the gangly aspect of my eldest son's growing frame. He actually looked quite dapper. "You clean up pretty good, sweetie. Let me fix that tie a little." I went to him and started fiddling with it.

"Do I gotta wear one of those, too?"

I looked over my shoulder. Chris scowled at us from the doorway. "'Fraid so. Sorry, Cee-Boo, but it's a requirement for today."

I looked back at Zach. "Your dad already leave?"

This close, he couldn't look away. "Uh-huh." He tried, though. "They needed him there early, you know, for the . . ."

"Procession," I finished; both the tie and the sentence. "I know. It would have been nice to go as a family, though. Zach, let me have one of your ties for Chris. Let's hurry, boys. We're late."

* * *

I had one of those surreal episodes when we entered the chapel; a short, freakishly intense bout of disconnection that rolled over me like a sneaker wave the moment my gaze fell on the front pews.

The whole Woodring clan was there: Earl and Louise, Sue, her husband and three kids, Mishelle's three brothers and at the very end; my husband. They filled the front pews.

There was no room for myself or my two sons.

I glanced back and forth as the unreal sensation grew. No one had saved us a place? The chapel was about half-full, but most of the seats near the front were taken as well. It was as if I'd been forgotten, overlooked; even demoted to the rear of the room.

It was silly, I know and maybe that's what snapped me out of it. "Huh. Okay boys, follow me."

We found our own pew; the third row near the end. I sat; still feeling a bit nettled and then cocked my head, listening. I could hear the music Dave had recorded playing softly, somewhere.

It almost made me smile: something by . . . Procol Harum? That was it: *A Whiter Shade of Pale*.

I listened, lost in that old, wandering melody.

Someone tapped me on the shoulder. I looked up, startled. Lori smiled down at me. "Hey, Michelle."

"Hey!" I nudged Chris. "Scoot over, boys. Make some room."

With only a little grumbling, my two sons moved over. Lori sat. She held two roses in her hands. She gave one to me. "I thought you might want one of these."

I took it. "Yeah, I do. Thanks, Lori."

She smiled at me again. The room finally seemed to come into focus and I heaved a sigh of relief.

"You're welcome, Michelle." She patted my arm as the pastor entered the room.

The crowd fell silent. She began with an invocation and I prayed numbly, not knowing really what I prayed for, but hoping with all my heart that all would be somehow for the best.

And then she began her talk and things went downhill from there.

The wheels didn't come off, fortunately. The pastor didn't say anything inappropriate or unpleasant; in fact, she didn't say much of anything at all.

I've never heard such a basketful of generalities in my entire life. It might have applied to *anyone*. There was no mention made of Mishelle's amazing list of accomplishments; no mention of her struggle for identity, no comments about her courage and her will to live or her wicked sense of humor or even her chess-playing ability, for Heaven's sake!

It was as if this woman who purported to speak for my friend and her life knew nothing at all about her.

Depressed, I realized that it was the truth.

I think I tried to shut off my ears at that point, with only limited success.

At least I didn't blubber like an idiot.

Mercifully, the pastor's talk was brief. I suppose one has to run out of generic pleasantries eventually.

When she was done, I stood and went to the casket. Lori and the boys trailed after me. Earl and Louise were lined up with Sue and her husband; a burly sort of fellow who looked like he could pick his teeth with you.

We all shook hands. I don't remember what I said, exactly; something innocuous; something reassuring. My eyes were getting a bit glassy by then.

I went to the casket and laid the rose across Mishelle's breast. Lori did the same. We looked at each other and nodded.

I took Lori's hand and beckoned to Chris and Zach.

My two sons went to the casket. Chris looked and shrugged; his face expressionless.

Zach took one look and shuddered. He closed his eyes for a second, then he and his brother joined us.

The shudder was very small, almost unnoticeable. But I'm his mother. I could tell.

Earlier, Zach had told me that he had no interest whatsoever in viewing Mishelle's body.

"That's not her," he declared in a quietly firm voice.

I agreed.

There was a short break before the actual graveside service, so we went outside. I've never been so grateful to breathe clean air.

I was standing on the front lawn, reminiscing with Sue when Nicky and Lynn approached us.

We hugged. Nicky looked solemn, for her. "I just want you to know that we are so *glad* that you and your family were there for Mishelle." She closed her eyes and sighed, a little theatrically, I thought. "She was so *happy*."

She opened her eyes and looked at me. Her expression was innocence distilled. "You gave her something we never could, you know."

I said: "Thanks, Nicky. She was lucky to have the two of you as caregivers." I hesitated, then: "But she loved you two as well. Don't ever forget that."

"I won't." She beckoned to me and before I had a chance to come closer, she leaned in and began to quickly mumble something in my ear. I had time to notice the words *detective* and *phone call* and that she reeked of stale cigarette smoke then I pulled away.

"Nicky, this is not the time or the place," I said firmly. "Call me later, please."

I didn't give her time to respond. The procession to the gravesite was preparing to move. My sons in tow, I marched off to my car.

I'll give Earl and Louise this: Mishelle would have loved the site. It was up on a hill, overlooking part of the valley and under a broad-limbed maple that looked like it had been there for a while and had every intention of staying put for many years to come.

The lush green grass rolled down the hill into the distance and under different circumstances, I might have been tempted to take off my shoes and wiggle my toes into the fat green blades. I think my friend would have approved wholeheartedly.

Perhaps I will, someday.

It's a lovely place to be laid to rest. But who does that matter to most, really? The living or the dead?

I suppose I won't know until it's my time.

We gathered at the grave.

Dave stood with Mishelle's brothers behind the hearse and they toted the casket to the hole. It was covered, of course. Carefully, the men set their burden down on the webbing sling that lowered the casket and took their places among us.

My husband came to stand silently beside me. His face was utterly without expression, but I patted him on the arm anyway, hopefully.

"Thanks," I whispered. He nodded, not looking at me.

The pastor went to the head of the casket and said a few more vague pleasantries, then asked if anyone would like to speak.

There was silence for a few heartbeats, and then Lynn spoke up. "I'd like to say some things, please."

The pastor nodded at her.

Lynn kept it brief and heartfelt and didn't weep. I thanked her silently. Again, there was silence.

The pastor glanced around the circle of faces. "Is there anyone else who would like to say a few words in memory of this fine woman?" she asked.

Silence.

I was clenching my teeth, just a hairsbreadth away from biting my tongue. The way I felt, I could've bit it clean in half.

I was looking at the stony expressions on the faces of the Woodring clan and all of the resentment, all of the anger, all of the hideous sense of shared betrayal I'd felt in the few months since I'd learned how abandoned my friend had been by her own blood was throbbing in my temples and wrists.

My heart felt as if it would explode.

There was a piece of paper in my purse containing a few jotted notes I'd planned to read but looking at those faces, I decided against it.

This was and still is a very good thing. I don't know what I'd have done if I'd tried to speak that day, but it's a safe bet I would have made a complete mess of it.

So I stood mute as the pastor concluded the service and then my family and I walked away from my friend's final resting place, my heart like lead within me, my throat clogged and eyes wet with tears.

If I'd been a dog, my tail would have been between my legs.

We went home. I did things, things I don't remember doing and it made it hard to find things afterward. I must have unloaded the dishwasher because I found silverware in some of the weirdest places, later.

The phone rang. I was dusting and the charger was close at hand. I picked up. "Hello?"

"Hey, Michelle, it's Nicky, how are ya? Gettin' over the funeral yet? Jeez, that was somethin', huh? I was gonna say somethin' but Lynn spoke up and then she kinda said what I would have, you know? And then I was kinda waitin' for someone else and then it was over and hey, you know, I called to tell ya that the police are gonna be following up on Julie's statement to them about all that suspicious stuff about Mishelle's death, you know?"

I uncrossed my eyes with a mighty effort. "Say what?" I said faintly.

"The police. The cops. They've started an investigation. Me and Lynn hadda go down to the police station and answer questions. You know?"

"No," I said. *Questions?* "Are you fuckin' kidding me?"

"No, I'm not fuckin' kiddin'." She almost giggled. "They were gonna stop the funeral, you know? And take her body in for an autopsy. But I guess they couldn't get a judge to sign off on the court order or somethin' so they took a needle and withdrew fluid from her real eye. Weird, huh?"

And that tore it; literally tore it.

I could feel things tearing within me; pain ripping through me and leaving nothing but shreds in its wake. Things tore . . . then burst:

"*Why?*" I screamed. "I did nothing but *care* for her! I *never* harmed her! My . . . I, my whole *family* showed her nothing but unconditional love and acceptance! How the *hell* . . .! Why would *anyone* think that I had anything to do with her death?"

I was grabbing at my self-control but it was a slippery bitch that day. "Nicky, you saw me count and dump the meds! *You signed the log as witness!* She wasn't even taking any meds the days before she died! They were all accounted for, every one of them!"

"Yeah, well." She sounded dubious. "I think they were more interested in your relationship with her than anything else."

The room spun crazily around me for about three seconds. I wanted to throw up when it steadied down. "My *relationship?* What . . . What about my relationship?"

Reluctantly, like a child faced with a plate of unwanted vegetables: "Well, all that kissing and hugging and stuff. They were really interested in that."

I'd been seasick once, on a cruise. Contrary to popular belief, they do *not* let you throw up overboard. I spent most of the afternoon and early evening hugging the tiny and amazingly smelly toilet bowl in our cabin.

That was a picnic by comparison. "*Kissing?* You kissed Mishelle, too!"

"Yeah. But . . . Well, anyway, Julie thought it was really inappropriate, you know?"

"What did I ever do to make her hate *me?*" I wailed.

"I dunno. But, well, there it is. Y'know?"

I said, "I have to go now," and hung up, trembling in every nerve and muscle.

The front door banged shut. I turned.

My husband stood in the entrance to the front room. His eyes were on me. "What?"

I told him.

His face sagged. His shoulders slumped and weariness radiated out of every square inch of his stocky frame. "I knew it," he mumbled. "I knew it the minute I saw her, I knew this . . ."

Dave shook himself and straightened. "It's all crap," he declared. "All of it. And that's all I'm gonna say right now."

He turned and left me standing, staring after him.

I didn't ask him what he meant. I didn't want to know.

I looked at the phone in my hand. I punched in a number with a trembling forefinger. It rang three times.

"Hello?"

"Renee? You're *not* going to believe this . . ."

* * *

I woke with a knot in my stomach that stayed with me the whole morning. It took every ounce of concentration I had, every technique I'd ever learned in class and in the field to keep focused and on task with my patients.

I was exhausted long before noon.

I was between patients, parked momentarily while I caught up on some charting when my work phone rang.

I flipped it open and stared at the tiny screen. It was Robin.

"Hello?"

"Michelle?" Robin's cool, calm voice was infinitely gentle and infinitely implacable. It reminded me of something more pleasant, if somewhat less immediate. "I just got off the phone with a homicide detective from the Kalispell Police department. He had some questions regarding your relationship with Mishelle Woodring. Is there anything you'd like to tell me?"

Anything? "N-no!" I stuttered. *Everything!* "What . . . What do you . . ."

"I mean inappropriate. Intimate, Michelle. Did you do anything improper?"

Tears suddenly stung my eyes. I could feel my stomach twisting itself into a tight, hard knot. "Robin, I, I . . ."

I stopped and swallowed the bile in the back of my throat, then washed it down with cold coffee; a combination I cannot in good conscience endorse for anyone not in possession of a cast-iron gullet. "Robin, I have *never*, would *never* do anything improper with any patient, with *anyone*, for God's sake!"

Again I wrestled with my self-control and it was a wildcat on that day; all claws and fangs and scrambled fury. "You've been in Hospice for years. *You* of all people should know what it's like to care so deeply for a patient, to, to . . ."

"Then why would the police ask me such a question?" Her voice was perfectly modulated and perfectly under control, perfectly unlike mine.

"*I don't know!* All I can tell you is what happened!" I tried, fumbling, to recount the weary, dreary details of the week before but she interrupted me:

"Michelle, I'm sorry but I have to go. The detective is here. I'll call you back."

She hung up.

I sat stunned, the phone still clutched in my sweaty hand. "Homicide?" I said, dazed. "*Homicide?*"

* * *

My friend once told me that she knew what Heaven was.

I know what Hell is.

Hell is sitting numbly in a well-worn car seat, waiting for the phone to ring, waiting to hear if you've still got a job; a reputation; a life.

Hell is waiting to hear that you're wanted for murder; that everyone thinks you did awful things to a helpless person; that you're the kind of person that would do those awful things.

Hell is waiting.

But the phone rang and a different kind of Hell presented itself. I soon realized that I didn't really know Hell, not at all; not yet, anyway.

"Michelle? Are you busy?"

"Not really. Between patients right now. Two more to go." I felt a bit light-headed. Lunch had been a bagel and the remains of the coffee. "What did the detective say, Robin?"

"Well, I can tell you this: it was Nicky who called the police."

Dumfounded, I opened my mouth but nothing came out.

"Michelle? Are you there?"

"Uh-huh," I said faintly. "Nicky? Really?"

"Yes. The detective was quite specific as to who filed the complaint. The law requires it."

"Oh. But she said . . ."

"Who?"

"Never mind. What did the detective say, exactly?"

"That they had been contacted by Nicky and that she filed a complaint against you accusing you of assisting a suicide and having an inappropriate relationship with Mishelle." Her voice was filled with distaste for that word; *inappropriate*. Welcome to the club, Robin. "You might be interested to know that Lori sat in on the conversation."

"Well, thank God for that," I mumbled.

"You could say that, yes."

"Did you show the detective the list of meds I disposed of?"

"Yes, he has a copy of that now. Lori went over the medication list with him and told him what each was for and why Mishelle was taking them."

She paused, and then said, "That's not all, Michelle. Lori told the detective about how we Hospice and Home Health workers tend to become emotionally attached, even deeply involved with our patients, that it's almost unavoidable in some situations."

There was another, longer pause. "Michelle, she emphasized that point continually. I think the detective finally realized what an emotional and spiritual journey caring for a terminal patient can be."

I wanted to put my head down on the steering wheel and weep. Instead, I said, "Has a cause of death been established yet, Robin?"

"Not officially, no. But Lori has spoken with Mishelle's primary doctor and his preliminary opinion, based on your report, is that she died from either a pulmonary or abdominal embolism. She relayed that information to the detective, too."

"An embolism?" I muttered.

"It's the most likely cause, given her symptoms, Michelle." I could hear her take a deep breath. "Try not to worry. This will all work out for the best, I'm sure."

"Worry?" Acid burned the back of my throat. I would have washed it down with more cold coffee but my cup was empty. "Robin, I'm under investigation for *murder*! How in the world can I *not* worry?"

Her calm, soothing voice neither calmed me nor was particularly soothing. "I know. Listen, you have a few days off coming up. Why don't you take some me time and relax, get in touch with your center?"

She hesitated again. "And I think that the detective wants to talk to you about this, too."

"Well, I should hope so! Since I'm the one under investigation!"

"Yes." I could hear papers being shuffled. "One more thing, Michelle. You may not be aware that the police have seized Mishelle's computer. They have someone going through it, checking for e-mails between you and Mishelle."

"Fine," I said grimly. "I've got nothing to hide. Do they want mine, too?"

"He didn't mention that. Not to me, anyway."

I picked up my empty coffee cup and glared at it. "Robin? Does Jodie know about all this? Or Donna, her boss?"

Robin sighed. "Jodie knows. Donna's on vacation and as far as I'm concerned, she has no need to know until she gets back. We'll cross that bridge when we come to it, okay?"

I crumpled the cup in my hand and watched the amber dregs dribble over my whitened fingers. "Great. Just great. I'm under suspicion for murder and you want me to go home and *relax*."

I tossed the cup out the window with rather more force than was required. *So arrest me for littering too!*

"Try, Michelle. Worrying about this will do you no good." Her voice sharpened. "Michelle, anyone who knows you or has worked with you knows you would never be capable of murder. That's ridiculous. Now, I suggest you go home tonight and put this out of your mind, as best as you can."

From Robin, that was about as strong a rebuke as I was ever likely to hear. I was properly chastened. "You're . . . you're right, Robin."

I swallowed. Unshed tears were stinging my eyes and clogging my throat. "Thank you for supporting me. Thank you for . . . Everything."

"Of course." Was there a mild rebuke in that as well? Looking back, three years gone, I can't say for sure.

But I was darn sure she was utterly sincere: "I know you. I've known you for years. You have nothing to fear because you've done nothing wrong. Now go and take a few days off, will you?"

"Thanks, Robin." I closed the phone, found a Kleenex in my purse and set about mopping up the spilled coffee.

* * *

"What am I gonna *do*?" I wailed against my husband's broad chest.

"What Robin said." His voice was a different kind of calm, one I was used to but it didn't work any better than hers. "Wait. Cooperate. Relax."

"Hah! Are *you* relaxed? 'Cause this affects you, too!"

"Don't think I haven't considered it." He shifted his arms around me and looked down, his face set. "I've done a lot of thinking since she died."

"And?"

"I was thinking that meeting Mishelle set off a chain reaction of events that almost *had* to lead here, today." His expression was impassive, like weathered granite. He regarded me, something smoldering in the back of his eyes. "You being the kind of person you are. And her being . . . herself. You two met and things *had* to happen. Like it was Fate."

"Or God," I added softly.

"Yeah, there's that. Kind of hard to argue with that. No percentage in it."

"Yeah."

He shifted position on the bed. "I want you to promise me something."

I shifted position too, but I was actually quite comfortable there in his arms. Dave can be very cuddly. "I won't promise you I'll relax," I warned. "I can't keep that promise."

"No, not that. Well, that would be nice, but I know you." Briefly, he grinned down at me; carved stone coming alive for a breath or two. "No, I want you to promise me that if the cops don't call you by the end of the business day, you'll call them and at least leave a message."

"Why?"

He shrugged. The Great Stone Face returned. "Call it pre-emptive. At least they'll know you're eager to cooperate. It might go a long way toward making you look less guilty."

Abruptly, I sat up. "I am *not* guilty!"

"I never said you were." Our faces were inches apart. His calm brown eyes held me motionless. "But they have to assume that you are; otherwise there's no point in gathering evidence, is there?"

Deflated, I nodded. "Right."

He glanced at the clock. "Two hours. Then call them." His implacable gaze fixed me again. "How many patients did you have today?"

"Five," I admitted.

"Sheesh." Dave glared. The rocks shifted and his eyebrows became a single line. "You *need* this time off, woman. Go take a bath or something, willya?"

So I did.

* * *

"I want to speak to Detective Scott Wardell, please," I said firmly.

The dispatcher who answered the phone sounded bored out of her skull. "Uh, he's left for the day, ma'am."

I gritted my teeth. "Will he be in tomorrow?"

"Just a sec'." She checked something, probably a duty roster. "Nope, sorry. He's off for the next four days. Vacation. He'll be back on Monday."

I took the phone from my ear and stared at it, put it back. "Is anyone else handling my case?"

"Uh, who'd you say this was?"

"Michelle Alexander. Detective Wardell is investigating me in connection with the death of Mishelle Woodring."

"Oh. Well, I can put you into his voice mail if you wanna leave a message."

My back teeth were beginning to ache from the strain of not screaming. "Yes, that would be very nice. Would you do that, please?"

She was gone and the phone emitted a ring tone. I waited until his message was done, then said, very clearly and as calmly as I was able: "Scott, this is Michelle Alexander. I understand that you need to speak to me regarding Mishelle Woodring's death. Would you please call me on my cellphone?"

I recited the number and closed the phone with an emphatic snap. Behind me, Dave cleared his throat. I spun.

His right eyebrow was raised perhaps a single millimeter. "Well?"

"It's gonna be a *long* weekend," I told him.

* * *

I moped. I sulked.

I had crying jags and moody silences when I would stare off into space and if my poor husband or kids happened to be present, they didn't have much to say about it.

Just as well. I probably would have cracked like old china and had a major meltdown.

Dave tried to cheer me up a few times then gave it up as hopeless. "You know, you'd look terrible in prison orange, hon," he joked over dinner Saturday night.

I was playing with my food, something I hadn't done since I was six. "Anything orange," I said absently, mashing my peas into paste.

"Fluorescent orange," Zach commented. "Like one of those road construction workers."

I looked up at him. "You'd better hope that I don't wind up as one," I said in dull tones. "They don't make much money."

There was embarrassed silence around the dinner table. "I was only jokin', Mom," my eldest said apologetically. "Sorry."

My eyes suddenly filled with tears. "Me too, Zach. Sorry. Sorry I got you all into this. So . . . sorry."

"I'm not." Chris spoke up. "I'm not sorry at all. I got to meet one of the coolest people ever. And I know you didn't do *nothin'* wrong." He forked in another mouthful of mashed potatoes and swallowed. "Anyone who says so is fulla crap."

"Wash your mouth out with soap?" his brother suggested.

"Aw, shut up. It's true."

"That's enough, you two." My husband doesn't do the father-voice too often but when he does, the boys listen. "No more talk like that." He eyed me. "Honey, you want to go lie down?"

I nodded shakily. "Yes, Yes, I believe I would like to do that, very much."

* * *

Sunday afternoon, in the middle of a particularly unpleasant daydream about my predicament, the phone rang.

I was imagining myself in a job interview, answering questions from a faceless recruiter: "So tell me, Mrs. Alexander. Why were you terminated from your last job?"

"Oh, nothing much. I just crossed a few boundaries, is all."

"Boundaries? What kind?"

"Oh, you know: phone numbers, home addresses, working off the clock for a special needs patient, that sort of thing."

"Hmm. Sounds serious. Anything else?"

"Well, I invited her to my home. Several times."

"How many times?"

"Six. I spent a lot of time at her place, too. Off the clock."

"You said that already. Anything else you like to tell me?"

"Yeah, I loved her. She was my best friend."

"Well, that's *really* serious, Mrs. Alexander. Don't you know that we health care professionals are supposed to remain detached, at arm's length from those we care for? Don't you know that becoming emotionally involved with a patient usually results in disaster?"

In my daydream, I said, "You had to be there."

I had that particular daydream a lot that long weekend. Sometimes I'd end the interview with something really smartass, like: "I gotta be me!"

I was inventing another cute comeback when the phone rang, effectively putting a stake through the daydream's evil heart.

I picked it up and saw that it was Lynn. "Hello."

"Hi, Michelle? This is Lynn."

"I know who it is. Caller ID."

"Oh. Yes. Well, I just called to see how you're doing."

"Pretty good, considering that I'm being investigated for murder."

There was dead silence on the line, and then she said, meekly, "Uh, Michelle. I just want you to know that Nicky is really sorry about what happened."

"She told you that?"

"Yes. Yes, she did."

"Then she's talking to the wrong person. She should be talking to *me*, don't you think?"

"Uh . . ."

"Better yet, she should march her sorry ass down to the police station and tell *them*." Warming to my subject, I continued. "And just out of curiosity, why the hell didn't you give me a heads-up on this? You knew she was going to do this, didn't you?"

"She discussed it with me," Lynn admitted reluctantly.

"And not once did you discuss it with me. Thanks, Lynn. Thanks a bunch."

"I was trying to do damage control," she protested.

"Nice job. You controlled the damage so well; the police came to my work and questioned my supervisors."

I could hear a sharp intake of breath that wasn't quite a gasp. "You weren't fired, were you?" There was a note of horror in her voice.

Hah! "No, I wasn't! You know why? Because I have a frickin' spotless record that I've worked my butt off for over twenty years to maintain, that's why! Because I haven't had a patient complaint in over ten years, that's why!"

I was breathing hard. *Top* that, *missy.* "Because I have integrity and responsibility and I put in the frickin' hours and I do it well, *that's* why!"

The silence was so brittle; I thought it might snap in two, leaving me on one side and the rest of the world on the other. Hesitantly, Lynn said, "Would you . . . Would you like to pray with me?"

And to my astonishment I said, simply: "Yes."

She led us. I don't recall it now but it seemed genuine at the time and I'm inclined to believe that it was, even now. I had no reason to trust her . . .

But I did.

I've not had occasion to question my decision, even now. I prayed then and I pray today that she of all people who knew Mishelle; who helped her on the move to Seattle; who was perhaps the first to truly know her as a woman and remain steadfast in that belief for much longer than myself; would understand why and how I came to the place I am today.

She alone might understand me because she understood our friend.

And so we prayed.

When we were done, she said, "Want me to drop by later? My afternoon is free."

"Yes. I could use the company. I've been . . . avoiding people."

"Me, too. See you in a bit."

"Okay." I clicked off and wandered outside.

It was a beautiful day. I blanked my mind and did nothing, something I was getting depressingly good at. When I heard her car, I felt a twinge that I tentatively identified as pleasure.

She came to me in my garden and we embraced.

We talked. Reminisced. Prayed again. Wept together and even giggled once or twice. I told a funny story about Mishelle and she added one from the Seattle years, when they'd visited her and supported her, even though she was many miles from Kalispell, their home.

When she left, I felt as if a great weight had fallen from my shoulders and a tightly coiled mass within me had uncoiled, releasing its dangerous potential energy.

I was still sitting there, musing and even managing to admire the flowers when Dave appeared.

"Hey." I looked up at him. "Did I just see Lynn's car leave? I was coming up the street when she passed me."

"Yes," I said placidly. "She was paying me a visit. She came over to apologize for the way things have turned out. She wanted to assure me that she was on my side with this . . . horrible thing and that she would speak to the police for me, too." I smiled up at him. "I think we can count on her, Dave."

His eyes grew big. His cheeks turned red. Detached and Zen as I was in that moment, I watched with clinical interest as he prepared to explode.

Explode he did: "Are you *crazy*! What the *hell* are you doing, Michelle? How in the world can you ever *trust* that woman? She's going to take everything you said to Nicky!"

I stared at him. "How do you know that?"

"Because she already has! She's already talked to Nicky about all this, hasn't she?"

That sick sensation was crawling back up my esophagus. With a slowly mounting sense of horror, I stammered: "But . . . but she was *sincere*. We prayed together . . ."

"So *what*? Michelle, *she went to the police station with Nicky*! Can't you get it through your thick skull that the *only* people you can trust right now are your family?"

My husband's face was beet red and his hair seemed to stand belligerently away from his scalp. "Do us all a favor, sweetheart. No more opening your heart to everyone, okay? Until this is over. No *more*."

The tears were back. Hello, tears. "I think I need to go lay down again."

I rose and tottered off into the house.

* * *

I hate Mondays.

Well, this time I had a good reason. I parked the Toyota in the office lot and marched in, head high once more; determined to stare down anyone foolish enough to question my character.

But once again, it was business as usual. I was plowing through some paperwork when Robin poked her head around the side of my cubicle. "Hey."

I jerked, startled and almost knocked over my coffee. "Hey, you. What's up?" For a second, my heart leaped into my throat.

She winked at me. "Just dropped by to tell you to hang in there. We're all pulling for you."

My heart went back to its proper place. I smiled at her. "Thanks, Robin. I really appreciate it."

Her smile warmed me clear through. "If you need to talk . . . Anything, Michelle. You know where to find me."

I nodded.

She eyed the mound of paperwork. "Busy day?"

"Four today. More tomorrow."

"Ain't it the truth?" She winked at me again. "Talk to you later, Michelle."

"'Bye." I sighed, stuffed the paperwork into my bag and hit the road for my first patient of the day.

* * *

The phone rang between number three and number four. I picked it up and saw that it was the moment I'd been dreading. *Finally!*

"This is Michelle."

"Uh, Mrs. Alexander, this is Scott Wardell from the Kalispell Police Department."

"Yes, Detective. I understand you've been wanting to speak to me? About my . . . Mishelle Woodring?"

"Yes ma'am, that's right." What he said next sent an arctic chill right through me: "Could you come down today, please? Around one?"

There was nothing else I could say: "I'll be there. Do you mind if my husband accompanies me?"

"Well, I won't be needin' him during the interview, ma'am. But if you want to bring him along for moral support, I guess that'd be alright. He can't come in while we're talkin', though."

I said, "I understand. Let me call him, please. I'll see you at one o'clock, Detective."

"Oh, you can just call me Scott." He sounded a touch amused. "Everybody else does. See you then, Mrs. Alexander."

"Call me Michelle," I said, but he had already hung up.

I dialed my husband. "Dave? It's now. Meet me at the police station at one pm. And don't be late!"

He started to protest, but it was my turn to hang up abruptly.

I called in and made arrangements for my remaining patient and then sat; darkly and silently considering many things, not the least of which was how I'd look in prison orange.

But Thy will be done . . . and so on and so forth. Besides, what choice did I have?

All my choices were so obvious that it might be said that I had none.

I stared though the windshield. "*No*," I whispered. I *always* had a choice. I could surrender.

Or I could fight, like her.

Just like her.

She chose to fight; to never surrender.

I could do no less.

CHAPTER TWENTY-FOUR
Closing the Circle

INISHED, I LIFTED MY HEAD TO LOOK AT HIM. He gazed back at me; his face bland as a preacher's.

"Is that all, Mrs. Alexander?"

I nodded. "So where do we go from here, Detective?"

He was jotting notes on the pad in front of him. "Well, we'll complete our investigation in a few weeks . . ."

"What about the fluid you took from her eye? When will the results be back from the lab?"

Surprised, he looked up. "Ah, you know about that, then. Yes, we withdrew a small amount of fluid from her right eye. Don't worry, we didn't leave any marks."

"You'd better not," I said grimly. "I'm giving you fair warning, Detective. If this goes any further, I'm hiring an attorney."

He nodded. "Which you have every right to do, of course. I wouldn't worry about it, though. I think . . ."

"You didn't answer my question, Detective."

He arched an eyebrow. "About six to eight weeks. It's a small lab and they handle a lot of State work."

"For what it's worth, they have my sympathies. What about *me?*"

He didn't answer. Instead, he looked down and doodled something. Without looking up, he said, "Why do you think Nicky reported you?"

"I don't know for sure," I admitted. "But I can guess."

"Humor me, please."

I shrugged. "Jealousy. She knew Mishelle for over three years before I arrived. Less than a month after we met, I was her best friend and she did everything with me when it used to be Nicky." That sad feeling was back, sitting on my stomach like a lump of cold oatmeal. "I don't blame her, really."

"And it wouldn't do you any good if you did. No feuds, please. I don't want to hear that you two got into it in the grocery store or something."

I glared at him. "Not frickin' likely," I snapped.

He looked up and nodded. "Good enough, ma'am. Do you have any more questions for me?"

"Yeah. Do you want to talk to my husband?" I was wondering about the letters and the laptop.

He shook his head. "That won't be necessary. I think I have all I need."

"Are you going to proceed with this stupid investigation?" I didn't quite growl at him. I try to keep a civil tongue in my head when I talk to police officers. Blame my mother for that.

The corner of his mouth curved in a quizzical half-smile. "No, as far as I'm concerned, this case is closed. I don't believe that you caused Mishelle's death. We haven't found any indications that she committed suicide."

An eyebrow lifted again. "Although I think I should officially warn you about crossing professional boundaries, ma'am. I hope you've learned a lesson from all this."

I stared at him. I wanted to laugh and weep and throw something. *Learn a lesson?* "I have," I said, my voice trembling. "But it's not officially closed until you get those test results, is that right?"

He nodded.

I was very close to tears right then and I desperately hoped it didn't show. "Well, what does that *mean?* Am I like, still under suspicion, officially? Is my name on some kind of hot-list and I'll be arrested if I get pulled over or something?"

"No," he said quietly.

"So that's it? That's *all?*"

He nodded. "Yes, ma'am."

"I'm free to go?"

"Yes, ma'am."

I stood, not taking my eyes from him. "And you'll call me when you get the test results back, is that right?"

"Yes, ma'am."

I held out my hand. "Until then, Detective."

He stood, took it and for one brief, goofy second, I wanted to hug him. Instead, I covered our joined hands with my left and looked into his eyes.

They were once again opaque. Friendly, perhaps even amused, but betraying nothing. We nodded at each other and I opened the door . . .

Let it close behind me as I took a deep, shaky breath. Musty old air knotted my stomach with sudden nausea and I hurried for the exit.

Dave bounced to his feet the moment I emerged from Scott's office and followed me down the hall, his expression anxious, what I could see of it.

He followed me outside, found me taking great gulps of fresh air and digging through my purse for my sunglasses.

"Well?" he asked after a decent interval. "How did it go? Are you still in trouble? Are *we* in trouble?"

I found my shades and slipped them on. The harsh Montana sunlight suddenly became bearable again. "No. No, we're not in trouble. Detective Wardell says as far as he's concerned, the case is closed."

He sighed with relief. "That's it, then? It's over?"

I looked at the sky, marveling anew at how vast and blue and full of light it could be.

"No, I don't think it will ever be over."

Epilogue:
December Nineteenth, 2009

No, it wasn't over; not at all.

Detective Wardell never called me as he'd promised. I waited almost eight weeks, frustration and worry burning in my chest like indigestion. I finally called the police department and was told that the tests had come back negative for any medication or drug that might have caused Mishelle's death.

Nobody from the Kalispell Police Department apologized to me or let me know in any way that they felt any sympathy for what I'd been through during those weeks after Mishelle's death. Not one.

I shouldn't have been so irritated. The police were only doing their job and I suspect that Detective Wardell never really thought that I'd murdered my best friend. From their perspective, I suppose it was mostly a formality; something they had to do because the law required them to do so.

Still . . . it would have been nice to hear an apology.

Blue the kitty went to live with Lynn. I visited her a few weeks before this memoir was completed to renew our acquaintance and talk about the events; to find some sort of perspective in what all of us had gone through those few short months in 2006. The gorgeous little cat recognized me immediately and came to sit in my lap, purring contentedly while Lynn and I reminisced and discussed my plans for this book.

The visit was very emotional.

Lynn and her husband Bob had known Mishelle for many years. They had been with her before her transition and stood by her when she made that fateful decision to become herself. They supported her in ways and deeds that would take another book to describe. They were close to her in a manner I'd never known and didn't realize until I began the preliminary research for this memoir.

Without them, she might not have been able to achieve her goal. I feel sure she would have, regardless. She was that kind of person.

Nicholas went to live with Nicky. I wasn't happy with that and I'm still not happy. At this writing, Nicky is nowhere to be found and I feel sad that there are two others in this story with whom I cannot achieve closure. Perhaps someday I can, God willing.

Mishelle's parents and family underwent their own transformation subsequent to her death. I came to know them quite well and finally realized that the distance between them and their daughter wasn't as great as she'd led me to believe. I knew that Mishelle wasn't above playing the sympathy card now and then and while everything she'd told me was accurate, the emotional content was colored by her perspective; necessarily limited by her disability and her own pain. Earl and Louise did care, would always care and even if they didn't understand, they accepted her as best as they could. I have noted many times that folks from the Depression generation tend to have great, almost overwhelming difficulty in talking about their feelings and Mishelle's parents were no exception.

I discovered that there was more to their relationship with Mishelle, much more than I could have ever suspected. The photos, writings and memorabilia they saved were invaluable in making this memoir more than just a dry recounting of events. For that, and so much more, I will always be grateful to them.

In many ways, I have come to think of them as part of my extended family. I hope that they feel the same way, but I doubt if they will ever be able to tell me that.

Chris and Zach arrived at their own sense of closure, in their own way and in their own time. Children are flexible and heal quite well if they receive enough nurture and love. Three years after her death, Chris still remembers his friend and adopted sister with affection and admiration. For quite some time following her passing, it seemed as though he still could sense her presence; feel her in ways that I as an adult could only guess at. He did not speak of her very much then and today speaks of her only when prompted. But there is sureness in my youngest son; a certainty of principle he and his brother share that gives me an unshakeable conviction that my two boys will be part of the fundamental change in values our world requires in order to continue and mature.

Perhaps a further anecdote about my son and his friend might shed some light upon that conviction. In the weeks following her funeral, Dave and Chris happened to be talking about Mishelle and my son misgendered her, called her *him* then stopped: mortified.

"What did you say?" my husband inquired gently.

From what Dave told me later, our son's face was beet red. "Uh, Dad? I know about Mishelle," he whispered.

"You do?" asked my husband.

Chris nodded. "Yeah, only don't tell Mom, okay? I don't think she knows."

After twenty-three years of marriage, my husband Dave and I have decided to divorce. Our decision was not arrived at lightly nor was it without its own measure of pain. It has also been filled with respect and compassion and yes: love. People change and sometimes they grow apart in that process. Dave and I were no exceptions to this. We both have our Path, he and I. It grieves me and always will that it is differing Paths we must now take.

And I? Only time will tell. I can tell you this, though: I made a promise to my friend and I will keep it. This memoir is the first step in that process. "And miles to go before I sleep." Yes, Robert Frost knew that each of us must journey, sometimes without hope or light. This story was meant to give others Hope and to shed Light upon the dark places within the human heart.

I pray, every day, that it will.

Michelle Alexander and Michelle Rose
Kalispell, Montana and Portland, Oregon
September 2006 through December 2009

Afterword:

Three Perspectives

—MICHELLE ALEXANDER—

It has been three years and nine months, 1,265 days and approximately twenty thousand hours since my journey with Mishelle began. There hasn't been a single day that has gone by when I have not thought of her, our journey and the impact that this experience has had on my life.

Have you ever wondered if there are certain people who are placed into our lives by God? If I had once wondered, I don't anymore. During the short four and a half months that I spent with Mishelle, I learned that one of the reasons she was placed into my life was so she could educate me about the inner landscape of the transgender person. It was up to me to take what she taught me and educate others. Sharing Mishelle's unique experience of being transgender and *blind* gave me hope that I could open some hearts and minds to the truth.

Initially, I was prepared to share this only on a small personal scale: my friends, my family and perhaps some of my co-workers. But shortly after she died, I realized that Mishelle wanted me to tell her story on a greater level.

I knew I was meant to write this book. When this came to me, I had to laugh. You might ask why? Well, I don't like to write. Not only do I not enjoy writing, I *struggle* with it. And frankly, I suck at it.For me, it's the most painful process imaginable; kind of like getting a tooth pulled without Novacaine. From the reluctant start to the bitter end of my first effort took two long years. I'm sure I must have gone through fifty reams of paper and probably the same number of ink cartridges. I had to free-hand everything first and then edit it and *then* type it into the computer, print everything and then re-do, re-do and re-do again.

I remember my very first draft. My husband read it, shook his head and gave me an A for content and an F for composition. I chucked it and went back to the drawing board. Dave tried to help me, but after many arguments we both came to the conclusion that he couldn't find my voice.

He could write the story from his perspective but not mine. It didn't stop me. A task that I felt I was given to do, I also felt *expected* to do.

During the time I spent with Mishelle, I had a nagging feeling that there was more that I needed to learn, more reasons that she was placed into my life. Eventually the answers started trickling in, one by one. I had to evaluate the lessons that she brought to me, learn from them and then apply them in my day-to-day existence.

This started me on a quest of self examination and self improvement. The first area that presented itself was my own spirituality. From the *knowing* after the Crusillo, to the *knowing* the day of her death and then watching things unfold exactly as I felt they would was truly a profound experience. How could I *not* explore the meaning? I really believed (and still do to this day) that this whole experience had been orchestrated by God. I had always considered myself to be a spiritual person to some extent. But after this experience, my spiritual growth took off. I began to devour books and CD's, looking at self-growth from a spiritual perspective.

Everything I listened to and read resonated deeply within. Even though a lot of the information was not necessarily new to me, the element that seemed to be missing in the many PMA (Positive Mental Attitude) books that I read was the spiritual content. Call it the aging process, wisdom, experience, perception or perhaps a desire to feel and experience something that had always been missing. But I knew that hunger was always there. I started to feel a deep connection not only to my Creator, but also a yearning to feel deep connections with others. I had a profound desire to become a more authentic human being, like Mishelle. It humbled me that someone so obviously ravaged and diminished by disease, abuse and neglect could be so aware and at peace with herself while I with my advantages and privileges could be so unfulfilled.

So: as I plugged along with the book, I continued down my path of becoming the best expression of myself that I could. I became interested on Dr. Wayne Dyer's teachings. In one of his lectures, he compared having a spiritual experience to a catapult; a sudden shift in what is truly important in your life.

I thought of it as a burning desire: I knew that I was to tell Mishelle's story and open hearts and minds to the inner landscape of transgender. So I began to exercise my faith muscle. Not once through this entire process did my faith waver. I began to pray regularly. I began to visualize the end result. I realized that there was a force out there that was greater than me. The more that I was able to simply surrender to this force, to remain open and allow it to happen, the more these synchronistic events began to occur. The right people began to appear to help me bring this book into existence. All I had to do was just stay out of my own way.

Let me be clear. There were times throughout this process that things seemed to be at a standstill. It was difficult for me to accept that none of this was going to be done strictly on *my* terms. (I can be very impatient at times!) But I soon realized these were necessary opportunities for me to do more internal work.

Eventually I realized that things were unfolding exactly as they were intended. I started looking for the lessons I was meant to learn in every circumstance and every contact.

I discovered Debbie Ford's work. I went through a few of her on-line programs and through her teachings and exercises; I began to peel back my own layers to get a good look at my own authenticity. (You might say that Mishelle was my biggest teacher in this area.) My discoveries led to an examination of my own limiting beliefs and behaviors, my internal dialogue and my relationships. I recognized my own responsibility in constructing them in ways that were no longer working. I reviewed those that needed nurturing, including the relationship that I had with myself. I examined my ego and my fear-based thinking. I saw what was working and what wasn't and began to reprogram the file system in my head.

I came to the realization that my self-growth and the evolution of my soul was a big reason that Mishelle was put into my life; for me, perhaps the most important reason. I needed to become the best expression of myself as possible and then help others to do the same, step by step if necessary. As Dr. Dyer says: "Where there are ladders, there will be rungs." I realized that life is a journey, not a destination. So simple, yet so difficult to grasp.

During this journey, I've had the opportunity to meet several other trans women. Again, I see each one of them having been placed into my life for a reason. They have all been an example to me in the true sense of living an authentic life. I cannot begin to fathom the amount of strength, courage and perseverance that it takes to fully transition. If these remarkable women can do this, then I have to challenge myself to become the best that I can be and to be the best ally possible to this community, if only because of what they have done for me.

Pay it forward. I must. I promised.

In the course of *her* journey, Mishelle had to take off her mask. Not only to others but to herself as well. I started to look at the masks that I wore as a means to be accepted and hide the flaws we all have. Most people struggle with this issue. We hide from ourselves and others until the hiding becomes bigger than the issues. I struggled to be accepted for myself, too. We *all* do; gay, lesbian, bi, trans and most certainly straight people. But I discovered that once I was honest with myself and took off my own masks, my own authenticity began to emerge. Once I found my true self and the courage to display my authentic feelings and vulnerability then I found the connections, the compassion, acceptance, support and encouragement that every human being thrives upon.

I learned the true meaning of unconditional love and acceptance. I learned what really matters. My dear friend Mishelle had to transform not only her outer shell, but her inner being as well. She had to integrate the inner and outer to be true to her authentic self. She had to meld her masculine energy and feminine energy, which I have come to realize, is part of every human being. She learned how to accept all parts of herself: the positive, the negative, the masculine and the feminine, the light and the dark.

Before she died, she was able to love herself unconditionally; accept herself as she was. I learned just how important this is if we want to share what we truly have, what we truly are.

I would like to believe that I am always learning, growing, applying and sharing. I realize that I still have a long way to go but I'm convinced that I'm on the right path and I owe it to my experience with Mishelle. From her, I learned what is really important: the human heart.

In May of 2007, an acquaintance gave me a list of freelance editors. Before I contacted any of them, a friend introduced me to a very nice woman from a publishing company who read the first few chapters of my book and gently told me that my writing sucked. She believed in the content but . . .

So I rewrote. The results were much the same. I never did contact those freelance editors. I just had faith that the right person would show up at the right time. But I couldn't give this story to anyone. I had a very specific idea of whom I wanted for this project. I was looking for a person who had some experience with the trans community. I wanted that person to be somewhat spiritual in nature and able to communicate from an emotional level. And it wouldn't hurt if they knew how to write.

I posted a few messages on Jennifer Boylan's forum. I'd discovered her site while following another thread, recognizing it as belonging to the author of the first book Mishelle had given me so many months before. Soon after, I met Michelle Rose. She read my post about my journey with Mishelle. I read about her journey and the parallels between this Michelle and my patient Mishelle astonished me.

So: I contacted her, just to say hi and get acquainted. She read about my journey with Mishelle, wrote back and with great conviction told me that I *had* to write this story. It could open some hearts and minds! (She said.) I wrote back and told her that I *had* written it but I'd taken it about as far as I could and I was just waiting for the right person to show me what to do next.

She said, "Perhaps *I* am the writer you are looking for?" And I *knew* without a doubt.

It's been a long year since then.

In the spring of '09, I took the opportunity to start life coaching classes. After attending the introductory session, I knew that *this* was what I was supposed to do! As I write this, I am in the final stages of the curriculum. My goal, my firm intent is to assist the transgender community in becoming the best possible expressions of themselves; each to her/his own expression and potential. But I am careful to remind myself that I have much more to learn from this community. I hope to share what I have learned with them. I pray that they will share their experiences with me.

Many people considered Mishelle different, odd, and even repugnant. But she was a child of God, no different than you or I. She had the same needs, the same desires. Some might call her complex, but she was quite simple, really.

All she was looking for was love and acceptance.

Aren't we all?

—MICHELLE DIANE ROSE—

Call me the Scribe.

That was my original intent when I approached this work: an edit job with perhaps a few addendums to smooth out what had already been written and Explain It All to you in a tasty, easy-to-swallow fashion.

It didn't quite work out that way.

To begin with, I discovered that my writing partner is a verbal person, not a writer. She works better one-on-one, eye-to-eye because she's most comfortable with interpersonal communication; not surprising, given her profession. There's nothing she enjoys more than deep conversation.

By way of contrast; I'm perfectly happy deep in my cave, my rear end parked in front of the computer, communicating with the rest of the world via the written word.

Strange, isn't it, how the opposite can be complimentary?

So what began as a task I thought would take only a few weeks turned into a year-long odyssey filled with many sleepless nights, much gnashing of teeth and a lot of phone calls for more detail.

About four thousand hours of phone calls, in fact. We looked at the cell phone bill in late summer and it shocked us speechless. It's a good thing she has unlimited minutes.

Also emails. *Dozens*. I questioned her endlessly. She responded with pages of descriptions and impressions and memories that seemed to pour out of her fingers through the keyboard, onto the screen and across the Net to me. (I saved every one of them.) Her writing style is entirely stream of consciousness and first person POV; a predictable outgrowth of her training as a nurse required to observe and record with utter objectivity.

Regrettably, this does not lend itself to an engaging narrative. I had to surf through that torrent of words and find patterns; episodes and encounters that meant something within the context of the overall story arc. It quickly became necessary to discard irrelevant material. It was *painful*.

It was well that we could agree upon what had to go. I shudder to think of the alternatives.

We eliminated incidents. We threw out interactions with other people that would have complicated the story arc unmanageably. We compressed events in time, although as little as possible because I longed to make that arc consistent and she agreed. As I plowed through her original narrative, I found episodes crowded together in the final four or five chapters that simply could *not* be ignored or even minimized. They opened like separate narratives unto themselves. I found myself wondering time and again how two people could cram so much into four and a half months. About halfway through this project, Michelle and I finally met and I stopped wondering.

I micromanaged, too. We reiterated conversations between her and Mishelle endlessly and no prosecuting attorney has ever dissected a ten minute conversation as I did with such protracted emphasis on detail, detail, detail. In retrospect, her patience with this mind-numbing tedium was astounding and probably the main reason such a varied palette was available to me at all.

I asked my partner for physical aspects of the story; things that Mishelle had owned or touched or interacted with in some way. She sent me half a dozen hefty packages containing pictures, clippings, postcards, letters, audio cassette tapes and memorabilia of every description. Included was a copy of Mishelle's journal. I made the mistake of reading it on a gloomy, rainy night. Be careful what you ask for!

At last, patterns emerged. The arc formed. I had a narrative, finally.

I did my best to make sense of it all. I'd like to think I did.

You decide.

I wasn't unaffected by this process. (A short pause please, while they give me a medal for Understatement of the Year.) But this story isn't about me, never was and may it always be so.

Would I have taken this on, had I known what it would entail?

Hell, yeah. It was the opportunity of a lifetime. And yet . . .

I don't regret my decision to take on this project, not one bit. I don't regret the long hours and the necessary disconnection from my community and friends to complete it. There is only one thing I regret:

I never knew her; Mishelle.

I will *always* regret that.

—CELIA CAMILLE EBERLE—

June Twenty-Second, 2009

I am following a white Toyota zipping through the narrow streets of Kalispell, Montana past churches and quaint houses; dodging parked pickups and passing through four-way intersections so small they don't even have stop signs. We arrive at a long tree-lined driveway that eventually leads to the grassy entrance of a large cemetery. Michelle drives like a bat out of hell and following her was no small task. (Now I know how she can visit so many patients spread across the Flathead Valley in a single morning!)

My daughter sits next to me. She's a trouper; coming along for a brief graveside remembrance for someone she didn't even know. Technically, I didn't know Mishelle either, except what I've read so far in the manuscript. But my daughter didn't really have a choice; we are a thousand miles away from our home in Colorado, a distance we will cover in the next couple of days and it was one of those parental requests that can't be ignored or postponed.

Many people wouldn't think of driving two thousand miles round trip over an extended weekend as their idea of a relaxing summer vacation. Throw in three national parks, a parade, two gigs with my band Cynova and the result is five hectic days. But the chance to meet Michelle Alexander in person and commemorate what would have been Mishelle Woodring's sixtieth birthday makes the trip worthwhile. The Color of Sunlight is at the halfway point (or so says the chief editor from her comfortable chair six hundred miles away in Portland) and I am captivated and anxious to meet Michelle Alexander and understand more about the community that is the backdrop for the events described in the yet-unfinished book.

From the entrance to the cemetery, I follow Michelle's Toyota up the hill in my trusty mini-van; the very one that shuttled my daughter, now twenty and on summer recess from college, to so many high-school soccer matches. It's a little blustery this morning, but it promises to be a wonderful early summer day in Montana. I'm full from the Father's Day buffet and the bucket of coffee we consumed at the hotel before we checked out to begin the thousand mile return trip to Colorado. In accordance with Michelle Rose's wishes, we are visiting the graveside visit to lay a dozen yellow roses and acknowledge the birthday that Mishelle would never experience.

The three of us place a dozen roses on Mishelle's marker. We all hold hands while Michelle marks the moment with a prayer. Before too many tears can set in, Michelle Alexander tells us the story about how she, Lynn and Nicky visited Mishelle's body in the funeral home, did her makeup and wrestled to change her into the gender-appropriate underwear. My daughter snaps a photo or two. More tears are shed, hugs are exchanged and my daughter and I climb into the mini-van to start the long drive home.

* * *

Only a few months ago, I didn't know Michelle Alexander. I'd never heard of Mishelle Woodring and Mishelle Rose was merely a friend I had made in Portland the previous year. I thought a Kali-spell was something a Hindu shaman would cast.

The unlikely tale of how the paths of these three women converged almost three years after the events described in *The Color of Sunlight* is miraculous in its own right. Time and again, the right people met one another and things happened at just the right time. I am lucky enough to have been a catalyst for some of these events, although Michelle Alexander and Michelle Rose did all of the heavy lifting. Carl Jung coined the term *synchronicity* for events like these and tried to explain them with psychological theory. But even for a hardened cynic like myself, witnessing the process of this book's inception has made me open to the idea that something greater was going on. Call it karma; call it faith; whatever you wish. The lives of these three women were meant to intersect and this book was meant to be, just as it is.

Portland Pride 2008 — Michelle Rose

I first met Michelle Rose at a dinner party in Vancouver, Washington, just across the Columbia from Portland, Oregon. Several local trans women had gathered for a snack and cocktails at a local Mexican restaurant. A visitor; Susan from Silver City, New Mexico was passing through on her way to see her daughter in Seattle. My friend Cheryl Lynne brought Michelle Rose along to meet the other women and generally expand her awareness and visibility in the community. The meal was predictable: ho-hum Mexican fare served in a classic dive that featured turquoise vinyl seats, overly sweet but underpowered margaritas and indistinguishable entrees; each camouflaged in a thick layer of broiled orange cheese. (Forgive me; I'm a frustrated restaurant critic!)

After meeting Michelle Rose, I was initially impressed with her intelligence as well as a list of accomplishments that included authoring a published S-F novel and her struggles in producing a CD for a band she played keyboards with. I suppose I'm a bit impressed by people that finish things since I have started a dozen creative hobbies that never seem to result in final products.

I saw Michelle again when we went to the 2008 Portland Pride Parade. I marched with a local UU Church group. She marched with the Northwest Gender Alliance. I'll never forget the tens of thousands of allied and supportive voices along the parade route. After an hour, my face was sore from all the smiling and acknowledging the love expressed by every person we passed. For those unfamiliar with this, Pride events are an annual parade and picnic held in cities across the country to affirm the dignity of and celebrate the Gay, Lesbian, Bisexual and Transgender community (GLBT) and its allies. Portland Pride is among the largest of these celebrations. Predictably, there are always a small number of protestors, hurling out-of-context bible quotes like rocks, all in the misappropriated name of Jesus. I would estimate that at this particular Pride, there were about forty thousand GLBT people and their allies and perhaps fifteen protestors expressing their hateful message. After the parade, Michelle and I set up camp in the beer garden and enjoyed the entertainment. We talked a lot, too.

Our friendship was cemented one evening at my place when we grilled some chicken, commiserated and laughed about the trials and tribulations of gender transition and played loud electric guitar until well into the evening; our laughter and riffs punctuated by an amazing thunderstorm, the likes of which I'd never seen in the Columbia Basin.

Later that year, I accepted a work transfer back to Colorado where I could be closer to my family. I had made many good friends in Portland and Michelle was at the top of the list.

The Book Project — "Michelle Alexander: meet Michelle Rose."

Actually, I didn't introduce the two. Mishelle Alexander and I were participants on a message board (forum) that was hosted by noted author Jennifer Finney Boylan (*She's Not There* and *I'm Looking Through You*). This forum was a daughter site to the *MyHusbandBetty* site that the pioneering author and gender theorist Helen Boyd (*My Husband Betty* and *She's Not the Man I Married*) has been operating since the early years of this last decade. Both sites were moderated by Helen's partner Betty Crow, now known as Rachel.

On paper, Michelle Alexander had captured the essence of her experience with Mishelle Woodring, but she was still trying to figure out how to get the work professionally polished and distributed to a wider audience. She contacted me, described what she had in mind and inquired as to whether I might be interested, perhaps for a fee? I declined, citing my lack of time and the lasting scars I suffered from narrowly passing my high-school English class years ago. (Honestly, I probably knew that I wouldn't finish it!)

On the same forum, Michelle Alexander met Michelle Rose. This project, both its content and timing, was perfect for Michelle Rose. She was in a particularly difficult time in her gender transition which was also compounded by some health challenges, notably a severe case of pneumonia and a recently diagnosed heart condition. Synchronistically, the mitral valve problem that Michelle was diagnosed with was also the condition that had plagued Mishelle Woodring all of her life; the result of the same childhood illness that had led to the loss of her vision.

Michelle Rose eagerly accepted the challenge and began the intensive task of reworking the initial notes and the eighteen chapters that Michelle Alexander had first written. The two Michelle's spent many hundreds of hours on the phone, working through the notes, extracting more details from memory and reviewing drafts endlessly. Somewhere in midst of the process, Michelle and Michelle realized I was a common friend, so I was assigned the relatively lightweight job of unofficial reviewer.

Like many transgender people, I have read dozens of transition memoirs over the last several decades in my quest for self-enlightenment. I have digested works from the likes of Christine Jorgenson, Rene Richards, Nancy Hunt, Jan Morris, Alecia Brevard, Lannie Rose, Calpernia Addams,

Matt Kailey, Donna Rose and Jennifer Boylan. All that time, I was looking for assurance that whatever it was that drove me to question something as fundamental as my identity was not something unique to me.

These days, one might think that writing a book is a necessary condition to transition. In fact, journaling is still one of the most widely recommended practices as a necessary adjunct to working with a gender therapist. Blogging has also brought a seemingly endless supply of gender transformation narratives available to one's fingertips.

But even with this abundance of stories, public understanding and acceptance of the important issues surrounding gender and transition in particular are actually at an all time low. There are television campaigns in various states equating natural gender expression variance with sexual crimes against children. In Congress, our community was stripped from the provisions in the Employment Non-Discrimination Act because its sponsors feared that an already-doomed bill would be utterly rejected if it conferred equal rights upon "a bunch of guys in dresses."

Why *do* we make people so uncomfortable? This normal and natural expression of identity is regarded by too many as a character flaw at best and a terrible sin and abomination at worst. Do some people envy other's freedom and self-awareness? Are we to sacrifice all happiness in this life to serve some greater purpose that another human being has rigidly defined for us? Regardless of who we love or who we are, are we all not worthy of love?

The story of Mishelle Woodring's life and its remarkable ending; how she taught Michelle so much about the human spirit ensures that *The Color of Sunlight* can stand among the many other fine works by transgender writers. But this book offers so much more. It raised my awareness to the daily challenges that blind people face as well as the whole of the process surrounding end-of-life care. As I write this, I struggle to remember that the transgender reader is only a part of this work's entire audience. It was written for the enlightenment of *everybody*. The fact that Mishelle was transgender is just one more facet of her brave character.

Kalispell Pride 2009

In another of the many spooky coincidences that aligned in the creation of this book, I found myself scheduled to travel to Kalispell, Montana for the state Pride event in June of 2009. Kalispell must have been where they were talking about when the phrase: "You can't get there from here", was coined. (Or was that Brooklyn?) So for me, a trip to Kalispell was highly unlikely!

That spring, I had joined a Boulder based folk-rock group: Cynova. At the time, I hadn't played guitar in a gigging band for almost thirty-five years. These wonderful women took me in and tolerated my rusty playing and lack of stage awareness while teaching me some beautiful songs full of soaring harmonies and gorgeous, intricate melodies. I'm very fortunate.

And it just happened that the first gig I was to play with them was for Montana Pride in Kalispell! I would finally meet Michelle Alexander.

Michelle is a Butte girl. (That means you don't mess with her.) She's pretty, vivacious and packs enough energy for ten people. Not readily visible though, is her intelligence, voracious reading capacity and a heart as big as all Montana.

I finally met Michelle in the flesh on the Friday night before my band's Pride show. Accompanied by my daughter, we sat in the hotel bar, intending to have a quick drink before we went out to dinner. Once we started talking, we couldn't stop. (My daughter politely excused herself after half an hour. All that boring grown-up talk, I suppose.) Four hours, far too many glasses of wine, two appetizers and three band sets later, we realized that we should stop. They were closing the bar down!

We talked about everything: the book, her background, growing up in Montana, her family, my family, my transition, Mishelle, Kalispell . . . you name it, we talked about it. It was an amazing experience.

We never did make it out to a restaurant.

The Pride event itself was uniting, terrifying and humbling all at once. Kalispell was hosting this event for all of Montana. A few hundred GLBT folks throughout Montana had converged on the town for the weekend. Unlike the Pride event in Portland, the Kalispell event was much more contentious. Over a hundred sign-toting protestors lined an entire side of the parade route. Every available state trooper in Montana was redeployed to Kalispell, along with a small cavalry of mounted sheriffs.

To everyone's credit, marchers and protestors alike, conflict was avoided. The parade culminated in a picnic at a local park. Everybody was well behaved except for a few haters with bullhorns that hung on the fringes of the park, shouting incoherent, religious gobbledygook at the peaceful crowd. The contrast between attending one of the largest Pride events in the country (in Portland) and one of the smallest (in Kalispell) was powerful in the extreme.

There was a special unity in the park on that day, given the hostile surroundings. I believe that the atmosphere created by the haters actually served to make everyone there more supportive of each other. Never before that day had I felt a community loyalty with *everybody*: gays, lesbians, bisexuals, transgender people and allies alike; all gathered together in peace in that small place. It's interesting how a common adversary can unite such disparate folk.

This was the environment into which Mishelle Woodring had courageously ventured years before. On that fateful day when she first appeared in public as herself, she walked among those haters and mockers and was proud and unafraid. I marvel at the strength of character that she must have possessed. I wonder what Mishelle would have thought of this event in her home town. Would she have proudly marched in the parade with her community?

Yes, I think so.

Later that day, I rendezvoused with Michelle at another little gathering of some Montana transgender citizens in one of the hotel meeting rooms. No, it wasn't planned; I just stumbled onto the session on my way to get my guitar an hour before the afternoon performance. Eight or ten transgender Montanans were there and about five minutes after I sat down, Michelle Alexander walked into the room and sat down next to me. She greeted me with a hug. I felt a tingle. Synchronistic forces seemed to be at work and ensured that we would both be there that day, at that particular gathering.

Michelle met some of the transgender activists in the burgeoning Montana community. Watching her network with them, I was suddenly struck at how tragic it was that Michelle Woodring had lived one lifetime too early to find this kind of peer support.

The rest of the Pride event was pure fun. My band's performance was attended by my daughter and Michelle and it was the best show we had ever played. People danced to the fast songs and I think there might have been angels in the room for the slow, healing ballads.

So What?

I have never been a person with a lot of faith in myself or in others, for that matter. For example: the seemingly mundane task of parking a car. My life-partner Lori and I frequently visit a wonderful restaurant in our town; the Rio Grande or simply the Rio. In my frustrated restaurant critic's humble opinion, it's a world-class eatery that serves the best margaritas on this planet, offers a menu featuring entrees which are actually distinguishable from one another and possesses an almost indescribable positive energy. Lori and I have spent countless hours in one of the many therapy booths in the back, working through the complex emotional issues of my transition, shedding a few tears and quaffing their delicious margaritas.

When we visit the Rio, we always seem to become entangled in a light-hearted debate on where we will park. If my dearest happens to be at the wheel, she always insists on heading directly to the restaurant and parking in one of the prized angle parking slots in front. "It's my parking karma!" she exclaims and I have no choice but to believe her because she nearly always finds a space.

On the other hand, if I'm driving, we're more likely to end up at a parking garage two or three blocks from the restaurant. Lori finds this incredibly amusing and even gave me a totem to hang from the rear-view mirror; the Patron Saint of Parking. (I think his name is Fred or something like that.) Her totem is a Buddha bobble-head that seems to project boundless energy and great good luck. I've noted that we seem to have much more success when she drives her own car. Even with the mojo inherent in Fred, the Patron Saint of Parking, I never seem to get the good spaces.

Maybe you just have to believe in something once in a while, even if it's only Fred.

Knowing a trans person doesn't have to be as remarkable as providing end-of-life care to a blind transgender person. More often than not, it's much closer to home: we are your daughters and sons, nephews and nieces, aunts and uncles and mothers and fathers.

To quote the legendary American philosopher Elwood Blues, Michelle Alexander is on a Mission from God. She has continued to expand her horizons and has recently become a certified life coach. I'm positive she will succeed in helping many of our community realize their dreams. She's one of the strongest possible allies the transgender community could have.

Michelle Rose continues to grow. She's still in school, working on her degree in communications, grinding away at a job that would drive me right out of my mind and occasionally taking a break to hone her extensive skills on the keyboard or guitar. I hope she continues to write and I eagerly look forward to whatever her plans include.

The legacy that Mishelle Woodring left lives on in Michelle Alexander and Michelle Rose and all those who choose to read this book and think, really think about its message. Still, there are many untold stories of how she prevailed against impossible odds, before and during her transition. I fervently pray that the two Michelle's can bring these amazing tales to the printed page someday.

Apart from my partner Lori and our two children, the three Michelle's are my heroes. I believe that, through this book and the phenomenal process of its creation, I have come to a renewed faith in myself, my family and friends and life in general.

So I'll keep on spending my days at work, playing guitar with my band and working with Lori on our evolving relationship at the Rio therapy booths.

By the way, that's my mini-van in the angle-spot right by the front door.

Celia Camille (CiCi) Eberle,
Jan 1, 2010

Acknowledgements

A project of this scope could not possibly come to fruition without the wholehearted cooperation of a small army of loyal supporters and advisors. The authors would like to individually and jointly recognize the following wonderful, hard-working and devoted folk.

Michelle Alexander:

First and foremost, I would like to thank Michelle Rose. If not for her dedication and commitment to this project, it might still be just a vision in my head. She immediately realized the importance of getting this story out to the world, even before knowing that I had already completed my version. She has spent countless hours, many sleepless nights and drunk countless pots of coffee to bring this to life, all the while working full time, undergoing transition and attending college. Her ability to see and write the memories from my perspective without ever meeting Mishelle still amazes me. I could never have done this without her.

I thank my husband Dave and my sons Zach and Chris for never discouraging me in the pursuit of my dream. Although they may have not quite understood my passion and drive for completing this, their support has never gone unnoticed. Thanks guys, for giving me the space to do what I felt was necessary for my own personal growth and self discovery.

I thank my extended family for their belief that I could complete this task. Although they may not have always understood my desire to assist the trans community, their support and belief in me was priceless. I believe that they now grasp the significance this journey has had for me and that their minds and hearts have been opened as well.

I thank Jeannie Painter for her knowledge, expertise and her personal time in formatting this book and assisting with the cover design. Also: many thanks to J.J. Walburn for her multi-faceted assistance because she truly is a gem. J.J. offered to help without knowing the contents of this book, found the image for the cover after several days of combing the Net and it just happened to be the very first image she showed me. When she finally heard the story, she climbed aboard with great enthusiasm and assembled a video presentation for my first speaking engagement.

I would like to extend my very sincere thanks to Beth Parker, former editor for Mountain Press for her advice about finishing this. Her belief that this book would be attractive to a publisher and her gentle encouragement to find a co-writer or take some writing classes was instrumental in finally reaching this goal.

My thanks to Mona Rae Mason, who helped clean up my speech for the Montana TDOR. Her constant encouragement was invaluable.

My thanks and love to Jean-Anne who supported this project even when it was stuck in the mud of its own making. She was one of the first to see the earliest drafts, believed in it and challenged me to persevere; to never quit, even when it seemed I would never finish. She continues to challenge me every day. Jean-Anne has been my friend for over two years and I'm honored that she holds me close to her heart.

My enduring gratitude to the many trans women I have met on this journey: Chris Paige, Kyndra, Bree, Bobbie and Amanda. All of these beautiful women have had a hand in the final shape of this book and I will be forever grateful to them.

My humble thanks to Jacquie Donahue and the Circle. Thank you for your encouragement, support and for opening your hearts and minds to the deeper meaning of this story.

My thanks to my coaching peers and instructors who showed me the possibilities and gave me the skills and determination to make a real difference in the lives of others. *Pay it forward.*

And finally: Dr. Wayne Dyer, Debbie Ford and Cheryl Richardson for giving me the inspiration and teachings to follow my passion, listen to my intuition, surrender and allow spirit to be my guide.

Michelle Rose:

Marilyn, who knew me first and hung in there for much longer than I had any reason to expect. She took a part of my heart when she left but that's okay; I gave it to her willingly.

My sister Erin, who accepted me and loves me for myself. Thanks, sis.

My brother Kelly, who wasn't surprised at all. Thanks, you knucklehead.

The members of our *ad hoc* peer review group: Elijah Brubaker, Nikki Handler, Mary Rae McPherson, Lily Witham, Renee, Jean-Ann, and of course; CiCi Eberle. Without their combined input, this memoir would have been very different.

My partner Michelle. She believed in me and still does. I haven't quite figured out why but give me time.

The authors jointly thank:

Professor Jenny Boylan of Colby College who listened to the opening notes and declared: "I say yes!" Professor Boylan is author of the first book that Mishelle gave Michelle #2 to begin her education. If not for her forum, we would never have met. We owe you a beer or two, Jenny.

Lauren Allis, who performed a meticulous line-by-line edit of the final manuscript for no compensation other than the sheer joy of it. She opened her heart to this story and her unswerving commitment and support helped carry us to the finish line. She is deeply connected, fiercely ethical and an undocumented national treasure.

Cami Anderson, who provided us with fresh eyes and a new perspective and in doing so, realized that she had much more to give than she had previously believed. She came to us near the end of this journey and her belief in its message opened her heart to us and ours to hers. Welcome home, sister.

CiCi Eberle, who with her daughter Kate accompanied Michelle #2 to Mishelle's gravesite and helped commemorate her sixtieth birthday, August twenty-second of 2009. (During Gay Pride, coincidentally enough. Or maybe not.) CiCi has been an invaluable resource, a diligent critic of this work and an unflagging supporter. We are proud to be her friends.

Dave Dutro, who saw the potential immediately and doesn't seem to mind that he underbid this particular job by a considerable margin. Without his enormous efforts, this project might not have made it past the first stage. With his direction, we learned how to expand this vision in order to pay it forward.

Renee, who knew Mishelle and loved her. Sometimes that's all you need. Her support through the grieving process with Michelle #2 was the start of a great friendship and her input on the emotional color of this work was priceless. Her recollections of Mishelle served to help bring this book to life.

The Woodring family: Earl and Louise, Sue and her husband, Mishelle's brothers and all the assorted cousins, nephews and nieces. Their stock of memorabilia provided the means to complete this project and their courage in allowing us to do so should serve as an example to all families with a trans person in their midst. Accept your loved ones while they are still with you for they are yours: your family and your blood.

Resources and References

The following is a list of websites, links and books which the reader might find useful. These are but a few and the reader is urged to follow the accompanying links and threads at will as there is much more available to inquisitive and open minds.

INFORMATIONAL WEBSITES:
http://www.wpath.org/publications_standards.cfm
http://www.annelawrence.com/twr/
http://www.tsroadmap.com/index.html
http://www.ncteqality.org
http://www.trans-academics.org/about_us
http://www.nodumbquestions.com
http://transfm.squarespace.com
http://www.straightforequality.com
http://add-www.transfaithonline.org
http://www.trans-health.com
http://ifge.org

FORUMS:
http://www.myhusbandbetty.com/community
http://www.genderlife.com/forum/ubbthreads.php/forum_summary.html
http://www.pinkessence.com
http://genderevolve.com
http://www.transfaithnetwork.org

BLOGS:
http://www.transadvocate.com
http://www.bilerico.com
http://www.pamshouseblend.com

PERSONAL SITES AND BLOGS:
http://www.jenniferboylan.net
http://www.juliaserano.com

http://www.myhusbandbetty.com
http://www.donnarose.com
http://www.crossingthet.com
http://ai.eecs.umich.edu/people/conway

INFORMATIVE SITES FOR AND ABOUT THE BLIND:

http://www.afb.org
http://www.acb.org/resources/index.html
http://www.bethel.edu/disability/resources/external/ahead-handout.html

PMA WEBSITES AND SOURCE MATERIALS:

http://www.waynedyer.com
Recommended reading: *The Power of Intention* by Dr. Wayne Dyer

http://www.debbieford.com
Recommended reading: *Why Good People Do Bad Things* by Debbie Ford

http://www.cherylrichardson.com
Recommended reading: *The Unmistakable Touch of Grace* by Cheryl Richardson

http://www.hayhouserradio.com
http://www.mylifecompass.com
http://www.tlcrn.com/Home_Page.php

BOOKS:

— *She's Not There—A Life in Two Genders,* 2004. *I'm Looking Through You—Growing Up Haunted,* 2008 by Jennifer Finney Boylan. Both published by Broadway Books, a division of Random House.

My Husband Betty Thunder's Mouth Press, 2003. *She's Not the Man I Married* Seal Press, 2007. (Berkeley, CA) by Helen Boyd

— *True Selves—Understanding Transsexualism* by Mildred L. Brown and Chloe Ann Rounsley. Jossey-Bass Publishers, 1996

Mark 947 by Calpernia Sarah Addams. Writers Club Press, 2003

Dress Codes by Noelle Howey. Picador Books, 2002

— *Whipping Girl* by Julia Serano. Seal Press, 2002. (Emeryville, CA)

The Uninvited Dilemma—A Question of Gender by Kim Elizabeth Stuart. Metamorphous Press, 1983. (Lake Oswego, OR)

ABOUT THE AUTHORS

Michelle Alexander was born in Butte, Montana and has been an RN for twenty-three years. She lives in Kalispell with her two sons and her cat, Momo.

Michelle Rose lives in Portland, Oregon and works for a non-profit. She is a speech and communications student at Portland Community College.